The Last War

The Last War

Racism, Spirituality and the
Future of Civilization

by

M. L. Perry

George Ronald
Oxford

George Ronald, *Publisher*
Oxford
www.grbooks.com

© M.L. Perry 2005
All Rights Reserved

ISBN 0-85398-491-3

*A catalogue record for this book is available
from the British Library*

Contents

Preface

In the late 19th century Bahá'u'lláh, the Prophet-Founder of the Bahá'í Faith, expounded a unique vision of the relationship between religion and human society. In many writings composed over the course of some four decades, during which He was a prisoner of the Ottoman Empire, He identified religion as the foundation for all civilizations. Only through the divine religions, He asserted, can human beings achieve a lasting, profound unity. The time has now come when the human race will enter the period of its long-awaited spiritual maturity. All nations and races will become united in a global civilization, a unity in diversity that will continue to evolve without end.

Bahá'u'lláh's vision is of critical importance for understanding humanity's transition from its turbulent adolescence to maturity and particularly for the resolution of racism.

Lest there be confusion – which is all too common in these days when words and concepts are rapidly evolving and subject to powerful ideological influences – we might bear in mind several points.

First, since our discussion focuses on the history of slavery and racism in North America we will be emphasizing the fundamental role played by Christianity in the rise of western civilization. However, much if not most of what we discover regarding Christianity is applicable to any of the other religions.

Second, we assume that religion is, if uncorrupted, a constructive and life-giving force for human society. If one were to understand our discussion as a defense of Christianity, such an understanding would be correct in part. It is, in fact, a defense of all truly spiritual religions and ways of life. But it should not be taken as a defense of traditions that inspire hatred and exclusion. We should be careful to distinguish between constructive, creative, positive religion and destructive, fanatical, negative religion;

to this point we shall devote further discussion. The truly religious life, irrespective of time or place, is a discipline that teaches the individual to love others, even under the most trying circumstances when love seems impossible. This discussion is not a defense of Christianity so much as an attempt to recover our original understanding of it, and not so much a defense of Christianity as a defense of the religious life in general.

Third, that our discussion is based on a positive conception of religion as a whole should in no way be taken to mean that we are adopting an uncritical attitude towards history. Nor should it be interpreted as a sign that we are ignoring or rejecting the importance of science in history and in our future. Bahá'u'lláh Himself clearly states that both science and religion are essential for the unfoldment of humanity's infinite potential. Let us, then, enter this discussion having left behind the ages-old debate between these two pillars of civilization.

Fourth, we should also avoid the conclusion that because our discussion asserts the fundamental importance of spirituality and the religious life, we are effectively advancing what might be understood in the current political culture as a conservative agenda of moral values. As shall be seen, Bahá'u'lláh's vision cannot be reduced to a simple formula that neatly fits into any political platform, whether conservative or liberal. It is fundamentally a spiritual vision, while at the same time it describes the evolution of human society as dependent on rational will. To reduce it to the level of politics yields little if any fruit. Although it shares some elements with ideas expressed in various philosophies of human society, ultimately it is a unique conception of humanity's history and future, and undoubtedly it will be the subject of much scholarly work in decades to come. Since political culture in the West dominates much of the writing in history and religion today, we need to remain aware that Bahá'u'lláh's conception of spiritual and moral teachings stands independent of what is politically fashionable.

Finally, since ours is a society that has been ravaged by corruption and our minds and hearts now are encased in the armor of cynicism, we find it difficult if not impossible to consider with an open mind any vision of a future for humanity that is glorious and transcendent. We dismiss it as the utopian dream of the deluded. Therefore we will attempt to relate Bahá'u'lláh's vision to the facts of human history, to ensure that at each point in the analysis we are looking squarely at past and present reality.

Having for generations locked ourselves into rigid camps advocating one or another world view, having been paralyzed by a crisis of will, we now thirst for the means to overcome the impasse. Let us view the study of Bahá'u'lláh's vision as an opportunity to transcend the dogmatic confines of contemporary social discourse and to see that when spirituality and material development combine they open doors that have been closed for most of human history. In the rise of civilizations past we have had but the briefest glimpses of human potential. Even the European Renaissance, with all its artistic and scientific glories, was, in the context of Bahá'u'lláh's conception of humanity's future development, but a small step at the beginning of a lofty road. Many times in the past we have stood, only to fall. Soon, Bahá'u'lláh assures us, we will become surefooted, for we are about to learn the ways of true civilization. Thereafter we will progress towards endless mountains, savoring unprecedented and unexpected victories, ever anticipating with both confidence and profound humility the peaks we have yet to climb.

Note from the Publisher

Racism is one of the major obstacles to world peace. The dignity of human beings is continually undermined by its persistence and the potential of whole groups of people is denied under its tyranny. The depth of the problem has reached even into the language itself. The terms used to describe people are often insensitive, derogatory, offensive and imposed by others. In a work such as this, it is important to try to use terms that people use for themselves. A style guide produced by the Native American Journalists Association recommends the terms 'Native American' and 'American Indian'. In this book the two terms are used interchangeably. The term 'Indian' alone is used for the sake of simplicity when the full term 'Native American' or 'American Indian' appears in the text preceding it. Similarly, instead of repeating the full term 'African Americans' the briefer 'African' is sometimes used.

For further information on this subject, please refer to:

Kara Briggs, Tom Arviso, Dennis McAuliffe and Lori Edmo-Suppah. *The Reading Red Report: Native Americans in the News: A 2002 Report and Content Analysis on Coverage by the Largest Newspapers in the United States* <http://www.naja.com/docs/red.doc>

Christina Berry. 'What's in a Name? Indians and Political Correctness'. <http://www.allthingscherokee.com/atc_sub_culture_feat_events_070101.html>

Borgna Brunner. 'What Style and Usage Guides Say: *American Indian* versus *Native American*'. <http://www.factmonster.com/spot/aihmterms.html>

Acknowledgments

For the past eight years I have on countless occasions remembered my good fortune to benefit from the unfailing support of the staff of the Lebanese American University Library, Beirut. This work was made possible by their meticulous professionalism and conscientious dedication and I cannot thank them enough.

I am deeply grateful to Dr Wendi Momen for her willingness to take on this project and her guidance and expertise in piloting it safely to shore.

Finally I also wish to thank the Lebanese American University Research Council for providing much valued assistance.

1

Introduction

Racism
Being an Outlaw in America

As a young child I watched a fair amount of television, which in those days was a small black and white screen set in a handsome wood cabinet. One of my favorite programs was *The Lone Ranger*. Every episode began with a scene of the hero in profile racing his horse across the tumbleweed-strewn landscape of the far West to Rossini's stirring 'William Tell Overture'. He was fearless, expert and dashing. His hat and his horse were white. With his trusty Native American companion, Tonto – whose constant presence contradicted the show's title, but never mind – he chased bandits and outlaws who wore dark hats and rode dark horses. The Lone Ranger upheld the laws; the bad men broke them. I was always on the Lone Ranger's side and felt deep satisfaction when every episode concluded with the bad men receiving their punishment and order and justice restored. Little did I know that I myself, in those days, was an outlaw.

My family was illegal in 16 states of the United States until 1967. Over the course of our country's history 38 states had had some form of 'anti-miscegenation' law. Gradually the states had voluntarily repealed these statutes. Between 1945 and 1967 anti-miscegenation laws were abrogated in 15 states: Arizona, California, Colorado, Idaho, Indiana, Maryland, Michigan, Montana, Nebraska, Nevada, North Dakota, Oregon, South Dakota, Utah and Wyoming. Yet until 1967 they remained on the books and more or less in force in Alabama, Arkansas, Delaware, Florida, Georgia, Kentucky, Louisiana, Mississippi, Missouri, North Carolina, Oklahoma, South Carolina, Tennessee, Texas, Virginia and West Virginia. That these laws still had teeth was evidenced by the fact that cases of intermarriage across state lines to avoid legal prohibitions in Georgia and Maryland were prominent in the media as late as 1966.[1] Not until 1967, when Richard and Mildred Loving, an interracial married couple, submitted their precedent-setting appeal for legal protection from the state of Virginia, did the United States Supreme Court rule the unconstitutionality of anti-miscegenation laws.[2]

These laws characterized people of mixed racial backgrounds as social and legal abominations.[3] Yet we, as children of African American and European American parents, were very fortunate, for we knew the unity of the human race as a reality, not an abstract concept or ideal. We knew it because we lived it every day. It entered our consciousness not through the mind but through our very being. We could not entertain any notion that one 'race' was different from another, just as we could never be told one's own hand belonged to another person. This background helped us keep our bearings in a world full of powerful false ideas regarding the origins and physical features of peoples, powerful because they were expressed repeatedly by governments, the media, neighbors, parents, teachers and books.

Global Nightmare

As we proceed further into the age of global consciousness we recognize that the struggle against racism is common to many peoples around the world. It has been a long global nightmare, a violent spiritual storm. We constantly discuss it, study it, write books about it, because we believe that this storm will be made to cease by the power of understanding. And as long as it roams freely throughout the United States and elsewhere none of us will be free. All of us will continue to be imprisoned by it, locked up for safety within the walls of our homes, never to venture out and see each other face to face in security and peace. It is as if the terror of the Salem witch-hunts – believed to have been limited to a small town in a distant past – has been overrunning our land for some 400 years. America, the 'land of the free', is a land of spiritual prisoners. We have been right all along to yearn for freedom; the irony is that we have been our own jail keepers.

Now we are beginning to witness a measure of self-liberation from superstitious traditions. More and more Americans of all races have of late been choosing to open the gates of their minds and hearts and throw away forever the locks of prejudices. It has been a slow and painstaking process but one that has abundantly proved its success nonetheless. It has proved that the superstition of racial prejudice refers to no true reality. It has proved that the acceptance of humanity as a single race, regardless of color or origin, does not lead to evil and the wrath of God but, quite the contrary, to greater peace and social advancement.

This constructive process has yet some distance to run, for regrettably the global nightmare of racism and superstition continues to plague the mind and soul of humanity.[4]

Defining Racism

Most societies and peoples experience racism and prejudice of varying degrees of intensity. While the form that racism takes differs from one society to another, the content is always the same: a profound lack of spirituality, a condition which we will explore in greater detail. Our discussion centers on racism in America. It is one of the oldest, most powerful and most deeply entrenched forms of racism in the world. Methods of oppression used against African Americans and American Indians have been taken as models by some other countries, most notoriously Nazi Germany. While in our era of global telecommunications many outstanding efforts to eradicate social ills have gained ground, persisting systems of prejudice and racism are rapidly spreading virus-like throughout the world. Moreover, as the leader of democratic nations, the United States has long been regarded by many peoples as the exemplar of modern civilization. For the exploration of racism, then, there is no better place to begin than American society. We bear in mind, of course, that many if not most of the basic truths we will explore are universal, relating to the human condition, and are not specific to any particular culture.

Racism is not a discrete phenomenon with specific boundaries that clearly demarcate what is and what is not racist behavior. Rather it is gradated. At one extreme is undeniable racist behavior: lynchings, use of racial epithets, inhumane laws and governmental systems, prejudicial religious doctrines and so on. At the other extreme is complete freedom from prejudice, social interaction with no regard for skin color or ethnic background. Occasionally in history, in certain places at certain times, it could be said that this ideal has been achieved if only tenuously. Melting pots wherein race has been forgotten or at least regarded as unimportant, and where diversity and mixing of races are considered normal, prove that the ideal is indeed possible. Such places include Islamic Andalusia, the interface between the European colonies and the early American Indian tribes of the East coast, Hawaii, Brazil, parts of the Caribbean, parts of California and New York City.

Between these two extremes is the 'gray area', society's mainstream wherein racism is systematically practiced, consciously or subconsciously, yet in all cases in such a way that renders people confused. Mainstream racism exists, yet it is either not detected or, if easily recognizable, not prosecuted by the law. Unlike extreme racism, mainstream racism faces no official or moral prohibition. Its conscious practice is considered reasonable and acceptable by law and its subconscious practice is considered non-existent. It is the most widespread form of racism in the world today and the source of most disagreement about racism. By carefully reasoned arguments its existence is justified or its nonexistence is proved.

One such argument is that European Americans also have their own stories to tell: how they have been mistreated, harmed or abused by African Americans or other minorities. Often blacks hear the stories of whites in which the white narrator is a victim of a black criminal and the seemingly inescapable conclusion is that racism is a legitimate white reaction to the behavior of blacks. Before our discussion can proceed we must resolve this difference of perspectives.

Let us agree that criminal acts committed by people of any race should be punished with justice according to the law. Nearly all black people would agree with this principle, especially since most crimes in America – over 80 per cent – are committed against victims of the same race.[5]

Let us also agree that when we are talking about racism we are not referring to white responses, justified or unjustified, to criminal behavior of blacks. Rather, racism refers to the oppression blacks face when they are *not* criminals, when they are law-abiding, when they have achieved a great deal in their lives, proved themselves outstanding, done everything their society asks its citizens to do – and yet are treated as criminals. In more ways than one this is the heart and soul of racism and this sort of treatment the vast majority of our European American brothers and sisters do not face.

Another central aspect of anti-African American racism is that, unlike prejudices against other ethnic groups, it is systematically supported by the society's institutions. 'Biases against rock music or Italians', Maureen Reddy explains, 'are not encoded into every social institution, after all, while racism is.' Moreover, this kind of encoded, systemic racism does more than cause hurt feelings: it has the 'power to affect its targets' life chances – where one lives, where one works, what sort of job one has, where (or if) one goes to school, what one thinks of oneself and of one's group'.[6]

Prejudice is my fear or rejection of someone out of ignorance. Prejudice is natural. We tend to assume things about people based on the little we know of them. But when ignorance is replaced by experiential knowledge, fear and rejection naturally disappear. A racist, however, will never lose that fear and hostility no matter how much experiential knowledge he may gain. Racism is the continuation of our negative assumptions even when, after getting to know the person, we recognize that these are false. We are racist when we take the 10 per cent of a group who do bad things or are negatively perceived and we apply their negative qualities to the remaining 90 per cent of the group. Racists perceive minorities through mental filters

4

that eliminate most, if not all, good qualities and achievements and allow to pass through only character flaws and misdeeds. In an observation from the late 1950s and early 1960s that is applicable today, John Howard Griffin stated that most newspapers 'adhere to the long-standing conspiracy of silence about anything remotely favorable to the Negro. His achievements are carefully excluded or, when they demand attention, they are handled with the greatest care to avoid the impression that anything good the individual Negro does is typical of his race.'[7]

Experiential knowledge does not register in the racist's mind, a cognitive dissonance that prevents him from recognizing, for example, that the African American neighbor has an outstanding character. Racism is therefore above all a belief system, a matter of faith that come what may, against all facts, the truth is something other than what it appears to be. It is a belief system that defines reality and is not influenced by reality itself.

Such a system hopes and expects to foster the white population's development while retarding and even arresting the development of African Americans – cultivating powerful abilities in one community and imperfection and social pathology in another. What the proponents of such a system do not realize, however, is that humanity is an organic whole, and sooner or later injury to one part of the human race will affect, materially and spiritually, all other parts.

But racism is also only one of many forms of what law professor Patricia J. Williams calls 'spirit murder': 'cultural obliteration, prostitution, abandonment of the elderly and the homeless, and genocide are some of its other guises'. Spirit murder 'produces a system of formalized distortions of thought' in which fear and hate, and the actions they inspire, are permitted.[8] Racism is thus a particularly powerful form of what is a much more general phenomenon. As we shall see, such spirit murder has been systematically committed in the West since at least the late Middle Ages, just at the time that the modern world was beginning to take shape.

Between Absurdity and Insanity

Although we can define racism and discuss it rationally, we should remember that if it is essentially a spiritual and social illness, as we shall argue, it is therefore a system of thought that ultimately makes no sense. Perhaps the best way we can understand the nonsensical nature of racism is through comparisons.

Some decades ago a small state in central Africa, following its hard won independence from England, promulgated laws that limited the rights of Europeans and citizens of European background – anyone with white skin. Whites were not permitted to enter certain hotels and restaurants. They were excluded from all lakeside beaches and swimming pools except those reserved for them. They were denied the use of the sidewalks in the wealthier areas of the capital city. Housing authorities instituted a concerted effort to gradually push them away from good residential areas into the less desirable estates and public housing. Whites were restricted to the worst hospitals. White children were permitted to attend a wide range of schools but were excluded from the best and were not permitted entry to the national university. Police favored Africans and discriminated against Europeans. The media highlighted international cases of white criminality, frequently publishing photographs of white criminals and rarely of black counterparts. White victims of crime were generally ignored. Although Africans observed common courtesy, they periodically reminded whites of their lower status in the newly independent state by suddenly – and thus all the more effectively – uttering racial epithets in their presence.

This was indeed a horrible, shameful situation. Such laws and practices would be rejected outright by any civilized society. How could this nation, even if newly independent, dare to create such draconian measures? Were they not sensitive to the wrongs they themselves suffered in history? Could they not forego revenge and practice forgiveness and justice? How could arrogance take hold of this nation so quickly and forcefully as to affect and even permanently maim the lives of innocent children and adults?

Let us now examine our emotions upon reading this account. Naturally one might feel emotions of hurt, anger, perhaps even outrage. Now let us consider the following: The example of this African country is not true. It is a fabrication. As far as I know, no African country has created such racist laws against whites. I merely took the laws created by racist societies in America, South Africa and elsewhere and placed them in an imaginary black society. When the laws are created by whites, do we feel the same emotions of hurt, anger, perhaps even outrage? If not, why not? As we shall see, our emotions are to a great extent not determined by a sense of justice but by the prevailing culture in which we live.

Let us further imagine that a proportion of whites in America, say 10 per cent, is excluded from learning and playing competitive tennis and is treated with contempt at the workplace no matter how senior they may be in the corporate ranks. And the reason for this discrimination? No reason at all; it is just the way it is. We forget that in reality, if we bear in mind the spiritual nature of humanity, such discrimination against blacks 'because they are black' is based upon no valid reason at all. Indeed, racial prejudice is literally *un-reasonable*. Therefore the best analogy would be random discrimination of a segment of the white community, a group who from early childhood would know their status, find it indelible and suffer from it all of their lives. They would be blonde and blue-eyed and turned away from the tennis club; blonde and blue-eyed and mistaken for the janitor;

6

blonde and blue-eyed and told to 'pick up those bags'; blonde and blue-eyed and suspected of thievery.

Shocking? Somehow when we see that the skin color of the victim of such discrimination is black or brown we are not shocked; it makes sense to us; it is part of the order of the universe. We are comfortable with it because it has been cultivated in us. We take it as natural, essential and true; yet it is but an illusion created by language and other means of socialization, as Lao Tzu and Chuang Tzu, among others, have taught. It is no more a part of reality than witches were in Salem. This comfort with something that is patently unreal is our self-imprisonment. It is our collective nightmare. We are haunted by our own imaginings, haunted because we take them not as imaginings but as reality.

And the story has not yet ended. If we expand our view of the scene we will witness something truly mind-boggling: the concept of random discrimination against a proportion of whites is not as far-fetched as it may at first seem. Do we not find this when we look at the world as a whole? A holistic perspective allows us to see many simultaneous forms of discrimination against whites across the face of the earth. You may be white but that is no guarantee you will be treated without discrimination. And as the perspective becomes more global, this discrimination begins to appear more and more random, more and more absurd. You may be white but you could be discriminated against if you are Jewish, or if you are Muslim, or if you are Protestant, or if you are Catholic, or if you are from the 'South' or from the 'North', or if you are British, or French, or from the 'East' or from the 'West'. You may face prejudice as a white person if you are poor, if you are a woman, if you have a certain kind of accented speech. Is this not absurd? The more we study the global situation, the more we realize that very few whites – indeed very few of any race – are safe from discrimination. And why so? Simply for many reasons that are completely incompatible and nonsensical. Hence, from the wider global and spiritual perspective, for no valid reason at all.

Yet many of us regard racism and prejudice as the very height of reason, the essence of social reality. We believe it is ordained by God, or a necessity of nature, or based on scientific truth. But this is nothing more than superstition. We are a people suffering from spiritual illness.

Let us now turn from thought experiments to real historical examples to illustrate how this absurdity manifests itself in our society.

Walter White (1893–1955) was from 1931 until his death the head of the National Association for the Advancement of Colored People. He was an African American but his physical appearance was that of a white man. In a late 1940s article in the national magazine *Look* he recommended the use of skin-whitening chemicals as a cure for racism.[9] Walter White had

7

suffered greatly as a child, witnessing his father's inhumane treatment in a racist hospital and subsequent death in a decrepit ward reserved for African Americans. His suggestion can be interpreted today not so much as a sign that he alone was out of touch with reality but as the natural response to a world gone mad. Even today skin bleaching has become the rage in parts of Africa itself, causing people to scrub themselves with special soap and shampoo and apply several powerful creams. The results lighten the color of the skin quite dramatically but also weaken the skin to the point where it cuts very easily and cannot hold stitches.[10]

About half way through his four-week journey in the South in 1959 disguised as a black man, John Howard Griffin, a white writer, found himself feeling tremendous guilt when speaking by telephone to his white wife. She had been completely supportive of the project from the start. Why such negative feelings, then, when he spoke with her over the telephone?

> I began to understand . . . that culture – learned behavior patterns so deeply ingrained they produce unconscious involuntary reactions – is a prison. My conditioning as a Negro, and the immense sexual implications with which the racists in our culture bombard us, cut me off, even in my most intimate self, from any connection with my wife.[11]

In a matter of days he had come to identify with blacks very strongly, even though he was merely in disguise. A similar transformation of mentality was experienced by white journalist Ray Sprigle, who in 1948 also traveled through the South as a black man. Both Griffin and Sprigle had lived all their lives as 'whites' and yet they became 'blacks' in thought and emotion in a matter of days. How real, then, can whiteness or blackness be? A University of Maryland student repeated the experiment of Sprigle and Griffin in the spring of 1994. Having chemically darkened his skin color and shaved his head, he had intended to travel alone through the South for 25 days. But then he had a change of plans. 'After all of two days, the experiment was over. Maybe I was weak, maybe I couldn't hack it. I didn't care. This anger was making me sick and the only antidote I knew was a dose of white skin.'[12]

In the Jim Crow period, in order to circumvent the anti-miscegenation laws, 'a white man would transfer blood from the African American woman he loved in order to assert that he was black himself'.[13]

According to the Jim Crow laws, a mixed-race boy who was born to a white woman would not be permitted to marry a white woman like his mother.[14]

> Around the year 1970 a black woman had a college friend who discovered, having lived her life as a red-haired, gray-eyed white person, that she was

one-sixteenth black . . . Before my eyes and despite herself, she began to externalize all the unconscious baggage that 'black' bore for her, the self-hatred that racism is. She did not think of herself as a racist – nor had I – but she literally wanted to jump out of her skin, shed her flesh, start life over again. She confided that she felt fouled and betrayed.[15]

In speaking of ghettos, Jonathan Kozol testifies to the absurdity of racism in New York City. He sees that 'ghettos serve a very important function for the privileged'.

In the early and mid-1980s, thousands of families became homeless in New York . . .

Inevitably these people walked the streets and stood outside the restaurants and theaters, and their presence was abhorrent in the middle of Manhattan. The civic boosters of the city were alarmed. This would hurt tourism. The last thing theater owners wanted was to have a wealthy couple spend $200 to see Les Miserables and then come out from the theater and see the real thing! There was often bitter irony in that situation. I walked by that theater sometimes and would notice people who had presumably been weeping for the poor children in Paris a few minutes before in the theater; now, coming out on the street, they were miserably offended by the sight of people begging on the sidewalk.[16]

CAVEAT

Studying the origins of racism is like studying the origins of the physical universe. At some point the observer recognizes that those origins exist outside the known reality, beyond history and historical events. Historical research, like physics, has its limits. The true nature of racism is beyond words and logical thinking. Any attempt to explain completely the nature of racism and prejudice requires one to comprehend the entire panorama of history, an impossible task. We can never know the absolute beginning of racism; this concept must be taken as relative.

Therefore in exploring the origin and nature of racism we must avoid the temptation to become too specific. We must remember that racism is the construct of a sick society and we are all affected to some degree. In severe cases racism manifests itself in the individual as symptoms of mental and spiritual illness but because these symptoms are shared in a community that is racist they do not appear as illness but rather as normality. Countless such symptoms have evolved during the history of the United States, including myths about food preferences, myths about the ability to swim and myths about sexual behavior. On the one hand, we are going to be clarifying the origins of racism and, on the other, we should keep in mind these symptoms and mental constructs of the racist personality. But it is not particularly fruitful to draw complete lines of causality from the origins of the spiritual illness to the symptoms. The person suffering from severe forms of this illness does not think rationally. Although his thoughts may be perfectly logical to him, his 'logic' is in fact fantasy. It therefore does not pay to follow him step by step into the wilds of his imaginings. Our task is to explain the rise of this wilderness in the midst of a complex civilization and its eventual fall, not to know all the pathways within.

AWAKENING

We naturally ask, if racist ideologies make no sense, why do we believe in them? Recognizing the absurdity and insanity of racism, we are prepared to look for a deeper understanding of the motivations and nature of racist behavior.

Superficially, racism in America seems to be primarily about the oppression of blacks and Native Americans. At a deeper level, however, it is something else. As we shall see, racism is not really about black inferiority, which in the final analysis is merely a red herring. Rather, the true goal of racism is white superiority. Racism targets blacks only in order to construct whites as the superior group of people on the planet. It is an attempt to define whites as supreme by default, by negating the values of all other groups. It is the habit of supremacists to declare themselves uniquely sacred, closest to God, supreme on earth, even gods on earth. Racial supremacists target blacks because they cannot openly and directly proclaim themselves supreme for fear of contradicting religious teachings that require us to love and show humility to all creatures.

'White studies' has appeared on the scene in academia and for good reason. 'Whites' come in many different colors; many are darker than people called 'black', as is well known. Many, including Irish, Italians and even Scandinavians, were considered not white until relatively recently. Noel Ignatiev has written: 'I even heard of a time when it was said in the Pacific Northwest logging industry that no whites worked in these woods, just a bunch of Swedes.'[17] Whiteness refers not to physical color but to an ideal ultimate reality. Being white is, in the supremacist philosophy, the only true reality and all else is false and illusory, all else is not truly human.

From the deeper spiritual perspective, however, racism is not even about white superiority. Here superiority, inferiority and race itself are illusions. What is real is the spiritual aspect of human life. The spiritual perspective focuses on the human race as a whole and our evolution towards a transcendent destiny. Much of our discussion, therefore, will not be about race *per se*, since the solution to racism lies far beyond skin color, beyond oppressed and oppressor, beyond policies of distribution of social benefits, economic resources and power, beyond history. The solution to racism lies in the way we intend to make our future as a people on this planet in building a true, spiritually-based civilization. In the context of the overwhelming possibilities standing before us like a blank canvas, racism and all other social problems are transformed from the center to the periphery and finally to ineffective obstacles in the inevitable rise of a global civilization. Racism appears interminable only because we mistakenly believe that ours is a true civilization.

Racism is not only symptomatic of false civilization; it is also a means to maintain the illusion that our civilization is true. Its purpose is not to make sense but to deceive. Karl Marx characterized religion as the 'opium of the masses', for it kept the proletariat in a deep sleep, a state of impotence preventing self-consciousness and the attainment of political unity against the ruling class. Although our discussion here is based on the reality of religious and spiritual truth, we can agree with Marx that at periods in history religion has prevented the healthy evolution of society. Yet there are many such opiates of the masses and among the most important must be racism. It is a very powerful opiate indeed. It is an induced and prolonged state of dreaming that has concealed the truth – not the truth of politics and class interests but the much deeper truth that we are all spiritual beings and that human society should be spiritualized, based on recognition and practice of the oneness of humanity. By diverting attention away from spiritual truth, racism succeeds in keeping open the door to the endless, superficial and ultimately destructive delights of excessive materialism.

Spirituality
Defining Religion

Most people believe that religious tradition has been the source of racist belief and action for centuries. But here we are turning this notion on its head, for we shall show that this is an incorrect interpretation of history. There are two kinds of religion: true religion and corrupted religion, both of which call themselves religion or faith. It is essential, therefore, that we differentiate between the pure teachings of the Messenger and the impure interpretations and corruptions we have introduced in the name of the Messenger's religion. In our discussion, the term 'true religion' refers to the original and pure teachings and nothing else. We are referring to spiritual life, the teaching and practice of universal love, wise usage of resources yet detachment from earthly desires, a life in balance and harmony with other people and with nature, a life that anticipates a transcendent existence after physical death. Religion that is truly spiritual is an effective remedy pre-cisely because racism is a form of extreme materialism.

Some researchers, such as Richard Dyer, have characterized Christianity as being materialistic, oriented to the physical body.[18] This is only correct if we equate misinterpretations and distortions of Christ's teachings with Christianity as taught by Jesus Himself. Therefore, on the one hand, researchers are correct in saying that the modern society that has evolved from Christianity is obsessed with the physical world and the physical body. On the other hand, they are incorrect because the teachings of Jesus were diametrically opposed to such a way of life. Physical objects and physical relationships are referred to in the New Testament as a way of conveying a spiritual truth. Only in a highly materialistic world view could the text be taken to emphasize the physical over all else. The text appears to be materially oriented only if we are not sensitive to the spiritual meanings these physical symbols convey.

Only a few references are needed to prove this point. Jesus likened the attitude of the Pharisees and Sadducees to people who wash the outside of a cup but leave the inside dirty. He was not speaking of dishwashing but rather the spiritual state of those who claim deep knowledge and yet are blind to the truth – in other words, hypocrites. Jesus warned against attachment to wealth and basically declared that wealth and spiritual life are incompatible, just as a camel cannot go through the eye of a needle. He also called upon one of His disciples to let the dead bury the dead, meaning that the disciple need not be concerned with the burial of his deceased father for others who are not interested in following Jesus will fulfill that duty. For Jesus, true death is the death not of the body but of the soul. Likewise, true life is not the physical life on this earth but the spiritual life of the soul and its nearness to God.[19]

Let us openly acknowledge that religion has been corrupted and misinterpreted for evil purposes throughout recorded history. Slavery and racism were defended by copious references to and sophisticated exegesis of the Bible.[20] Nevertheless, however materialistic the interpretations, traditions and rituals that have encrusted Christianity and other religions, it is our duty to recognize the original teachings of the Messenger and not the false teachings that others have ascribed to Him. We are confused because we have a problem of terminology. When we say Christianity or religion we mean one thing and other researchers mean another. We ought carefully to distinguish between this and that. We ought not describe Christianity as materialistic when what we really mean is humanity's interpretation of it. By true Christianity we mean here the teachings and life of Jesus, which were obviously so far removed from materialism as to have caused Him and His disciples for generations after to suffer persecution from the authorities of a deeply materialistic age. If His had been a materialistic view of the world it would have comfortably, quietly and conveniently sunk into the morass of the materialistic culture already firmly established throughout the Roman Empire, becoming just one more of many new cults arising around countless local beliefs, visions, gods and superstitions. Christianity was and is far beyond the clink of gold, the step of be-robed authority, the formulaic manipulations of angels, saints and sinners. Christianity has always been the teaching of love and the life of the spirit, the preparation of individuals and society for an existence beyond the physical world.

Revalidating Spirituality

In several statements Bahá'u'lláh sets forth a conception of human civilization as based on truly spiritual religion.

All men have been created to carry forward an ever-advancing civilization.[21]

The well-being of mankind, its peace and security, are unattainable unless and until its unity is firmly established.[22]

The purpose of religion as revealed from the heaven of God's holy Will is to establish unity and concord amongst the peoples of the world; make it not the cause of dissension and strife. The religion of God and His divine law are the most potent instruments and the surest of all means for the dawning of the light of unity amongst men. The progress of the world, the development of nations, the tranquillity of peoples, and the peace of all who dwell on earth are among the principles and ordinances of God.[23]

Should the lamp of religion be obscured, chaos and confusion will ensue, and the lights of fairness and justice, of tranquillity and peace cease to shine.[24]

Here Bahá'u'lláh presents three fundamental principles of humanity's social evolution: we are destined to build an 'ever-advancing civilization' that inevitably will encompass the entire globe; civilization will not be possible without unity; unity will not be possible without religion. This concept of society as religiously based compels us to completely revise our understanding of history. Whereas most social scientists attribute the major forces in social evolution to secular institutions and processes – economics, politics, war – in reality, Bahá'u'lláh states, the true cause of social evolution is the spiritual development of the individual, the community, the nation and the human race as a whole.

Also implied here is the relationship between spirituality and religion. Spirituality is an innate potential in human beings; religion is the means for realizing that potential. One practices religion in order to develop spiritual qualities. Without true religion these qualities remain dormant.

SKEPTICISM IN SOCIAL SCIENCE

Talk of spirituality tends to bring academic and political discussions to a dead halt. Most contemporary social science rejects religion not only as irrelevant to the solution of social problems but also as a historic contributor to the problems themselves. This attitude is a legacy of the anti-clerical movement that gave rise to the secular state and its supporting philosophies, of which social science was a central part. The modern social sciences are predicated on the principle that all problems are material in nature and their solution is only a matter of rearranging material relations between people – their money, land, jobs and so on.

Prior to our materialistic understanding of human society the prevailing view was based on religious dogma. Society was seen as the outcome of the growth of the religious community. Humanity was not merely a collection of individuals but the creation of a personal, transcendent God. Society was not in humanity's hands but in God's. There was, therefore, no room and no need for a 'science' of society with which to study and resolve problems; they were the result of sinful behavior, which could only be corrected by repentance or by God's intervention.

The analysis presented here subscribes exclusively to neither of these approaches but rather takes parts of each. It accepts the premise that human behavior can be studied, analyzed and corrected making use of rational, scientific means. However, it also accepts that science and rationalism are limited in the study of human behavior. It argues that humanity is not only material but also spiritual in nature and thus a purely materialistic approach would fail to account for the totality of human experience. It therefore includes the paradigm that spirituality and its laws are real and that human society must also be understood in terms of this spiritual reality. It examines the interface where the spiritual and the material meet. Only when both are accounted for can an accurate understanding of social problems be obtained and an accurate solution formulated.

Materialistic social science argues that slavery and racism arose because of economic forces: the desire for cheap labor, especially as the industrial revolution emerged and stimulated a vast international demand for raw materials. Many social scientists, politicians, economists and philosophers of all stripes have offered countless remedies for racism, typically centering around an ostensibly pragmatic solution involving governmental and economic policies, voting systems, civil rights, housing resources, educational opportunities or a combination of these. They propose manipulations of money, political power, symbols. Such remedies consist of strategies, agendas, logical arguments, analyses of the mechanics of society, an almost scientific 'physics' of the push and pull of human emotions and their relationships to material wants and needs. Social scientists are the plumbers of civilization who tap here, knock there and come up with a diagnosis and solution to replace, rebuild or repair a particular element in the system by which we live. Many of these perspectives are reasonable, at least in part, for racism manifests itself as various social and economic problems. The difficulty is that purely materialistic solutions have not yielded satisfactory results. The system continues to be as faulty as ever, no matter how many new policies, adjustments or strategies are implemented.

This is so because the heart of racism, the disease itself as opposed to its outward symptomatic manifestations, is not social but spiritual. Doubtless the social symptoms must be addressed but their resolution, although necessary, is not sufficient. In fact, the much deeper issue is the religious disenfranchisement of African peoples who were thereby set up to be exploited. And if racism is essentially a spiritual problem, then so too is its solution. But since traditional social science believes that spirituality is not a true reality, it fails to understand the essence of racism.

It is a modern myth that spirituality and morality have no bearing on the development of society and the twists and turns of history. All material factors – politics, economics, psychology, demography, culture, the weather and natural phenomena, diseases, and science and technology – are believed to play powerful roles. But because Marx said religion is the opium of the masses, because science says it is at worst a harmful delusion – as Freud saw it[25] – or at best sincere hopes, most social scientists have concluded that religion, and the morality it attempts to convey, is false, bankrupt and of no relevance to the study of humanity's true nature. The separation of Church and state has meant that spirituality has no business in the unfolding of history and the scholarship that interprets it.

We tend to ignore Christianity's moral collapse as a key factor in the rise of slavery and racism because of a subtle assumption: Most modern historians join Freud in assuming that Christian love was merely a myth, that the teachings of Christ to love one's neighbor as oneself, and to love one's enemy, to be spiritual and not materialistic, were never taken seriously and were never applied with diligence in the Christian community except among a small handful of fanatical believers, monks, priests, nuns and assorted eccentric ascetics. It is assumed that only a saint – or a madman – could follow these teachings. Today spiritual ideals are not relevant to our profit-based culture and so we cannot see them as having ever been relevant in the past. Christianity is myth, theory, sentiment, not reality. Because of this assumption we have not been able to unravel the cultural evolution of western society that led to slavery and to modern racism. If we assume that Christianity was never a reality, that spirituality is only an unattainable ideal, then we cannot understand the workings of the modern western mind in its death-struggle with the guilt of slavery and racial oppression. The historians who base their work on a Freudian assumption of a psyche essentially amoral in content and operation are blind to the elephant in the living room of American culture, the contradictions at the heart of America's quintessential problem.

The fact is that spirituality is real, its operation powerful, its neglect fraught with dire consequences. The lack of brotherhood, the absence of spirituality, make possible the inhumane treatment of one by the other. Racism and slavery are the symptoms or consequences of the ebbing of spirituality from the social landscape. The entire enterprise of modern social science has failed not because of a lack of scientific skill but because social scientists have been determined to disenfranchise spiritual concepts and institutions in order to make way for their own newly ordained secular clerical order and academy. Such disenfranchisement denies the existence of what has been at the heart of social life for most of human history: a primal concern for the non-material aspects of life, for the higher emotions of love and compassion, for the need for human unity. Any honest effort to understand humanity – which is the stated goal of all social science – must see, appreciate and acknowledge human being in its entirety. Social science has failed because it has accepted only a false humanity as the subject of study, an edited humanity, an artificial humanity, an academically constructed humanity. We study not ourselves but some creation of the laboratory of the mind. And unfortunately, all too often we social scientists become like our laboratory creation: alienated from the world, from human society, from ourselves.

If we are to understand history accurately we must not impose our contemporary culture on the past. If we are not spiritual in our day, we cannot assume that past generations were likewise unable or unwilling to practice spiritual ideals. Not only must religion be taken into account when investigating history but also the *spirituality* of pre-corrupted religion, the actual practice of the seemingly impossible spiritual ideals of the Bible and other holy books. If we are to understand our current society, we cannot ignore the fact that spiritual love was at some time past not a myth, not a dream, but a reality, that what we now refer to as brotherhood or solidarity actually first appeared in our western civilization among the followers of religious teachings, not unions and political parties.

SECULARISM

Many people believe that it is hopelessly idealistic to heal racism with religious platitudes and moral principles, to argue that the problem would disappear if people would obey the rules of religion, like the Ten

Commandments, or secular moral principles like the pledge of the Boy Scouts. They tend to dismiss such idealism as illusions and clichés that, as Marx argued, merely mislead the masses and prevent them from understanding the true nature of society. Such illusions, they believe, are worse than empty of value; they are, in fact, the remnants of a false ideology that only fools would follow.

But it is equally idealistic and reductionist to argue that secular principles will save the day, that all we need do, for example, is follow the principles of the free market. Having banned religion and spirituality from their social space, secular institutions have become dangerously amoral. As Peter Marin states, secularism has promised much but delivered little to the world.

> Freud's view of religion can stand in general for the standard secular view of religion, a view which runs all the way back to the Enlightenment and has marked almost all secular thought since then. The great dream at the heart of secularism has always been that religion would slowly wither away, giving way, as it did so, to reason and a generosity of spirit or a morality rooted not in a fear of God or the hope of heaven, but in a sense of community and a belief in the common good. The fear and fanaticism engendered by faith would gradually be replaced by a maturity of vision, an understanding of self, and an ethical complexity that would leave behind, as part of the infantile past, the illusions, fantasies, and superstitions which had marked the childhood of man. The religious divisions and hatred separating us one from another would disappear, and the senses of gratitude, awe and indebtedness traditionally felt for God would be transferred to the human world and relocated in a universalized community. Values would no longer be enforced or maintained through oppression or fear, but instead would rise naturally and directly from human reason, instinct, and sympathy. Men and women would give freely to one another what had once been demanded by God.[26]

Yet Marin, who describes himself as a dedicated secularist, admits that after centuries of predominance in the West secularism has failed to fulfill these noble goals.[27] If secularism has proved itself to be a failed dream, we then must question the secular method of solving problems and we must at least investigate the role of spirituality in social life. We have struggled to implement scientific and political solutions for decades without satisfaction. The failure of secularism forces us to realize that spiritual principles cannot be regarded as false. We ignore them at our peril. They are not scientific, yet they are essential to the formation and preservation of any society. Now it is time to embrace a spiritual conception of humanity – however strange it may seem to us, we who have been educated so consistently in a secular context – and apply it to the heretofore insoluble divisions of race, class and culture.

Corrupted religions have earned for themselves the scorn and skepticism of the masses in most countries. In the West, criticism of ecclesiastical iniquity has become a venerated tradition and a means of expressing civil morality. But what the opponents of religion are criticizing is religion without spirituality and, indeed, who could disagree? For when religion loses spirituality it becomes an institution of great political and material power lacking morality and as such becomes harmful. However, in the process of making society free to pursue market activity unfettered by religious laws, we not only limited the powers of the religious authorities but invalidated spiritual life as a whole. We threw the baby out with the bath water.

The culture of the West that gave rise to racism produced first a materialistic tradition that could justify and support it, a philosophy that has so dominated our history that we fear to break free of its influence. We fear being labeled irrational, unscientific, emotional and simply wrong. But this tradition is quickly becoming bankrupt. We have tried the purely rational method and found it wanting. This should not be taken as a criticism or dismissal of science and technology, for the rational mind is essential to civilized life. But beyond it is the spirit, a mysterious, transcendent and mystical power that operates in conjunction with the mind yet is quite distinct from it. Liberation from the scourge of racism lies down that mysterious path wherein material qualities are recognized as having no ultimate reality. As we enter the new millennium, spirituality is regaining the attention of scholars and doers throughout the world, for they realize that the essential truths common to all the religions, far from hampering the work of governance and problem-solving, speak directly to critical human needs.[28] We are recognizing that spiritualization, far from boding ill for society, answers a fundamental need which science and rational method cannot fulfill. We can no longer impulsively conclude that spiritual language necessarily precludes scientific and rational discourse and thus implies an inquiry without worth to the field of practical action. The consensus is growing that spirituality and scientific reason are not incompatible; spirituality can indeed be investigated, discussed and applied by reasoning minds. Social science and spirituality together form a holistic discourse. One cannot be divorced from the other if we are to make progress in resolving racism in particular and social problems in general. Science, technology and religion are the central elements of civilization. The rapidly spreading acceptance of spirituality's role in human life is a sign of humanity's gradual maturity.

It is often argued that you can't legislate love, morality or spirituality, that it is best to leave them to the home life. For example, the 'separate but equal' doctrine established in 1896 by the United States Supreme Court in *Plessy* v. *Ferguson* was predicated on the notion that 'legislation is powerless to eradicate racial instincts'.[29] The American social scientist William Graham Sumner strengthened this concept of human nature when he argued in a 1907 publication that 'legislation cannot make mores' and 'stateways cannot change folkways'. President Eisenhower said, 'I don't believe you can change the hearts of men with laws or decisions.'[30] But the whole point of morality is that it applies to the society as a whole; if it is relegated only to the home life it ceases to be morality and becomes only a private spiritual practice. By its very nature morality is public. In any case, America's legal history, as we shall see, proves that hearts can be changed by enforced legislation. Indeed, what are law and morality but the training of the heart?

BROADENING THE CONCEPT OF RELIGION

Spirituality in much of the Christian world is now but a Sunday morning thing, platitudes, holidays of strangely empty-hearted gift-giving and loneliness – a reduction that is not religion's doing but ours. What we experience in western civilization is the remnant of the initial religious impulse. The core of spiritual love is gone but the outer shell remains. Since from the outside it looks like religion, many people conclude that it must be religion on the inside as well. But nothing could be farther from the truth. One cannot help but recall Jesus' criticism of the Pharisees who would clean the outside of the cup but leave the inside unwashed. One need not reiterate all that has been said over the centuries since Martin Luther in order to prove that Christians and other religious peoples themselves have long been aware of this problem.

The call for spirituality should not be equated with a call for everyone to 'return to the church'. Religion is a word that must be carefully recovered, for it cannot be understood the way popular culture defines it. In speaking about Christianity we must bear in mind that it is not a political movement or the basis of a party. We are so used to hearing of the 'Christian Right', 'Christian Democrats' and such groups that we gradually have begun to accept that the term 'Christian' is by its very nature a political one. It most definitely is not. It is a spiritual term and we must reclaim its true meaning.

Spirituality is not a matter of simply going back to the church just as holistic lifestyles are not simply 'back to nature'. We have to study carefully what we mean and see the details. For example, the simple 1960s ecology movement has evolved into a very complex set of powerful principles and practices that require of us a far more sophisticated understanding of ourselves and of nature. We are beginning to understand that life on this planet requires us to establish new systems to reduce, reuse and recycle materials; to transform the basis of our energy system from fossil fuels to renewable sources – wind, sun and hydropower; to transform our agriculture from a chemical to an organic basis; to restructure our cities so that their size does not exceed the carrying capacity of the available natural resources; to build strong economic and cultural ties between urban and rural areas, ties that in the end eliminate the artificial barrier between them. What began as a simple slogan, 'back to nature', has become a new way of life at a higher standard.

Religion, however, has been so identified with the past that we have not allowed it to evolve. Stagnating religion is clearly not what is meant by spirituality, which is a powerful complex of culturally diverse principles and practices that require of us a far more sophisticated understanding of ourselves and of religion than we ever had in the past. We cannot reduce spirituality to outmoded notions of weekly church-going, just as we do not reduce ideas of technology to notions of the cranking, smoke-belching, steam-powered industry of the past. Just as science, technology and the holistic health and ecology movement have been allowed to evolve, so too the practice of spirituality must be released from the prison of tradition to evolve as society matures.

Relevance

It is all well and good, one might argue, to speak of religious and spiritual ideals, but we are in need of remedies now, not a profound transformation that may or may not come in the future, a hope that might not be fulfilled and that has remained unfulfilled for most of recorded history. How is this talk going to be of any practical benefit to the issues and problems of our lives on the ground today?

When dealing with racism it is very easy to lose track of the fundamental issue. We become easily distracted by cases in the news that fill us with partisan emotions: the Stephen Lawrence case; white farmers in Zimbabwe; police brutality on the streets of Los Angeles, Cincinnati, Miami, London and elsewhere; genocidal campaigns against Native Americans, Australian Aboriginal peoples and others; the growing call for reparations for slavery. These cases, which smolder and flare up year after year, cause such raw feelings of anger and outrage that many of us instantly forget the truth that we are all sisters and brothers, and we see instead only illusions. Surely these are cases that involve wrongs that must be rectified through justice. But planting the mighty tree of justice in the heart of a society is not possible by addressing the branches and leaves; rather we must deal with the roots.

This discussion is not meant as an exhaustive study. It merely attempts to provide an opportunity for reflection on the underlying causes of racism and convincing evidence that spirituality is a key factor. Partisan politics have attempted to solve racial problems for many decades and have failed. Clearly it is time for a more fundamental approach.

It is all too easy to become entangled in a myriad of conflicting interests: politics, economics, ethnicities, politics, culture, media, politics. One of the most distinguished scholars in the history of American social science, Harold Lasswell, wrote a brilliantly straightforward classic with a blessedly simple and revealing title: *Politics: Who Gets What, When, How.* In our discussion we are not interested in who gets what. We want the truth. We want to get to the spiritual foundation and from there unravel this tangled web with justice. So for the moment let us not think of who did what to whom in recent specific cases; we will be better able to deal with these issues if we first explore the eternal principles of our existence on this planet. For they are not irrelevant, they are not so abstract as to be impractical. Rather they are the key to knowing ourselves, our errors and our future development as a global civilization.

Therefore, first we must explore how the collapse of the practice of spirituality in society led to the rise of systemic racial prejudice. Once we understand despiritualization, we can then discuss ways of respiritualizing society and, finally, the boundless potentialities that spiritualization unlocks through the maturation of human society. It is hoped that this analysis will allow us to return to any specific cases with fresh insights of the spiritual nature of humanity and to contribute to their resolution.

Despiritualization: The Archeology of Racism

The Organic Evolution of Racism

In this study we are approaching racism as an archeologist explores a massive site which is partly visible above ground but mostly deep below the surface of the earth. Racism is a vast structure of many strata, each of which was created at a certain period in history according to the circumstances of the time. What we see today is the cumulative effects of all these cultural strata operating simultaneously, though some have greater importance than others. Fortunately we do not need to have tools in hand or special clothes; we do not need to travel; we do not need to ward off 'unfriendly natives', deal with snakes or rivals or pay high fees to the host government. All of this is the archeology of the mind and of the culture that surrounds us. But it is nonetheless real for we take actions on the basis of these cultural strata. Although they are constructs of the human mind, they have so powerfully influenced our behavior as to make us go to war and take lives.

We should bear in mind three aspects of history, archeology and indeed the study of all organic systems. First, things that are powerful and highly influential today were very small and seemingly insignificant when they began centuries and millennia in the past. A giant sequoia, the largest living being on the planet, can grow to over 300 feet in height and yet it begins its life as a tiny seed no larger than a child's fingernail. Mighty cities that today are home to millions of people were originally clusters of huts by a river. Chicago began as a tiny trading post in the swampy woods along footpaths near the shore of what is now called Lake Michigan. Old cities like Beirut and Jerusalem are built up of historical strata. The buildings in use now are standing atop layer upon layer of older periods of history. The superstructures of one period became the foundations of the next.

Consider a river like the Rhone. It begins in the high Swiss Alps, mysteriously remote, hidden, almost secret, and it winds its way down to the Mediterranean. It is quite narrow as it emerges beneath the shadow of its namesake glacier. Towards its mouth it is a substantial body of water, filled with power to alter the landscape and the lives of the people living along its banks. History is like this. Just as the Rhone builds and builds to a climax, magnifying its power as it descends, so too does culture magnify its habits with time, not losing the past but building upon it and sweeping it along, carrying it ever with the present. Racism at its source is a seeming nothing, a mere wisp of a belief. But at its mouth – the present – it is a powerful, complex, fast-moving torrent that can sweep away whole nations and flood a culture off its foundations. Apologists for racism tend to look at the history of their country and dismiss racism because they do not find its origins to be at all powerful. Denial is feasible. One can, as it were, point to the source of the Rhone and deny that it is any kind of threat anywhere in the world. But while whites point to the source some centuries ago, blacks point to the mouth today.

A second important principle is the constancy of change. In the course of their flow through history beliefs evolve. At their origin they may be subconscious. They may then become transformed and enter the social consciousness. In the course of further transformation they may return to the subconscious level, perhaps further from conscious thought than ever. Such is the evolution of the specific beliefs associated with racism. Today we see only the leaves and outer manifestations of a vast tree-like network of beliefs on race but the original roots are hidden from view and can be discovered only through historical investigation.

Such, likewise, is the evolution of society's unwritten laws.[1] They are unwritten because they are part of society's subconscious belief system. Indeed it could be argued that some of them remain unwritten precisely because society does not wish them to be brought to the level of conscious thought. As we shall see regarding the absence of any explicit reference to slavery in the United States Constitution and the Declaration of Independence, society is ashamed of itself because of them.

Thus on the one hand we have the conscious thought in the written law. Often this law is so revered that it is regarded as sacred and the word of the law becomes an icon in and of itself. On the other hand is the unwritten law that is so obscure that it is only in the subconsciousness of society. The evolution of society and its beliefs flows between these two extremes, the manifest and the concealed. We should be prepared to draw the connections between facts that at first seem utterly unrelated, just as leaves seem quite independent of the unseen roots on which they depend.

We should also keep in mind a third quality of archeology: The closer to the present we are in our exploration the easier it is; conversely, the further we dig down in our site – that is, backtrack in history – the more complex and difficult. The deeper our retrospection, the more taxing become recognition, analysis and understanding, and the more necessary patience.

Let us begin our exploration of this extensive and deep archeological site called racism. There is no better place to start than at the surface, the top stratum which we will call Level One.

Level One: Denial of Racism

At this level the sun is shining, the wind blowing and we can roam freely over the top of our archeological site, the ancient mound called racism. We have an unobstructed view but in reality we see very little. The racist is, at this level, wearing a mask but he doesn't know it. He believes the mask is reality. We see people in everyday life, with all the attitudes, emotional expressions and habits they display in public. But these things do not tell us much. In fact they hide more than they reveal. Maureen Reddy observes:

> Race, I believe, operates in some (often hidden) way in every aspect of life. The very hiddenness of race's workings creates massive problems unknown before the outlawing of certain discriminatory practices. Derrick Bell calls white American attitudes 'racial schizophrenia': the very same whites who welcome blacks into their lives in some roles carefully discriminate against blacks in others.[2]

This masking, Derrick Bell argues, is the cause of frustration, alienation and 'a rage we dare not show to others or admit to ourselves'.[3]

At this very superficial level, western society for the most part denies or ignores the existence of racism. We see this often with archeological sites. You are traveling along a road that traverses a flat landscape. Suddenly a large hill appears. The road continues right on over the top and down the other side. Alternatively, the road circles around the hill. We don't stop to investigate what the hill is. People even build houses on the hill, a village with shops, a house of worship and a town square; or farmers plow it and plant a vineyard to catch the sun. Little do they know that underneath the surface are the remains of an ancient city, with a temple dedicated to unknown gods and a king's palace of many marble pillars. Likewise we tend to ignore the existence of racism.

In the late 1950s and early 1960s public discussion of racism in America raised consciousness so much that by the late 1970s A. Leon Higginbotham, Jr., could write optimistically that we were about to begin uncovering this hidden complex of ideas and exposing it to the light of day:

Today, America is finally at the point where it has the potential to resolve in a positive way so many of the problems of the past. If we dare ignore this opportunity, the alternative will be to drift into further polarization. The ultimate direction in which this nation moves may well depend on how it interprets the legacy – both to its black citizens and to its white – of centuries of slavery assured and guaranteed by the law.[4]

But two decades later Randall Robinson testified that we had missed this opportunity:

African-Americans, perhaps still placated by the fool's gold of integration as an endgame achievement, seem not to have noticed our worsening condition with any alarm. At some point beyond the peak of the civil rights movement, we lost our bearings, as if sleepwalking. When we thought about it at all, we reckoned that we were forward of where we had been before. But if we had progressed, it hadn't been by much. Our longitude had changed but our latitude was virtually the same. If the new social terrain looked unfamiliar, it was only because we had drifted sideways, if not backward as well.[5]

Racism is not in our vocabulary. If it exists at all it is considered a construct of the imagination of certain people in society who have not succeeded and therefore wish to blame somebody or something for their failure. It is a figment of the imagination. It is merely political rhetoric employed to wring some funds from the government's annual budget. It is not brought up in polite conversation because, like UFOs, it causes embarrassment among mature, well-educated realists and rational thinkers. Racism is a myth.

It is like the city of Troy, which did not exist except as a Greek legend. So many people wasted their time thinking and dreaming about the glory of Troy as described in Homer. We were foolish, taking from epic tales some idea of history, little realizing that what we read was the stuff of fantasy in an ancient culture. Racism is like Troy and by this reasoning we can be done with it, declare it a myth, clear our slates and consciences and celebrate, dancing in the streets.

The problem is that although Troy was indeed a legend, the legend was transformed into a reality when in 1870 Heinrich Schliemann discovered it on the coast of what is now Turkey!

It is here at Level One that we find the common belief that African Americans should have done what other ethnic groups did when they arrived in America – the Irish, Italians, Germans, Poles, Slovaks, Jews, even the Chinese, Japanese and refugees from Vietnam, Laos and Cambodia and the Latinos. They should have hunkered down, disciplined themselves and

25

pulled themselves up by their bootstraps. These immigrants faced racism and succeeded. Why can't the African Americans? This kind of statement is a perfect example of the denial of racism. It ignores a difference between Africans and immigrants. Africans were forced to come to the United States to labor until death as slaves under the full weight of a totalitarian system created and enforced by local, state and federal law. Immigrants willingly chose to live in the New World, had few or no legal restrictions upon their freedom to build a life for themselves and their families, were free to retain their cultural identity, keep their language and religious beliefs for as long as they wished, keep their money and their property, keep their own children and raise them as they wished and keep their own spouses. African slaves were able to do none of that. That is a big difference. But we're getting ahead of ourselves; let's not start digging just yet. Why don't we look around and pick up a few samples of how this denial and ignorance really works today.

What we find most often in everyday life at Level One is the statement, 'This has nothing to do with racism.' At Level One most people really believe this; they take the mask as reality. They are not aware, or do not allow themselves to be aware, that they live according to racial beliefs and practices.[6]

Not many years ago in suburban America many homeowners proudly displayed near the entrances to their houses what were called 'lawn ornaments'. These included such items as pink flamingoes, sculpted cherubs, Italianate fountains, even plastic deer. Some were more abstract, such as shiny red or blue metallic spheres. But perhaps the most famous of all such ornaments was the 'lawn jockey'. Typically it was a three-foot-tall sculpture of a black man dressed as a jockey on which a horse's halter could be tied; later it became a decorative item. Clearly it represented a slave or a post-slavery servant. Most of these have disappeared since the civil rights movement.

Uncle Ben and Aunt Jemima are commercial images evoking slavery and post-slavery culture. Their smiling faces give us comfort – and their corporate owners significant profits – when we prepare and eat rice or pancakes. They are survivors of what was a pervasive usage of slave images to sell products. The fact that they survive indicates the strength of the commercialization of race in American society even after the civil rights movement.[7]

Commercialization of race goes well beyond African Americans. Quite a number of professional, college and high school sports teams are named after Native Americans or some impression of their culture: Washington Redskins, Cleveland Indians, Kansas City Chiefs and so on. There are too many to mention here. Numerous organizations, campaigns and websites are devoted to the issue. Grotesque stereotypes in cartoons and costumes, many employing sacred religious symbols and artifacts, offend not only American Indian cultural identity but also religious sensibilities.

As we look across Level One we see that American society is quite littered with these kinds of practices that are racist yet denied as such. They are in popular films and music, television, school textbooks, paperback novels. They are in corporate decisions about the kinds of clothes, cars, food and banking services marketed to minority groups. They are in university policies regarding housing of students and courses of study. European Americans are quick to assure African Americans, American Indians, Hispanics and others that no, this is not racism, you need not feel uncomfortable, everything is fine. The problem is that those sensitive to the hidden racism feel that European Americans should not be the only ones able to define what is and is not racist.

From here we cannot go further into the subject without descending to Level Two. For we cannot understand what is on the surface without studying what supports it.

Level Two: Covert Racism, Present to the 1960s

No need to get out our trowels. They won't be necessary for a good while. A lot of work has been done on this archeological site by many researchers who have already dug an exploratory trench down through quite a few levels. We can descend some stairs into this open area below the surface. Here we can no longer see the surface but we are not far from it, just a few feet down. The light is very good here and the open sky is still all around us. We have very good viewing conditions, less wind.

Let us take a look around and see what we have. Many artifacts have been exposed, discovered and well analyzed by researchers in recent years. The term *covert racism* refers to the conscious but discrete practice of racism. It is similar to Level One in that the racism is denied but it is different in that here the racism is deliberate, not unconscious. Here the racist is wearing a mask but he knows it. We can see, therefore, how covert racism gradually evolved into the unconscious deniable racism of the succeeding level. As each generation continues to wear the mask the children grow up with it and think nothing of it, becoming unaware of its existence.

Level Two is the period in which the European Americans reacted to the civil rights movement of the 1950s and 1960s. Many of them became pro-African American and dedicated themselves to eradicating racism and prejudice from their own lives, their families and their communities. But many others decided to continue their traditional way of treating African Americans, only to do so underground, as it were. There was a backlash, a term which was coined in 1963 to describe the extreme reaction of whites

27

against the civil rights movement.[8] The white backlash is perhaps best summarized by the final outcome of what was originally thought to be the civil rights movement's greatest victory, the integration of the public schools. Speaking of Thurgood Marshall, the lawyer who won the Supreme Court case of *Brown v. Board of Education of Topeka* – a case that required the overturning of segregation laws – and who later became the first black member of the United States Supreme Court, his biographer Juan Williams states:

> When he first joined the high court in the late 1960s, almost two thirds of black students were in integrated schools. When he died [in 1993], however, two thirds of black students were back in mostly segregated schools.'[9]

Responding to the civil rights protests, marches and legislation that made overt racism illegal, and in order not to cause further provocation, practitioners of covert racism removed the overt signs of the Jim Crow era that publicly declared and enforced racial segregation. They restrained themselves from using racially offensive language. They learned to get along with African Americans. They hired them at the workplace and instituted affirmative action programs, civil rights legislation, housing and school integration. It was a time of seeming openness and change but it did not last. These measures may have been started by sincere workers for racial unity but they were transformed by the less than sincere into an effective mask that permitted the preservation of the *status quo*.

Let's examine seven examples, starting with something close to the top of Level Two. It dates from the late 1990s, an account from the nation's capital. Written by Randall Robinson, then head of the prominent human rights non-governmental organization Transafrica, it describes the experience of his young daughter, Khalea, at an elite school in Washington DC.

> Hazel [Robinson's wife] and I attended a parent-teacher conference at Khalea's school. Khalea attends Beauvoir, a highly rated private school situated on the well-manicured lush grounds of the Washington Cathedral. She had tested as a gifted child, and we were not surprised to learn that she was doing well in class. Everyone associated with the Beauvoir family was warm and friendly . . . Khalea's teacher that year . . . was no exception. As our successful conference drew to a close, Hazel thought to clarify a matter that had only just occurred to her.
>
> 'What does this "time out" mean?' Hazel asked.
>
> 'Children are placed in time out for disciplinary reasons,' explained [the teacher]. 'They go to a corner alone and remain apart from the class and quiet for a period of time.'

'Khalea tells us that all of the black girls in her class have been put in time out and none of the white girls. Is this true?' Hazel asked.

There were three black girls in the class in addition to Khalea. One was Vanessa, whose mother, Gayle Williams, sat on the Beauvoir governing board. Kristin was the daughter of Jack White, a columnist for *Time* magazine. Erica was the daughter of Judge Eric Washington of the DC Superior Court. They were well-behaved girls. Kristin was so quiet, I'd not have known her voice, although she came to our home often to play with Khalea.

'Yes, that is true,' said [the teacher].

'How can that be so?' Hazel asked, more mystified than upset. 'I know these girls and they are well mannered. Yet all of them have been isolated from the class and not one of the white girls has been disciplined in the same way. Doesn't that seem odd to you?'

'No,' replied [the teacher]. 'Studies show that black parents rear their children to be more aggressive.'

Later, there would be profuse apologies from the school, copious tears from the teacher. But the damage was done, mirroring in its particular and personal way the problems we face on a global scale.[10]

Thus we see the microcosm of reward and punishment imprinted on the minds and hearts of young children even in one of the most enlightened schools. The problem is not the existence of rewards and punishments but the fact that they are distributed not in accordance with justice, and often exactly contrary to justice.

We can see how this example exhibits signs of both Level Two and Level One. The teacher was very apologetic and apparently indicated that she was not aware that her decisions in disciplining students in the classroom were racially determined. One can almost hear in her statement the phrase, 'This has nothing to do with racism.' How could it be racism if 'studies show' the reality? But it also exhibits very strongly aspects of Level Two. The teacher is consciously categorizing African Americans as being inferior and threatening to European Americans.

Now let us reach down a little deeper, to something from the early 1970s. In high school William Lee, an African American who would become a graduate of the United States Air Force Academy and a major in the Air Force, found that his counselor reacted negatively to his ambitions.

... the thing that really made me want to go in the military – actually to the Air Force Academy in particular – was a guidance counselor. She looked at me, and I was an A student. My guidance counselor said, 'Well, Bill, you're an all right boy. You got some real good grades and stuff. But I don't know.

I think the best you can do is to try for vo-tech [vocational-technical training]. You ought to try for vo-tech. And I think you'd do real good in that.' I wanted to go to Auburn, I wanted to go to Alabama. As a matter of fact, my grades, my SAT scores ... were high enough to get into Georgia Institute of Technology on an academic scholarship.

I said to myself, 'How can she?' And here I was, I had twelve letters, okay – *had twelve letters* [awards for outstanding athletic achievement]. Basically three or four letters every year since the ninth grade. All-state, all-district, everything. On the student council. The corps commander of air force ROTC [Reserve Officers Training Corps] detachment, junior ROTC. In the 'A Club' and everything else, plus an A student. And this woman says, 'Well, I don't know. I don't know if you're college material. You probably can go to a good vo-tech and do real good in vo-tech.' And I said, 'Hey, I can't believe it.' But fortunately, I had a teacher who was my math instructor, who said, 'Hey, yeah, go for it.'[11]

There are two important points about this example. First, the counselor was aware that she was limiting the student's future because of racial considerations. She did not verbalize it; it was tacitly understood, hence covert. Second, there was nothing necessarily malicious about the counselor's action. She may genuinely have been trying to help William Lee avoid problems in life. Nevertheless William Lee's future was being mapped out according to a racial program that disadvantaged him and privileged European Americans.

Both of these examples deal with the subject of education. We shall come across this theme again and again as we continue the dig and we will find that it is central to the entire structure of racism. If after the Civil War African Americans had had full and equal access to educational opportunities, racism probably would have been far less severe and perhaps even have disappeared. One of the most convincing proofs of this assertion is the fact that in order to prevent slaves from becoming literate and their descendants from entering good schools, universities and training programs, racists exerted the utmost effort and maintained an almost incredible diligence decade after decade. They saw the power of education as an Achilles heel and they were right.

These examples help to answer important questions. We know that racial discrimination at this level is being hidden but why? What is the purpose of hiding it? From what is it being hidden? Racism is concealed at this level because the civil rights movement demanded justice and instituted laws to achieve it. Racism is a quintessentially unjust system of society, in which African Americans are unfairly punished and European Americans are unfairly rewarded. It is this unfair system of reward and punishment that is being hidden from the public view so as to avoid open criticism, protest and corrective action.

Bryan Shelton, an African American tennis player, recalled his experience as a young rising athlete in Alabama in the early 1980s.

> There were tournaments at certain clubs that I didn't try to enter as a kid because my family knew that blacks weren't welcome there . . . I suppose we could have made an issue out of it, but we didn't. I remember one tournament I played in when I was thirteen, in Birmingham, and I won it. The next year I wasn't invited back. The message was pretty clear.[12]

Bryan Shelton eventually became a successful tennis professional but as a youngster he was punished for succeeding. Why? Had he been a European American would he have been 'invited back'? Would he have been encouraged to continue to play and learn and succeed? Yes, he would have been highly rewarded. And one wonders how much more rapid and how much greater his success would have been had he and other young African American athletes received encouragement from the wider society.

More recently, in 1998 – the heart of an era in which meritocracy, free competition and just rewards to the deserving have been strongly championed in the popular culture – America witnessed the attempt of corporate sponsors to ban Kenyan runners from competing in professional races held in the United States. The sponsors felt that the Kenyans were succeeding too well and they wished to give the Americans, that is, European Americans, a better opportunity to win and to give themselves white champions who they felt would serve best as stars of their advertising campaigns.[13]

The ideal of meritocracy in America, the principle of just reward and just punishment, needs strengthening. Many observers, however, point to the bright examples of Tiger Woods and the Williams sisters as proofs that racism is rapidly waning, if not already at an end. These African American athletes are breaking down the barriers of country club exclusivity, succeeding in sports traditionally unwelcoming to African Americans. This is indeed a victory not only for them but for the international sports world and American society as a whole. Yet history has shown that Althea Gibson, Zina Garrison and a host of outstanding athletes before and after them were unable to bring an end to racism in professional sports, let alone American society. Tiger Woods and Venus Williams both faced powerful racial attacks early on in their professional careers. Undoubtedly they have won the hearts of many, black and white, yet it is equally clear that there is yet much work to be done to open the doors to potential stars of all races. Must there be only one Tiger Woods? Could not tennis host more than two black stars? More than ten? How would professional tennis be regarded with, say, 50 black stars in the top ranks? One recalls that into the early 1960s professional basketball was governed by an unwritten rule that prevented the number of black players on the court at any time from exceeding a certain percentage of the total number of players.[14]

Let's follow the traces of meritocracy into the hallowed corporate boardroom. Journalist Ellis Cose interviewed an African American corporate lawyer, 'not only a senior partner in one of the nation's premier law firms, but a bona fide rainmaker'.

Under his polite prompting, I briefly summarized my work-in-progress. I was dealing with rage, I told him, specifically with the rage of the black middle class, with why so many people who had so many things to celebrate seemed to be angry. 'Well, I can tell you why I'm angry,' he said, launching into a long tale about his compensation package. Despite the tens of millions he had brought into the firm the year before, his partners were balking at giving him his due. 'They want you to do well, but not *that* well,' he grumbled. The more he talked, the more agitated he became. What I had originally thought would be a five-minute conversation stretched on for nearly an hour as this normally restrained and unfailingly gracious man vented long-buried feelings.

Much more was on his mind, it quickly became clear, than the fact that his partners were still 'fumbling with my compensation'. One source of immense resentment was an encounter of a few days previous, when he had arrived at the office an hour or so earlier than usual and entered the elevator along with a young white man. They got off at the same floor. No secretaries or receptionists were yet in place. As my friend fished in a pocket for his key card while turning towards the locked outer office doors, his elevator mate blocked his way and asked, 'May I help you?' My friend shook his head and attempted to circle around his would-be helper, but the young man stepped in front of him and demanded in a loud and decidedly colder tone, 'May I help you?' At this, the older man fixed him with a stare, spat out his name and identified himself as a partner, whereupon his inquisitor quickly stepped aside.

My friend's initial impulse was to put the incident behind him, to write it off as merely another annoyance in an ordinary day. Yet he had found himself growing angrier and angrier at the young associate's temerity, and his anger returned as he related the event. After all, he had been dressed much better than the associate. His clients paid the younger man's salary. The only thing that could have conceivably given the associate pause was race: 'Because of his color, he felt he had the right to check me out.'

At this point the conversation turned to the concept of racism we discussed earlier: that it is punishment not only when the black person is innocent but when he or she has fulfilled the responsibilities of good citizenship.

He paused in his narration and shook his head. 'Here I am, a black man who has done all the things I was supposed to do,' he said, and proceeded to tick off precisely what he had done: gone to Harvard, labored for years to make his mark in an elite law firm, married a highly motivated woman who herself had an advanced degree and a lucrative career. He and his wife were in the process of raising three exemplary children. He had surmounted every hurdle life had thrown in his way. Yet he was far from fulfilled . . .

When I described the encounter to [psychologist] Ron Brown, he said the man's reaction was totally consistent with what he had seen a thousand times. When the partner had been blocked by the young associate, 'it was the momentary and ultimate sign that you're not in . . . You manage that over a lifetime. You take the slights. And you manage the ability to take the slights. Then, at some point [it all comes tumbling down]' . . .

My experience with that lawyer was far from unique. In encounter after encounter with successful, confident black professionals, I ran into a reservoir of despair so deep that it seemed a blessing (or even a life-sustaining miracle) that their good humor and high spirits had survived.[15]

This lawyer's success was qualified, compromised, mixed. He had garnered rewards, yet each of these was accompanied by a regular diet of undeserved punishments. His past achievements were not only partially ignored, they were held against him, resented and duly punished. The racism he faced was covert. It was not specified in words – there were no signs, no verbal epithets prohibiting his presence. Yet his presence was openly considered illegal by the young associate, who felt free, unconstrained, to judge and condemn this senior lawyer. He felt right to do so, since he was not *specifying* race by word. Of particular importance in this example is the issue of the associate's previous learning about race. If he felt free to behave this way at his law firm, one wonders what he had learned about race among friends, colleagues and authority figures in his law school, college, high school, community and family.

Charles Ogletree, a professor of law at Harvard, argues that this sort of systematic punishment of blacks is part of a pervasive environment of racism which is designed to prevent any escape. He refers to the fact that the everyday suspicion of African Americans is more than the well-publicized phenomenon aptly and ironically named 'driving while black' – a pun on the traditional police terminology DWI, driving while under the influence of alcohol, a legally punishable offense. Police have the well-documented tendency to stop and question black drivers who have committed no offense or violation. Being black is *de facto* illegal in this perspective.

As much as we talk about the drivers, there is also a crime called 'riding while black'. And for those of you who walk through the cities of New York, Washington DC, Los Angeles, Chicago, and Houston, there is a crime called 'walking while black'. And we don't see the books as much but those of you who jog through Central Park or Lincoln Park in Washington DC or any park in Anywhere, USA, there is a crime called 'jogging while black'. There is also a nondiscriminatory crime that crosses gender lines called 'shopping while black'. You get all the tension in the world in department stores, so we all really have the phenomenon called 'living while black'.[16]

We see in these examples the consistent fact that the African American presence in sports, in the corporate world, in education and in daily life is either discouraged or punished. The question then arises: In such a society, who then is rewarded? Virtually everyone agrees that the rewards go to the European American community. What is debatable is whether or not these rewards are just or unjust; but if racism is real, then it must be true that they are unjust. Consider the following:

In 1987 Mr Harry Thomas, a black cook working in Louisiana for the Shoney's restaurant chain, was fired. He claimed his dismissal was racially motivated. After a thorough investigation the Equal Employment Opportunity Commission agreed with him and issued a reprimand to Shoney's, specifically citing the discriminatory actions of the chain's regional manager under whom the cook had worked and insisting that he be 'disciplined so he no longer has any authority or responsibility involving hiring, firing or disciplining employees'.

> The Shoney's attorney who handled the case . . . agreed to the EEOC's terms and even thanked the agency in a letter: 'We appreciate your fine work and cooperation in resolving this matter as contemplated by the [civil rights] Act and look forward to working with you again should the need arise.' Harry Thomas accepted $1,000 to settle his claim, and he agreed to find another job elsewhere. A month after the settlement, though, [the regional manager], instead of being terminated, removed from his supervisory duties, or disciplined in any way, was transferred from Louisiana to Kansas City, Missouri, where he continued to work as an area supervisor for Shoney's – with a $270 biweekly raise.[17]

The injured party was essentially punished; he lost his position and walked away with insignificant compensation. The individual who had broken the law, however, was not punished. On the contrary, he was rewarded with a new position at a higher salary. His racially motivated behavior was thus encouraged by society.

The pattern of unjust punishment in all these examples is easily discernible. Granted, injustice is part of life because the world is inherently imperfect. But racism is not about imperfection, not about the inherent way of the world, but about artificially induced destruction, the prevention of civilization. Therefore it ought not be dismissed as purely natural, purely inevitable. It is the conscious or unconscious cultivation of the world's imperfections, rather than the cultivation of humanity's abilities to overcome imperfections.

Here in Level Two the cultivation of imperfection is conscious yet hidden. All the decisions and actions taken to discourage African Americans in these seven examples were deliberate, not unknowing. A teacher's decision to punish unjustly; a counselor's decision to block a student's aspirations to excel in university as he excelled in high school; a tennis tournament's decision to refuse an invitation to the previous year's champion; a decision by sponsors of a road race to ban Kenyans from participation; the decision of a junior member of a law firm to rank himself above a senior member on the grounds of race; the decisions of police to question the rights of African American citizens to go about their daily lives unsuspected; a company's racially-motivated decision to fire an African American employee, and the court's decision to levy an inconsequential fine and allow the company to reward the racially-motivated manager – these actions are well crafted, carefully executed and systematically repeated. Here racism is not open but it flourishes underground, beneath the laws that supposedly prevent it.

The European Americans who commit such actions justify them by pointing to reasons other than race: the aggression of African American parents, not their racial background; the practicality of vo-tech education for an African American student, not his own personal limitations; the need to encourage European American runners and strengthen their abilities to compete; the right and need of police to 'profile' possible suspects; the need for companies to maximize their customer base in order to maximize profits. Every possible reason is cited, except race. The ideology is still there but it is not publicly identified as such.

This is what African Americans and other minorities in the United States and elsewhere in the West have been facing since the 1960s. Overt racism is no longer acceptable in the international community, which of course is cause for optimism; but it is not cause for celebration for there is yet much work to be done. The surface manifestations of the disease have disappeared but symptoms are still working their way silently and invisibly through the body of society.

Level Three: Overt Racism, 1960s to 1860s

If we continue down into this well-worked dig we quickly come to Level Three. The wind is no longer felt here. The light is much softer yet more than adequate, although at the bottom of the level we have to exercise care and patience. As we survey our surroundings, which are narrower than Level Two yet still quite spacious owing to the excellent work of many previous researchers – our trowels are still not yet needed – we find that unlike the first two levels we are face to face with artifacts that are not familiar to us, with which most of us have no immediate experience. We are beginning to enter a different world, a culture which no longer exists except indirectly through the support it gives to Level Two. The uppermost two levels are the culture in which we live today but this is something alien – it is what makes archeologists and historians get down on hands and knees to look closely. Yet we must ever bear in mind that however alien the site becomes as we descend, it is all, in the final analysis, still our world, the world that our forebears built, the world that we inherited.

Overt racism was as open as covert racism is hidden. It was a slap in the face. There was no mask. In some ways that openness was better because at least it was honest. In most ways it was far worse because racist behavior was more or less quite legal and therefore much more harsh and frequent. We recall the two samples regarding education from Level Two: a teacher was confronted by African American parents for unjustly punishing black children; a counselor discouraged an outstanding African American student from applying to university, recommending vo-tech. Now consider the following from Level Three.

One of the most dramatic passages from *The Autobiography of Malcolm X* describes his school experience in Michigan. The year was 1940. He was one of the best students in his otherwise all-white eighth-grade class. One day a teacher he highly respected asked him what occupation he wished to pursue. Malcolm Little answered that he intended to become a lawyer. The teacher was taken aback and then calmly advised, 'We all here like you, you know that. But you've got to be realistic about being a nigger. A lawyer – that's no realistic goal for a nigger.' The teacher pulled the rug out from under Malcolm's hopes, turned his world upside down, counseling him that rather he should plan to pursue carpentry or some similar craft or trade. Needless to say, Malcolm was devastated – and never forgot.[18]

The uprooting of hopes has happened not only to Malcolm Little. As we saw in Level Two, it continues even today. But the key aspect of Level Three, the striking contrast with Level Two, is the openness with which European American authority figures exercised the right and power to weaken and maim the African American community. Their pronouncements against African American potential were categorical and without appeal, and race, pure and simple, was the one and only basis for such destructive actions. Before World War Two, beyond the ubiquitous Jim Crow signs 'For Colored' or 'Whites Only', it was common to see more explicitly racist signs that read, 'This is a White Man's City' (Baltimore, 1899); or 'This Part of 135th Street Guaranteed Against Negro Invasion' (Harlem, New York City, 1910); or 'No Jobs for Niggers Until Every White Man Has a Job' (Atlanta, during the Great Depression).[19]

Racism was not a myth. It was the truest of all realities. European Americans, far from hiding their racial beliefs, proudly, publicly and without apology made their decisions and took their actions with racist ideology ever in mind. Similar open statements of racial prejudice were directed at some European groups, such as the Irish, Italians and other southern Europeans, and Eastern Europeans, but not with the force of law and police power that supported anti-African racism.

Open racism was what led to the dramatic and revolutionary civil rights movement, which we see here at the top of Level Three. Much has been written of this subject and therefore we need not review it. However, we should point out the primary qualities of racism during that turbulent period, for they provide an excellent introduction to what we will see in the earlier decades below. The first quality, which we have already mentioned, is that racism wore no mask; it was open and public. Second, it was characterized by implied or realized violence. Violence was ever in the air in and around African Americans, whether at home, in the agricultural fields, in the woodlands, in the town or in the city. Third, violence came not only from the police but also from male citizens. Fourth, European Americans, in acting out their racist beliefs in public, could instantly become extremely emotional on the subject of race. The emotions of those times are difficult if not impossible to recapture. We can only get a glimpse of them from viewing photographs and film footage of Ku Klux Klan rallies, the opposition to school integration and so on. But even this audio-visual documentation cannot really convey the vibrating tension that filled school classrooms and hallways, that caused such fear on the streets and even in the privacy of African American homes. It is not mere coincidence that the treatment of Jews in Austria and Germany as the Nazis rose to power bears many similarities to the lynchings and mob violence visited upon African Americans, for they were manifestations of the same extreme emotionalism.

Melba Patillo was one of the group of African American students chosen to integrate Little Rock High School in 1957. In her memoir of that time she vividly evokes a medieval atmosphere of unbearable tension. When she was finally able, with the aid of armed soldiers, to enter the school building, she found herself surrounded by hostile students and adults staring and shouting racial epithets at her.

> I was alone, in a daze, following a muscular, stocky white woman with closely cropped straight black hair. Up the stairs I went, squeezing my way

past those who first blocked my path and then shouted hurtful words at me. 'Frightened' did not describe my state; I had moved on to terrified. My body was numb . . . I was panic-stricken at the thought of losing sight of my guide. I ran to keep up with her.

'Move it, girlie,' she called back at me.

'Pheeew!' one boy said, backing away from me. Others stopped and joined in his ridicule. For an instant, I stood paralyzed.

'Don't stop!' the woman commanded. Her words snapped me into action. I scuffled to move behind her. Suddenly I felt it – the sting of a hand slapping the side of my cheek, and then warm slimy saliva on my face, dropping to the collar of my blouse.

A woman stood toe-to-toe with me, not moving. 'Nigger!' she shouted in my face again and again. She appeared to be a little older than my mother. Her face was distorted by rage. 'Nigger bitch. Why don't you go home?' she lashed out at me. 'Next thing, you'll want to marry one of our children.'[20]

Not all the students in the school were racist. Melba Patillo points out that non-racist students, although very small in number, had a significant presence and were able later to provide her discreet support. But otherwise Little Rock Central High School represented medieval culture rather than the dawning space age, was more akin to a madhouse than a schoolhouse, for within it and in the surrounding school grounds and neighborhoods racist beliefs, statements and actions had free reign.

These raw emotions were not created by the turbulence of the civil rights era of the 1950s, for they had been in evidence on a regular basis since the beginnings of slavery. The daily life of African Americans had always been like walking through a minefield. Odessa Boone, a young girl living in Georgia shortly before the civil rights movement, found herself in deep trouble when she was told by the father of her white girlfriend to refer to his daughter, who had just turned the age of 13, as 'ma'am'. 'Odessa could not understand why her good friend should suddenly be treated as a superior. She refused to call her "ma'am" or anything other than her name. The girl's father summoned Odessa's own father and warned him to get his uppity daughter out of Georgia. If not, he said, she might end up hanging from a tree one night. The next day Odessa was sent to stay with her aunt in Philadelphia.' Odessa has been residing in Philadelphia ever since.[21]

In his memoirs former president Jimmy Carter, who also grew up in Georgia, described a very similar transition. From around the time he turned 14 his African American friends suddenly began to show him deference. This was a generation earlier than Odessa and in this case there was no thought of refusing the tradition.[22] But even then, the generation of children before World War Two were making choices if they could. In the same period a young African American boy living then in Missouri was talking with his friend as he walked down the street of his town. There was a white woman nearby. Suddenly a white man rushed up to the two boys and shouted, 'Boy, don't you ever do that again.' Apparently he felt that they had dishonored the white woman in some way by talking about or looking at her. The young boy decided then and there to leave Missouri and he moved to South Dakota, where his family still lives.[23]

Quick-tempered racists would unleash their violence against any black who they considered had taken a 'false step'. The violence became particularly vicious and, significantly, controversial after World War Two, when black veterans returning from the war were unwilling to tolerate subjection to the very culture of racism that they had fought against overseas. There are, alas, many horrific accounts of this spectacular clash of newly empowered African American veterans and the forces of racist conservatism in America. Only in order to understand the depth of overt racism in the mid-20th century, and to understand that the civil rights movement gained momentum in the wake of the war, we cite two cases described by writer Juan Williams in his outstanding biography of Thurgood Marshall. Both occurred in 1946.

An altercation sparked the first race riot in the South following the War:

> Dozens of people, black and white, exchanged gunfire in Columbia [Tennessee] on the night of February 26, 1946, after a white store owner slapped the mother of a nineteen-year-old black navy veteran. James Stephenson, a tall, athletic boy, and his mother, Gladys, had gone into the Caster-Knott electrical appliance store at about ten o'clock that morning. The Stephensons were upset because the store's repair shop had not fixed their radio – even though they had paid to have it repaired. The repairman, Billy Fleming, age twenty-eight, said that he had fixed it but that Gladys Stephenson had broken it again. When the woman argued that she had done nothing to the radio, Fleming slapped her and pushed her out of the store. The woman's son became enraged and punched Fleming, knocking him through the store's plate-glass window.[24]

The police, siding with Fleming, arrested the Stephensons. By the early evening the area around the police station in the center of town was filled shoulder to shoulder with an angry mob. The police chief, who was not in favor of any extra-legal action, was able to secretly conduct the Stephensons through the back of the station into a waiting car that sped them out of town to safety.

We must put ourselves in the shoes of the Stephensons. When they woke up that morning and got themselves ready for the day, they had a chore before them to complete in town. Little did they think that this simple task would result in a store clerk slapping Mrs Stephenson across the face and pushing her out onto the sidewalk, or James engaging him in a bloody fight, or their facing death at the hands of a raging mob. Their world that was sunny with the safe return of their veteran son from the war had suddenly become dark within seconds in a little country store.

The second case also involved a veteran of the war, Isaac Woodard.

> The day of his discharge from the army, after fifteen months of jungle fight-ing in the Philippines, Woodard was on his way to visit his mother. At one stop he delayed the bus driver while using the bathroom. At the next stop, in Aiken, South Carolina, the driver asked him to step off the bus for a moment. Two policemen were there to greet him. The driver shouted that Woodard was drunk and creating 'a disturbance' on the bus.
>
> When Woodard protested that he had done nothing wrong, the police-men clubbed him and put him in their car. Once they got Woodard to the jail, they beat him with a blackjack and nightstick. At one point, as Woodard was on the ground and helpless, the policeman purposely shoved the end of his nightstick at both of Woodard's eyes, completely blinding him.[25]

These incidents of horrific violence committed by whites against blacks were all too common throughout the United States – not just the South – in the age of overt racism. And they even continue today in the age of covert and denied racism, as we know with numerous documented cases of police brutality against African Americans characterized not as racism but as firm policing action. What was different after World War Two was that African American veterans, having served in most of the branches of the military, including the Army Air Corps, with great distinction in the global fight against racism and fascism, were no longer willing to accept racism within the ranks of the military itself, nor within American society as a whole. They were speaking out and standing up and this sparked a tre-mendous reaction among racists who wished specifically to give all African Americans the message that whatever we did to oppose racism abroad, it was to be business as usual at home. This time the lines of battle were very clearly drawn, more so than in the Civil War, which was a fight between two factions of the white community. This time the blacks were stronger and more united and took the field themselves on one side. This time there was no backing down, for it was not merely a sporadic riot here and there as in the past. This time the culture of the African American community had changed and there was no turning back. African Americans were empowered as they had never been before by the sacrifices they had made in the war, by the consciousness of racism that the war had raised throughout the world and by the simultaneous rise on the home front of a powerful movement of lawyers and civil rights advocates, black and white, led by Thurgood Marshall among others, to force the government authorities to uphold the laws ensuring equity and justice. The combination of sacrifice, legal skills and public relations proved unstoppable and led directly to the full-blown civil rights movement.

Usually such open violence was not in evidence. It didn't need to be. Much more common – as, ironically, in Nazi Germany – was the kind of calm, confident and comprehensive racist acts that Malcolm Little faced that day in school. Such acts were the stuff of daily life. They were what defined a well-bred person. European Americans did not shrink from taking racist actions in public; rather, they relished the opportunity to do so, for it reinforced their sense of superiority. It was always a source of deep satisfaction, one that almost never caused them to pause and reflect or to become conscious of the meaning of their beliefs. It was like any tradition – pumpkins on Halloween, trimming the tree at Christmas, hunting for Easter eggs. It was a source of inner joy, of confirming that all was right with the world. Racists in this period would treat African Americans as they treated their farm animals. They were useful as employees but they could turn dangerous and must be dealt with firmly and comprehensively. As long as they stayed in their place there was peace but the moment they got out of the pen or stable all heck would break loose and everybody had to join together to get them back where they belonged. When it was all over everybody could have a good laugh over a job well done.

But not everything is so cut-and-dried at this level. Yes, racism is unconcealed. But there is also the beginning of doubt about white supremacy after World War Two. The pride is not so secure as in earlier decades, the confidence not as strong. The deeper meanings of the war were having their effect on the culture and eroding America's racial tradition.

In 1946, the same year as the Woodard and Stephenson incidents, Marvin Holladay was a 17-year-old teenager living in Chanute, Kansas, and quickly developing the musical talent that would enable him to become a highly respected and successful jazz saxophonist. He was also quickly developing a personal opposition to racism, which he, as a European American, was beginning to face as he continued his close friendships with local African American musicians. He was at this time a member of a small band that had one black musician nicknamed Smitty.

> Every night after the job, we'd head back into town and I would ask Smitty
> if we could stop and get something to eat at a restaurant. All the guys in the

41

band would be there. He always had a reason to get home, usually church the next day, which was understandable, since I had to do the same thing and sing in the choir as well. I always asked and when he said, 'No', I'd take him home and go back downtown and join the guys in the restaurant. This went on for some time until finally one night Smitty said, 'O.K., let's go eat.' This was great for me because now I wouldn't have to come back later to get something to eat.

We found a place to park near the restaurant, went in, walked over to the table where the guys in the band were sitting and joined them. The waitress came over and took our orders and then announced that Smitty could pick up his plate at the counter. I said, 'What for?' and she told me that Smitty would have to take his plate outside and eat it there. Of course, this brilliant young kid [Marvin] had to ask [again], 'What for?' and watch her stummer and stammer as she tried to figure how to identify Smitty. She was able finally to get out that he was a 'niii – gro' and that they didn't serve them in the restaurant. It took all that for me to finally get the message. Now I realized what Smitty had been trying to tell me, without telling me, all this time.[26]

The waitress was confident and had the situation in hand – until she had to explain what usually did not need explaining. She stumbled in trying to articulate the very beliefs that were the heart and soul of America's social hierarchy. To identify people and their relationships to oneself is not a hard task: This is my mother, this is my boss, this is the carpenter, this is the doctor and so on. It is not even so difficult to talk about social groups: She is Baptist, while he is Episcopalian; their people come from Sweden; our family is originally Scottish. Fine. And it is clear that African Americans were constant subjects of discussion in those days: what they wanted; how they behaved; what their future would be; their profile in the media, on radio programs, in music; their styles of dress and how they danced. But she stumbled. Racism was there, open and unmasked, yet its foundation was clearly no longer strong enough to prevent her from feeling ashamed.

The explanation for this open yet unconfident racism lies in the happenings of previous decades, a series of confrontations between the forces of racism and of anti-racism. The first and most well known was the long battle between the advocates of slavery and the abolitionists, leading to the Civil War. But this was a wave of change that receded and was only partially effective. For the Civil War did not end racism. It did not even end slavery, which continued under various other forms – such as 'sharecropping' – until it was finally shaken in the civil rights movement. The southern partisans continued to fight for new forms of slavery using primarily the Ku Klux Klan. Founded in the winter of 1865–6 in Pulaski,

Tennessee, its creators were former Confederate officers, among them Nathan Bedford Forrest, the first Grand Dragon of the Klan. By 1877 the Klan had achieved a spectacular victory: Through constant acts of terrorism the occupying troops of the North eventually tired of dealing with an unrepentant South and the Hayes Compromise was struck, allowing the South to retake control of their state governments and have virtually complete sovereignty, as long as slavery was practiced under a different name and was slightly disguised either as sharecropping or the repayment of debts.[27]

In the early 1920s the Ku Klux Klan enjoyed a popularity in the United States that made it the dominant political power in the state of Indiana and a true player on the national scene. The Klan's rise climaxed in 1925 with marches in Washington DC and other cities by tens of thousands of white-robed members. At that moment it seemed nothing could stop this grassroots racist juggernaut from consolidating its political power, increasing its organizational structure to include larger and larger swathes of the 48 States and, election by election, seizing the offices needed to install governments at the local, state and national levels that would do its bidding. White supremacy had everything going for it.

At the zenith of this triumph the head of the Klan in Indiana and one of its national leaders, D. C. Stephenson, was arrested, tried and convicted of murder. In the full light of a long-awaited glory, before the gaze of the entire nation, it brought upon itself a shame that in an era still strong with Christian morality could not be covered up, explained away or spun by media pundits into insignificance. Although the Klan did not die, it suffered in this event a blow from which it never recovered.

The second wave followed World War One. African Americans' migration from the rural South to take war-time industrial jobs in northern cities, and their loyal service in the military abroad, gave their entire community a first taste of the fruits of economic and political empowerment. Great was their shock when in the war's aftermath their hopes were ruthlessly dashed by the reassertion of strict racist laws and practices. Even greater, however, was the shock of the nation when the African Americans arose in unprecedented strength and conviction to oppose this racist revival, leading to the worst 'race riots' in American history.

Soon thereafter, Americans' awareness of Nazi philosophy, and of its defeat by the victories of Jesse Owens at the 1936 Olympics and of Joe Louis in the ring against Max Schmelling in 1938, had effectively brought racism to a showdown with world opinion. Whereas the Civil War had brought a showdown over slavery, now the ideas underlying slavery were being tested and found wanting even before the first shots of World War Two were fired.

By the late 1930s, as many writers have noted, Hitler gave racism a bad name.[28] The war was remarkable in that it achieved what decades of vociferous debate could not: it crystallized a consensus against racism and prejudice. The establishment of the United Nations in the war's aftermath cemented that consensus in a perpetual institution which most nations wholeheartedly supported. What had been a vague, philosophical ideal now had become a living reality. The popularity that racist philosophy had enjoyed before the war was now cast into doubt not only by the evil of Nazism but also by the international agreement to banish the conditions that made the war possible. The first international blow against racism was struck and there was nothing racists could do about it, no place to hide, for it was a global consensus, one of the first in history. At the local level racists could carry on as usual but their conscience was pricked by the rapidly growing awareness that the vast majority of peoples beyond the West – who were the vast majority of the globe's population – were dead set against racism. Even in the United States itself the offices of the federal government in Washington DC – which had been segregated, ironically, by Woodrow Wilson – and all branches of the military were gradually desegregated on the order of Harry S. Truman beginning in 1948.

Central to Level Three is the establishment and enforcement of the Jim Crow laws, practices which to all intents and purposes perpetuated the social and cultural conditions and much of the economic structure of slavery. And of all the Jim Crow laws, the most important, the most meaningful, the most weighted with superstition and emotionalism, was the law prohibiting sexual and marital relations between blacks and whites and particularly between African American men and European American women. Although this law was declared unconstitutional by the United States Supreme Court in 1967, the emotional aversion and fear surrounding this tradition has remained in the hearts of most Americans and determines much of how we interact and communicate, both in person and through the media.

The Jim Crow laws derived directly from slave society. If we understand slavery, we will understand everything about Jim Crow. Therefore we descend to Level Four.

Level Four: Slavery, 1860s to 1500s

Welcome to Level Four. The light here is rather weak, so we will have to turn on our lamps. That is much better. As you can see now, there are many, many artifacts *in situ*, a perfect jumble uncovered by previous researchers, so you have to watch your step. There is a lot of space to cover – Level Four is quite extensive – but it is a labyrinth of passageways leading into and out of each other, so although there is much room, it is easy to get confused. And it is confusing especially because, as we shall learn, the people of this time were themselves confused. Slavery and racism were born right here in a society that was mentally and spiritually sick. They built around themselves this rather large structure which to them was the very height of rational civilization. But now, just look at it! We can barely make head or tail of it. To a degree we have to begin thinking like them in order to understand what we are seeing. Fairly soon we recognize the pattern and move about easily. We want to become accustomed to Level Four because we are going to be here for a good while. Formal, legalized slavery in North America lasted from the mid-1600s until 1863–5 and illegal slavery continued for some time thereafter. If we include the slavery practiced in other parts of the New World by the Spanish and Portuguese, we are looking at over 300 years. Here we will discover truths that will give us the answers to questions raised in the upper levels.

New Primary Laws
Anti-miscegenation

The basis of racism in America is slavery. And the basis of slavery consisted of five simple laws: 1) All children of slaves shall be slaves; that is, slavery is hereditary. 2) Slaves remain slaves for life; that is, slavery is perpetual. 3) Africans and Europeans may not intermarry. 4) Slavery is confined to Africans. 5) Conversion to Christianity shall not change an African's status as a slave. All of these laws were, in one form or another, in existence in the Old World in systems of slave labor created by the Portuguese, Spanish, Muslims or English. The difference in the North American colonies, however, was that these laws were applied with a hitherto unseen intensity and inhumanity that was possible, as we shall see, because there was no spiritual authority to stay the hand of the slave-holders from the excesses to which they were driven by their quest for unlimited profits.

In Islam, as in the Greco-Roman world, slaves were of all skin colors, races and ethnicities and were able to rise to the highest levels of society. The English word 'slave' derives from the most prominent slave trade conducted by Muslims, which was between the Ottoman Empire and the Slavic regions of Europe. There was indeed racial prejudice and discrimination regarding slaves. The Ottomans considered the most prestigious slaves to be those from Europe, the lowliest from sub-Saharan Africa and the intermediate rank was filled by the Ethiopians. As a general rule, the higher the slave's prestige, the better he was treated and the higher his potential rank in society. Many such slaves, as in the Greco-Roman period, were able to attain seats of power, even sovereignty. But the converse was also true – that the slaves of East Africa below the Sahara were generally treated poorly, given the most menial tasks and had few opportunities if any to advance in the society. But even with this qualification it is clear that a significant number of black African slaves rose to the highest ranks in the Islamic world and that the slavery practiced in the Middle East was greatly mitigated by the influence and laws of Islam, which required that slaves be treated humanely and be free to join the ranks of the believers with all due rights. There was nothing in Islam that prevented a free person from marrying a slave, no matter the slave's racial or ethnic origin. And the Qur'án states that among the actions of the truly righteous believer is the manumission of slaves.[29]

North American slavery went far beyond the long tradition of slavery of past societies, particularly in the slave's complete lack of rights. Whereas slaves in the Greco-Roman world and Islam could acquire literacy and learning, American slaves generally could not; whereas Greco-Roman slaves were able to make contracts, own property, legally marry and in general have a recognized legal and spiritual personality, North American slaves could not. It was a form of slavery that, W. E. B. DuBois asserts, was 'on a scale and with an elaborateness of detail of which no former world ever dreamed. The imperial width of the thing – the heaven-defying audacity – makes its modern newness.'[30]

Of all these unique laws of slavery created in North America, the one that has been the source of the greatest emotionalism in the United States even to this day, and that even now influences the thoughts of most people in the country, is the law against intermarriage. Not only were anti-miscegenation[31] laws central to the practice of racism but they continued in force until 1967, a century after the demise of slavery itself. Their imprint is longer and fresher in the American psyche. It has long been known that sexual relations between black men and white women is the very center of racism in America and in similarly racist states elsewhere. Nothing arouses the violent emotions of racists more readily and powerfully than this subject. Before slavery was well established interracial marriage was legal in the colonies, tolerated, even sanctioned by local clergymen. But as time wore on and the forces of racist politics grew in strength, the outrage that was evoked in defense of white supremacy intensified. By the late 19th century lynchings of African American men became common and were often based on supposed sexual assaults of white women. Even after World War Two lynchings were still carried out. One of the most notorious such cases was that of Emmett Till in 1955. A 14-year-old African American boy raised in Chicago, he was visiting family in Mississippi when, as a result of racist reactions to his alleged attempt to flirt with a white woman, he was kidnapped and brutally murdered, apparently at the hands of a group of men that included members of the local police. His body, found weighted down at the bottom of a river, was positively identified despite the complete disfigurement of his face from the beatings he had suffered. The acquittal of all suspects sparked international condemnation of America's racial policies and further fueled the march towards the abolition of the Jim Crow laws.

The civil rights movement took the first small steps towards reversing this tradition but it was a long road, as illustrated by a 1959 production of *The King and I* by a consortium of African American college students, the Atlanta-Morehouse-Spelman Players. The king was played by a black student and the British teacher by a white student. In one scene, when the king put his arm around the teacher's waist to demonstrate the style of dance he preferred, 'there was an audible murmur in the audience. In the year 1959 that was a bold theatrical event.'[32]

Even today the suggestion that blacks and whites might freely inter-marry or date produces a reflexive negative reaction in American society, in both the South and the North. In 1994 a white high school principal in Wedowee, Alabama, threatened to cancel the annual prom because of intense controversy surrounding his alleged opposition to interracial dating. Emotions ran so high that along with debates and protests, the high school was burned to the ground by an unknown arsonist.[33] A prominent and progressive private school in New York City conducted an anonymous survey in the early 1990s on the racial attitudes of the white parents of students at the school. The parents generally favored interracial friendships and scholarships for minority students but when it came to interracial dating 90 per cent expressed opposition to it.[34]

Let us therefore concentrate on the anti-miscegenation law, for we shall see that it is the root of the later laws and cultural norms that became the Jim Crow system.

In 1661 Maryland, which was not a state at that time but essentially a private fiefdom, promulgated the following law:

> And forasmuch as divers freeborn English women, forgetful of their free condition, and to the disgrace of our nation, do intermarry with negro slaves, by which also divers suits may arise, touching the issue of such women, and a great damage doth befall the master of such negroes, for preservation whereof for deterring such freeborn women from such shameful matches, be it enacted: That whatsoever freeborn woman shall intermarry with any slave, from and after the last day of the present assembly, shall serve the master of such slave during the life of her husband; and that all the issues of such freeborn women, so married, shall be slaves as their fathers were.[35]

A similar law was established in 1691 by Virginia, a society which in many ways served as a model for other states to follow in establishing their legal systems in support of slavery.[36]

> And for the prevention of that abominable mixture and spurious issue which hereafter may increase in this dominion, as well by negroes, mulattoes, and Indians intermarrying with English, or other white women, as by their unlawful accompanying with one another, Be it enacted by the authoritie [sic] aforesaid, and it is hereby enacted, That for the time to come, whatsoever English or other white man or woman being free shall intermarry with a negro, mulatto, or Indian man or woman bond or free shall within three months after such marriage be banished and removed from this dominion forever, and that the justices of each respective countie [sic] within this dominion make it their perticular [sic] care, that this act be put in effectuall [sic] execution.[37]

In 1924, 233 years later, Virginians had matured beyond what they were in the colonial era – or so one would think. But that was not the case, at least with regard to the question of intermarriage. For in that year the laws were made more specific by the promulgation of 'A bill to preserve the integrity of the white race':

> It shall hereafter be unlawful for any white person in this State to marry any save a white person, or a person with no other admixture of blood than white and American Indian. For the purpose of this chapter, the term 'white person' shall apply only to such person as has no trace whatever of any blood other than Caucasian; but persons who have one-sixteenth or less of the blood of the American Indian and have no other non-Caucasian blood shall be deemed to be white persons. All laws heretofore passed and now in effect regarding the intermarriage of white and colored persons shall apply to marriages prohibited by this chapter.
>
> If any white person intermarry with a colored person, or any colored person intermarry with a white person, he shall be guilty of a felony and shall be punished by confinement in the penitentiary for not less than one nor more than five years.
>
> If any white person and colored person shall go out of this State, for the purpose of being married, and the intention of returning, and be married out of it, and afterwards return to and reside in it, cohabiting as man and wife, they shall be punished as provided in [section] 20–59, and the marriage shall be governed by the same law as if it had been solemnized in this State. The fact of their cohabitation here as man and wife shall be evidence of their marriage.[38]

By this law, and by its subsequent actions, Virginia remained faithful to its word of 1691, for even as late as 1967 the Lovings would have been banished forever from the state had it not been for the intervention of the United States Supreme Court.

Interracial sexual relations, and the resulting children, were punished by most of the colonies and states, both in the North and the South. Wherever these laws were enacted, any free white person who had sexual relations with an African, whether in or out of wedlock, would forfeit his or her freedom for a period of years. Any free African or part African who engaged in marital or sexual relations with a white person would lose his or her freedom for a period of years or even for life. Later laws also provided that the white person would be required to pay a heavy fine and might suffer a term in prison. Banishment from the colony and severe whipping were also common punishments. Generally the children of these relationships were made slaves for life or for very long periods, often till the age of 30.

The Myth of Natural Repulsion

Recent scholarship is confirming that the land-owning class in the American South created race-based slavery to maintain a strict separation between the white and black labor forces and thereby prevent rebellion against the quasi-feudal system established in the New World.[39] Anti-miscegenation laws were promoted by whites to forestall social unity between potential anti-establishment social forces, as James Johnston explained in 1970:

> It is . . . to be believed that the planter wished to develop an attitude of race superiority on the part of the poor white and the Negro groups through a fear that at some future time the poor white might lead the mulatto and the Negro in revolt against the established order. Reflecting this sentiment in part, even in the North, Judge Horsmanden, who published a very complete account of the Negro plot at New York in 1741, claimed that the purpose which led him to publish this book was to warn the other colonies of the danger that he believed had been narrowly averted in the city of New York. This judge placed much emphasis on the evidence of the inter-marriage of Negroes and the lower white element of the city, warning that disaster might be expected to come to other colonies if association between Negroes and the poor whites were permitted.[40]

Before this interpretation appeared, however, many scholars, most notably Winthrop Jordan, attributed the anti-miscegenation laws not to any conscious or unconscious desire to control labor and thereby secure the source of wealth in the New World but to a supposed feeling of natural repulsion between the African and European races. According to this argument, the differences in skin color, physical form, language, culture and thought were so great that it was only natural for Europeans to fear the Africans and to maintain distance from them. Obeying thus the dictates of nature, the European colonists were blameless.

The most obvious problem with this reasoning is that it contradicts the historical facts. While the emotions of fear, apprehension and antipathy existed among some Europeans during their first encounter with Africans, much historical evidence shows that these negative feelings were not sufficiently powerful to set a permanent barrier between the races and were often overshadowed by more positive attitudes towards the African. The early colonial period witnessed a social circumstance of the utmost importance in our understanding of racism and prejudice in America. The first generations of Africans in America had an ambiguous social status. Jonathan Bush writes, 'For the first few decades of English colonization, there was likely no slavery in practice and certainly no mention of slavery in law.'[41] Upon their arrival Africans were not culturally identified as evil, nor legally defined as slaves; in fact their status was roughly equivalent to that of European indentured servants and could be significantly raised by the profession of Christianity until law prohibited this possibility beginning in the mid-1600s. The colonists brought to America no legal or social category of 'slave' such as we now associate with the American plantations and thus American slavery was a unique institution developed *ad hoc*, not a natural inevitability based on inescapable laws of racial antipathy.[42] There was no category of 'slave' in English common law. As Joseph Boskin points out, 'no Englishman could be denied a place within society'. All members of English society were regarded as having some protection under the sacred laws of the society. They were all recognized as being within the pale. The lowest status was 'one of relative "unfreedom"', that is of bonded servitude. But even this status allowed for fundamental privileges and rights. When the first groups of Africans arrived in the early North American colonies they 'were accepted into society as relatively "unfree" servants and, as such, enjoyed whatever privileges as were granted to white indentured servants'.[43] James Johnston agrees: 'In the early days little distinction was made between the white indentured servant and the Negro slaves, and what is regarded as race prejudice was, in these days, very closely akin to English class prejudice.' Colonial leaders were therefore simply 'building on English class prejudice'.[44]

We should not oversimplify the matter: It is true that the elements of African enslavement were already in place on plantations in the Mediterranean area, Sicily, Majorca and elsewhere; these, however, were slave systems run by the Portuguese and the Mediterranean principalities with whom they directly traded.[45] Nevertheless, Basil Davidson states plainly that at the beginning of the Atlantic slave trade 'European attitudes toward Africans in those early times displayed a wide range of contrast . . . [but] they supposed no natural inferiority in Africans.'[46] Although the Africanization of the slave trade was accelerating at that time, it did not translate into an assumption of racial inferiority for blacks and superiority for whites.

Eyewitness accounts of visitors to the African coast in the 18th century give us some idea of the degree to which fabrications of racist minds in America distorted the reality of African life and culture and the European perception of Africans. It was not so negative an encounter as the myth of natural repulsion would have us believe. In harmony with the thought of his contemporary Rousseau, a visitor to Senegal in 1754 wrote:

> Which way soever I turned my eyes on this pleasant spot, I beheld a perfect image of pure nature; an agreeable solitude, bounded on every side by charming landscapes, the rural situation of cottages in the midst of trees; the ease and indolence of the Negroes reclined under the shade of their spreading foliage; the simplicity of their dress and manners; the whole revived in my mind the idea of our first parents, and I seemed to contemplate the world in its primitive state: they are, generally speaking, very good-natured, sociable and obliging. I was not a little pleased with this my first reception; it convinced me, that there ought to be a considerable abatement made in the accounts I had read and heard everywhere of the savage character of the Africans. I observed, both in Negroes and Moors, great humanity and sociableness, which gave me strong hopes, that I should be very safe amongst them, and meet with the success I desired, in my inquiries after the curiosities of the country.[47]

A European visitor to the coast of Guinea in 1726 testified to the great intelligence displayed by the people there:

> They were a civil, good-natured people, industrious to the last degree. It is easy to perceive what happy memories they are blessed with, and how great progress they would make in the sciences, in case their genius was cultivated with study.[48]

A most significant statement of this same travel narrative conveys the observation of another European who had lived in coastal Guinea for ten years:

> . . . the discerning natives account it their greatest unhappiness, that they were ever visited by the Europeans – That the Christians introduced the Traffic of Slaves; and that before our coming they lived in peace.[49]

A European who traveled far up the river Senegal during the same period wrote of the rich agriculture and orderliness of the societies:

> The farther you go from the sea, the country on the river seems more fruitful and well improved. It abounds in Guinea and Indian corn, rice, pulse, tobacco, and indigo. Here are vast meadows, which feed large herds of great and small cattle; poultry are numerous, as well as wild fowl.[50]

The same traveler also visited the region south of the river Gambia, where he found 'land so well cultivated; scarce a spot lay unimproved; the low grounds, divided by small canals, were all sowed with rice; the higher ground planted with Indian corn, millet, and peas of different sorts, beef, and mutton very cheap, as well as all other necessaries of Life'.[51] He also found the people 'generally good-natured and civil, and may be brought to any thing by fair and soft means'. From another observer of this society a similar comment: 'They are a sincere, inoffensive people, and do no injustice either to one another or strangers'.[52] The resemblance of these descriptions of Africans with early descriptions of the American Indians is striking. Columbus wrote in 1493 of the Indians: 'They manifest great love towards all others in preference to themselves'.[53] Both were regarded as of high moral character, peaceful, highly organized, expert in farming and making use of natural resources, and generally cooperative.

It is true that Europeans harbored racial prejudices against Africans, as expressed so powerfully by Shakespeare's *Othello*. The identification of blackness with evil in Christian theology, which had begun as early as the time of Origen (ca. 185–254), paved the way for the extension of the analogy to dark-skinned peoples, particularly in the development of lasting hatred of the Saracens during and after the period of the Crusades.[54] Yet these accounts of travelers to Africa clearly show that the anti-black prejudice was not all-pervasive and certainly not powerful enough to determine the direction in which the culture of the American colonies would develop. It was a weak prejudice, probably present in all classes of society though expressed articulately and with greater frequency and vehemence by the upper classes, who gradually became aware that they had vested material interests in the despiritualization of Africans. As we shall see, the primitive church looked favorably upon Ethiopians as representing the most distant branch of humanity that had won spiritual victory and proved the universality of Christianity by converting to the new religion. And in the medieval period, Joe Feagin notes, positive images and understandings of dark-skinned peoples were also well established in Europe itself:

> ... there was still significant diversity in European perspectives on Africa in

the Middle Ages. African (Ethiopian) Christian groups were well regarded and present at European church councils in the early 1400s, and some African religious figures were viewed in a positive light by many European Christians.[55]

One of the most prominent and deeply respected African figures in the history of the Roman Catholic Church is St Maurice (died ca. 287). As the Christian general of a Roman legion, the members of which were also Christian, Maurice defied the emperor's command to wipe out a community of Christians in what is now Switzerland. When he and his men refused to return to the pagan religion and offer sacrifices to the gods, they were themselves massacred on the order of the emperor. Historian Joel A. Rogers, who rediscovered and popularized the forgotten history of St Maurice, states that the martyrdom of St Maurice had wide repercussions: 'This singular example of devotion gave great impetus to the faith. It heartened the Europeans by proving to them that the church in Africa was as firm as in Rome . . .' Many towns have been named after him, including the famed alpine resort of St Moritz, the site of the massacre. But St Maurice was only one of many Africans revered in the Church, including Simon of Cyrene, who helped Jesus to carry His cross, Candace of Ethiopia and the eunuch who taught her the faith, St Augustine, St Cyprian, Tertullian, Origen, Clement and St Athanasius.[56]

For the sake of argument, let us put aside Europe's embrace of Christian Africans in that time. Even if we argue that Europeans and Africans in the early North American colonies were for the most part quite alien to each other, both in physical appearance and cultural habits, nevertheless the historical record shows that they proceeded – contrary to the theory that fear causes irreconcilable disunity – to intermarry. Edmund Morgan wrote, 'Up to and perhaps through the 1660s it is difficult to document any indisputably racist feeling about miscegenation.'[57] James Johnston notes, 'In the seventeenth century the association of the indentured servant and the slave was very close. They were often subjected to the same treatment and held by the master in the same esteem. Such associations led to many of the marriages that have been recorded.'[58] And even after the anti-miscegenation laws were promulgated they did not really succeed as well as had been anticipated. The slave-holders were hard pressed to maintain a social barrier between the African slaves and Europeans of all classes. In fact, from the mid-1600s until today, Gary Nash argues, a mighty struggle has been ongoing in the United States over the direction of the nation's development: towards a mixed-race future or towards a future which is primarily white. At times the struggle was open, as in the Civil War, and at others hidden. But there is already much evidence that the faction favoring a mixed-race population has had many significant if quiet victories. The mixing of races has occurred with far greater frequency in American history than is supposed by most historians. Nash cites the existence of a number of tri-racial societies descended from African slaves, American Indians and whites on the East coast surviving even today: the Wesorts, the Lumbees, the Red Bones and the Brass Ankles. Indeed, most Indian tribes along the East coast took in Europeans and Africans and welcomed them as full members of their community. Most of the American frontier as a whole was characterized by the intermarriage of all races meeting there, particularly in the areas dominated by the French and the Spanish.[59] In modern decades the profile of mixed America has become even more conspicuous. Thurgood Marshall's entire professional career was devoted to the cause of racial integration. It is common in the South for white families to have a set of cousins in the African American community. The Creole community of New Orleans is another quintessentially mixed group that, unlike the smaller groups on the East coast, achieved a measure of fame, cultural power and even economic strength. Thus, while the mixing of races is well known in Latin America, it is no less true in North America, the only difference being that North American society tends to suppress this knowledge, deny it, hide it and to prevent further mixing.

These earliest decades of the North American colonies exemplify the human spirit's tendency to unite, a tendency seen throughout history in migrations, conquests and colonization. The fear that may exist in our reactions to new people is overwhelmed by the greater tendency to interact with them.

As the colonies evolved, demographic considerations caused slave-holders to increase their opposition to the intermarriage of blacks and whites. In the mainland British colonies, blacks in 1680 numbered three thousand or 6.25 per cent of the total population. By 1780 they were 220,582, or 41 per cent. One can clearly see that had intermarriage proceeded unhindered, the 'white race' in the colonies would have been married out of existence and the entire ideology of race-based slavery thrown out of balance and quite possibly brought to an end.[60]

By the early 1700s intermarriage between blacks and whites was prohibited in most southern states. Laws forbade any clergyman from performing a marriage ceremony for an interracial couple. Pennsylvania, however, had become at that time a haven in which blacks and whites could legally intermarry. By the mid-1800s intermarried couples were common there, as the state was also a primary refuge for fugitive slaves. Despite many complaints to the state government and requests for the institution of a law banning marriage between the races, no such law was ever established there. Carter G. Woodson summarized:

> Marriages of whites and blacks eventually became so odious [in Pennsylvania] that they led to disturbances as in the case of the riot of 1849, one of the causes of which was that a white man was living with a Negro wife. This was almost ineffective, however, in the prevention of race admixture. Clandestine intermingling went on and tended to increase in enormous proportions. The conclusive proof of this is that in 1860 mulattoes constituted one third of the Negro population of Pennsylvania.[61]

Pennsylvania was not the only colonial society witnessing interracial marriages. Such couples were forming constantly throughout the colonies despite the legal pressures against them. Large numbers of whites – indentured servants, free persons and even members of the slave-owning class – simply did not believe in the profaneness of Africans. While marriage between the races eventually became severely restricted and in most places completely stamped out, nonetheless interracial socializing tended to be common, especially in the larger southern cities. Urban life in the South afforded many opportunities for interracial fellowship, including masked balls, social establishments on the fringe of propriety and even religious gatherings.[62] C. Vann Woodward notes that a 'frequent topic of comment by Northern visitors' to the South during Reconstruction 'was the intimacy of contact between the races', which included 'the sight of white babies suckled at black breasts, white and colored children playing together, the casual proximity of white and Negro homes in the cities, the camaraderie of maidservant and mistress, employer and employee, customer and clerk, and the usual stories of cohabitation of white men and Negro women'.[63]

Regarding this last phenomenon – white men's frequent sexual relations with slave women despite the resistance of the black community and even many whites – James Baldwin summarized the imbalance neatly. Speaking to a European American southerner during a televised debate, he said: 'You're not worried about me marrying *your* daughter. You're worried about me marrying your *wife's* daughter. I've been marrying your daughter ever since the days of slavery.'[64]

We are often told that the anti-miscegenation laws were the Europeans' *response* or *reaction* to Africans. We are told that it was natural for Europeans to take these legal actions, since it is normal for people to oppose that which they fear. These interpretations of history are inaccurate and unreasonable. First, although humans are emotional and subject to deep fears, we also recognize that they have consistently overcome fears in order to explore, create, achieve and conquer. Second, humanity has shown throughout history a constant ability to adapt to new circumstances, new experiences, new environments, new aspects of reality. Indeed, taken as a whole the history of human civilization is nothing if not the expression of these two qualities. Third, the historical record shows that there was very little if any fear between whites and blacks in the early colonies. It must be concluded, then, that the inhumane laws of slavery in America were not a *reaction* to the Africans. These laws were promulgated so as to *create* Africans as a pariah class. Edmund Morgan writes that even if, as Winthrop Jordan argues, the establishment of slavery in North America was an unconscious development, the concept of natural repulsion between blacks and whites was not:

> ... if Negro slavery came to Virginia without anyone having to decide upon it as a matter of public policy, the same is not true of racism. By a series of acts, the [Virginia] assembly deliberately did what it could to foster the contempt of whites for blacks and Indians.[65]

According to Woodson, intermarriage between Europeans, Africans and Indians was too common for any rational system of race-based slavery to survive without the support of strict legal measures.

> Persons who professed seriously to consider the future of slavery . . . saw that miscegenation and especially the general connection of white men with their female slaves introduced a mulatto race whose numbers would become dangerous, if the affections of their white parents were permitted to render them free.[66]

The racism that we encounter in Levels Two and Three did not arise from a natural feeling of repulsion between the races, did not originate in white emotions of distaste and hatred of Africans. Quite the contrary, it was precisely because whites and blacks were becoming socially united that the economic and political leaders of the colonies became alarmed. Emotions that tended to unite whites and blacks were all too prevalent well into the 19th century. Slave-holders had a devil of a time trying to keep control of their labor force and they used every tool they could find to do so, including the creation of draconian laws and pernicious myths and superstitions. Racism, therefore, was and is not natural. It is an artificial creation, fabricated by the pens of lawyers, judges, legislators and slave-holders.

THE ORIGINAL AMERICAN DREAM: ENGLAND WEST

One of the primary motivations for the establishment of colonies in North America was the shortage of land and resources in Europe that became acute in the 16th century. The New World served as a safety valve and an opportunity for the ambitious to achieve the high social status that eluded them in a continent experiencing 'population saturation, food scarcity, and runaway inflation'.[67] Slave-holders feared they would lose control of their laboring class and thus the dream of America as a vast field for the expansion of the landed gentry would abruptly end. Andrew Hacker has made this point succinctly:

> Europeans who colonized the Western Hemisphere sought to recreate it in their image and to transform North and South America into 'white' continents. With conquest comes the power to impose your ways on territories you have subdued. The treatment of Native Americans simply ratified that view.[68]

Gary Nash concurs:

> The farther inland English settlers moved, the more likely they were to cross racial boundaries. But all along the eastern seaboard, from the early 1600s to the 1800s, white settlers endeavored to re-create English society rather than mix it with others.[69]

From George Washington's carefully preserved household records we have a clear picture of how the slaves were used to recreate the manor life in the midst of the American wilderness. Washington serves as a primary example, for he was one of the wealthiest of all Americans, owning some 36,000 acres and 216 African slaves.

> Slaves washed his linens, sewed his shirts, polished his boots, saddled his horse, chopped the wood for his fireplaces, powdered his wig, drove his carriage, cooked his meals, served his table, poured his wine, posted his letters, lit the lamps, swept the porch, looked after the guests, planted the flowers in his gardens, trimmed the hedges, dusted the furniture, cleaned the windows, made the beds, and performed the myriad domestic chores . . .[70]

Slaves were very expensive resources vital to the success of the plantations as profit-making enterprises and only the wealthy could make such investments. In order to prevent their slaves from slipping away into freedom through marriage, and from demanding and attaining independence through cultural adaptation, the slave-holders instituted the strict and powerful laws forbidding free association and legal intermarriage between blacks and whites. These laws were promulgated and enforced as much to keep whites on their side of the fence as blacks on theirs.

Without the separation of the slaves from the non-slaves, the investment would be lost virtually overnight, a fact which the slave-holders themselves came to recognize only gradually. At the very least, the loss of slaves would mean a severe curtailment of the luxurious, servant-based English lifestyle that was the heart of the original dream of landed gentry in America. Just as a modern farmer could not tolerate his dearly priced bulls and cows to walk away on their own accord, so too the slave-holder would incur heavy losses, and even face bankruptcy, by any limitations to the practice of slavery as a perpetual institution. Just as the calves born to his prize livestock represented a lucrative future, so too the children born to his slaves represented the continuation of his profits for the benefit of his descendants.

What we see, then, is the gradual development of a social system designed primarily to separate not the races *per se* but slaves from non-slaves so as to preserve and sustain the former as a renewable resource. Race, or color, was the secondary quality which served as the means both to *identify* the slave population wherever they may be in the wider society and to *justify* their lower status. In short, the separation of the two populations and the development of an ideology of race were the means of rationalizing the cultivation of slave labor. Indeed, the same rational approach to agriculture as expressed in the discipline of the plantations – the neat rows, the organization and categorization of tools, equipment, harvested produce, types of animals, obedience to a strict schedule according to the seasons, coordination with supplies and with customers in the markets both locally and abroad – this same exacting, disciplined rationality was applied to the task of organizing, managing and perpetuating the slave populations. Thus, the identity of slaves achieved a kind of sophistication, of perfection, following the agricultural model. Africans were divided up into numerous categories, according to material characteristics: gender, age, height, build, teeth, skills. They were further categorized according to 'blood': pure Africans, mulatto – derived from the term 'mule', the offspring of a horse and a donkey – quadroon (one fourth African), octoroon (one eighth), a system that in some states extended literally *ad infinitem* with the advent of the 'one drop' rule. Thus by declaring all human beings with even one drop of African blood as slaves by law, the slave-holders were dutifully obeying the dictates of a capitalist culture that strove to the utmost to account for every penny of its investment, that shunned any loss or wastage, that regarded it as the highest expression of civilized behavior and honor to make theirs an ordered world under their complete control.

Legalized slavery was a vast and unfortunately all too successful experiment in social engineering that owed at least some of its success to the experience of the English in Ireland. For similar reasons – more obviously revealing of the political and not biological concerns – the English in the 14th century had outlawed intermarriage with the native Irish to support their colonization efforts in Ireland. Such prohibitions of intermarriage are indeed profuse in the political history of most cultures and nations of both the East and the West.[71]

BIRTH OF COLOR CONSCIOUSNESS

The colonial era was a turning point in modern history, for then the Europeans – especially the English – began to refer to themselves as white in order to distinguish themselves from other populations intended to be reserved as slave labor pools. Prior to the advent of the construct of whiteness, colonists referred to themselves and others by nationality – Englishmen, for example – and by religion. When slavery was justified by the excuse that the slave was not Christian, the system was vulnerable to the process of religious conversion – which, after all, was one of the stated aims of the colonies. The legalistic mentality of the colonial intellectuals simply shifted the justification from the variable quality of religious identity to the more or less fixed physical quality of skin color. Thus the colonists took advantage of a convenient accident of nature. The first usage of the term 'white' as meaning a race of people was in 1604. It became common first in the American colonies and this only after some 70 years of Africans and Europeans coexisting there.[72]

Consciousness of the visibility and permanence of skin color had profound implications, for it exaggerated the material and marginalized the spiritual. Referring to slavery in Europe's colonial period, Victor Kiernan reasons, 'An urbanized aristocracy wants its servants very distinctly marked off from it, as a different species of humanity . . .'[73] Of particular value, for the sake of capitalist enterprise, skin color passed on to the next generation, that is, it enabled slave status to be easily and cheaply reproduced. The practical political shift became gradually loaded with ideology, until over the centuries skin color in Europe and America was completely mystified in popular culture, bearing countless meanings. Under the evolving system of racist philosophy in Europe, the Americas and wherever European colonies were established, each shade and hue of skin became a heavily weighted text. Children were taught from a young age to read and understand these texts; it was a primary duty, the failure of which they knew brought severe punishment.

THE CHURCH AS GROUND ZERO

If these primary laws were the seeds of slavery and racism in North America, the segregation of the Christian Church was the fertile soil in which they grew. The denial of full access to Christian brotherhood for the African made possible the criminalization and moral condemnation of interracial marriage.

John Howard Griffin, while in the guise of a black man, experienced two kinds of encounter with religious institutions during his investigations for *Black Like Me*. On the one hand he met with some positive reactions. A church bookstore was willing to cash his traveler's check when no other store would. A monastery welcomed him for a few days of retreat: 'The contrast was almost too great to be borne,' he recalled. 'It was a shock, like walking from the dismal swamps into sudden brilliant sunlight.' It was a place where he, as a black man, was accepted. 'Here men know nothing of hatred. They sought to make themselves conform ever more perfectly to God's will, whereas outside I had seen mostly men who sought to make God's will conform to their prejudices.' On the other hand, he was also 'deeply shocked to be driven away from churches that would have welcomed me any time as a white man.'[74] The Christian community's ambiguity regarding race can be traced to the very origins of slavery.

Beginning in the mid- to late-1600s slaves in Virginia and other southern colonies were denied membership in the Christian Church. Slave-holders opposed the Christian conversion of the Africans 'because of the belief that the equal association of the races in religious matters made the Negro dissatisfied and . . . aspire to other forms of association. The same forces that were opposed to conversion were opposed to intermarriage for similar reasons.'[75] By the time of the Revolution, one South Carolinian could write plainly that the slaves were 'excluded in a manner from the pale of the Christian Church'.[76]

Even when slaves later received permission to become Christians they were never accepted as full members of the Church and were restricted to worship outside the church building at the windows or in a separate section of the church, a gallery above the main congregation or back pews. While it was also the case that class determined seating amongst whites – the wealthy in the front and the less wealthy behind – the slaves were always considered the least welcome. In either case, whether the hierarchy was class-based or racial, it contradicted the spirit and the teachings of Jesus and effectively stifled the development of spirituality among whites and blacks alike.[77]

Moreover, throughout nearly the entire duration of slavery, laws forbade slaves to learn to read and thus denied them direct access to the Bible. If society in the West was founded on the loving fellowship and mutual respect fostered by religious practices, then these facts have the utmost significance. Yet they tend to be overlooked or given secondary importance. To this subject we shall return.

The successful operation and acceleration of the capitalist economy required a dual society: on the one hand, a careful balancing between adherence to the spirit and laws of Christianity in order to maintain social unity and, on the other hand, freedom from the obligations of the Christian spirit and laws. The solution: Slave-holders segregated the churches in the late 1600s to limit the ideal universal association at the foundation of Christianity. Segregation was an uneasy compromise between the Christian and the capitalist powers. Slaves were allowed to practice Christianity but only in such a way that the brotherly mutual association which Christianity naturally engendered amongst its followers was truncated and tightly controlled – as the tremendous potential energy latent in a free-flowing river is controlled by a dam. It was a Christianity that fenced off the religious domain, rendering brotherhood finite, exclusive.

The most far-reaching effect of the segregation of the Church was manifested in the institution of the family, for the Church was the basis upon which the prohibition of interracial marriage was laid. The possibility of intermarriage independent of the Church was very rare, since marriage – that is, legitimate, legalized and socially honored marriage – like all institutions of the society, was based on the Church and American courtship patterns have tended to be related not so much to family ties, as practiced in aristocracies and tribes, but to Church membership.[78]

The early colonists eventually realized that an integrated Church would naturally lead to interracial fellowship and intermarriage and that intermarriage between slave and free person would give rise to an integrated populace, new generations of mixed heritage capable of comprehending both the domain of the master and the domain to which the slave had been assigned. The psychological controls separating the slave and the free populations would fail. Mutual association between whites and slaves would be legally instituted and sanctified. Slaves would then be *de facto* under the shelter of the religious law, within the religious domain. 'The result of such unions,' writes Edmund Morgan, 'could be a blurring of the distinction between slave and free, black and white.'[79] The dual society would become unified, association would become universal and the planters and entrepreneurs would then be deprived of their unlimited source of 'non-human' labor. Again we see here that the dread of intermarriage originated not from an aesthetic, visceral repugnance towards 'race mixture' but from the slave-holders' efforts to eliminate a primary means by which the slave population could enter the religious domain and thus subvert the established economic order.[80]

Although the Christian doctrine did succeed among African Americans, the Christian Church may rightly be considered the first and foremost segregated institution in American history. The segregation of this single institution, which is the very foundation of modern western society, generated the segregation of all superstructural institutions, from nurseries to schools, lunch counters, beaches, hospitals and cemeteries.

Peer pressure to be racist is bad enough. But this is far outweighed by the legal and moral pressure from the Church and the state themselves, the highest authorities in the land. Together these institutions caused the metamorphosis of racist philosophy from dry law and social policy into powerful conscious and subconscious superstitions bearing the threat of sin, of blasphemy and of eternal damnation.

If the Christian Church in North America had never become segregated, never been a locus of racial discrimination, American society would not have produced extreme racism. This is not to say that all of America's problems would have been solved had the Church been free of spiritual corruption; such would be an oversimplification. But it is to say that extreme racial prejudice would not have received the sanction of the highest spiritual authorities in the land and thus would not have become a part of what it means to be a true, faithful Christian and good citizen. It would not have become normalized but rather would have been rightly recognized as deviance from the Christian teachings.

By this reasoning we can better understand why American churchgoers have tended to be more prejudiced than the unchurched.[81] However immoral the idea of racial prejudice may be, its practice in the form of segregation has long been honored as a moral institution in America because of its genesis and perpetuation in the churches of American Protestantism. Insofar as many Americans identify these churches as the true essence and form of Christianity and, more importantly, as the embodiment of the divine will of the Creator of the universe, it is logical that they uphold the practice of racial prejudice as a proper element of the Christian life; whence, moreover, the close association between racial and biblical beliefs in the doctrines of race supremacy groups.

THE CENTRALITY OF THE WHITE WOMAN

The focus of the secular laws and religious norms establishing slavery, specifically those prohibiting intermarriage and condemning the children of slaves to be slaves themselves, is the white woman. The entire structure of slavery and racism depended on the deliberate maintenance of the white woman in a state of ignorance and powerlessness. This is seen in two important facts.

First, the white woman could not have sexual freedom. This is not to say that there were no sexual or marital relations between white women and black men during slavery. Eugene Genovese states: 'Despite the legend, white women of all classes had black lovers and sometimes husbands in all parts of the South, especially in the towns and cities,'[82] a fact that reinforces our understanding that racism was an artificial construct fighting an uphill battle to keep the races separate. But such relationships were suppressed by the entire society, were illegal and were very often punished. Edmund Morgan argues that one of the reasons for this strict control of white women was the gender imbalance in some of the colonies. In Virginia the ratio was three men to two women and the fact that illegitimate mulatto children were common showed that 'black men were competing all too successfully for white women, even in the face of the severe penalties'.[83]

The white man regarded himself free to have sexual relations with black women because the resulting children would be raised completely in the slave culture and would be safely ensconced in a slave mentality. However, the white man could not grant the white woman the same freedom. Were she free to choose a black husband she would give birth to a black or brown child who would be culturally free, that is, would grow up with her own free mentality and culture. If the white woman were to have this same sexual freedom, the 'production', 'reproduction', perpetuation and definition of the African population would go out of the control of white male hands and into the control of white female hands, at least in part. James Johnston noted that the threat to the white society was particularly acute if the mother of the interracial child was white.[84] We may argue – as Johnston neglected to give any further explanation of his point – that this was because it is through the mother that the child receives the great majority of his cultural training and education. Oliver C. Cox argued that 'it has not been the Negro man but the white woman who presented the greatest problem to the oligarchy', for she represented a 'cultural bridge' between the slave and free populations.[85]

Second, the white woman could not be free to be a mother. Motherhood and sexuality both had to be taken away at one stroke, lest the freedom to be a mother would lead to the freedom to choose any husband regardless of color. The white male brought the black female into the white family structure not only as his sexual partner but also as the mother of his white children, to nurse them, feed them, bathe them, clothe them and lovingly raise them to adulthood. The white woman was considered too sacred and holy for this function but actually this was a cover, a deception: the white woman would have become too powerful if she retained the responsibilities and authority of motherhood. If free to be a mother, she would see herself free to be a lover, just as the white male was. The white males were fathers to white, brown and black children. Naturally the white females would follow suit and become mothers to white, brown and black children. But unlike the coldly calculating, financially motivated white male slave-holders, the white woman would identify herself with her brown and black children and would emotionally reject their enslavement and oppression. She would become a firm obstacle standing between the white male slave-holders and the African slaves.

Thus, the myths concerning the slave man's relation to the free white woman, by centering their fearful expressions on him, concealed the true threat posed by the white mother as the potential educator and hence liberator of the slave children, as the destroyer of the society's uneasy, artificial duality. By making her too sacred and holy for sexual life and for motherhood, the white male power structure rendered the white woman politically, socially and culturally impotent. The white men knew very well how powerful white women could be in disrupting and disbanding the delicate structure, the tissue of psychological illusions, myths and theories, on which racism and slavery were based. They knew that white women were the weak link in the system, because they recognized that these women would fall in love with black men just as they themselves had fallen in love with black women. But the difference between these two forms of love is that from time immemorial, while fathers had been relatively distant from children in European society, mothers had identified themselves with their children and sacrificed themselves for their upbringing. Were free white women to lovingly raise brown and black children, such a relationship would lead directly to a breakdown of the slave mentality among the brown and black population. Rather than risk this grave threat to their economic and political system, white men effectively isolated white women from the rest of society.

The denial of freedom to white women contributed greatly to a long course, still ongoing, of significant mental illness on an individual, group and social basis in the South. White women watched as their children were taken away and raised by black surrogate mothers; they watched as their husbands took black lovers; they watched as they became objects of idol worship; they watched as they became abstracted into a mythical existence removed from reality, from their children, from their husbands; and they watched as they were forever cut off from any possibility of relations with black men.[86] Although it may seem to us farfetched for a white woman or girl to fall in love with the lowly black male slave, in those days it was not farfetched at all. This the white male slave master knew all too well and therefore he pruned the white woman's human nature, eventually uprooting it and leaving a permanent scar in the psyche of white society in the South. While for Africans slavery was chains and irons, for white women it was a gilded cage but a cage nonetheless.

Moral Vacuum

The primary slave laws created by the new class of merchant rulers in America effectively bankrupted morality and terminated observance of the Golden Rule among the masses in the American colonies. Secondary laws, rules and traditions were also created to provide additional support to the slave system: slaves were prohibited to learn reading and writing; they were not permitted to travel away from their owner's land without a pass from the owner; owners had the right to buy, sell and trade any slave or slave child; although excessive violence against slaves was illegal, in practice it was permitted; although sexual relations with slaves was illegal, it was very commonly practiced by white male slave-holders.

The agrarian capitalists in America felt free to create these laws so contrary to European practice because the great distance from Europe, and the impression of both the New World and Africa as wildernesses, encouraged them to shrug off past restraints associated with Christian civilization. America was wild, a place where materialism had free reign. God and His Church were back in Europe.[87]

Law itself had a tenuous position in the early decades of the New World colonies and in the American Revolution much of what had been instituted from the Old World was swept away, giving free rein to the bourgeoisie to devise their own best world. Jonathan Bush states that the American colonies were essentially private fiefdoms in which the English common law – which definitely did not permit slavery as it developed in the New World – for the most part did not apply. 'South Carolina, Pennsylvania, and Maryland were granted to private proprietors under charters that, like their medieval models, gave the lords proprietary a wide ambit in organizing and governing the new colonies.'[88]

> The colonies began as lands in the king's possession but not under parliament or common law. Instead, they were dominions, governed by the royal prerogative and either annexed to the Crown or granted to lords proprietary. This prerogative framework permitted divergent local practices. Thus, despite the common law's traditions of antislavery rhetoric, doctrinal conservatism and centralization, there were few obstacles to prevent the colonists from making their own local slave law . . .
>
> The critical point for the development of colonial slavery is that however the medieval precedents were glossed, the 17th-century versions of conquest doctrine allowed *all the colonies* a private space in which planters and merchants could deploy slave labor with little oversight from England . . .
>
> . . . the privatization of the medieval manorial serf is a model for colonial autonomy under the prerogative. Prerogative theory held that the early colonies were military or commercial enterprises, under the quasi-feudal lordship of their promoters and indirectly under the king, and that the royal as well as proprietary colonies were not necessarily under common law. As Charles Andrews put it, '[I]n reality these settlements were not colonies; they were private estates.' Hence, early governors adopted laws

at variance with the common law . . . The irony of all this was that, long before the 17th century, private ordering had come to apply only to certain frontier zones; generally, it had fallen into sharp disfavor . . . Everywhere in 16th and 17th-century Europe, the trend was towards the breaking of old private and feudal social relations. Thus, when 17th-century lawyers applied conquest law to the new colonies, they were taking a highly unusual step.[89]

In such private realms the proprietors, and the plantation owners living under their wing, were free to create rules with which to fill the vacuum left by the impotence of English common law.

The master-slave relationship, which implied the complete removal of the slave from the public sphere, was particularly open to elaboration outside of law. And the developing political culture of plantation slavery, emphasizing values of personal autonomy and paternalism, made it likely that slave holders would use law as but one means of implementing their mastery. Within the private world of the master, the formal underdevelopment of slave law was offset by private 'rule making', described in plantation manuals and rule books and enforced with whipping and other punishments, including death.[90]

Freedom from Europe's traditional laws and legal authorities – the Church and the monarchy – enabled racist thought and action to evolve from generalized notions to specific legal measures. Regulations, codes, rule books, plantation manuals – all creating new laws, new offenses, new punishments, new criminals – evidenced the high degree to which slavery and racism quickly made use of the exquisite rational systems of thought rediscovered from the Greeks and Romans in the late Middle Ages and the Renaissance. The rights of Africans were rationalized and legislated out of existence in a world free of oversight by genuinely spiritual religious institutions.

Insofar as these laws established what is right and wrong, good and bad, they identified blacks, who were unable to be freed through conversion, as false Christians, as evil. These laws and their cultural residue have made Africanness in America foreign, unpatriotic, illegal; they are still culturally powerful and many of them have yet to be abrogated by all ranks of government.

CIVILIZATION'S END

Some interpretations of American history assume that in promulgating these laws slave-holders were merely following the practices of their time, that the historical context not only permitted slavery but demanded it and that therefore they were not morally culpable. But then the question arises: Why was slavery *not* practiced in England and most of Europe on such a large scale as was later found in the New World? Why, if it was so economically and socially useful to the colonists, had slavery not been established before, or even later, in Europe itself?

The answer is quite simple: it was illegal. The European colonists in both North and South America broke civil and religious law in establishing slavery – particularly its extremely inhumane form in North America. English common law, Jonathan Bush notes, strongly opposed slavery.

> It is . . . a different and more difficult [historical] matter that English and colonial law came to accept slavery, given the strong rhetoric in English legal culture rejecting slave status and celebrating freedom. No less remarkable is that the law adopted slavery in the way that it did: quietly, without ever formally introducing the new institution – an 'unthinking decision', in Winthrop D. Jordan's apt phrase. Instead, a startlingly new labor regime, repudiated at home [in England] for centuries, was introduced by rapacious planters and merchants; as local practice [in the colonies] it was enshrined in provincial statute and allowed indirectly under common law – from start to finish, a passive, almost stealthy process of legal accommodation.[91]

Here we might question Winthrop Jordan's characterization of the genesis of American slavery as an 'unthinking decision'. Its institutionalization was quiet, informal and stealthy, as Bush suggests, precisely because the slaveholders knew that they were treading an illegal path. These violators of English common law, busily sowing the seeds of a slave-supported society in the New World, were well aware of their guilt and they were ashamed. A. Leon Higginbotham has made this point very clearly:

> The [United States] Constitution accommodated the institution of slavery without ever *explicitly* using – prior to 1865 – in any article or clause the word 'slavery'. But the drafters' coyness about using the word 'slavery' did not necessarily reveal an aversion to the institution of slavery. Rather, it suggests a reluctance to sully the great document with a word that most of the founders realized, despite their protestations to the contrary, denoted a fundamentally evil institution.[92]

Consciousness of the shamefulness of slavery caused strong opposition within the white community. James Madison advised that the Constitution should not include an explicit reference to the 'idea that there could be property in men'.[93] Luther Martin, a writer of the revolutionary period in

America, asserted, referring to the framers of the Constitution: 'They anxiously sought to avoid the admission of expressions [i.e. "slavery"[94]] which might be odious in the ears of Americans, although they were willing to admit into their system those *things* which the *expressions* signified.'[95] In 1841 John Quincy Adams wrote: 'The words slave and slavery are studiously excluded from the Constitution. Circumlocutions are the fig-leaves under which these parts of the body politic are decently concealed.'[96] This violation was too shameful to be mentioned in the country's fundamental legal documents. In the capitals of Europe this was the grossest violation of the tradition of Christian civilization but in the wilds of North America colonists felt themselves too isolated across the Atlantic, too tempted by the potential to make fabulous profits, to concern themselves with moral niceties half a world away.

As we argued in our characterization of the American colonies as England West, many if not most of the Europeans in America were not seeking to create a high, complex civilization. To them, high civilization and Christian behavior lay across the Atlantic, in the realms hallowed by the memories and remains of Rome and Athens and the power of the Church. America was a realm where civilization's laws were irrelevant, rightly transgressed with impunity. Whereas force of circumstances led the French and Spanish, most of whom were explorers in the interior without families, to abandon the ways of the Old World and be open to intermarriage, the English Protestants on the East coast insisted on recreating English society – but only its pastoral form.[97] Many were English plantation owners who, like their peers in rural England, sat content in splendid rural isolation, with no hint of the development of any great civilization on the horizon. Their goal, consciously or unconsciously, was to bypass high civilization and its requirements and strictures and directly establish themselves as landed gentry. They more than matched the success of great landowners back home but without the benefit of the high streets, the universities, the arts, the great cities. In a time when 90 per cent of the population was engaged in agriculture, they turned their backs on the city life as 'corruptive, encouraging luxury', states Meyer Reinhold, and were following instead the ideal of the contemporary British gentleman farmer as well as the ancient example from Roman political theory, which advocated a 'free agricultural commonwealth composed of self-sufficient, economically independent farmer-soldier-citizens'.[98]

America's slave-holders were well aware that slavery and racism and cosmopolitan urban culture are incompatible. City life inherently involves systemic cooperation, unity in diversity and constant skills development, the hallmarks of civilization; in such an environment slavery and racism could not easily survive. The citizens recognized, consciously or not, that the goals of the city are more important than those of slavery or racism. City life, C. Vann Woodward wrote, was 'hostile to slavery. It corroded the master's authority, diminished his control, and blurred the line between freedom and bondage.'[99] It would of course be an oversimplification to suggest that the solution to slavery and racism lies in building up cities. And yet we must recognize in C. Vann Woodward's statement that the solution must include creative urban culture as a central factor. We have, therefore, made civilization a primary subject of our discussion and one to which we shall return. A critical goal of the social laws and codes of slavery, and later the Jim Crow laws, was to maintain a strict separation between slaves and the civilizing effects of cities and urban culture in general and to maintain strict identity between slaves and nature. Segregation was not merely to separate the races but to carefully circumscribe cosmopolitan urban life for European Americans' benefit and thwart its influence on African Americans. As long as slaves were identified with nature, there was no guilt in their enslavement; on the contrary, it was an achievement to tame them – a civilizing act in itself – just as it was to tame the wilds of America. This clarifies the seemingly self-contradictory statement of slave-holders that slavery civilized the Africans: If African life was the freedom of wild nature, then subjection to the discipline of slavery was equivalent to the reduction of wilderness to orderly fields of useful crops.

According to this logic, it was an abomination for African American slaves, who were considered part of the natural world, to enter the civilized world, just as it would be an abomination for any animal to do so. As law professor Christopher Stone put it:

> We are inclined to suppose the rightlessness of rightless 'things' to be a decree of Nature, not a legal convention acting in support of some status quo. It is thus that we defer considering the choices involved in all their moral, social and economic dimensions . . . The fact is that each time there is a movement to confer rights onto some new 'entity', the proposal is bound to sound odd or frightening or laughable. This is partly because until the rightless thing receives its rights, we cannot see it as anything but a thing for the use of 'us' – those who are holding rights at the time.[100]

It is for this reason that Justice Taney's famous dictum, the slave has no rights which any white man is bound to respect, was believed to be true, for it followed the basic principle of slave as nature. This also explains the often infuriating difference between blacks and whites in discussing slavery and racism, as if the two sides speak two entirely different languages. For white racists of the old South, racism is a matter not of hatred but logic. The result is an attitude of cool detachment, of lightness, of laughter, of ease with brutality and violence; it is the attitude of farmers towards plants and animals. For blacks, it is not a matter of natural philosophy and logic but of spiritual violation. The essential conflict, then, is that for whites it was outrageous to allow Africans to join civilization, while for Africans it was outrageous that whites tried to prevent them from doing so.

Preventing slaves from learning the ways of western civilization, and imposing the boundaries of nature upon them, the slave-holders, despite their grand mansions and plantations, their emulation of England's landed gentry, necessarily kept civilization from themselves. Thus the South, with but few exceptions, never created a thriving culture, and only in recent times, despite the fabulous wealth generated by slave labor, could it be said to generate the diversity of resources and skills characteristic of cosmopolitan Europe.

Even in the 20th century the city mitigated racism; it was a haven and promised land for blacks migrating from the rural South after World War One. The challenge for racists, then, was to transplant racism to the large metropolises of the North, that is, to prevent civilization from flourishing in the city – obviously a profoundly contradictory goal. But unfortunately they succeeded and for the most part without changing their methods. Education and skills training were denied, public declarations of the sanctity of African Americans were prevented, the family was disintegrated, natural passions were systematically encouraged by the easy availability of intoxicants. The development of unity in diversity was stifled and ultimately snuffed out by segregation. But, of course, in the process they snuffed out the civilizing influence of the city as a whole. The city became a dead space and whites escaped to the suburbs, where the failure to create the institutions and processes of civilization deepened.

American culture thus emerged between two powerful restrictions: the control and condemnation of nature and the severe limitation of civilization in order to prevent its influence from raising the status of the Africans. The destruction of nature and the restriction of cosmopolitanism has led directly to what we now see dominating American society: a culture greatly exaggerating technology and individualism. To this subject we shall later return.

FROM WORD OF GOD TO WORD OF MAN

We have seen that the slave-holders in America liberated themselves from the legal and moral obligations of Christian Europe and from the ages-old obligation to build up a thriving cosmopolitan culture. These were quite radical changes. The colonists were able to make them because they had discovered – or rediscovered – the power of the written word to create anew not only laws but meaning and morality.

The power of society to create good and evil, right and wrong, is well illustrated by the tradition in some American Indian tribes of opposites, 'crazy dogs' who would always act contrary to the expected norm. Numerous mystical religious concepts teach that our earthly existence is but illusion, that we are at fault if we take it to be absolute reality. The crazy dogs assist us to remain conscious of that fact. European Americans cast slaves in the role of immoral opposites, for a new capitalist society needing a new moral foundation. As Toni Morrison wrote, the oppression of Africans

> is the vehicle by which the American self knows itself as not enslaved, but free; not repulsive, but desirable; not helpless, but licensed and powerful; not history-less, but historical; not damned, but innocent; not a blind accident of evolution, but a progressive fulfillment of destiny.[101]

In this context we can see that the manmade laws of a society are not essential but tenuous constructs. They create a seemingly incontestable reality, yet the society is in the end an illusion fabricated as we wish it to be, a dream that changes on our whim, first in this direction then in that. It was very easy for the southern plantation owners to create a world that was the exact opposite of that described in English common law, the Declaration of Independence and the United States Constitution. They were, with respect to these moral and legal documents, and especially with respect to Christianity, contraries, yet claiming to be the exemplars of morality. And the double irony is that the planters claimed that the true contraries were not themselves but the Africans.

We can see unfolding before us a wider structure in which one group after the other, like dominoes, blames the next for contradicting truth and morality. The Church leaders blame the commercial leaders, who in turn blame the slaves. Or perhaps it is better viewed not as dominoes, a linear model, but as a web, a multidimensional model, in which each identity, a node on the web, blames all its neighbors for being contrary to itself, the ideal.

In the course of formulating and instituting the laws of slavery and racism in this web of simultaneous multiple possibilities, two important influences led to the perpetuation and spread of this spiritual infection: violence, which is well understood, and the iconic word. Usually the product of scholars, theologians and lawyers, the iconic word is that powerful expression which becomes an authority in and of itself. It is the word of men as opposed to the Word of God, a word that is deliberately used to achieve a material purpose. It imitates yet contradicts the Word of God. It influences individuals, communities and nations, sets the direction of social development and limits human thought.

Through the promulgation of explicit codes and laws the European Americans consciously identified the African Americans with the profane and the illegal. They tore to shreds the fabric of African humanity by the relatively simple acts of public declaration through the written word, enforced by the legal and justice systems. They thereby created slavery and racism out of thin air, as it were, by the power of the pen. In this, literary skill played a great role. As Gary Nash states, racial extremists in the South were not only backed by the threat and the reality of physical violence, they were also '[a]rmed with literature from some of the nation's best educated men'; a 'huge body of literature undergirded the increasingly harsh racial ideology of the period, strengthening the prejudices of the man in the street by giving them the blessing of academic and scientific authority', just as *The Bell Curve* performed the same function in recent years.[102] We shall see that such scholars played a prominent role in the earlier rise of the witch craze in Europe.

Slavery's apologists had inherited a long tradition of wordplay which had been infused with a powerful new life in the revival of classical humanism and in the age of reason. They were paid to practice an old craft – often considered most honorable – that asked them to prove day night and night day. When applied to the issue of slavery – only some 150 years after Martin Luther's rebellion against this sort of clerical and scholarly deception and manipulation – this craft spelled the doom of spiritual life in the colonies, for its aim was to conceal a massive moral failing. Slave-holders did not wish to see themselves or be seen as violators of the religious law. But at the same time they wanted freedoms which the laws and morals of Europe did not allow. They therefore charged intellectuals, both ecclesiastical and secular, to find the way to allow the freedoms without violations. The key, therefore, was the word and its manipulation. The word was no longer seen as divine and spiritual but as fundamentally material; if not manmade, it was at least under the control of man.

Only the violence of the Civil War was able to halt temporarily the march of this spiritual disease. But the iconic word of racist laws and theology lived on through the fire of that war, undiminished in power, until the civil rights movement and the end of Jim Crow. Many argue that this deceptive word continues to be central to racist thought and action even today.

Respiritualization requires the recognition that these words are not reality but illusion. We who have worshiped them as idols must now, fearlessly and candidly, break them. This is the purpose of the newly arisen nationwide movement to repeal racist laws from state constitutions and local statutes.[103]

Long-term Effects

The result of the slavery laws, and the thin tissue of illusion they created, was that in time the mere presence of an African American became at face value an offense, the mere presence a threat, the mere presence a disturbance of the social order, the mere presence a call for defensive and offensive measures to control it. The devil is in our midst and thus any means are justified to ward off his evil representatives and purposes. Such a culture doubtless had long-term effects on the lives of African and European Americans alike. Let us consider the effects of the witch-hunts on the development of women in European history, addressed by Anne Llewellyn Barstow in what is the first history of the witch-hunts from a feminist perspective. She argues that

> no historian of the period has considered the *effects* on European society of one hundred thousand or so public executions for witchcraft or of the targeting of its own women as victims. The nature of beliefs about the crime itself, considered so horrifying that it justified any means of punishment, indicates a high level of fear; the form of execution, most often by burning, confirms a high level of violence. That torture and execution took place before large crowds shows not only the blood-thirst of the age but even more the desire of church and state, local and national, to control their citizens through intimidation. In the witch-hunts, violence bred violence. The effects of the 'solution', which . . . were unsettling rather than healing, became in turn the cause of further persecution.[104]

Clearly this passage presents many parallels with slavery, which induced in the white population a tremendous and perpetual fear of Africans. The level of violence against Africans was consistently high during and after slavery, most of it in the privacy of the plantation. Torture and execution were commonplace; there was rarely any pretense to judicial proceedings. These had a powerful effect on the white population, particularly those of the working class. As we have seen, recent research argues that the patriarchal landowners in the colonies controlled the masses of poorer whites, and prevented them from seizing power and forming a more democratic society, through the doctrine of racism and the violence inflicted upon Africans. The doctrine gave the poor whites a sense of satisfaction in psychological superiority, while the violence instilled in them a fear of the ruling authorities.

We can hardly underestimate the longevity of these effects. It is clear that slavery established a culture of violence that permeated not only the South but the entire nation with regard to African Americans in particular and minorities in general. Anne Llewellyn Barstow asserts, 'Not until the mid-nineteenth century did the status of Western women begin to recover from the witch-hunts. It can be argued that we have never entirely recovered since.'[105] If the witch craze has had such a powerful influence on the West and involved the public execution of some 100,000 women across two centuries in Europe, one wonders at the depth of the influence of the enslavement of millions of Africans in America over roughly the same length of time.

PHYSICAL EFFECTS

Not far from the foot of the Brooklyn Bridge in Manhattan, near New York's City Hall, a construction crew in 1991 unearthed an old cemetery. Archeologists and historians determined that the site was the burial ground for African slaves from the late 1600s until 1796. In 1993 another construction crew working some 200 yards away from the old cemetery site also discovered human remains, and one observer from an archeological museum saw there 'piles and piles of dirt with bones popping out all over the place'.[106] They too were part of the African burial ground, which now was revealed to be far more extensive than originally had been imagined.

In time archeologists and physical anthropologists learned much more than most people would imagine possible from bodies long buried. It is now recognized as 'the earliest and largest anthropological find for interpreting African-American history'.[107] The bones were in excellent condition and provided powerful evidence of the lives of the slaves. Michael Blakey, an anthropologist at Howard University and the director of the New York African Burial Ground Project, has taken pains to publicize the physical findings that testify to those long forgotten lives, testimony which is all the more striking as it speaks of slave life not in the deep South but in the North and in a relatively urban area no less. This fact does not contradict our earlier argument that urban cosmopolitanism is a primary factor in resolving slavery and racism. The practice of slavery in New York and other cities was, according to C. Vann Woodward and others, in the long run mitigated by the need for the urban culture and economy to build up social relations. It is not merely coincidental that it was New York City itself that became the fertile ground of the Harlem Renaissance.

If there was ever any doubt, the New York African Burial Ground provides incontrovertible and vivid proof that the lives of the slaves were filled with incomparable suffering. First, disease and malnutrition:

> Premature mortality was high. One-half of the population died in childhood, and nearly forty percent of those children died as infants. These rates are nearly twice the rates of infant mortality among the colonial English in the colony of New York. (Interestingly, although today's infant mortal-

ity is much lower, African-American infant mortality remains twice that of Euro-Americans). Children often show evidence of infectious diseases (twenty-five percent of skeletons have bone lesions associated with generalized infection). Fifty percent of dead children show evidence of metabolic disease, the vast majority of which indicates anemia (most likely to have resulted from malnutrition and disease, while approximately ten percent of anemia might easily have a genetic basis). Children (two to twelve years of age) often show evidence of growth retardation in which bone growth lags approximately two years behind developmental ages assessed on the basis of dental development. Furthermore, about sixty percent of children have developmental defects in dental enamel resulting from bouts of malnutrition and disease.

Second, stress from labor:

Our historians are showing that enslaved Africans in colonial New York City were engaged in a diversity of occupations that included skilled crafts, but tended more often to involve arduous labor as mariners, stevedores, porters, and domestic workers. They also worked in farming, clearing land, construction, mining, ferrying, and just about every form of physical labor involved in the building and maintenance of the colony. Our biological data shows that the strains of load bearing and other physical labor usually stressed their musculoskeletal systems to the margins of human capacity and often even beyond that capacity.

Muscle attachments become enlarged when muscles undergo frequent strain. Most of the population of men and women have enlarged muscle attachments in the neck, arms, and legs. It has become commonplace for our technicians to find women's bones that are so robust as to be indistinguishable from those of men. Were it not for the presence of more specific indicators of sex, many of the women's skeletons would have been misidentified as men's skeletons.

When muscles undergo strain beyond the capacity of their bony attachments to anchor them, muscle tears will occur at the attachments, creating deep bone lesions and calcified connective tissue. The majority of both men and women from the African Burial Ground exhibit such effects of excessive strain, most frequently involving the muscles – pectoralis major in the upper arm, brachialis in the lower arm, and the adductor muscles along the linea aspera at the back of the thigh. These muscles are involved in heavy, power lifting, in addition to many other muscular tasks.

We think that heavy lifting is a most likely cause of such extreme muscle strain, because all of the aforementioned muscles are used to lift heavy objects to be carried on the head. The extreme arthritic changes often found in the bones of the neck are also consistent with this historically verifiable, African load-bearing technique. What is more, we often see fractures of the spine, including healed fractures of the first bone of the neck, that result from traumatic loads or force to the top of the head. There are also at least six cases of ring-shaped fractures of the base of the skull, resulting from collision between the spine and the base of the skull, causing death. If this trauma was not deliberately induced, it serves as evidence of being worked to death. Axial loading (bearing loads on the head) is a very efficient technique, but may have been abused.

These factors, disease, malnutrition and hard labor, combined to cause the destruction of childhood:

It is often said that a society can be judged by the treatment of its most vulnerable members. In this respect, one example from the African Burial Ground is suggestive. The individual known as Burial #39 is a six-year-old child. We do not know whether #39 was a girl or boy. This child has dental developmental defects showing that he/she was ill at birth, implying maternal ill health as well. The orbits of the eyes show pitting, characteristic of active anemia at the time of death. There are lesions in the outer layers of bone caused by generalized infection. The growth areas (sutures) of the skull have closed extraordinarily early in development; we are not certain whether this resulted from load-bearing or brain growth retardation due to malnutrition. Burial #39 has lesions at the arm attachments where the brachialis muscles strained, and muscle attachments in the arms are enlarged. The first and second cervical vertebrae (neck bones) are partially fused due to force or heavy load trauma to the top of the head. The only artifacts associated with this burial are the shroud pin stains evincing the care with which the child was interred by members of his or her community.[108]

Some six months after this article was written, CNN was able to broadcast a sharp summary of the site with the benefit of more complete laboratory data:

The bones show the hardships the Africans faced the moment they stepped off the slave ships; in some cases they literally were worked to death.

'You have so many individuals who have trauma or injury to the bone, broken neck bones because they were forced to do that kind of labor,' says Ena Fox of Howard University.

As Blakey demonstrates how the knee bones work, he tells of the enlarged muscles or torn ligaments the slaves would have experienced. He says half of the [population] died before they became teenagers; others died within the first two years of their arrival.

Fox, who's been collecting data from the teeth that were found, says defects in the tooth enamel were caused by malnutrition.

Further examination of the bones and teeth reveal [that] Africans who were enslaved as children and then shipped here had more [cases] of metabolic illness and malnutrition than children who spent their childhood in Africa and later died as adults.[109]

This is the testimony of the physical remains that, surprisingly, have survived in 'pristine' condition beneath the streets of Manhattan for two or three centuries. It is valuable testimony because it cannot be dismissed as subjective or biased. In a scientifically oriented society this kind of evidence speaks the language currently in vogue in courts of law and elsewhere. But the physical effects are only part of the story. They serve as the background for understanding the far more significant enduring effects on society.

SOCIAL EFFECTS

Today many European Americans argue that they have never owned slaves and that the United States has been free of legalized racism for decades. The claim is often made that the effect of racism over time ended in 1965 with the introduction of civil rights legislation.

But in reality social processes do not start and stop instantaneously. They have inertia. Civilization is an organic process over generations. It is akin to the painstaking and time-consuming training of a fruit tree by a gardener. What can be expected after three centuries of deliberately malicious and harmful anti-training? What kind of tree results and what is needed to alter it? Can it be retrained in three decades of neglect? As journalist Jill Nelson writes, 'Why would we think that after in excess of two hundred years living in slavery that when emancipation came black people could simply walk away from the plantation, physically free and psychologically unaffected?'[110]

It is more than merely an issue of segregation. Rather, we are dealing with laws that prevent learning and hence civilization-building. The power of laws is that they set blanket conditions for large populations into the future. All anti-African laws were designed to have long-term effects, to stunt generations *ad infinitum. This was their very purpose.* But the laws became powers unto themselves, entrapping whites as well like the miscast incantations of the sorcerer's apprentice.

One of the most profound concomitants of racism is social retrogression. Worse is substituted for better. Let us consider a simple example that illustrates much of what has been occurring throughout American society. In his recent investigation of racism in a large chain of restaurants in the southern states, Steve Watkins found abundant evidence of the substitution of worse for better. A former manager in one of the restaurants has stated that he was instructed by his superiors to

> limit the number of black workers in his restaurants and hire as many whites as he could instead, no matter how poorly qualified they might be. In fact, [he] says, there was a joke often made in the company about the single requirement necessary for hiring white workers to avoid having to hire blacks. 'The joke that went around in the personnel department,' he says, was, '[they] told me that they [were] to stick a mirror under their nose and if they fogged it up, to hire them.'[111]

Such actions and attitudes cause the decline of standards, of civilization as a whole, a fact that was observed by Benjamin Franklin and Alexis de Tocqueville, among many others. Franklin wrote that slaves 'pejorate the families that use them; the white children become proud, disgusted with labor, and being educated in idleness, are rendered unfit to get a living by industry.'[112]

Racists' claim that blacks are incompetent or less qualified than whites is beyond ironic, for one of the key aims of racism is to promote less qualified whites, a well-documented fact in virtually every aspect of society, from racial restrictions on housing, to the exclusion of minorities from unions, to the systematic denial of bank loans to minority businesses. As a result the whole society is deprived of the advancements African Americans would have contributed. Social progress slows, stalls, ends and decline accelerates. And to this day the South, which was the economic and political leader of the colonies and the United States from the mid-1700s until the 1850s,[113] has less than its share of fine universities, museums, orchestras, far less considering the immense wealth it generated during the centuries of slavery. Feagin finds that this deficiency affects blacks and whites alike even today.

> Today, southern states still reflect this racist heritage in critical ways. As a group, these states not only have larger proportions of poverty-stricken citizens but also generally weaker public schools and colleges, public health programs and other important public programs providing for the general welfare of their citizens than do the northern states . . . The weak public sector is one of the continuing legacies of the authoritarian eras of slavery and segregation – and of the openly racist, one-party governments in place in most southern states until the 1970s . . . And the South has provided [only] a modest share of the nation's intellectual and scientific leaders and innovators – one striking consequence of its historically weaker public educational systems.[114]

Eugene Genovese argues that the failure of the South to develop a more complex and rich culture is the direct result of the slave economy.

> What slavery could not do, despite its economies of scale and its financial advantages, was to lay the foundations for sustained growth and qualitative development. Nowhere did it advance science and technology, generate self-expanding home markets adequate to encourage industrial diversification, accumulate capital within its own sphere for industrial development, or encourage the kind of entrepreneurship without which modern industry would have been unthinkable. It produced spectacular growth in response to the demand of an outside society but simultaneously guaranteed stagnation and decline once that support was withdrawn.[115]

In the pre-Revolutionary period laws barred African Americans from basic social rights: marriage, freedom, property ownership. Then the United States Constitution denied their humanity. These slavery laws created a sort of primeval soup, a social and cultural matrix of attitudes, emotions and beliefs both conscious and subconscious. One of the most powerful of them, more powerful even than the denial of human status in the Constitution, were those granting slave-holders the right to separate children from their mothers to enhance sales of slaves. The long-term effects this one practice caused are unimaginable.

Out of this potent mix, secondary laws – many resulting from the 'private rule-making' to which we have already referred – arose, barring African Americans from enjoying a wide variety of resources available to the white public: restaurants, motels and hotels, bathrooms, telephone booths, waiting rooms, hospitals, cemeteries, beaches, parks, golf courses, tennis courts, swimming pools, circuses, primary schools, high schools, colleges and universities, dormitories, churches, libraries and cafeterias, elections, public office, most employment, unions, most transportation and most professional sports.[116] Even the simple sidewalk was a battlefield upon which African Americans were to fall daily. As a boy growing up in the 1930s in the neighborhood of Old West Baltimore, Maryland, where blacks and whites frequented the same commercial district, Walter Carr 'remembered the indignity he felt while on Pennsylvania Avenue. "You were supposed to walk out in the gutter when you saw white folks walking down the street. My grandmother knocked me in the gutter half a dozen times."'[117]

Beginning around the turn of the century Jim Crow laws reached new heights of complexity and comprehensiveness. Factories in South Carolina systematically prevented the mixing of the races 'in the same room, or using the same entrances, pay windows, exits, doorways, stairways

. . . or the same "lavatories, toilets, drinking water buckets, pails, cups, dippers or glasses" at any time.'[118] Copies of the Bible for swearing in legal witnesses were segregated according to race. 'North Carolina and Florida required that textbooks used by the public-school children of one race be kept separate from those used by the other, and the Florida law specified separation even while the books were in storage.' 1930: Birmingham banned interracial checkers and dominoes. 1932: Atlanta banned amateur baseball teams of different races from playing within two blocks of each other. 1935: Oklahoma banned interracial fishing and boating.[119]

The long-term effects of all these restrictions inevitably led to the underdevelopment of skills among African Americans. Forgetting the causes of these restrictions, whites conveniently or naively forged their own privileges and sense of superiority on the cliché that 'Blacks can't'. 'Blacks can't swim' because it was *illegal* for them to do so at pools and beaches. 'Blacks can't play golf, tennis, can't ski, etc.' because it was *illegal*. 'Blacks can't do art' because it was *illegal* for them to exhibit their work.[120] 'Blacks can't manage a baseball team' because it was *illegal, de facto* and previously *de jure*, hence the development of the Negro leagues. 'Blacks can't be professionals' because it was *illegal*, hence the creation of parallel organizations: the National Bar Association, the National Medical Association, and unions. But today we remember the causes; we remember that they are artificial, not innate in the character and body of the African American.

If blacks did not have expertise it was because they were obeying the law. To gain such expertise they would have had to *break the law*, to exacerbate their already tenuous legal status, to steal the expert knowledge and experience and lessons, just as slaves had to steal the ability to read. Once the law had shifted away from a Christian basis the duty of citizens likewise was transformed and it became illegal to help the slaves. According to this system whites who are racist cannot be regarded as immoral or blameworthy, for they are doing their best to obey the law as it is presented to them by the country's duly recognized authorities, stretching as far back as the founding fathers. To do otherwise would be tantamount to being disloyal and unpatriotic.

If these laws had not been promulgated and enforced, Tiger and Althea and Zina and the Williams sisters would not be so rare at all. These laws have powerfully shaped not only sports, the performing arts and business in America, they have shaped the society as a whole. For African Americans, acquiring these skills meant not only being 'uppity' but disloyal, criminal, traitorous. For blacks, loyalty to the nation meant denying themselves these skills.

But what of the civil rights laws enacted in the 1960s: Did they not remedy the situation? The principle of inertia applies here, as Jill Nelson has pointed out. Society is like a pail of cold water. The addition of a small amount of hot water will make very little difference in the overall temperature. A society that is predominantly racist over several centuries will not change its character in any fundamental way by the promulgation of toothless token laws. Although the overt laws against blacks have been struck down or forgotten, there has never been a corresponding set of laws favoring or protecting them with the same vigorous and universal application of state and federal powers as were the slave laws and Jim Crow system. From the mid-1960s we have had some promising anti-racist legislation but no enforcement comparable to the nearly 300 years of systemic racist oppression.[121]

It is not surprising, then, that while African Americans have developed a profound sense of self-worth that enables them to survive the tremendous mental strains of American society, they also must battle against an inner conviction of worthlessness constantly evoked by the sirens of white supremacy. The 1954 United States Supreme Court case of *Brown v. Board of Education of Topeka* was won partly because of the psychiatric research done by Dr Kenneth Clark, who found that black children preferred a white doll to a black doll, a clear sign of self-hatred. Almost a half century later writer Randall Kenan, visiting a breakfast program for very young African American children in Atlanta, found the same phenomenon well entrenched in their minds and hearts.

> I asked Salah . . . a freshman at Morehouse from Buffalo, and the chair of the breakfast table, about the program's goal. 'The other day,' he told me, 'we sat down and told the kids stories. I was reading them a book, and in the book there were pictures of many different colors of kids. I asked them how many thought the black one was pretty, and all the children said, She's ugly. And I say, Why? And all the little kids in unison said, Because she has a black face. So we're here to give them breakfast, but we are also here to start to combat the stigma that society is placing on them at such a young age.'[122]

SUPERSTITION

As the social effects of the slavery and Jim Crow laws evolved, multiplied and became more complex, like a tree's endless organic ramifications reaching skyward from hidden roots, they led to profound distortions of the mind. It is ironic, though not surprising, that the extremely rational legal language of the anti-miscegenation laws gave rise to powerful and enduring superstitions. In the following two cases from 1949 we can easily discern parallels with the Salem witch-hunts and the consistent identification of African Americans with evil.

Occasional reports in the newspapers of the enforcement of anti-miscegenation laws give us a hint of the suffering that occurs when race laws destroy a marriage. Davis K____ of Ellisville, Mississippi, was sentenced to five years in jail in 1949 for his marriage to a white girl, although he had lived his life as a white in the white part of town and came from a family that had been considered white for the seventy years that older residents of Ellisville could recall. He had no negroid features. But rumors had circulated, and trial and conviction followed. K____'s last futile defense was that if indeed he had a trace of nonwhite blood it must have been American Indian, not Negro.

In the same year, a young man was brought to trial in Roanoke, Virginia, because his mother-in-law one night had a dream in which he appeared black rather than his customary white. Clark H____ had visited his girl's family often while he was stationed at a nearby naval base, and had been well received. The wedding was performed by a Baptist minister who later said, 'He seemed to be a white man . . . He seemed to be very genteel and nice and I invited them to join my Bible class if they settled in Roanoke.' Then relations cooled. The father of the bride afterwards recalled that 'he seemed to be getting darker after they were married', and then within weeks came the dream and the arrest.[123]

American law had other quirks regarding intermarriage indicating not only irrationality but social insanity:

> Arizona once had a law so involved it made marriage of a mulatto to anyone, even another mulatto, unlawful. The law did to him what nature had done to the mule. But the law was repaired. The mulatto was given a measure of relief: he could marry an Indian, but he was still forbidden to marry a Negro, a Caucasian, or another mulatto.[124]

SPIRITUAL EFFECTS

However deep racism's wounds on the body, the mind, the community and the economy, the deepest long-term effect is on the human soul. What must be its impact, we wonder, on the spiritual growth of a child, of an entire population? When we consider that slavery and racism ruled the lives of African Americans for over 300 years, the suffering and lost potential boggle the mind.

Let us consider several examples. The first concerns psychological development and the simplest aspects of daily life in a loving family. The language of love is filled with looks, gestures, touches. It is subtle and yet very powerful. Indeed, a well-known anthropologist has written an entire book on the subject of touching alone.[125] It is well established that animals that are isolated from contact suffer permanent behavioral damage. But it is perhaps less well known that this is also true for human beings. Cases of ferality in children, most famously that of Genie, who was discovered in California in 1970, prove that children isolated from human contact will lose the ability to communicate and understand the world; they will suffer permanent mental retardation.[126] But if this is true with an individual soul, it must also be true when an entire community is prevented from expressing the language of love. What spiritual harm could African Americans have sustained as a result of being unable to communicate love except only furtively, ever fearful of punishment under what was arguably the most totalitarian social system yet known? Clearly full-blown ferality is not the issue here, for slaves were in contact with others, both Africans and Europeans. But it is also clear that this is a matter of degree. Moreover, what spiritual harm could European Americans have sustained in prohibiting themselves from ever legally loving African Americans? For whites' expression of love towards slaves was illegal and even among slaves themselves it was difficult to sustain loving relationships, whether between husband and wife or parents and children. What could the effect be of the centuries of neglect of this language of love? How does that deliberate neglect affect black and white souls? We can only ponder.

Secondly, the isolation of slaves involved not only separation from loving others but also from nature. Although strictly identified with wild nature as juxtaposed with civilization, ironically slaves were not permitted to be a part of nature. They could never experience the infinite qualities of the planet's surface. They could not walk as they pleased for as long and as far as they wished. They could hope for but never approach the horizon. Slavery was, plain and simple, imprisonment for generation after generation, from at least the mid-1600s until some time after 1863.[127]

For over 200 years an entire population, a nation, struggled under an early but all too effective form of totalitarianism. They were deprived of both man (civilization) and nature. They occupied a purgatory on earth, the spiritual and psychological effects of which we are only now beginning to understand.

INVISIBILITY

Ralph Ellison's concept of the African American as an *invisible man* implies that all African Americans constitute an *invisible nation*. They are not recognized in the United States Constitution. But then neither are Poles or Jews, for example. The difference, however, is that Africans were pointedly and deliberately denied recognition in that document; in other words, their non-recognition, their invisibility, was officially and legally recognized.

In this context, therefore, the United States denied African Americans basic human rights not because they were dark in skin color but because European Americans claimed they did not exist as human beings. Racists wield racial epithets in order to identify those particular human beings who have no rights because they are, paradoxically, nonexistent, invisible, dead.

This paradox is at the heart of the surreal nature of racism wherever in the world it is manifested. It is well illustrated in the habit of whites to usurp Africans' identity and reality. For example, the invisibility of Africans in South Africa was enforced by the concept that whites constituted a *tribe* in the country and that this white tribe therefore had not only a right to exist but by implication priority over every other people or tribe. The tribeness and, more importantly, the indigenousness of Africans had thus been usurped by the whites.

In the United States we see a similar technique to eclipse African Americans. Elvis and the Beatles rendered the original black groups they copied invisible. The Jackson Five were subsumed by the Osmond Brothers. This usurpation of African American culture is deeply layered. For example, we see the Carpenters doing a Beatles song, which itself was an imitation of an African American pop song. In this instance the African Americans have been given two coats of invisible paint. Any casual observer of American society would naturally assume that Africans and African Americans have done nothing and certainly nothing original. When he was teaching jazz at a university in Michigan, Marvin Holladay, after many disturbing experiences at music festivals and competitions, decided not to have his students participate in them any longer. He found that performances of jazz ensembles were routinely and strictly judged by what he considered were white interpretations of the genre and black ensembles usually did not receive any substantial awards or prizes, even if they were, in his view, by far the best performers. White jazz educators were not willing to recognize the skills of African American musicians performing the music that emerged from their own culture.[128]

The same process of invisibility is found in Native American history. James Loewen's *Lies My Teacher Told Me* explains in detail how achievements in the Native American culture, from agriculture to social and political organization, have been systematically assigned to white culture. A most striking instance of this is the Iroquois influence in the origins of the United States Constitution. The explosive popularity in the 1960s of Native American arts and crafts was harnessed by whites who gained control over their sale and marketing. Even today the artists are left with precious little gain or public recognition.[129]

The invisibility of African Americans is also found in academia. The most astonishing fact about D. B. Davis's classic award-winning treatise

The Problem of Slavery in Western Culture is that not once does he cite the views, opinions and experiences of the slaves themselves – as if they were not part of the western culture mentioned in the book's title. It is all well and good to discuss the philosophy and law of slavery, its finer points in intellectual discourse, but it is another thing to discuss the spiritual meaning and reality of *loss of freedom*, which he does not do. It is like a history of the Nazi holocaust without putting in a word or two from any victims.

Moral and spiritual truths have been removed from academic discussion of racism and slavery because whites have long controlled and defined the discourse. Could it be that the African Americans are experts on the subject; the Native Americans know most about their history; women are the best sources for interpreting their own struggle? To each of these groups we are obliged to turn for enlightenment. For white males to say otherwise is for them to attempt a rearguard action to protect their academic and cultural interests. White scholars, through meticulous research, may indeed have better knowledge of an endless catalogue of facts – everything from the kinds of languages spoken by slaves to the style of dress the slave women wore in 1783 in the Piedmont. But such facts, however interesting and valuable, do not provide *understanding* of slavery, of racism, of genocide, of oppression.

One is struck by the fact that throughout the veritable sea of scholarship on the history of slavery and racism many if not most of the works are dedicated to analyses of theories, explanations and competing contentions among white scholars. It is a problem of not seeing the forest for the trees. The suffering of humanity in slavery and racism is completely lost in the jumble of academic jargon and concepts. And very often, as in Thomas D. Morris's *Southern Slavery and the Law*, we find that a book that claims to be about slavery says very little about European behavior, European attitudes, European culpability, and instead focuses on the behavior of blacks, their violation of laws, the threat they represented to society, their culpability. For blacks, slavery was really about white behavior, just as for women patriarchy really is about the actions of men. Morris writes:

> People of color were slaves, but that was only the initial policy choice. Slaves were in bondage to provide labor, and it was to assure control over that labor that many legal policies were adopted. A persistent internal danger to the social order was the 'obstinacy' of the slaves, and Southerners adopted a wide range of policies to reduce the danger: some were ruthless uses of criminal law, some were police regulations, and some were more gentle adaptations of noncriminal law rules.[130]

Here the African Americans are invisible in three ways: First, the consistent neutrality or even positive bias of the language with regard to the whites. Slavery was only a 'policy choice'. Could a historian of World War Two get away with reducing the holocaust to only a policy choice? The system of slavery was a set of 'legal policies', 'a wide range of policies'. Some were 'ruthless' but all were legal, careful, conscious, orderly, according to regulations, even 'gentle' – in a word, civilized.

Second, the open use of negative terms to characterize the African slaves. They were 'a persistent internal danger to the social order'. Could it not be said that the whites' slave system was the true danger to the social order? Why must the historian speak from the point of view of the European colonists: is their perspective inherently objective and the slaves' not? Was the quest for freedom a danger? Only if the reader is taking the white point of view. This is a disservice to history, to scholarship and to the reader.

Third, the use of quotation marks to make possible a highly negative and traditionally racist condemnation of the Africans. It is as if the quotation marks render the word 'obstinacy' not racist in this context; Winthrop Jordan used this technique consistently and frequently throughout *White Over Black*. It is as if the author is free of any guilt for having written a racist characterization of Africans because he is hiding behind the remarks of someone else.

In this example it appears that the African American slaves are clearly visible, yet they are not. What is apparent is the scholar's image of them. What remains hidden is the African American's own voice, her own reality, her own experience.

It is a logical error to take the writings of European intellectuals in the time of slavery's genesis and evolution as fully representative of the society. Certainly this is the standard method for study of intellectual history but we ought not confuse this with a complete picture. For example, we cannot accept intellectuals' arguments on the reality of witches as representative of the entire population – except if we take these clergymen and intellectuals as the sole class fit to represent the far more diverse population of men and women of various classes, experiences and beliefs that constituted Europe. Therefore what writers such as Richard Hakluyt (1552–1616) wrote with their powerful pens was actually extremely limited, a distortion of reality, as proved so clearly by the plain fact that a very large percentage of blacks and whites in the American colonies did not agree with their anti-black beliefs. We can no more take these writers as representative of their societies than we can take some of today's intellectuals for ours. While propaganda tells us something valid about a historical period, it should not be identified as history in all its completeness. The eventual dominance of slavery and racism should not blind us to other historical realities, namely that without such overwhelming violence racism would not have become established, for it was not in fact a dominant belief among the masses, most of whom, like the innocent victims of the witch-hunts, were more spiritualized than the extremists who ruled them.

Conclusion

Slavery in America was not a natural inevitable phenomenon but a carefully constructed artificial order. Its simple initial laws were intended to preserve the slave system over a long period of time and in this they succeeded. As slavery aged the laws evolved, became more detailed and complex, producing not only secondary laws and rules governing everyday conduct but also a host of intricate and subtle social, psychological and spiritual constructs – from ghettos to superstitions – that have greatly affected the American culture. The resulting long-term effects of slavery continue to pervert American culture to this day, to convince individual European Americans that Africanness is, always has been, and always will be, illegal. The concept of Christian love and brotherhood has been unable to break this constructed barrier of illegality. Africans were placed outside the domain of the Church's protection. The formation of separate, segregated churches for African Americans only served to cement the disunity, to severely truncate the practice of Christian brotherhood in both the black and the white communities. The social laws of slavery in the end had profound spiritual effects that further manipulation of laws and social institutions has been unable to overcome.

Level Five: Justifications

Now that we have had a good look at the key laws that created slavery, the question arises: on what basis were these laws constructed? To answer we must descend a few more steps down our ladder to a slightly earlier period.

Here we see immediately that the illegality of Africans rested on two fabricated justifications. The first was a religious basis. The original rationale for the enslavement of Africans was that they were heathen, distant from God, their dark skin a sign of His punishment for their sins. Christian colonists argued that dark skin color was the curse placed by God on descendants of the sinful Ham;[131] thus it was not only a convenient brand for ease of identification, it was also divinely ordained. No matter how excellent an African's character, his skin color gave the lie and proved that God Himself had already condemned him. White-skinned persons had no choice but to condemn the inherently profane Africans out of pious obedience to God's will.

This religious basis of African illegality, however, gradually evolved into a secular understanding. For soon it became clear that as sinners the Africans were called by Christianity to repent, turn to Jesus and enter His Church, which they did. Their conversion created a spiritually contradictory situation in which the planters were enslaving not brutes but their own brothers in Christ who had been baptized and hence cleansed of sin. The planters therefore carefully crafted a second justification: they defined Africans as animals, as enemies of civilization, their only redeeming quality being their service to civilized people. African Americans became known as outlaws not because of sins against God but because of crimes against society. Contemporary racism continues this theme of blaming African Americans for secular ills; they deserve to be ostracized not because of theological sins but because of social sins: 'aggressiveness', anti-social behavior, criminality, primitiveness, violence.

Although secular condemnation of blacks is overtly rational, expressed in countless state and federal laws and statutes, there remains always an echo of the original religious impulse. Today we may not be conscious of the original theological justification for slavery, yet the content remains fundamentally the same. The black or brown skin is proof of sin and identity with the devil but also of primitivity, lower status in the evolutionary scale, less intelligence, a more animalistic personality. Black or brown skin indicates first a violation of God's laws and then of secular laws.

Each of these justifications developed into a complex set of ideas and relationships between Europeans and their world. Together they described a duality: the sacred and the profane. The Africans were enslaveable because they were part of the profane realm and were, like the witches of Salem, guilty of association with evil and the devil. The Europeans for their part were entitled to be slave-holders because they were part of the sacred realm and were supported by God's favor. Richard Dyer writes:

> All concepts of *race*, emerging out of eighteenth-century materialism, are concepts of bodies, but all along they have had to be reconciled with notions of embodiment and incarnation. The latter become what distinguish white people, giving them a special relation to race. Black people can be reduced (in white culture) to their bodies and thus to race, but white people are something else that is realized in and yet is not reducible to the corporeal, or racial.[132]

In short, racist philosophy saw a profane African body juxtaposed to a sacred European soul.

Profane Society: Africans as Nature

As materialism spread throughout European society, God and the holy were replaced by an all-pervading consciousness of nature, of its value as a storehouse of resources, as the basis of unlimited wealth. All things, including human beings, became vulnerable. The realm of the sacred became ever more restricted and that of the profane expanded plague-like with astonishing rapidity.

The universal brotherhood of Christianity was lost. Race, denomination, language and other non-essential distinctions became important. All humans existing outside the pale of one's own Church were to be considered not humans but alien objects. European slave-traders defined the Africans as existing outside the pale of the Church's protection, in the animal world, and therefore as constituting a freely available economic resource in the same sense as animals in the agrarian economy.[133] Where the religious law ended, nature began. The Decree of Gratian (ca. 1140), for example, denied heretics the right to hold property because they were protected by neither the secular nor the Church law.[134] By the late 13th century the laws of the Church tended to regard the heretic as an inhuman thing. 'Excommunication and interdict in those days were no empty words. To be placed outside the communion of the Church was even more than being outlawed from the Empire, equivalent to being placed outside civilization; it was to be deprived of all rights, made any man's legitimate prey.'[135] Any member of the Church was free to ignore Christianity's laws when dealing with the heretic. Yet within the domain of one's own Church, the ideal of brotherhood remained intact. European Americans applied the tremendous social forces of their Christian unity to the systematic exploitation of people beyond the pale – the Africans, Indians and others beyond the sacred domain and defined as aliens, as soulless laboring bodies.

We see here the duality of society: a religious domain in which the legal society is primary, sacred and preserves powerful institutions; a second, external domain which the legal population perceives as profane unsocialized *nature*, subject to neither the obligations nor the protection of the religiously based law. Although these two domains are quite distinct, the boundary between them is a realm of ambiguity; indeed, one of the fundamental paradoxes of American race relations was the desire of planters to associate with and dissociate themselves from slaves simultaneously – whence the complexity of the slave codes and Jim Crow laws and the contradictory, illogical nature of racism.

Within the matrix of this dual society the European capitalist colonization of North America seen on Level Four organically evolved through two simultaneous actions. The first action was the creation of slavery in West Africa and the second was the creation of racist philosophy. Slavery has been a common practice throughout history. Many cultures and nations have had some form of slavery. It was typically the way that captives of 'the enemy' were assigned a position in the captor's society. Although African societies commonly practiced slavery, their slave systems were not comparable to those created by Europeans in America. Indeed, in parts of West Africa some scholars have found that 'no form of slavery existed at all until European demands produced it'.[136] Wars between African tribal groups were generally localized, limited and short-lived, and resulted in few captives. On the whole slavery in Africa before the coming of the Europeans was 'basically benign, family-dominated' and characterized by the treatment of the slave as a kinsman.[137] Martin R. Delany, an African American abolitionist who visited southern Nigeria in the late 1850s, described the stark difference between slavery there and in America:

> It is simply preposterous to talk about slavery, as that term is understood, either being legalized or existing in this part of Africa. It is nonsense. The system is a patriarchal one, there being no actual difference, socially, between slaves (called by their protector sons or daughters) and the children of the person with whom they live. Such persons intermarry and frequently become the heads of state.[138]

Thus the slavery of the Europeans in the Americas was their own creation, not an imitation of an African or even an Islamic institution. Meltzer summarizes that while both parties, the Europeans and the Africans, knew slavery, each party understood something completely different by that term. Gradually the Africans became aware of this. In 1526 King Affonso of the Congo wrote to the King of Portugal in complaint:

> We cannot reckon how great the damage is, since the merchants are taking every day our natives, sons of the land and the sons of our noblemen and vassals and our relatives, because the thieves and men of bad conscience grab them wishing to have the things and wares of this Kingdom which they are ambitious of; they grab them and get them to be sold; and so great, Sir, is the corruption and licentiousness that our country is being completely depopulated, and Your Highness should not agree with this nor accept it as in your service ... We beg of Your Highness to help and assist us in this matter, commanding your factors that they should not send either merchants or wares, because it is our will that in these Kingdoms there should not be any trade of slaves nor outlet for them ...[139]

Like the gold fever of a later age, the trade in slaves swept like wildfire through African societies and caused not only an epidemic of kidnapings and raids but the rise of warfare between tribes, a situation that made the trade all the easier for the European factors and their African agents. It was not that slavery flourished there because the region was naturally in chaos before the arrival of the Europeans. Rather the voracious, insatiable trade in slaves fueled by the newly arising capitalism naturally brought chaos to West Africa.

The second, simultaneous action was the creation of race as a justification for this unprecedented form of slavery that was illegal in traditional Christianity. Whereas the legal structure for American slavery was developed *ad hoc* on American soil,[140] the basis for the inhumane treatment of slaves was created in Europe, even before trading on the West African coast had begun. For it was in Europe that the brotherhood of Christianity was inexorably failing. In the wake of this collapse many marginalized groups – women, heretics, Jews – were defined as being outside the pale of the Church and subject to ever harsher treatment. What had begun as the limited excommunication of individuals and specific European sects became a more powerful and generalized exclusion of whole populations on the basis of easily formulated and easily accepted justifications. The new rule was inevitable: all on earth – humans and other creatures – were profane unless proved otherwise, and conveniently available for economic purposes without entailing the inconvenience of a guilty conscience.

In contacting the Africans, Europe had stood at a critical crossroads in which its decision was influenced by both Christianity and capitalism, yet was finally swayed by the economic tide whose institutions eventually proved politically superior to the Church. Gradually the Africans were legally and psychologically separated from the Europeans and were assigned to the domain of nature for the purpose of accelerating the engine of material development in the New World, while the Europeans retained their place in the religious domain. The capitalist economy thrived on the decay of the religious law in the Old World and on the absence of the institutions of that law in the New.

This context helps us understand Protestantism's contradictory attitude towards slavery and racism. What Protestant missionaries took to the slaves in America, and often to indigenous peoples elsewhere, was religion without the religious law. 'In the end,' as Higginbotham has written, 'the colonists imposed religion on the slaves without love, the same way they forced children on slave women.'[141] Religion was becoming so divorced from the practice of colonial government that it had no influence on social matters. Even if the slave or native were conceded a soul, civil law rendered the Church increasingly powerless to protect and sanctify her legal identity. Civil law became a correspondingly powerful and autonomous instrument which the Europeans designed to order and utilize the material world; by its unsurpassed authority they defined Africans and Indians as rich fruits and nothing more. Civil law and religious law, waxing capitalism and waning Christianity, together constituted the components of a dual society and opposed one another in an enduring struggle over the planter economy and the American conscience.

EUROPEAN INDENTURED SERVANTS

Why was the European indentured servant not also considered enslaveable, not also assigned to the natural domain? Was not the European's labor just as valuable as the African's? We can admit that certainly a factor of psychological identity and sympathy based on common physical and cultural characteristics may well have been involved in the planters' eventual granting of higher status to the European servants. But we cannot assume simply that the difference in physical features alone inspired the colonial powers to enfranchise the European and not the African. Clearly other issues were of equal if not greater importance.

First, in the eyes of the colonial entrepreneurs, the European servant represented the home population, which needed to hear favorable reports from the distant colonies in order to increase its support of these rather risky ventures.[142] News of poor treatment of the European servants would quickly spread to the mother countries and dampen the zeal of potential colonists. As it was, accounts of the poor treatment of African slaves in the American colonies had the same effect.[143]

Second, and more importantly, the sheer inertia of the brotherly tradition in Christianity was still significant. Like the indigenous people of Ireland, the European indentured servants were, despite their servile condition and their distance from the home country, indelibly associated with the laws and institutions of the religious domain. They had institutional protections, hence their 'troublesome European notions of their rights', as C. Duncan Rice wrote. `Unlike white indentured servants, even Irish or Scottish ones, blacks had no one in England or America to whom they could appeal for redress if their liberties were curtailed or if they were generally maltreated.'[144]

The British regarded the Irish much in the same manner as they later perceived the Indians and Africans in America: as barbaric, animalistic and deserving of severe treatment.[145] They justified their harsh actions in large part by condemning the relatively provincial form of Christianity in Ireland as true paganism. They therefore assigned the Irish to the animal domain outside of the law, where it was logical that force alone could govern.[146] The critical distinction, however – and one which applied equally well to the European indentured servant in the American colonies – was that the Irish 'barbarians', from the 6th century, had been decisively within the pale of the Church and therefore were, unlike the Africans, inescapably identified in the British psyche with Christian history and law. Oppression of the Irish was possible only to a limit, beyond which such abuse as perpetual slavery would tend to adversely affect the Church as a whole and thus the British themselves. K. G. Davies argues:

> Some Englishmen thought that the Irish could and should be treated the way Spaniards treated Indians, as a people reduced by conquest; but this was not a universally held doctrine. For one thing the Irish, with nowhere else to go, resisted better than the Indians; and for another, they were more or less Christians already which induced scruples whether they could be justly dispossessed and killed if they demurred.[147]

Chattel enslavement of the Irish was a legal contradiction that the British society could not tolerate, not because the Irish were 'white' but because they had long been recognized as Christians – however feeble or faulty their faith was perceived to be. True, the British oppressed the Irish very much like they oppressed the Africans and Indians in America; yet any observer recognizes the great disparity in the outcomes of those two forms of oppression: the Irish became literate and developed a complex society, while the African Americans and Indians remain at a very low level of development. Of course there are other factors, primarily the fact that the Irish remained in their own homeland. Yet history shows that displacement alone is not a significant determinant in the development of society. The social environment determines the group's development, not the fact that it was transplanted.

Thus the Christian identity of Europeans protected them from total enslavement both in Ireland and in the American colonies, while the Africans, originally lacking the Christian identity and later denied access to it, were assigned to the domain of nature beyond the pale, denied the spiritual protection that would have greatly mitigated their circumstances.

UNITY THROUGH SCAPEGOATING

Ages-old identity with Christianity, however, was not the sole cause of the European indentured servant's relatively high status. Another factor was of equal importance: the need for unity in a schismatic society. The European rulers of the colonies realized that because of the extreme competition in their society they lacked unity and that without unity the colonies would fail. Hence they took advantage of the situation to create the Africans as a common 'enemy', following the ancient method of primitive social organization known as scapegoating.[148]

Until Europeans began slavery in the New World they had practiced the tradition of subduing, controlling and exploiting their political or religious enemies while at the same time allowing them to become integrated into the society, an integration that eventually led to complete assimilation if not full citizenship with all due rights. But in North America the enslavement of Africans took a decidedly different turn: they were not permitted to become citizens and they never lost their status as 'the enemy'. Hence when Africans were labeled with racial epithets, described as 'devil', 'lazy', 'stupid', 'a threat to white women' and so on, they were no longer regarded simply as a labor source. Their lives were being interpreted differently, becoming burdened with far more onerous meanings. For these terms were all various means to keep afresh their identity as *the enemy*. The situation paralleled the Salem witch-hunts, in which any unusual female was considered a potential witch, meaning she was an enemy of God and of the people in the colony. The African was always feared because of his potential to rebel against the slave masters. But in reality he was also feared because he was always considered an enemy of the state. He was even described as God's enemy in that he was the descendent of Ham. He was the universal and perpetual enemy.[149] It was in no small measure by such scapegoating that European American colonists, who were notoriously divided by language barriers and national, religious and cultural prejudices, were able to forge a union.[150] Their unity, so spectacularly successful in some ways, was quite superficial in others. Even to this day some observers have noted that when whites disagree politically or culturally, one of the quickest ways they can renew a bond of brotherhood is to refer to racial code words, concepts, criticisms and even jokes.[151] D. W. Griffith's *Birth of a Nation*, by its very title, is perhaps the best illustration of this phenomenon. True spiritual unity amongst European Americans was to remain elusive.

CONTRAST WITH LATIN AMERICA

We can better appreciate the North American Protestant construct of Africans as profane by contrasting it to Catholic Latin America's attitude towards African slaves and American Indians. Catholic conquistadors and capitalists were as destructive of Indians and Africans as Protestants were in North America. Why, then, was Latin American society so much less negative towards them than its northern counterpart?

We begin to see an answer when we look at the Latin American colonists' attitudes towards intermarriage. They believed in racist ideas, yet intermarriage was common and never outlawed as it was in North

America. Gary Nash cites three primary reasons. First, whereas the peoples of the British Isles were isolated by geography from much of Europe, let alone other continents beyond, the Spaniards and Portuguese had long associated and intermarried with peoples of Africa.

Second, the laws of the Catholic Church and the Catholic monarchies tended to protect all peoples regardless of race. One of the characteristics of Roman Catholicism that has distinguished it from Protestantism is its overarching unity of doctrine, law and organization. David Brion Davis writes:

> Du Tertre pointed to a fundamental difference between the Catholic and Protestant Churches which was bound to affect their relationship with American slavery. Catholics might be very slow in providing slaves with meaningful religious lives, and might long discriminate against even freedmen of the proscribed race. But in time, the Catholic emphasis on universality would remove most of the distinctions that barred the descendants of slaves from spiritual equality. The relative exclusiveness of the Protestants, which was associated with their emphasis on individual responsibility, presented an additional barrier to the Christianization of Negro bondage.[152]

Therefore 'spiritual equality' took priority over 'race' in Latin America – at least to a greater degree than in North America. Even though the Church permitted the enslavement of Indians and Africans following the ancient examples of the pre-Christian Roman society, it ensured that slaves were recognized as souls endowed with spiritual and social rights, including the right to be married under divine authority and sanction. Elkins states that the marriage of slaves in the Catholic Church 'was a sacred rite and its sanctity protected in law'. Similarly, Frank Tannenbaum wrote that in Latin America 'the slave was married in the church, and the banns were regularly published. It gave the slave's family a moral and religious character unknown in other American slave systems.'[153] Thus the slave in Latin America, wherever the Church was able to enforce its will, possessed a legal and divine personality. Moreover, in Brazil there was no law against the slaves becoming literate.[154]

Third, it is a historical fact that intermarriage was permitted because there were very few European women and in some areas none. Yet this does not reduce the significance of the Church's *sanctification* of these unions, thus giving 'minorities' a sacred identity. Moreover, the many European male colonists who took Indian and African women as concubines were not overlooked. The Catholic clergy moved to bring these couples into the wider unity of the Church. Doubtless this could be interpreted as a self-serving move to consolidate clerical authority but it also consolidated the social unity of the masses nonetheless.[155] Although we of a later age may criticize the clerical corruption of that time, we cannot be blind to the successes, however inadvertent, the Church achieved despite its shortcomings.

In Latin America the Indians and Africans benefitted from the protection of the Catholic Church, whose legal structure was much stronger and more systematic than those of the disparate Protestant denominations of North America. 'Accordingly,' writes Eugene Genovese, 'the white racism and cruel discrimination that inevitably accompanied the enslavement of black to white emerged against countervailing forces of genuine spiritual power.'[156] Catholicism is distinguished from Protestantism by the presence of a comprehensive unified structure of laws and legal institutions and by the fact that, unlike most Protestant denominations, it was the basis of monarchies and thus its laws had teeth. In Catholic Latin America a system of priests traveling regularly to plantations provided some protection of slaves' rights by forwarding information regarding their treatment to the attorney general of the region. This fact demonstrates the close and cooperative relationship in colonial Latin America between the civil and ecclesiastical legal systems. In Cuba, for example, the Church took action to prevent abuse and neglect of spiritual needs. It was in the cities of Cuba 'where Spanish law and Catholic religion were most likely to protect' the slaves. Catholic anti-slavery arguments 'did keep alive concepts of the slave's right to religious institutions, protection of his family relationships and redress against brutal physical treatment'.[157]

We can see a clear pattern: In the places where organized religion and religious laws are strongest, slavery and racism are less. In Europe, which is the source of religious life for westerners, slavery was basically forbidden. 'It had been received doctrine in England,' writes Theodore Allen, 'at least since before the publication of Thomas Smith's *De Republica Anglorum* in 1583, that Christians could not hold Christians in bondage.'[158] As we go further away from Europe the practice of slavery becomes more prevalent. In Catholic Latin America slavery exists but it is significantly mediated by the Church. African and Indian slaves were given rights to marry, to enter the Church as full members and to have a spiritual identity, to be recognized as a *human being*, as a *soul*, rather than as chattel. There is no doubt that slavery was often as brutal in Latin America as in North America, and that it lasted longer in Brazil than anywhere else, but we cannot take these facts to mean that the Church played no role. In any case, Genovese argues that the Church's presence, its legal and moral authority, its sheer power, were able to mitigate many of the evils of slavery that were realized in North America. And the results are clear: while today there is racism in most of

Latin America, there is also a far greater degree of racial integration there than in the North.[159]

Even in North America the Catholic Church continued the pattern, having a profound effect on the direction of slavery and race relations, as Joseph Butsch suggested in a 1917 article. The 'Code Noir' – not to be confused with the oppressive 'black codes' in the Protestant areas of the South – was created in 1724 by M. de Bienville to systematize and publicize the spiritual rights of slaves in Louisiana, rights which were never to be permitted under Protestant slavery on the East coast. The Code Noir

> ordained that all slaves be instructed and that they be admitted to the sac-
> raments and rites of the Roman Catholic Church. It allowed the slave time
> for instruction, worship and rest, not only every Sunday, but every festival
> usually observed by the Church. It prohibited under severe penalties all
> masters and managers from corrupting their female slaves, and provided
> for the Christian marriage of the slave. It did not allow the Negro, husband,
> wife or infant children, to be sold separately. It forbade the use of torture or
> immoderate and inhuman punishments. It obliged the owners to maintain
> their old and decrepit slaves.[160]

Throughout the Americas, Roman Catholic and Jesuit institutions acted systematically to protect slaves; and despite the outlawing of these institutions in parts of the South, even there they were able to realize a number of their pro-African humanitarian goals.[161]

Before turning to the Protestants we must address the contradiction between the fact that the Church of Rome gave unparalleled spiritual recognition and social protection to slaves, thereby mitigating racism, and the facts that 1) the Catholic Church, as Orlando Patterson points out, not only permitted slavery but was 'too compromised by its large-scale holding of slaves' to 'take a stand' against it[162] and 2) it was the corruption and despiritualization of the Church, as we shall discuss, that enabled the rise of slavery and racism in the first place. These facts do contradict each other and we cannot lift a finger to resolve that contradiction. Such is the accretive aspect of history. On the one hand the spiritual legacy of Christianity was a lamp that still represented the light of unity; on the other the inheritors of this lamp were gradually becoming interested in material things. Both processes were flowing simultaneously in the same historical riverbed. It is an irony that the source of mass enslavement eventually proved more sympathetic to the slaves' plight than the Protestants. But do we not see many cases of such irony throughout the evolution of society: Martin Luther gave to Christians freedom in religion, yet denied political freedom to the peasants; Americans who fought tooth and nail against Hitler did likewise on the homefront against the growing civil rights movement; some of the largest oil companies are aggressively supporting the development of alternative and renewable energy sources. The key point here is that the Catholic Church was possessed of multiple powers and one of them was clearly effective in promoting the human and spiritual rights of African slaves. Often an investigation leads us to find what we are looking for in the most unlikely places.

North American Protestant society differed from that of Roman Catholic Latin America in several respects. It had no centralized, united authority and administration. Churches in the American South were independent and under the complete control of local planters. All laws were fashioned by secular courts. In fact there was no effective religious law whatsoever. Clergy were disparate and hobbled, lacking the support of a vast and powerful international organization, their legal authority and moral influence severely restricted by the slaveholding class. The Protestant Churches were established on the very principle of individualism and dissent, the right to disunite, which weakened not only Church organization but also the sanctity and operation of Christian law throughout Protestant society. Even where it was strongest in the South, the Anglican Church never managed to establish direct ties to England; parish churches eventually fell under the complete control of the leading citizens of each locality, who typically were slave-holders and who ensured the continuing weakness of the Church's authority.[163] By the strict separation of Church and state, Protestants throughout North America divorced religious authority from the economic system which they believed would generate unlimited wealth and precluded a genetic unity between Christian laws and political authority such as existed in Catholic states. Capitalism, especially after the Revolution, was able to flourish free of those restrictions imposed by ecclesiastical and royal laws that elsewhere were limiting its growth.[164] Consequently no sacred protections were available to slaves.

It was not so much that the Roman Catholic Church yet retained more spirituality than the Protestants in America. Rather it was that without the moral restraint of a religious organization the Protestants in America were free to be more radical, to break cleanly not only from the king of England but also from their Christian morality. The Declaration of Independence was not only about political and economic freedom but also about freedom of moral choices. Hence the document focuses not on the obligations of the believer to follow the laws of his faith but on his freedom to make his own world, a self-centered world, to pursue his own happiness free from interference. In other words, the North Americans rejected the Old World and its morality, while Latin America remained firmly tied to it despite the profound inhumanity of the initial centuries of conquest. As expressed so powerfully in the writings of Las Casas, among others, the Catholic world could recognize that it had made grave moral errors in persecuting the other but the Protestants could not because they defined the institutions and morality of religion as irrelevant to their lives; hence there was no error to recognize. Unlike Latin America, North America's moral institutions had been deliberately swept away; as we have noted, there existed no moral frame of reference against which one could measure one's actions, only a deafening, blinding vacuum into which the new morality of capitalism inexorably flowed.

By this reasoning, then, it is logical to conclude that the American South was the least religious of all the regions we have so far examined. 'In the colonies where slaves were most numerous', wrote Marcus Jernegan, 'a vital interest in religion was lacking.'[165] The South was also the most secularized, the furthest away from reference to religion and religious institutions in legal affairs and moral questions in daily life. We need not look far to find evidence of this. The leaders of the nation were themselves setting the example. Is it mere coincidence that Thomas Jefferson, who kept numerous slaves with a conscience undeterred by any strict religious morality, excised from the Bible all verses that offended his rational sensibilities? Is it not unexpected, according to this reasoning, that religion was a primary pillar in the anti-slavery movement in North America and that the first social group to actively and systematically oppose slavery in North America was a fervently devout community of religious dissenters, the Society of Friends?[166] Thus the decline of slavery in North America was in large part due to the fact that devout Protestants were able to gain significant social powers like their Catholic counterparts in Latin America and thereby to alter or eliminate the slave-holders' assignment of the slaves to the realm of profane nature.

FEAR OF NATURE

In controlling and condemning slaves as profane nature, whites in the North American colonies were expressing their fear of the natural world, a fear alien to the African and Native American cultures. Even today much of western culture, particularly in America, can be interpreted as a dichotomy of nature and the sacred. To be black means to be close to and submerged in natural processes – hence the many racist references to dirt, disease, odors, physical features, physical cravings, death.[167] Whites identify themselves with the sacred and flee nature inasmuch as they identify it with evil, which justifies their brutal exploitation of it. To be white means to be ever farther from nature, to surround oneself with the artificial, with only manmade things, with immortality. We now witness the willy-nilly race of European science and business to discover, manipulate and exploit genetic structures, to create artificial organs and life, to create artificial intelligence, to freeze the body in a cryogenic hope of immortality. It is ironic, therefore, that western culture, which prides itself on its sophisticated understanding of natural phenomena, nevertheless neglects many truths of the natural world. In western materialistic culture heaven on earth is the opposite of the natural environment: it is a manmade, increasingly machine-made environment, and the more artificial the better.[168]

Consider, for example, farming. Among the most fundamental of all absolutes in humanity's material life is agriculture. The individual can experience reality by seeing the direct effects of the elements on crops, soil and the wider environment. A farmer has no leeway to indulge in the relativity of deconstructionism. He or she knows that to obtain the maximum yield the dictates – the absolute dictates – of nature must be satisfied. The farmer, who is working with nature daily, is forced to believe in it. The 'green revolution', a hope that even the dictates of nature could be superceded by technology, has now been proved false. Thus at every turn the farmer is bound to accept reality in the form of the scientific laws that determine agricultural outcome. One of the reasons why modern society in the West has embraced moral relativity is because it no longer has regular, direct experience with such absolutes.

Modern urbanites are completely out of touch with these dictates of nature. Their world is manmade. They are surrounded by buildings, streets, vehicles, clothing, sights, foods, sounds and other sensations that are partially or completely artificial. Many urbanites are born in the city, grow up there, live their entire adult lives there and die there, never experiencing nature directly, never planting a seed, harvesting fruit or vegetables, drinking water from a natural source, building a fire. They know little or nothing of the process by which natural fibers are grown, spun, woven and then sewn into garments. They do not feel the contours of the earth, its valleys, hills, mountains and plains. They do not see the stars except for the few brightest and never the Milky Way. They do not see the turning of the leaves into fall colors, the barren branches of winter, the coming of spring. They do not experience and do not even imagine the cycle of life. For theirs is a world of machines and the products of machines. They do not see the power of nature, they do not think about it, they do not feel it, nor do they ultimately believe in it. They feel themselves in complete control of their world. At the heart of modern western culture, wrote Francis M. Cornford, science, as opposed to religion, seeks absolute *control*.

> In one very important respect, the scientific tradition differs from the mystic. Ionian science supersedes theology, and goes on its own way, without drawing any fresh supply of inspiration from religion. Science, with its

practical impulse, is like magic in attempting direct control over the world, whereas religion interposes between desire and its end an uncontrollable and unknowable factor – the will of a personal God. The perpetual, if unconscious, aim of science is to avoid this circuit through the unknown, and to substitute for religious representation, involving this arbitrary factor, a closed system ruled throughout by necessity. The gods may be exiled to the intermundane spaces, or pensioned off with the honorary position of First Cause; what science cannot allow is that their incalculable action should thrust itself in between the first cause and the last effect. Thus, science turns its back on theology, and works away from it with what speed it may; it reaches, in a few rapid strides, a very simple and clear model of the structure of reality, from which the supernatural has all but disappeared.[169]

This is perhaps one of the reasons why the slave-holders were so inhumane. They sought absolute control for the sake of the scientific development of capitalist agriculture.

Our built environment, especially in the cities, convinces us that the world is manmade, that all creation is our work and that we are the gods. This is only natural since most objects and events in our daily lives are manmade. Even in the rural areas of the American West, the straight-lined, rationalized farmlands have rendered nature so controlled as to no longer possess the overpowering mystical qualities experienced by Africans, Indians and others in the non-western world. But once we step outside the city, the town and the industrial farm into the wilderness we immediately *feel* the undeniable reality of things transcending us, most directly through the power of the earth itself to foil our plans, to take us out of self-control and render us impotent, swiftly, suddenly and completely. Of course this can happen in cities as well, but relatively rarely, since cities construct defenses against the effects of nature.

Western urbanites are conditioned from childhood to believe that all of life's aspects are subject to human manipulation and control. God was declared dead, and so too was nature, leaving the human being absolutely free to create any 'reality'. But this is an illusion that can be sustained only so long as the urbanites remain within their cityscape. The moment they step into the wilderness they find themselves at the mercy of powers that dwarf the city.

In reinforcing these two extremes, the blackness of nature and the whiteness of the manmade world, western culture has forgotten the true sense of civilization. In the clash of these exaggerated constructs the reality of civilization as a balance between the natural and the manmade never took root. So much energy was misspent on preserving these extremes that the manmade world in America never approached the rich and balanced diversity of skills and qualities essential to true civilization. We have created the asphalt jungle, a perfect and ironic manmade reflection of the natural wilderness so feared by western culture. The heart of American culture is therefore the abortion of true civilization. It is the generation of sterile wealth, the suppression of the universality and balance essential to civilization.

The new class of capitalists in colonial North America justified the enslavement of Africans by defining them as profane nature. Africans and the natural world were held to be opposed to the sacred realm of the Church, to be evil. Slave-holders were able to institute their definition because, unlike in Latin America, they faced no opposition from a spiritual counter view. In Virginia agrarian capitalism was able to flourish in a setting 'where no prior traditional institutions, with competing claims of their own, might interpose at any of a dozen points with sufficient power to retard or modify its progress'.[170] Had the practice of Christianity been strong, Africans and nature would have been protected by laws. A culture of violence against them and inhumane exploitation of them would not have arisen. Sacredness would not have become understood as belonging to a relatively small, exclusive elite but would have been understood as existing within all created things and all human beings. With the weakening of Christianity, the concept of the dual society became established, in which the world was divided into two parts, the sacred and the profane, that enabled the one to gain endless wealth from the other by severing the sense of identity and spiritual brotherhood between them.

Sacred Society: Europeans as Divine
FEAR OF DIVINE CONDEMNATION

The scapegoating of the African slaves had other purposes beyond serving as the means for uniting white society around a common enemy. It strengthened the white conscience in a time and culture wherein the conscience weighed heavily on the individual, superstitions were extremely powerful and the fear of God's condemnation was ever present.

With the rise of the merchant class, the new capitalist economic order and secularization, and with the fall of the religious and spiritual ideals of the Church, the Europeans – especially the bourgeoisie – became psychologically and culturally confused. The old pattern of economic life and the needs of the people had evolved and the feudal form of society was inadequate. It was a period when identities became fluid. Africans and others could be assigned an identity; likewise the European identity became subject to creative and destructive tides. Yet it was difficult for some to break from the traditional patterns of belief, the ancient superstitions and religious concepts. In the face of the ages-long tradition of rule by kings and clergy, the bourgeoisie, we often forget, needed all the psychological, legal, cultural, military and material power it could muster in order to establish themselves as a new independent social class never before seen in world history. It was as if they were a rocket struggling to break free of the earth's gravitational pull for the first time. The traders wished to be free of the ancient system of monarchy, yet some of them feared this very freedom, not knowing what would happen to their souls since, as far as they knew, such freedom had never before been attained or practiced in Christendom. To change the social order, which, according to venerated tradition, had been established by Jesus Himself, was to risk the possibility of divine wrath. No doubt this fear convinced many of the colonists to side with the loyalists and move to Canada after the American Revolution. In the 16th and 17th centuries to claim independence from the king, who yet ruled by divine right, and to seek unlimited wealth by means of violent greed were acts which resonated strongly with opposition to the ideals of Christianity. Such acts meant the essence of evil both in the political and religious realms.

We cannot afford to forget that societies of the past – including the society we ourselves have inherited – were radically different from ours. Whereas today most of us are secularists, our direct ancestors, the founders of our own society and culture, were for the most part strong believers in God, in the Church, in the Prophets, as well as in the supernatural and superstitions. On more than one occasion in the early 1600s, for example, Christopher Marlowe's *Faustus* was performed so well that members of the audience got more than they bargained for: a terrible fright by what they perceived as real devils on stage. Even the players themselves were susceptible. During a performance at Exeter the players 'were overcome by the conviction that "there was one devell too many amongst them; and so after a little pause desired the people to pardon them, they could go no further with this matter; the people also understanding the thing as it was, every man hastened to be first out of dores. The players . . . contrarye to their custome spending the night in reading and in prayer got them out of the town the next morning."'[171] This belief in the immediate presence of the supernatural and mystical is a reality that cannot be erased from our history and ought not. Even if we now regard such beliefs as error, we only distort our understanding of history if we insist on misinterpreting or ignoring them.

Europe and America in the first centuries of capitalism were cultures saturated by the supernatural: visions, amulets, potions, prayers, sacred places, magical formulae and rituals. God, gods, spirits and superstitions were not only near but were actively, immediately involved in every practical aspect of life. The cradle of capitalism was, ironically, a quint-essentially nonrational culture. However rational merchants and capitalists were regarding money issues, they were nonrational in their continuing belief in the supernatural. Max Weber's analysis could well be interpreted to mean that for Protestants capitalism was magic, a powerful means of divining and even creating one's destiny. The capitalists became more like priests controlling access to heaven and hell than rational interpreters of fundamentally rational laws.

The 'division' between the secular and the religious is thus highly misleading. In capitalism the religious did not disappear but only changed form. Capitalist culture ought not to be regarded as rational. Slavery and racism were not purely rational responses to market forces; they were based on ideas of the supernatural, the devil, witchcraft and magic. We have become misled by written historical documents – legal, governmental, financial – into thinking that the basis of slavery and racism was sober, rational and theological deliberation. But in reality the cultural milieu stated firmly and universally that the devil lurked everywhere, that magic was real, that God blessed and God condemned. Money was a part of this culture, a symbol of it and not some bright and shining first light of a completely independent rational culture.

As a prime example let us consider the psychological relationship between women in Europe accused of witchcraft and their accusers. Anne Llewellyn Barstow's analysis argues that in that period, beginning from about 1550, the economy of Europe was failing owing to a number of factors: inflation, overpopulation, enclosures, land consolidation in the hands of the wealthy, the transformation of the masses from peasants working on the land to landless workers seeking wages, much of this due to 'a flood of wealth from the new colonies in the Americas'. R. I. Moore points out that the reintroduction of money itself caused great cultural and social disruption.

> The dislocations associated with rapid economic change and particu-larly with the growth of cities are familiar enough in several periods of European history. In this one, however, money stands for an additional dimension of change. Its coming into regular, day-to-day use for the first time since antiquity involved replacing a system of exchange which was ruled by the ethics of the gift to one which conformed to the values of the market-place.[172]

In this profound economic upheaval, Barstow finds, women were the most vulnerable. Left landless in the wake of the enclosures, they could no longer provide for themselves and their family from gardens they had tended around their homes. If they were unmarried, they were likely to fall into poverty. With the 'alarming increase in female beggars in western Europe, who so discomfited their better-off neighbors', those who prospered under this new system needed to assuage their feelings of guilt. They had 'reason to fear their [the poor people's] hatred and revenge'. This was 'a society that believed in evil magic' and that 'hatred could kill' and therefore the wealthy felt justified in taking action to rid themselves of the potential harm from impoverished women. This confluence of circumstances resulted in the 'classic case of the original offender being unable to deal with his guilt, then projecting the guilt outward onto the original victims, making them into witches *so that they could be done away with*, thus ridding the original offender of the source of his guilt'.[173]

In America as in Europe, Barstow writes, this was an age characterized by confusion, guilt and violent resolution.

> These New England farmers and their European counterparts were not yet capitalists, for all their greed over land, but they had ceased to be medieval peasants. They were a transitional class, living under the strain of a rapidly changing economy that challenged their religious beliefs about what one owed to one's neighbor. Thus they lived with a sometimes unbearable amount of inner conflict and guilt over their growing ambitions. Witch accusations, with their clear-cut demarcation between who was good and who evil, and who was master and who the subordinate sex, reassured these confused souls, while at the same time enabling them to increase their wealth.[174]

Here Barstow is referring to 'what one owed to one's neighbor', which in the Christian tradition was love. We clearly see in this analysis the direct conflict between the Golden Rule of Christianity and the new rules of capitalism. And so through witch-hunting the 'transitional class' arranged to have its cake and eat it too.

Persecution of accused women was not the only way in which the new merchants operating in the wilderness of North America regained certitude that God approved their goals and methods. If capitalism and democracy were radical, world-shaking social experiments giving colonists an unprecedented freedom to pursue wealth independently of the Old World monarchs and clergy, slavery was the lifeline tying the colonists to the ancient shore of hierarchical civilization. Through slavery kingship was preserved, albeit in a new form. Within their private fiefdoms colonists held the legal authority, status and power of kings. The ever-present subservience of African slaves, which strengthened the illusion of legitimate sovereignty, bolstered their confidence that their actions were morally correct. Most importantly, by the mere fact that they resembled and behaved like kings, they acquired by association, as it were, the patina of divine confirmation that is the hallmark of the aristocracy. The later conversion of slaves to Christianity, moreover, saved the European soul as much as the African by granting Europeans missionary success and divine right of conquest.

ASSIGNING SPIRITUAL BLAME

Defined by Europeans as 'crazy dogs', as we saw in Level Four, the African slaves served as a convenient 'lightning rod' – in Freudian terms a subject onto which emotions could be projected, into which all feelings of guilt and fear could be deposited. This is related to yet distinct from their role as scapegoat. According to the European reasoning of the day, one could hardly be considered deserving of divine condemnation oneself if one's black servants, marked as the cursed descendants of Ham, represent the true infidelity, the true heathenism, the true devil. The practice of racism is therefore the daily practice of ensuring that every evil quality is assigned and constantly identified with the Africans and every good quality with Europeans.

A. Leon Higginbotham describes the Europeans' self-identity as a function of the creation of the Africans' identity:

> Many of the colonists had left the Old World, rejecting a society that to them was 'unacceptably permissive, ungodly, and undisciplined.' They had arrived in the New World, finding an unformed land that promised them 'God's law . . . born of the detestation of human license and corruption'. In the colonists' eyes, the Africans embodied all they had tried to leave behind. Yet, as threatened as they may have been by the presence of the Africans, the Europeans could not have afforded to send them back to Africa or to assimilate them fully into the new society they were trying to build.
>
> The dark, savage, ungodly, and licentious Africans were the perfect image against which the Europeans could favorably contrast the pure, godly, and prosperous selves they dreamed of creating in America. The colonial concept of freedom did not exist in a vacuum. Rather, freedom existed only as it could be highlighted by and contrasted to slavery. The colonists knew they were free because the slaves were not. They knew they were pure and godly because African Americans were licentious and ungodly.[175]

The more the Africans were held suspect, the more the Europeans became cleansed of any sin against God and king. The witch-hunts of Europe also possessed this function, as Anne Llewellyn Barstow has written: 'Among the possible meanings of a woman's life in early modern Europe, the most shocking was that she could stand for all that was utterly evil.' 'The European ruling elite valorized certain European women much as it did African slaves and conquered natives, as objects to exploit and as useful symbols of all that European men claimed they were not.'[176] Orlando Patterson summarizes the relationship between slave-holders and slaves in America: 'Without slavery there would have been no freedmen.'[177]

The irony is that the European slave-holders could act like the devil and still be welcomed into heaven, whereas even if Africans were perfect angels they could never pass beyond hell's gates. This was so because according to the Protestant culture one's place in heaven was signified by material success. Wealth was the primary key and all else, even morality and spirituality, was irrelevant. The more the Europeans oppressed the Africans, the greater their wealth and their nearness to God. But wealth was not the only key to open the door to heaven; as we shall see, whiteness itself gradually became an alternative, especially for those who were unable to accumulate wealth.

The colonists needed the Africans not only for economic gain but also for psychological and spiritual protection. Through the Africans, the colonists were able to believe that they themselves were not wild, for the wild ones were the African heathen. Disoriented in the wilderness of the New World, European colonists derived comfort from the presence of Africans identified as God's enemies. The colonists therefore proved themselves as God's chosen ones by juxtaposing themselves to the 'crazy dogs'. The whites became racist not because they sought mere superiority but because they sought to confirm that God was blessing them and their deeds. In the culture of that period, every endeavor's success or failure was a sign of God's favor or condemnation; likewise in the weather, the happenstances of the day – in everything were seen signs of God's judgment. And the greatest of these signs was the black skin and the 'deserved' chains of the slaves, signs confirming the rightness and blessedness of the colonial endeavor.

Even in American society today this identification of African Americans with evil continues. In an interview from the late 1990s an African American woman recounts the experience of a nine-year-old African American girl.

She's in a Christian school. And the teacher told the kids that black, black children are born with their sin. And the little girl went home and she asked her mother, she said, 'sit down,' and told her mother. She said, 'I just wish I was white.' And she's only nine . . . And [the] little girl had said what the teacher had said, and she said, 'Black people were born of sin, let's pray for the black people.' And now the little girl is really scarred, but you don't know how scarred . . . and that kind of stuff makes you angry. You take a little child that doesn't know anything about prejudice, and this is the way you plant it . . . in all these little white children's heads . . .[178]

DIVINE CONFIRMATION OF SELF THROUGH SOCIAL CONDEMNATION OF OTHER

Weber's theory of the Protestant ethic strongly argues that the primary motivation for Protestants' economic behavior was their fear of not attaining the blessing and approval of God. He describes the culture of Calvinism as one in which 'the after-life was not only more important, but in many ways also more certain, than all the interests of life in this world'. In this life there was one primary concern: 'The question, Am I one of the elect? must sooner or later have arisen for every believer and have forced all other interests into the background.'[179] Puritanism led to a unique answer fraught with powerful consequences. In Calvinism, he wrote, 'two principal, mutually connected, types of pastoral advice appear.

> On the one hand it is held to be an absolute duty to consider oneself chosen, and to combat all doubts as temptations of the devil, since lack of self-confidence is the result of insufficient faith, hence of imperfect grace. The exhortation of the apostle to make fast one's own call is here interpreted as a duty to attain certainty of one's own election and justification in the daily struggle of life. In the place of the humble sinners to whom Luther promises grace if they trust themselves to God in penitent faith are bred those self-confident saints whom we can rediscover in the hard Puritan merchants of the heroic age of capitalism and in isolated instances down to the present. On the other hand, in order to attain that self-confidence intense worldly activity is recommended as the most suitable means. It and it alone disperses religious doubts and gives the certainty of grace.[180]

Protestantism was a movement opposed not only to Roman Catholic authority but to authority in general; it found salvation in individual endeavor and self-confidence, not in obedience to traditional authority whether ecclesiastical or secular. We can argue that western culture's history is a series of steps continuing in the same direction: away from the Pope towards increasingly secular kings, towards parliamentary democracy, towards the flexibility of the law, towards the relativity of law and of reality (deconstruction). The fruits of freedom – untaxed profits, opportunities to create and to transcend class and economic restrictions of the Old World – had their price: the individual became less and less sure of his salvation in the next world, which never ceased to serve as the ultimate background and context of life even for many of the most commercially dedicated bourgeoisie.

The role of racism becomes clear. As morality became more flexible and relative, claims of righteousness and God's blessings could be made only relative to manifest evil. The standard was no longer a universal law – for such law could no longer be enforced by the weak Church – but rather a universally recognized standard of evil, namely Africanness and darkness of skin, which defined their opposites as good and blessed. Whereas the New Testament taught the need to love one's neighbor, this new doctrine taught the need to recognize his failure before God. As we have seen, Weber found that in Calvinism the 'consciousness of divine grace of the elect and holy was accompanied by an attitude toward the sin of one's neighbor, not of sympathetic understanding based on consciousness of one's own weakness, but of hatred and contempt for him as an enemy of God bearing the signs of eternal damnation.'[181] While one's own election was assured through successful and intense worldly activity, the damnation of one's neighbor was likewise proved by his failure to escape his status as slave. The spiritual law of love that recognized the infinitely transcendent soul and ignored the body was replaced by a substitute doctrine that absolved the self of responsibility to lead a spiritual life and to love the other, a doctrine that rejected the transcendent, the infinite, the metaphysical, and emphasized the body and social rank as the sole proofs of one's spiritual status.

WHITENESS AS HEAVEN

Since race is just skin, so a common argument goes, there is no reason to give it great importance. But the issue of racism is more than skin, for skin color is taken as a symbol of whether or not God favors you. It is a symbol of where you go after you die, heaven or hell.

Often in encountering an African American who has become materially successful, a racist European American feels a visceral objection, which is traditionally expressed in a variety of forms: threats, cross-burnings, bombings and worse. Even today reports are common of blacks who move into white neighborhoods and are pushed out by the hostility and violence of the neighbors. More revealing is the widespread and highly emotional condemnation of affirmative action in higher education and employment for African Americans and the silent acceptance of affirmative action for European Americans who are children of alumni and members of 'old boy' networks. Why such an emotional and negative response? Does not black material success refer to the basic principles of fairness and equality of opportunity at the heart of the American dream, the pursuit of happiness? Why are these principles applicable to whites but not blacks? It is because there is a hidden paradigm at work here. And that is the paradigm of spiritual election. Every black material success produces tremendous cognitive dissonance in whites because the entire culture teaches them that they are God's spiritual elect. They have been taught this sometimes explicitly but more often tacitly through all the educational systems and information media that surround us in our culture. Everything we see signifies the election, the sacredness of white people. Their faces are honored in beautiful photographs, their works are revered, their names are perpetuated, while the faces, works and names of minorities are disparaged or in shadow.[182]

Truly spiritual religions impose no entrance examination or fee. One believes and enters the community of believers because of one's love and faith. Tests may come afterwards but these are perceived as God-sent, not manmade. How very different, then, is the Protestant culture Weber describes, which redefined Christianity as a closed, exclusive order.

White racism understands life in terms of inclusion and exclusion, of acceptance and excommunication. For whites, the chief social paradigm is the inquisition. Although inquisitions have been primarily identified with the Roman Catholic Church, which did not officially abolish them until the 19th century, they in fact were practiced throughout the spectrum of denominations, including the Puritans. Inquisitions, denominationalism, sectarianism and whiteness are all expressions of the root paradigm of belief in God's selectivity and the exclusivity of heaven. Christianity became more an identity than a spiritual practice. It became what was essentially a social definition that permitted the individual who belonged to enjoy exclusive privileges. It was, by the time of the colonies, understood as a birthright rather than a message open to all. Racism and slavery fused whiteness and Christianity into a single identity. To be Christian was to be white and to be white was to be Christian. (In that age there was no such thing as white atheism or white communism or white membership in alternative religions except Christian sects.) To be white and Christian was to have the birthright to enter heaven. To be anything other than a white Christian was to be denied entrance to heaven, was to be forever condemned to hell.

We begin to see that the paradigm of exclusive spiritual election is both relative *and a matter of degree*. There are three principles at work in this aspect of the Protestant culture in North America that evolved into racism. First, the community of believers wished to assure themselves that they were God's favored and chosen ones. Second, this election was accomplished by accumulating personal wealth as a sign of God's blessing and by juxtaposing themselves against a group of outsiders, the Africans, who were assigned the identity of being God's enemy. Relative to this socially condemned group the white Christians could feel confident that their social and economic success proved their spiritual success.

The third principle is what interests us here. Beyond the issue of relative distinction the white Christians were also concerned with the degree to which they were elevated in God's heaven. It was not simply a matter of establishing a difference between themselves and the others. Of course, this difference did indeed create a spiritual 'value', so to speak, for the whites but they wished to go beyond that. God's blessing upon them increased as they increased not only their wealth but also their social exclusivity. Not only did they want to be sure of entering heaven but they also wanted to garner for themselves the highest rank possible.

As Protestantism evolved in North America, many white Christians who were not wealthy wished to have the same assurances of God's favor and spiritual election. Their desires caused the Protestant theology of race gradually to expand and include new social rather than financial methods for assuring election and high spiritual status. Thus they gave those who were not wealthy the means to assure themselves of entering heaven. But they also influenced the thinking of and became adopted by the wealthy. Just as wealth was used to create and increase exclusivity, so too social laws were used for the same purpose.

Primary among these new social methods were those preventing interracial marriage. We can best understand the significance of anti-miscegenation laws by imagining the opposite scenario. If interracial marriage had never been banned, and it occurred regularly between whites and blacks, how would that have affected the Puritan concept of their election? It would directly refute the concept of an exclusive heaven because it would show that the community of believers was wide open and infinite. Whiteness would no longer be an irrefutable sign of inclusion among the elect. It would no longer be a sign of anything either social or spiritual. Skin color could not be associated *systemically* with any social, spiritual or material reality. Exclusivity means finitude, whereas interracial marriage means infinite combinations precluding any assumptions. Thus Puritans would lose all value in their investment in race.

Hence it was not good enough for the European Americans simply to be white and Christian. They realized that they could increase, confirm and strengthen that exclusivity – in other words lock the doors of heaven – by instituting laws that prevented whites from going out and others from coming in. These laws constituted a celestial iron curtain. Whether you liked it or not, you were in for good and you had better not seek to exit, for then you would devalue our heaven and perhaps even expose it as an artifice having nothing to do with God.

In more recent centuries much of this has been secularized. Private organizations and clubs are all derivative symbolic manifestations of heaven. Each club practices the paradigm by setting up the concept of the ideal 'angel', judging prospects, accepting few and rejecting most.

DEIFICATION OF THE SELF

Since the witch-hunts in Europe and America, Christianity in the West has placed great emphasis on the existence of evil. Consciousness of the near presence and power of the devil strengthens the believer's attachment to God, who is the protector and savior. But this consciousness also strengthens the believer's self-confidence by identifying the devil with alien others, outsiders, such as racial and ethnic minorities. If the other is identified with spiritual failure and evil, then the self can be seen as belonging to the spiritually elect. Each community reproduces this paradigm in different ways: one community identifies the devil with Africans, another with Mexicans, another with American Indians, another with Japanese and so on. What is important is not the 'race' or the skin color of the minority chosen but the practice of bringing into reality the devil, making him come alive in the form of a minority community.

From a global perspective we see the same process in many other cultures, both religious and atheistic. Some Japanese reify the equivalent of the devil in Koreans. Some Hindus do so with Muslims and vice versa. Tribes do so with each other in Africa and elsewhere. Even when we are freed from the devil we continue to increase the degree of electivity, to reaffirm our election relative to others. And so a new devil is identified and condemned. As this process of identifying the presence of evil with minority others unfolds, ultimately we end up worshiping God not through love but through hatred. We redefine religion as the worship not of spiritual realities transcending material life but the worship of the tribe, the deification of the collective self, which can only happen if the collective other is reified as the devil.

Nearly every society has a sacred–profane paradigm of inclusion and exclusion. But true Christianity, like other religions, has taught that all humanity is sacred; it explicitly teaches us not to judge and condemn others. Why then do we, consistently throughout history, take the divine paradigm of universal sacredness and transform it into a sacred–profane paradigm? We do so because we are not worshiping God but, as Durkheim argued, using religion as a cover to worship representations of our own selves.

The Evolution of Justifications

The definition of the European self as sacred and the African other as profane, the root justification for slavery and post-slavery racist oppression, became widely popularized and reinforced by intellectuals, theologians, scientists and politicians. As with most ideas, however, it did not remain fixed but rather evolved as it faced opposition from various quarters. Out of this clash there appeared numerous secondary justifications. As one became debunked another would take its place. In the end they all weave into each other to form a complex tapestry of racist ideology that still functions today.

LEGALIZATION

One of the most powerful yet deceptively simple justifications has been the use of laws, rules and regulations, both written and unwritten.

We have discussed in detail the use of written and unwritten laws, rules and codes in America's past to label African Americans as outlaws, both from a religious and a civil or secular viewpoint. But let us now take as an example an incident that occurred not in 1949, 1959, 1969 or even 1989 but in the year 1999.

> In Florida just before Thanksgiving 1999, a restaurant owner was ordered to pay $15 million and have his employees undergo sensitivity training. The company settled a lawsuit over the fact they were charging a 15 percent gratuity directly to the check of black [patrons] and not whites. When the manager was informed, he said, 'It was added because you black people don't tip well.'[183]

Just as in the 18th century, when the new merchant rulers of the American colonies were free to set up their own private fiefdoms and private laws which greatly disadvantaged and oppressed African slaves, so too today private companies still claim the right to create and enforce rules that permit exploitation by placing blame on African Americans.

INTELLECTUALIZATION

The Civil War tore down the legal basis of slavery at the national level and effectively prevented its legalization at the state and local levels throughout the reconstruction period. In place of legalization arose a new justification for racism based on intellectual, academic and scientific arguments. These new voices reasoned that the legalization of slavery and racism was not the critical issue because in any case, however the laws and courts may be disposed, at the end of the day scientific evidence and rational investigation prove that Africans by their very nature cannot be equal to whites and therefore must neither be treated as equal nor permitted to aspire to equality. Herbert Spencer took the theory of Darwin and adapted it to support this approach. An intellectual descendent of Spencer's work is the theory that African Americans generate amongst themselves a 'culture of poverty'.

Perhaps best known of recent works in this genre is *The Bell Curve*. Although its argument and motives have been soundly opposed by many academics, the book's significance lies in the fact that it serves as a symbol declaring intellectual support of white privilege. It attempts to quell the tide of questioning so that the masses can return to the *status quo* satisfied that even if they have not studied well the issue they need not do so, because the best minds have settled the question. The average person can confidently conclude that he and his society are free of guilt and sin, because the scientists have pronounced that racism does not exist, that the suffering of African Americans is for the most part self-inflicted and therefore there has been no violation of Christian principles in the founding, development and current pattern of American culture.

MEDICALIZATION

Closely related to the intellectual justification of racism is its medicalization, which argues that African American aspirations for equality are futile because the physical body of the African American does not permit him to achieve it. This argument has been expressed in terms of brain size, the presence or absence of certain genetic features, and psychological qualities – we recall the teacher's characterization of all black children as being raised to be more aggressive.

POLITICIZATION

During slavery planters insisted on employing heavy violence against slaves because they perceived the Africans to be a dire threat to the security and well-being of the community. The slaves were a foreign enemy in their midst, able and ready suddenly to overthrow the institutions of government, culture and religion. It was not a question of the planters' greed and violation of Christian principles but of their need to protect themselves from potential violence from the enemies of civilization.

Following World War Two African American aspirations for freedom from racism were defeated in part by the use of political arguments. The cold war dictated that the country stand firm in the face of an insidious enemy who would attempt to disrupt the solidarity of the American domestic scene. A 1960 'Appeal for Human Rights', written by African American college students in Atlanta, Georgia, and published in the *Constitution* newspaper, was condemned by the governor of Georgia as 'an anti-American document . . . obviously not written by students' and he further hinted that 'it does not sound like it was written in this country'.[184] The struggle for racial equality was interpreted by many as agitation provoked by the political propaganda of America's enemies. The substantive issue, then, was not the problem of unbridled greed and oppressive materialism, not the needs of African Americans, but loyalty to the state.

MARKETIZATION

This point argues that the economic failures of the African American community are due to a lack of economic skills within the community itself. If blacks suffer from poverty it is because they are not hardworking, not disciplined, not competitive in the job market. They lack the merit needed to earn the places to which they aspire. A secondary economic argument states that no free market system can hope for full employment. Unemployment is needed in order to maintain the steady flow of job-seekers essential for expansion and for the prevention of inflationary pressures.

CRIMINALIZATION

This approach argues that the behavior of blacks tends to be criminal. As criminals, blacks cannot participate in the brotherhood and unity essential for society. Criminality naturally separates them from the civilized world. Civilization must at all times be protected from the threats of criminality; hence it is logical to separate blacks from the white society. Segregation is needed not because they are the subjects of violent greed but because they are criminals.

SUPERNATURALIZATION

Racism argues that the bodies and the personalities of African Americans are supernatural. It claims that African Americans cannot be treated as equal because they are proved to be abnormal by unusual physical features – shape of lips, nose and other parts of the anatomy. They particularly emphasize the claim that the sexual behavior of African American men and women is evidence of their passing beyond the bounds of normal, natural human being and behavior. Such claims no doubt recall the accounts recorded by Herodotus of legendary peoples possessed of superhuman powers or extraordinary qualities.

Beyond the body, however, is another facet of this claim, which is that African Americans practice witchcraft, voodoo, and therefore are possessed of the powers of the devil. They are particularly insidious threats to humanity because these powers are hidden, kept secret, and provide them means of superhuman strength and seduction against which society cannot easily protect itself. Simple fear of African Americans that might exist due to ignorance thus evolves into paranoia.

TRIVIALIZATION

If we argue that blacks represent evil and the devil in western culture, we then need to explain the pervasive stereotype of blacks as lazy, shiftless, stupid and harmlessly inept. The image of Steppin Fetchit seems to contradict that of the black man as devil. One of the most common disguises for racist violent greed is the trivialization of the minority group and its complaints. Trivialization's most simple expressions attempt to dismiss the needs and human rights of African Americans by reducing them to mere subjects of jokes and caricatures. Blacks cannot be taken seriously, cannot be considered victims of violent greed, because their lives are so laughable and ridiculous. They are identified with childish obsessions with certain foods. They are considered physically incompetent in certain respects (swimming, winter sports, team leadership). Bodily features such as hair and feet, the darkness of skin, are the keys to release tensions and fears in collective laughter. Such laughter confirms to the racist group that African Americans have no claims to justice, are not part of the 'normal' human world, and thus are not the cause for any feelings of guilt or remorse for whites' unspiritual actions against them.

More complex forms of trivialization have to do with historical revisionism. African Americans are said to have no valid complaint based on slavery or any other experiences in the past, for these experiences, it is argued, were not harmful but enlightening, civilizing, Christianizing. Even if slavery were harmful, whites cannot be blamed because every society practiced it, even societies in Africa itself. It was an all too common feature of the historical landscape for which whites cannot be singled out and given undue responsibility. There was nothing remarkable about European enslavement of Africans. It was a natural development of society. Hence Europeans ought not be blamed for it. This argument is plausible but it cannot be valid in the context of the Christian teachings, in a society that knew slavery was wrong and was too ashamed even to mention it in its founding legal documents.

Conclusion

All the justifications for the practice of unspiritual behavior in the form of slavery are also present in modern racism. We easily discover them in conversations about the subject, in media interviews and talk shows, in popular culture. The deeper the subject is probed, the more diverse the explanations for the continuing suffering of African Americans and the social superiority accorded to whiteness; yet we never seem to reach the core issues of spirituality and morality. These stratified justifications act as veils that obscure, that distract and provide plausible explanations, that seem to satisfy the urgent questions and challenges. As an organic system of thought these strata have themselves become unified and their interaction has produced endless subtleties that bewilder the mind and effectively prevent African Americans and European Americans alike from discovering the reality of racism as the violation of spiritual laws and principles. In this organic development racist thought resembles a system of religious beliefs because it is vast, complex, possessed of dogmatic authority and held sacred by its adherents. But it resembles religion most of all because it is based on faith, a faith that allows materialism through the economic exploitation of a group to be considered in harmony with Christianity's teachings that explicitly forbid such behavior.

By defining themselves as sacred and the Africans as profane, European colonists in America were able to convince themselves of the righteousness of slavery and the inapplicability of the Golden Rule. In the process, whiteness itself, like material success, became a sign of spiritual election and God's favor. Possession of white skin absolved the individual and the community of the duty to practice Jesus' teachings to love the other without regard for material qualities of body or social status. Whiteness was a substitution for the religion of Jesus, a shortcut to heaven. But it was only one of a number of such substitutions that appeared and flourished as Christianity gradually collapsed.

Level Six: Substitute Belief Systems

In Level Five we clearly saw that the justifications for slavery and racism are falsehoods. What we have yet to clarify is the process by which the great majority of European Americans could accept the false as truth, even though it openly contradicts the teachings of Christianity. The answer lies here in the level below, where we shall find that across centuries before, during and after slavery western society had gradually undermined Christianity while keeping its name and established in its place a number of substitute religions and ideologies that served as the basis for new, looser forms of morality. These substitutes would later underpin the justifications for slavery, racism and other unspiritual practices.

Racism as Red Herring

The red herring, a cured fish possessed of a powerful odor, has been used as a favorite device to throw off hunting dogs from the scent of their target. It deceives the otherwise undeceivable. Earlier we introduced the idea that racism is, in the final analysis, a red herring. Its purpose is to distract the people from the culture of violent greed, from the fact that violent greed is contrary to the Christian law of love and brotherhood, and from the fact that wealth and prosperity are not dependent solely on the generation of private cash. These truths are lost in the vociferous statement and restatement of the importance of race in determining the outcome of individual and collective human life. Like an experienced magician, racism draws the people's attention away from what is actually occurring; their minds are therefore filled with non-reality, false justifications and superstitions, and they can no longer recognize the violation of spiritual law. Let us now examine more closely the nature of this deception.

BLAMING THE VICTIM, CONCEALING THE VICTIMIZER

Today many people in America fall into a linguistic trap that allows racists to frame and therefore control the discourse on racism. Norma Akamatsu told her daughter 'that Grandma Haru was discriminated against when she was a girl because she was Japanese ...' Similarly, one little girl recalled another teasing her saying, 'We don't want to play with you because you have dark skin.'[185] One feels uneasy about this reasoning. There is something missing. To say I was treated badly 'simply because of the color of my skin' is to leave a big hole in the picture. It is in fact a deception. Racism is not due to the victim's nationality or color but rather to the inhumanity of the racist, the lack of spirituality, the violation of religious law and teachings on the part of the racist.

Maureen Reddy puts it succinctly in describing a visit to her child's school to complain to the principal that children in her son's class were abusing him with racial epithets. The principal said, 'Sean is such a nice little boy. It's a shame that he has to put up with this kind of name calling.' She countered,

> Mr Walsh, you're unclear on the point here: Sean does *not* have to 'put up with' this kind of name calling, and it's your job to make sure all the students know that no black child has to 'put up with' being called 'nigger'.

That same day,

> a poem on 'black' was being posted outside a classroom in the school. A line in this poem, which was written by fifth-graders, reflects the same perceptual error I pointed out to Mr Walsh. 'Black,' a white child wrote, 'is why Rodney King got beat up.' Well no: *white* is why Rodney King got beaten.[186]

The accusation of witchcraft in 16th- and 17th-century Europe was used by wealthier peasants to attack and control weaker and poorer members of the community and to defend their own relatively higher status. It was therefore not only an offensive strategy but also a defensive one: the accusation of witchcraft was a red herring to escape the religious law to love others.[187] Likewise the first means used by slave-holders to disguise their violent greed and materialism was religion. Slavery and racism were justified by certain interpretations of the Bible that claimed: 1) Africans were the descendents of the sinful Ham, had earned the wrath of God and hence were deserving of further punishment and 2) Africans were brutes in the wild and only the influence of Christianity could elevate them from their debased state. In either case, the Bible was taken to justify the treatment of Africans as slaves, thereby disguising the true motives of the plantation owners. Thus racism, like the accusation of witchcraft, is and has always been a red herring for defending white status and the practice of violent greed.

Secular strategies also played a part. In the Cape Colony the Europeans made freedom dependent on a number of specific conditions which they alone, conveniently, defined.

> As for the full-blooded slaves of the [Dutch East India] Company, they were to be considered *eligible* for manumission after thirty years of service if imported or at the age of forty if born at the Cape, provided that they had been converted and spoke Dutch. Although this policy may seem generous in its implications, it fell short of implementing the principle that Christians could not be kept in chattel slavery. The manumission of baptized slaves who had two heathen parents was made a privilege rather than a right, and the eligibility requirements applied only to slaves of the Company and not to those in private hands.[188]

This was clearly a ruse, a series of catch-22s, that made it appear that freedom and enslavement were all bound up in and dependent on solely the body, mind and soul of the slave. But in reality the fact of slavery was bound up in and dependent on the body, mind and soul of the European. The point is not only that Africans were slaves; it is also that Europeans were *enslavers*. We often say that Africans were slaves in America. But actually from the holistic perspective we must also say that Europeans were enslavers in America.

A passage written by George Fredrickson, in describing the ideology of slavery, exemplifies the tendency to focus on qualities of the captive Africans rather than the perpetrators of slavery.

> Empirically speaking, the enslaved can be described as nonwhite heathens who were vulnerable to acquisition by whites as a form of property, either because they were literally captured in war or because a slave trade existed or could be inaugurated in their societies of origin. On an ideological plane, it was the combination of heathenism and captivity that was initially stressed.

Winthrop Jordan similarly argues that the cause of slavery and racism is the heathenism and the appearance of the African:

. . . it seems likely that the colonists' initial sense of difference from the Negro was founded not on a single characteristic but on a congeries of qualities which, taken as a whole, seemed to set the Negro apart. Virtually every quality in the Negro invited pejorative feelings. What may have been his two most striking characteristics, his heathenism and his appearance, were probably prerequisite to his complete debasement. His heathenism alone could never have led to permanent enslavement since conversion easily wiped out that failing. If his appearance, his racial characteristics, meant nothing to the English settlers, it is difficult to see how slavery based on race ever emerged, how the concept of complexion as the mark of slavery ever entered the colonists' minds.

Here it is clear that the scholar doth protest too much. But he goes on.

Even if the colonists were most unfavorably struck by the Negro's color, though, blackness itself did not urge the complete debasement of slavery. Other qualities – the utter strangeness of his language, gestures, eating habits, and so on – certainly must have contributed to the colonists' sense that he was very different, perhaps disturbingly so. In Africa these qualities had for Englishmen added up to *savagery*; they were major components in that sense of *difference* which provided the mental margin absolutely requisite for placing the European on the deck of the slave ship and the Negro in the hold.[189]

This kind of interpretation of history – an interpretation that focuses primarily on material qualities, not the soul – makes it appear as if the Europeans themselves had nothing to do with the initiation and perpetuation of slavery and that Christianity had no bearing on the matter. The enslavement of Africans was made to appear as a natural and inexorable development in the world. But this is simply not true, as we have seen, for two reasons. First, the initial status of blacks tended to their inclusion, not exclusion – and this must be recognized. Indeed, there was so little aversion that slave-holders in North America believed that the commonness of intermarriage between Africans and Europeans threatened to overthrow the entire system of slavery. Second, we know that most European colonists in America believed slavery was not at all natural, was in fact an abomination, inasmuch as they were too ashamed of slavery to mention it in the founding documents of the United States.

This is not to say that the facts cited by Fredrickson and Jordan are incorrect. I do not doubt that many people, especially among the learned who wrote chronicles, legal opinions, theological treatises and other documents of those times, were reflecting the true feelings of at least some groups in colonial society. But we cannot jump to the conclusion that such an aversion was universal and natural among whites, that the enslavement of Africans was therefore natural and inevitable, that the origin of slavery had nothing to do with conscious vested commercial interests and that therefore the Europeans were blameless drifters on the tide of history. This is plainly wrong. The leaders among the European slave-traders and slave-holders – if not the class as a whole – were fully conscious that in practicing slavery they were violating the civil laws in force in Europe, desecrating the laws of Christianity and promoting a deeply corrupted interpretation of Christianity in order to assuage their guilt and obtain public approval.

Nowhere in Jordan's analysis quoted above are the inhumanity, the responsibility, the spiritual hypocrisy and violent greed of the colonists cited as causes of slavery. This is why Jordan's analysis, although useful and enlightening, is ultimately unsatisfying, because the white colonist remains in a way merely at the mercy of forces beyond his control, is subject to the dictates of human nature and has no conscious or willful role in the rise of slavery.

Someone following Jordan's argument would conclude that lawmakers have no right to force whites to accept blacks since their separation is only natural, as history proves. But history proves exactly the opposite: that people *naturally* were uniting across national, cultural, religious and racial borders and that lawmakers with vested interests – slave-holders, lawyers, legislators and judges – forced the citizenry to accept legal barriers of separation that were extremely artificial, taught them racism and yet had no right to do so. Slavery and racism were, in the colonial period and ever since, contrary to humanity's nature and spirit and a source of deepest shame and guilt for the perpetrators.

Slavery was ideologically condoned and considered compatible with Christianity because of the obsessive focus on the status of the African as heathen or captive of a kind of religious war, a focus which allowed the Christian European conscience to be blind to the blatantly un-Christian materialism of the slave dealer. The Europeans enslaved Africans because they had become materialistic, the very opposite of what Jesus taught them to be. Not wanting to admit this, they used race and heathenism as red herrings simply to write themselves out of the picture. In this they were only partially successful. Spirituality and moral responsibility were alive then as they are today and no degree of corruption made them disappear completely from the human conscience.

HYPOCRISY

We must call the American attitude towards race hypocrisy, which in this context essentially means the appearance of satisfying spiritual law while pursuing a materialistic life. Thomas Jefferson is an example. He gave brotherly, Christian ideals to the founding documents of the nation. Then he opposed those ideals, saying Africans are not equal. He then had a long-time African mistress. He never acknowledged his children by her. And he claimed a united destiny for whites and Indians, yet by 1813 he sought a solution through their extermination or exile.[190]

The question is, why did our leaders behave this way? Why did they not simply say what they truly believed and intended to do? Why did not the Europeans, in making their laws, just simply state boldly and bluntly from the outset that they wanted to use slave labor to become wealthy and therefore would not free their slaves under any circumstances? While this question has many implications, part of the answer is clear: they could not achieve social unity without at least the pretense to high ideals. No large society could emerge on the basis of inhumane beliefs. Openness would jeopardize the entire enterprise because we must remember that, despite all this materialistic culture, Europeans themselves were to a great degree spiritualized. The masses, who recognized they would most likely become victims, would never accept, and since they as labor were the source of wealth in society, the whole colonial project could not be launched without them. People would not join. Imagine a constitution setting down as fundamental principles concepts exactly opposed to the Christian culture. It would be rejected out of fear of God, fear for self. Therefore Jefferson and others wrote beautiful spiritual words that all could agree upon, that could serve as the basis for overcoming differences and for building an overarching unity out of a very diverse group of contentious colonies. These early colonists were, however strange their theologies, strong believers in the existence, power and wrath of an almighty God. The masses could not easily tolerate open violation of religious principles. They felt that their new nation would be doomed without God's blessings; therefore it was of paramount importance that 'their Creator' be referred to in the founding documents, so that the believing masses would be able to sign on. They could accept violation only if they themselves were assisted to interpret violation as somehow God's will. By confusing the issue through legalisms and red herrings the merchant leaders succeeded in wresting from the popular conscience slavery's approval. Otherwise there would have been a fight. As it was, the northern states were not completely favorable and in the long run the matter split the country and led to devastating war. We may conclude that from the very beginning the slavers and their courts were sensitive to the fact that slavery was not popular in the European conscience; they knew they were sitting on a ticking time bomb; they knew that the system was threatened not only by slave rebellion but by European rebellion. For this reason the slave culture in the South aimed its large ideological guns at blacks and whites alike and the slave laws were aimed against the potentially liberating force of white women.

But the key aspect of racism is that it made the inhumaneness of violent greed permissible. The 'Founding Fathers' did not want to be humane or spiritual or Christian; they wanted to be financially successful and to replicate English culture. They believed that great wealth was only obtainable through great violence, which the Spanish and Portuguese used successfully in Central and South America. But in the early North American colonies, alas, there were no great mines of gold or silver. Desperate to save their investment, and save face, they turned to cash crops and applied the same techniques of managed violence. It worked like a charm. The problem was, few Europeans would join the colonies for fear of being subjected to violent oppression, a reasonable reaction. The Founding Fathers reassured them with a racism meant to substitute for true Christianity: This violence threatens not you, our white Christian brothers, but only the Africans and Indians, the heathen and the dark, which you are not. Come; God is watching over our prospering nation and will ever watch over you.

Golden Calves: Shortcuts to Heaven

Substitutions are common today. We can surf and snow-ski indoors. 'Natural flavors' are manufactured in chemical laboratories off the New Jersey Turnpike. Clothes made with natural fibers are now relatively rare. Natural materials for the construction and decoration of houses are being replaced by plastics. And there is the supposed ultimate substitution, something called virtual *reality*. Clearly, sometimes substitution is good and necessary: prosthetics, and veggie burgers in this age of BSE, for example. But it is equally clear that substitution must not be excessive. Otherwise we become phony, as *The Catcher in the Rye* complained. Unfathomably insincere, we become lost even to ourselves.

But the most harmful of all is substitution of religion, keeping the form but changing the content. This is more than adding adulterants to milk and honey. This means serious long-term trouble and eventually spiritual death, the end of brotherhood. We spend our lives seeking love, yet paradoxically the search becomes sidetracked, misdirected towards inadequate and ultimately unsatisfying or harmful substitutes: power, sex, money. From a spiritual perspective we know that love of humankind, of the unknowable Creator is essential to our being. We thirst for this love. Yet though we have this thirst we expend our utmost energies in order to push our way to the edge of salty springs.

Once the Christian faith became replaced by racist and other materialistic beliefs all the subsidiary institutions and cultural practices in society became an open market for substitution. If the Church does it, it must be right. I can therefore offer fool's gold for the real thing and feel morally righteous in the process. A domino effect ensues, leading to the moral collapse of the entire society, from the church altar to the newspaper stand. And the key point is that we can still call the one religion and the other civilization.

In the moral vacuum left by rising secularism and waning Christianity a number of substitute religions arose that took the reins of moral authority and leadership. These golden calves assumed many different forms, for if they fulfilled *the role* of a substitute religion, they did not need to be a religion in the traditional sense.

RACISM AS A SUBSTITUTE RELIGION

It is not surprising that many racists are also religious fundamentalists, for racism itself is a substitute religion. They consider their racist behavior to be morality's essence. The history of civilization shows that we have always tended in this way to substitute an easier and cruder morality for a more difficult and subtle one. But why? Among the greatest challenges humans face, according to all religious teachings, is not the conquest of nature – the seas, mountains, outer space – but the conquest of ourselves, our habits, our faults. In times of weakness we tend to turn away from great challenges, especially if we perceive no specific reward in return. But in the case of morality there is a great reward: confidence in knowing one has followed 'the correct way', one is 'right', 'favored of God', 'blessed'. We wish to have this blessing without the great effort, to have our cake and eat it too. And so with a fateful wink and nod, blithely ignoring the long-term consequences, we compromise and substitute our way out of the dilemma. Perhaps the best examples of this were the Catholic practice of indulgences and its Protestant successor, the quest for spiritual certitude through accumulation of wealth described in Weber's *The Protestant Ethic and the Spirit of Capitalism.*

The Protestant Reformation suddenly removed a clear and simple guarantee of heaven: regular confession of sins and absolution. Max Weber theorized that a substitute was established by the Protestants: the degree of one's ascetic accumulation of wealth and capital indicates the degree that one is favored by God. Sociologists tend to emphasize Weber's conception of capitalism as the result of Protestantism's ethical character. But here we are emphasizing something different: that a substitution for Christianity was made by Protestants, a shortcut to heaven and God's grace was concocted and established, a golden calf.

But we need to go beyond Weber's argument. As Protestant culture focused more and more intently on materialism as a key to heaven, the one key became two: first, the original key of accumulated wealth; second, a substitute and supporting ideology – exclusivity based on race. As we have seen, racism was an especially effective ideology for those who were unable to achieve wealth.

Like the golden calves raised up by the followers of Moses, by the creators of indulgences and by capitalists, racist philosophy substitutes a material value – skin color – for moral achievement. Thus, while all evil was associated with Africans, all holiness and righteousness belonged to European Americans, who were therefore assured of receiving God's grace and entering heaven.

As long as the black race was the source and end of all evil, it defined the white race as free of sin, free to enter heaven. The dichotomy of the colors white and black in the description of Europeans and Africans is so strictly observed, despite the reality of countless shades of skin colors, because the terms white and black symbolize, respectively, the ultimate dichotomy between heaven and hell. The colors cannot be gradated simply because there is no gradation between these two ultimate destinies. Defining the Africans as profane logically led to the definition of Europeans as sacred.

This idea of gaining and guaranteeing access to heaven by proving one's relative goodness explains the curious puzzle why whites tended to keep blacks with them, both physically and psychologically, despite their supposed profound hatred of them. Uncle Bens, Aunt Jemimas, lawn jockeys, grinning black caricatures, stereotypes in popular radio and television programs and jokes, together formed a consistent background that made possible the daily reinforcement of the sense of white superiority. As long as blacks or other minorities existed in the consciousness of the white individual and the white community they helped remind the whites of their superior status, spiritual station and destiny. The Africans' lower status, plainly and pervasively evident – nowadays especially in roles in television and film – served a psycho-religious need.

To be racist is often proclaimed a natural right equivalent to the right to choose and practice one's own religion. Indeed, it is a religious right because it concerns a deeply felt belief, a perceived fundamental truth that cannot be easily relinquished. We recall the late 1990s case of the nine-year-old African American girl who was told in her Christian elementary school that black skin signifies deep sin.

The more we study racism the more we see that logic, rational thinking, reason and science have little or nothing to do with it. These are merely tools racists use to convince themselves and others of what they believe. Racism is a comprehensive philosophy that, like any folk myth, answers all questions, from why the sky is blue to why human beings wear their hair in a certain style. Racists are able to explain everything in existence, ready to answer any challenge. They inhabit a dream world of their own making and they intend to make the outer world a perfect reflection of it. They expect all people to conform to their world view, to fulfill roles in the drama they have written in their imaginations. In psychiatry this is called psychosis but when it is a group behavior, pervades a large mass population and crosses from one generation to the next, it clearly has a religious form.

There is much evidence that shows the religious form of racism in America: worship of the Confederate flag; visceral reaction to the breaking of any Jim Crow taboos, taboos that compare to the strict caste separation in India and elsewhere; imposition on all citizens, whether they agree with it or not, of a single Bible interpretation claiming that God demands the separation of the races; honor, respect and in the end reverence required to be shown to whites as a priestly caste empowered to interpret Christianity and implement its teachings.

The Roots of 'White Male Privilege'
EUROPEAN MALES AS SECULAR PRIESTS

Religion and its substitutes are at the foundation of what has recently been termed 'white privilege'. One researcher has described this term as referring to 'an invisible weightless knapsack of special provisions, assurances, tools, maps, guides, codebooks, passports, visas, clothes, compass, emergency gear and blank cheques', available to whites alone, and especially to white males.[191]

Maureen Reddy, a white woman married to a black man and mother of their children, provides further details of the contents of this knapsack of privileges:

> Through my experiences with Doug [her husband], I learned about the other side of racism, white skin privilege, which within a few years appeared to me like a vast underground network, whose surface I initially had mistaken for the whole. In myriad ways, white people's skin color smooths our paths, making our lives easier than the lives of people of color. We can expect to find housing in any neighborhood we can afford, for example, or (if we are men) to have our qualifications for job openings taken seriously. We can blend into most crowds – in restaurants, classrooms, corporations – if we wish, or if we prefer *not* to blend in, can assert our individuality in whatever manner we choose. We can see people like us in most films, television programs, advertisements, and public life, read about such people in newspapers, magazines, and our culture's 'classic' works.[192]

Jane Lazarre, also a white woman married to a black man and mother of African American sons, finds in that knapsack something even more valuable: innocence.

The whiteness of whiteness is the blindness of willful innocence. It is being oblivious, out of ignorance or callousness or bigotry or fear, to the history and legacy of American slavery; to the generations of racial oppression continuing; to the repeated indignities experienced by Black Americans every single day; to the African cultural heritage which influences every single American, long here and newly arrived; to the highly racialized society that this country remains.[193]

All of these special privileges, powers and qualities grant to white males a unique authority to which we submit ourselves. They are leaders, for these privileges, powers and qualities define them as relatively perfect. They inherently possess the good that we inherently lack. They are the most sacred of the sacred.

The role of white males as secular priests is most visible in the university. Originally founded for the training of clergy, the university has inherited two focal points from the Church: the book and the priest. These have become transformed into the textbook and the professor.[194] It is no accident that the professor continues to wear priestly robes at the high points of the academic calendar.

The professor is a recognized authority not only because of his years of learning but because of the institutionalized role he has come to fulfill: the replacement of the priest. He therefore has not only authority but a residue of sanctity associated with his person above and beyond whatever works of scholarship he may achieve.

White males in the general population have benefitted from this social order in two ways. First, even if they do not choose the path of priesthood, they have traditionally always been eligible to be priests. They carry the necessary sanctity, whereas racial minorities and women do not. Second, being thus identified as the most sacred section of the population, white males have traditionally been the primary if not the sole object of educational programs. It was for them that the great institutions of learning – schools and universities, monasteries and seminaries – were built. Literacy was a skill reserved solely for them; racial minorities and women were excluded from access to it – most notoriously in the slave system of the American South. With relatively easy access to literacy, with the institutional encouragement to learn, use and benefit from the written word, white males were further identified with the sacred through their ready access to the Bible and its successor, the academic and scholarly text.

By contrast, minorities and women have been at a cultural disadvantage, never having been historically associated with the priesthood's high social authority and sanctity. Society tends not only to dismiss them as nonauthoritative but also to stigmatize them as unsanctified, unholy and hence evil.

It can be argued, therefore, that race prejudice is in part rooted in the earlier division within the Christian community between the sanctified officers of the Church and the relatively profane members of the congregation. This dichotomy, when affected by a powerful secularizing movement, led to the dichotomy of secular society as a whole, between those blessed with advantages and those denied them.

The white male's holy status was reinforced and even exaggerated in the New World. A new group of men were subsuming the priests' authority: the businessmen, the lay leaders working in the world. As the mighty process of secularism continued to weaken the social and political power of the Church and raise the power of the merchant class, a vacuum of moral authority appeared which the new moneyed class naturally filled. They founded colleges and universities as the new churches and hired social scientists as the new secular priests. They raised business to a function of untouchable sanctity, arguing that the entire foundation of western society rests on the proper functioning of business above all else. Of the origins of Puritan economic activity Tawney wrote:

> From [the] reiterated insistence on secular obligations as imposed by the divine will, it follows that, not withdrawal from the world, but the conscientious discharge of the duties of business, is among the loftiest of religious and moral virtues . . . The labor which [the Puritan] idealizes is not simply a requirement imposed by nature, or a punishment for the sin of Adam. It is itself a kind of ascetic discipline, more rigorous than that demanded of any order of mendicants – a discipline imposed by the will of God, and to be undergone, not in solitude, but in the punctual discharge of secular duties. It is not merely an economic means, to be laid aside when physical needs have been satisfied. It is a spiritual end, for in it alone can the soul find health . . .[195]

New cathedrals of business arose in the cities, skyscrapers as monuments far transcending the highest spires of any houses of God. Banks and other commercial buildings even today are designed in the style of Greek temples, places of worship inspiring awe. Captains of business built for themselves offices akin to priestly chambers; they surrounded themselves with staff totally dedicated to the enterprise, all else being profane. Into this rarefied world minorities and women could never be accepted. The pattern of this world is rooted in the European male-dominated Church, a Church in which the priest is firmly established as the symbol of sanctity and holiness, all else needing his blessing. The profane are impure and hence unfit to lead or to participate in the priestly functions; they are only tolerated by the new Church insofar as they receive the priestly blessing.

EUROPEAN MALES AS WITCH-HUNTERS

Illogical and contrary to scientific facts, racism is superstition, the ultimate state to which a distorted belief system falls. In one of His talks in America 'Abdu'l-Bahá stated plainly that 'racial assumption and distinction are nothing but superstition'.[196] But like most superstitions its life is strong and not easily overcome. How often is it the case that all the powers of scientific reasoning cannot convince people that a long-held superstition is false. It is not mere coincidence that the inquisitions occurred precisely during the period of European history when the relatively new (or revived) paradigm of scientific reasoning was becoming firmly established and was challenging the ideas of the Roman Catholic Church. Revived superstition allowed the Church to compete effectively with the new paradigm of science. The search for the devil and his assistants – witches and other evil infidels – constituted a supreme *raison d'être*, an authority and purpose which placed the Church above the authority, function and value of science. Or so the clergy hoped.

Such an institutionalized superstition is American racism. It was and still is akin to the inquisition. It is no wonder that there was a striking resemblance between the search for witches and the search for alleged outlaw African Americans. Blacks as witches is not merely an analogy or metaphor. For if we merely scratch the surface of European culture during the colonial period we find the close identification of black skin with the devil, the most famous example being Shakespeare's *Othello*.[197]

Who were the 'clergy' of the institutionalized superstition of racism in America? Clearly during Reconstruction and for several decades after it was the Ku Klux Klan. Not surprising, then, the inquisition-like qualities of their rituals: the robes, the solemn ceremonies, the burning crosses. It was the inquisition come alive again. It was a movement to ensure purity not only of race but of belief, both among whites and blacks. Those whose beliefs did not agree with the superstition were branded as infidels and duly punished.

But since the Klan's demise the priestly role of the white males has evolved. They do not wear robes but they fulfill the same office. When we observe carefully we see that white males have other 'clerical' organizations in form and function. Union clubs, country clubs, social clubs, business clubs, universities (until recently: Yale and Princeton first accepted women as late as 1969, Harvard in 1970 and Columbia in 1983), many sports (some until recently and others continuing). Indeed, a 1995 study found that '97 percent of the senior managers of Fortune 1000 industrial and Fortune 500 companies are white; 95 to 97 percent are male'.[198]

But perhaps the most common sanctuary for the white male is the white residential area, with its home-owners association. Here all the elements of institutionalized superstition become united, revealing the white male's clerical role: to uphold authority, sanctity and exclusivity, to condemn any prospective black resident as bad luck, as evil. In this context it is no longer surprising to see the consistency and persistence with which whites reject black neighbors. The perception of the black as a witch demands such an action; it becomes an individual duty and an institutional imperative to rid the community of the witch, otherwise the white male would lose his ancient status as priest.

Fighting the Devil

Most of us, as children, have been raised with notions of good and bad, of the righteous and the sinful, of those loved and those condemned, of heaven and of hell. Naturally it is virtually universal throughout all societies that individuals wish to identify themselves with the good and oppose evil. It is natural for a child to identify with the hero, with the beloved, with the good, and to shun the evildoer.

Why, then, do we have so much evil being done in the name of good, of Christianity, of heroism? One thinks of the hatred shown to Elizabeth Eckford in 1957 as she attempted to approach her new high school in Little Rock, Arkansas: parents and students screaming in her face with such hatred one would think that Elizabeth, silent and calm, was the devil himself. But she was not the devil himself. She was a teenager going to school. In the minds of the white parents and students, they themselves were the heroes battling against evil incarnate but in the minds of the African American community their violent hatred represented evil.

What we have, then, is a community that has accustomed itself to doing evil by convincing itself that what it does is good. It cannot do evil knowingly because it was raised from childhood to identify with good. Therefore it has cleverly confused the good with evil. It has become the bad guy but wears the white hat. It has identified goodness not with actions but with the white hat – or the white skin. So that whatever is done by the white hat/skin is by definition good and whatever is done by the black hat/skin is by definition bad. This gives to the white community a freedom that lets it have its cake and eat it too: immoral behavior along with constant identification of the self with the good.

By screaming at Elizabeth Eckford the citizens of Little Rock were proving to the world their righteousness and Christian goodness and declaring their opposition to the devil. Because of their hatred of the devil, how could they be anything but good Christians? Christianity and being good therefore depend merely on identifying a devil – any devil – and opposing him or her. The more the devil's fortunes would decline, the more the Christians' fortunes and spiritual station would rise. Is not this simply a corollary of Weber's theory of the Protestant ethic? If a Christian's spiritual station would rise from material accumulation, so too it would rise, relatively speaking, from the material decline of others. Slavery and post-slavery racism reflected the Protestant ethic but in reverse; the same persnickety, detailed and unwavering dedication to the accumulation of wealth, penny by penny, was devoted to the accomplishment of the material decline, penny by penny, of an oppressed class.

Would all this oppression and violence really be for the sake of attaining assurance of and improving one's spiritual station or are we exaggerating the matter? We must remember that most of history has been lived through the medium of religious experience. Secular society is a very new and very brief phenomenon. The great sweeping movements of history have all occurred in the framework of religions, their rise and fall. Human societies are, according to historical experience, universally religious; yes, religious life takes thousands of forms but that practice of spiritual experience is everywhere and cannot be dismissed. It is real, meaning that it informs daily life, it determines actions, it sets the course for the development not only of the individual but of whole societies and civilizations. One might argue that religions have not set the course but rather corrupt individuals in the name of religions. The point here is that the masses of people have ordered their societies in response to religious beliefs, whether corrupted or pure.

Whether or not religious life has become corrupted, the fact that religion has been universal in history shows that the goal of attaining a high spiritual station, or of assurance of an afterlife, has overwhelming and universal importance in human experience. For intellectuals and academics in the West in the 20th and 21st centuries this may not be the case but for the vast majority of peoples throughout the world today and in the past it most certainly is. And if the assurance of spiritual glory and eternal life is so powerful a motive, it is not at all farfetched that a corrupt society would do everything and anything to win these goals.

So to summarize: Am I saying that somebody yells out the car window, 'Hey you [racial or gender epithet]!' because he is seeking a higher spiritual station? Yes, but he is not aware of it. What he is aware of is that he is expressing his feeling of white supremacy – or male supremacy, or ethnic supremacy. But what is supremacy really? It is a feeling of overarching power; to be supreme means to surpass, to go beyond, to be far higher, to transcend. It really means to be god-like relative to the oppressed other. And to be a god is nothing other than to be immortal, to have the highest station in heaven. His behavior is free; he curses and commits violence without remorse, with absolute freedom, just as a god throws his lightning bolts at will.

One might argue that this is not the behavior of Jesus. True, but he is not following Jesus as a messenger of God; rather he is following a substitute for Christianity. He is focusing on the devil. He is defining his behavior as righteous by the simple trick of defining the other as the devil.

The focus on the devil is very clear throughout the oppressive periods of western society. We see it in the inquisitions and the witch-hunts and the slavery and post-slavery racism periods. The Confederacy's defeat meant that the southern white males' righteousness was suddenly pulled out from under them. They desperately needed to regain their status as priests and so their fight against the devil went temporarily underground and returned above ground when the power structure fell back into their hands and Jim Crow was established.

Cross-burning, which seems to be a most contradictory practice for a group that claims to be devout followers of the Christian faith, reveals many aspects of the fight against the devil as a substitute religion. The Klan members stand in reverence and awe in a great circle around the burning cross. Why? And why do they burn crosses on the lawns of folks whom they despise? It is because they regard the burning cross as a symbol of the devil, of the reality of the devil, the living power and presence of the devil, the hell-flames of the devil that come to overwhelm the quintessential symbol of the Church. The reality of the flames consuming the holiest Christian symbol proves the reality and immediacy of the devil; it therefore proves the Klan's right and authority to identify the devil, locate him and punish him. A cross-burning on someone's lawn or on a church property simply says: the devil is here. Only the Klan can burn the holiest symbol; no one else would dare do it. Only the Klan has the power to punish the devil. The focus of the Klan is the devil because the devil's existence justifies the Klan members' claim to superiority. It is not exactly devil worship but it is devil dependence. Without the existence and immediacy of the devil, the white male's authority decreases and even disappears; as the devil becomes more present, more powerful and more prolific, the power of the white male increases to stamp out the menace, as seen over and over again throughout the inquisitions and witch-hunts.

Symbolic Immortality

We have seen how western society has established substitutes for Christianity: racial superiority, inquisitions, witch-hunts, practices that define the self as following the correct path. But where does this path lead? The ultimate goal was to escape death.

The Native Americans believe that sacredness is universal and all life must be respected. They gave refuge to Africans because they revere all life. Europeans, however, rejected Africans because they made sanctity exclusive and private. Whereas Indians revere and focus on life, Europeans in America have been focusing on death. The materialistic culture of Europe in America teaches that life can only be enhanced through the systematic practice of the manifestation of death in nature and among people. By spreading death and destruction, yet leaving their own people and places untouched, Europeans were expressing themselves as sacred and were indirectly aggrandizing and even deifying themselves.

The tradition of lynching is most illustrative of this. Whites would lynch a black person and in so doing derive satisfaction, renewal, joy, reunion, revitalization as a community. These 'positive' qualities of lynching have been mysterious and incomprehensible to most observers. How could such positive results be associated with such a negative act? The lynched man was the scapegoat. He was identified with all that is negative and, above all, with death itself. Those who conducted and participated in the lynching knew themselves as alive in stark contrast to the death before them. Their own lives were made all the more vivid and potent. And thus it was a cause for celebration. Indeed the lynching was a perverse celebration of life, a celebration of the fact that white skin brought symbolic immortality, especially for those who could not obtain symbolic immortality through wealth.

The role of violence is clear in this regard. As Erich Fromm (1900–80) argued, by destroying I feel greater than my mere self. I consume and control the world; I become greater than the world, I transcend existence.[199]

We tend to regard extreme violence as a rational tool for the purpose of controlling naturally rebellious populations, namely women and slaves. But what we find in history is that the practice of violence had a second underlying goal because it was too irrational to be viewed simply as social control. The hidden goal of violence was control of the entire supernatural realm, the world beyond the physical, the realm of death. Violence against Indians, slaves and witches was the means to manage an economy of death. Through the control of violence the ruling elites gained the sense that they controlled death itself and hence life. They decided who approached death and who attained it, who was spared and who was condemned. It was a sense of power which was reinforced every day that such violence was successfully applied. Whereas money was, in uncertain economies, a weak symbol of control over death and immortality – for it might be here one day and gone the next – violence was guaranteed to give a sense of control because the physical body's response to violence is universal and invariable. The key to the control of death was to look not at the soul, as Jesus taught, but to recognize the body as a physical instrument that responds without fail to techniques of control. Inquisitors, witch-hunters and slave masters all had the control over death and hence, like gods, they were able to bestow life and death according to their words and actions. This, they believed, made them closer to God and to heaven, for the God of the Old Testament was perceived in this way. As gods, practicing daily the power of life and death, they were able to maintain their own sense of personal immortality.

Thus the slave states' way of life was in a sense more important than the money it generated. It was really about the imitation or illusion of immortality. This is why they were so loathe to relinquish it. This is also why racism or *de facto* slavery continued after the Civil War until our day, because it is not only – and not even primarily – about money but is a means for the white self to identify with immortality through the control of life and death among slaves, women and other minorities. Whites saw themselves as modern Olympians; to say that their culture revolved around money reduces it severely. Theirs was the culture of Olympia and money was merely a means and a by-product.

We have come to this conclusion because of the European male's attitude to the death of the other. We do not find the white male regretting, grieving or mourning the death of the slave or the witch. Quite the contrary, we see him relishing it, valuing it. This is the exact opposite of the teachings of Christianity. Europeans in the age of capitalism did not turn Christianity on its head solely for the sake of money; rather, they also used the capitalist system as a means for gaining control of the keys to heaven and hell, keys that had previously been in the hands of the Roman Catholic clergy.

White supremacy in America, then, means the systematic practice of death to non-whites and to nature as a method to enhance life within the white community and specifically to achieve symbolic immortality. By bringing death to others and to nature whites felt they had control over death, and thus could keep it away from themselves. Conversely, by treating white lives with respect and a sense of solidarity each white person's life was enhanced, rendered sacred and confirmed as immortal. In his analysis of scapegoating, René Girard has identified this as an ancient form of society, in which social coherence depended on ritual sacrifice.[200]

By contrast, many Native American traditions require that for any resource taken from nature – a fish, a deer, a tree branch – a sacrifice of a bit of tobacco or other item of value be offered in sincere prayer. This is a spiritual recognition of the sacredness of all things, the supreme importance of life. It recognizes life as an eternal cycle and thus it need not stave off death by trying to control it. Without fear of death, it sees the life of all things as good.

From this perspective we can explain another curious aspect of white racism in America. White supremacists have always had the strange attitude that Jim Crow and other oppressive laws, even slavery itself, were too good for the Africans. This seems to be rather unfathomable on the face of it. How could the deepest oppression be regarded as a benefit begrudgingly given by the oppressor? It is because white supremacists have believed that death is the only proper destiny for Africans and for nature. To give them anything else, to spare their lives in any way no matter how oppressive, is to give them a great bounty which they deserve not. Hence the bitterness and anger of whites against blacks, even when the blacks were suffering terribly under the weight of racist laws. According to racist culture, the blacks should not exist except as dying creatures sacrificing themselves for whites and not for black families and black communities. For blacks to expend their energies for the sake of other blacks is, according to the white racist point of view, a waste of this energy; but even further, for blacks to live, even if under oppressive laws, is to violate the whites' sense of control over the power of death. The existence of blacks flourishing as free persons offends the substitute religion of white supremacy, just as the existence of flourishing nature is offensive. Their very existence is blasphemy, causes outrage and anger. White racism can only find satisfaction, can only feel that the world is in proper order, can only believe that white life is properly immortal, when it views all other life systemically coming to an end, all life dying but white life. White supremacy is none other than the cornering of the market on life itself.

Pollution, poverty, disease and destruction are kept outside the white communities, while all things perceived as alive and good are hoarded within. White communities are increasingly gated in a further attempt to monopolize life itself. White supremacy is therefore the fear of death, disbelief in a spiritual existence beyond this one, lack of faith in Jesus' teachings about the kingdom of God, and instead belief in the substitute religion of clinging to physical existence.

This aspect of white supremacy is even more fully exemplified by Nazi Germany, which systematically destroyed life and through that destruction attempted to create immortality. Wherever in the world people practice destructiveness on a systematic basis, contrary to spiritual laws, there we find the same desire for symbolic immortality, the same futile attempt to escape physical death. It is a vicious circle: whoever worships material things and material life cannot accept his own physical death; it is a trap. And therefore he is bound to spend all his wealth and energy in search of an escape from the limitations of that same physical existence he worships.

By 'worship of material things' is not meant that Europeans worshiped the very existence of all things; that would resemble the spiritual attitude of Native Americans. Rather, what is worshiped in a materialistic culture is the self's possession and consumption of material things. Through possession, consumption and control of material things the self is enhanced, strengthened, enriched, empowered and hence farther from weakness, threats and death. The materialistic view is that the spirit lives and grows only insofar as one's life is enhanced by material wealth. This is really the spirit of capitalism. One accumulates wealth not as a sign that one will go to heaven but rather because that very material wealth *is* heaven, is the perpetuation and strengthening of the spirit, is the escape from death, is the means for immortality.

Mercantile Europe had already become so enamored of physical life, so identified with the acquisition of wealth, so distant from the spiritual teachings of Christianity, so deeply devoted to materialism, that by the time of the founding of the American colonies it already had begun searching for an escape from the trap of physical death. While Europe, the Old World, was the premise, the New World and its material wonders was the consequence. The entire American culture, and its peculiarly virulent forms of slavery and racism, must be viewed as the natural outcome of a culture in Europe that left worshipers of the material life – the leaders of capitalism – no future spiritual existence. To love material existence to the exclusion of all else necessitated a search for the means to perpetuate that existence, to escape from physical death through symbolic immortality. Spiritual people did not need symbolic immortality because they did not regard themselves as essentially physical beings. But materialistic people were and are desperate for it. They will do anything for it when they find physical death waiting for them at the end of the road.

Racism can be summarized as a material philosophy that attempts to substitute a material form of symbolic immortality, an earthly greatness based on wealth and skin color, for spiritual immortality. It has become so powerful, so fanatical, precisely because it can never fulfill our spiritual needs. It is but a psychological intoxicant that seems to feed the soul but is only an illusion of spiritual fulfillment. The dissatisfaction it deposits on the heart and mind causes the seeker to return to it again and again with increasing commitment yet he tastes the bitterness of the illusion ever more keenly.

Racism as a Cult

As a substitute for religion, racism in America resembles a cult. Tight-knit racist communities prevent minorities from integrating their schools and neighborhoods and prevent their own members from befriending minorities. They often speak of and base their existence on love, yet this 'love' is false and turns out to be primarily a tool for psychological manipulation of the members. The result is a cultic environment in which independence of thought and action are strictly forbidden.

In extremist groups racism's cultic qualities are clear; the Klan's symbols, rituals, costumes and even sacrifices are obviously representative.[201] The Klan has regressed from modernity and the practice of Protestantism and returned to a pre-Christian form of socio-religious organization, substituting a tribal order and identity in the place of modern Christianity.

History, therefore, cannot be understood in linear fashion. It is not accurate to construct our society's evolution as a timeline in which we move from one stage to the next and the next, like stepping stones across a river. History is a far more organic process; it is often not discrete but rather continuous and in many ways amorphous. While some parts of society might move to a new stage, at the same time other parts might return to an older stage. We have the simultaneity of social forms in our culture. We do not advance to each new stage by making a clean break from the old one. Rather, we often bring the old stage along with us, as a secondary or auxiliary form that we stubbornly preserve and employ at will. Social evolution is therefore accretive. This is not to say, however, that profound transformation, or even complete metamorphosis, is not possible. Indeed, history shows this to have occurred in countless periods and places. Nevertheless, whereas western scientific and material development has been utterly metamorphic, western spiritual evolution has been limited and tenuous, tending to cling to relatively primitive patterns. And whereas America is a diverse, modern society, yet with respect to racism's function as a substitute religion, it encompasses social elements retaining tribal and cultic forms.

Race as the Primary Symbol

If we accept that within European American society there exist elements that have survived from ancient cultic traditions, then we must also accept that America is not purely scientific, rational and modern. On the one hand modernity and science obviously play a central role but on the other hand pre-modern, pre-literate folkways yet have influence. America, for all its technological mastery and spectacular scientific progress, is only a few generations removed from a time when belief in witches and the threat of the devil were commonplace, when superstition and the interpretation of symbols equaled if not exceeded the importance of science and reason. We note that even today some 95 million adult Americans 'lack a sufficient foundation of basic skills to function successfully in our society'.[202] In semi-literate and pre-literate societies symbols have great importance. Shops are identified by bold designs of fauna, flora, handcrafted articles and other easily recognizable representations. Clothes are important in identifying various ranks of society. Religious ideas and identities are embodied in simple symbols – the star, the cross, the crescent.

Despite the endless technological sophistication of our contemporary global society we yet witness the strength and importance of symbols in everyday life. Some of these symbols are weak and others powerful. Some are subtle and others crude. Some are inspiring, giving life to the soul, and others lead to abasement and degradation. Because symbols are so varied and are constantly evolving, they require interpretation. A cross worn as a piece of jewelry hanging from the ear, for example, does not necessarily have the same meaning as one worn by a nun. Symbols are varied: clothes, car, hair, language, accent, home decoration, jewelry, tattoos, posters, graffiti, choice of school, hobbies and sports, musical taste, hair color, nose shape, smoking – skin color. Even today our society's functioning is partially based on a hidden language of symbols and their interpretation, a language which advertisers and marketers are trained to understand and use with all the force they can muster.

A job applicant is judged primarily according to a set of symbols. The symbols are judged, not the person, because only the symbols are known, not the person himself. The symbols are public, are shared, while the person's life is private – only his family and closest friends can say they *know* him. The curriculum vitae and application are filled with symbols: names, degrees, titles, companies, ethnicity – and race.

All too often every symbol is completely eclipsed by race. It has overriding importance. Witness cases of plainclothes black police officers arrested while attempting to perform their duties at crime scenes. When black officers present their badges they are not recognized by white police. The black skin is recognized and recognized as illegal. The blackness takes precedence over the official symbol of legal authority and responsibility. A recent study by economics professors at the University of Chicago and MIT finds that job applications submitted by fictitious candidates with names associated with African Americans receive 50 per cent fewer calls for interviews than applications with typically European American names.[203]

Conversely, sometimes if you're white, well then, all right. Elizabeth Nill, a tall blonde student at Northwestern University, seems to be set for life as far as employment is concerned, for there will always be a place for her at Abercrombie & Fitch. 'At no fewer than three Abercrombie stores, she says, managers have approached her and offered her a job as a clerk.' More than a few other companies aiming at the upscale market have the same aggressive hiring strategy. It's a new day when customers coming to spend their hard-earned cash are offered a contract instead of a hard sell, no interview, no resumé, no questions asked. Not all customers, however, are so favored: as it turns out, there is allegedly a small catch having to do with race, which has led to a number of lawsuits around the country. Although if you're white, everything's all right; if you're black, you'll most likely have to get back: in the case of several African American and Hispanic complainants who had applied for jobs at Abercrombie, 'store managers steered them to the stockroom, not to the sales floor'.[204]

Racism is a social state in which the 'race' of the individual takes precedence over all other symbols. It is the ultimate meta-symbol, more significant than even religion, for it is a symbol that signalizes the immediate and complete halt of the symbolic language of spirituality and love shared among the people in a united society. Race is the fundamental element of social life; in its oppressive shadow the spirit is defined as irrelevant, even nonexistent. The skin color, the body, is, contrary to Jesus' explicit teaching, all-important. Language revolves around the color of the body. Civil laws revolve around the color of the body. Symbology in advertising, mass media and the arts revolve around the color of the body. This language of the body has written the spiritual world quite out of existence.

Our society, like all others, is not a pure structure but a complex system built up of accreted layer upon layer of subsystems. We may point to two or three systems as our national identity – say, Christianity, science and democracy – but our actions point to others as well. If our actions reveal our true beliefs, we cannot be considered purely religious, scientific or democratic but also racist, for we *act* on deeply held racist beliefs. Racism has thus replaced religion, science and democracy as the dominant belief system for many people in the United States. For them racism is not theoretical or hypothetical but the most fundamental determinant of social action.

Militarization

Although many substitutes for Christianity have been old, often pre-Christian religious or philosophical ideologies, we ought not assume that technological, scientific and pseudo-scientific systems of thought have played no role. As we shall discuss, modern social science was created in great part to replace state religion following the collapse of the old order in the French Revolution. But the rise of social science and its influence on government was to a great extent a conscious movement, a strategy promoted by the empowered bourgeois rulers of a newly secularized Europe. What is far less recognized, however, is the heavy influence of military culture throughout the West, perhaps for the simple reason that warring is so far removed from religion that the former cannot logically be considered a substitute for the latter. However strange this proposition, we nevertheless can make the case that it is true. Let us begin with an exploration of institutionalized compassion.

Emergency services in the United States are probably the best in the world. Rapid response medical teams, mountain rescuers, lifeguards, coast guards, fire fighters: these all are dedicated to saving lives no matter what the circumstances, no matter what the race. Although it could be argued that in impoverished areas emergency services are very poor and even nonexistent, the fact remains that where they do exist they are exemplary of the best spirit of humanitarian assistance and compassion. Indeed, many members of these services are willing to risk their lives repeatedly for the sake of others. What more could a society ask for?

Yet somehow this sense of compassion is truncated, limited to a small set of social circumstances. If your house is burning, if you are in a car accident, if your family member has a heart attack, we are there to help you and we will even risk our own lives to do so. But if you are suffering from poverty, from homelessness, from hunger, we show you the door and say you are on your own. Why this strange bifurcation of moral sense? It is all too easy to answer by simply saying that it is the way of capitalism, that Ebenezer Scrooge and all misers long ago set the tone of how we conduct things in this world. This is too easy an answer because it does not explain to us how and why Scrooge became a miser in the first place. Is miserliness something to be accepted as the natural course of things, part of the unfathomable essence of the universe? Scrooge regained his sense of compassion through an experience that terrified him out of his wits and out of his bad habits. Is this terror always necessary to awaken us from moral corruption?

Scrooge is perhaps the best known Christmas character other than St Nicholas himself and for good reason. It seems that his story is a powerful modern-day parable because it speaks of profound truths about human nature. In the West most of us have these miserly qualities to some degree. Scrooge's personality has become generalized in the population. The growth of the middle class is the growth of Scrooge culture. Of course, many suburban home-owners, law-abiding taxpayers, would immediately object to such a characterization. But the truth is that we are taught to hoard our money, to avoid generosity and above all to blame the poor for their circumstances. We shun the guilt of enjoying our wealth in the face of suffering of the masses. We turn our backs upon the poor and bring down a series of gates to keep them out of our sight.

With our excellent emergency services we will help you to live but beyond that we cannot go. Our culture says you must stand on your own two feet. Fair enough, but should not compassion go beyond that limit? Does compassion somehow prevent the downtrodden from standing on their own two feet? Can we not assist others to stand and walk and run and progress, while at the same time being compassionate? Are these two goals incompatible? Quite the contrary, they are two sides of the same coin.

One answer to the origin of Scrooge culture is, as we have seen, the Protestant quest for certainty of the self's election, causing the self to value superiority relative to neighbors. A more subtle but equally powerful source is the militarization of culture in the West.

The military makes men out of boys by forcing them, pushing them, bullying them, beating them, denigrating them. To be a man is to take abuse, to forswear the need for compassion and to give abuse in one's turn. Compassion has no place in the military because there we are trained to use deadly force against an enemy. It is one of the heaviest responsibilities in the human world because the need for defense is deemed paramount in society.

War is a primary pillar of western culture – a tragic, ironic and shocking fact. By it we orient ourselves in history and create and recreate our national identities. Our recent wars are only the latest in a series of powerful processes binding western culture to a military ideal of civilization. It is no wonder that we glorify wars as seminal events and sing praises of them; laud military leaders and heroes; base our national histories on them and our corporate, educational and governmental structures on them. Thus the Marlboro Man, John Wayne, James Bond, the serious stiff-necked models of machismo, represent and are icons of the triumphant, ever-victorious soldier in a civilization based on military ideals.

The 1960s youth rebellions were not counterculture movements against the Vietnam War specifically but against the culture of war and the military as a whole. In great part they succeeded, for it is no longer taken for granted that youth will adopt the military as a personal style paradigm, as was the case of the buzz-cut 1950s and early 1960s. Moreover, youth rebellion since the 1960s has continued and has more or less aimed at the most immediate representative of military culture in local communities: the police.

But the militarization of culture constitutes a profound challenge not easily met, for it is a process that has been unfolding over centuries. Much of modern society's very rationalization and uniformity began, according to William H. McNeill, with the revival of Roman lock-step military drill techniques in 17th-century Holland.[205] It was further encouraged by the rise of mass production techniques, particularly the assembly line. To round out the picture of this cultural movement, we recall that it is not merely coincidental that among the first products to be mass produced were firearms, making use of Eli Whitney's design of a gun composed of interchangeable parts. The military basis of American culture became clearer after World War Two, when barracks-like Levittowns sprang up for the next 50 years and became the epitome of America's cultural bankruptcy and white suburban segregation.

The pervasiveness of military culture in America – its glorification, its centrality as the primary reference for the definition of national identity, its heroes as the Founding Fathers and political gods of the state – prevents the flowering of compassion, for it is the harsh voice of the drill sergeant that sets the tone for business culture, for the hospital, the school. We are made to do, we are ordered, we are not loved. The sense of compassion, of sympathy, of spirit is lost, for in the military there is no place for feeling and emotion and sympathy. While blacks give full expression of the heart in a rich musical tradition originating in the black church, whites, deeply affected by the militarization of their culture, find it rarely possible to indulge in such expressions. Since the early jazz era they have consoled themselves vicariously through the performances of white artists who adopt the latest emotive styles of unmilitarized African–American, Caribbean and Latino culture. And only sporadically have masses of whites been so bold as to embrace the work of African American pop artists directly.

Clearly the Protestant ethic and military culture are closely related in their origins. They both emerged from a Europe becoming oriented to materialism and individualism, in which action at the highest levels – particularly the colonial commercial enterprises – were predicated on achievement without concern for human feelings. The equating of business success with spiritual election meant the end of interpersonal sympathy and identity; success and prosperity took priority over humanity itself. The Renaissance therefore ended in a new cloud of glory – the glory of individual success – which obscured humanity and gradually but firmly closed the Christian principle of the eternal identity between self and other.

To be western, therefore, means to have no sympathy for the other. In this culture the absence of feeling for others is, ironically, a demonstration of strong faith. For the one most detached from the suffering of others is most able to amass from that suffering the greatest wealth. This is quintessentially the soldier's attitude towards the enemy.

Of course we need proper military defense but there must be a balance. For when the cold-bloodedness of the military seeps into the general society it destroys the very civilization which the military is charged to protect. The military has its place but so too does the practice of compassion. They must both be properly ordered, respected and practiced according to society's true needs.

How are the needs and balance to be determined? The answer is deceptively simple but most difficult to practice. They are determined by observing what results in the enhancement of life and what results in the diminution of life. That which is healthy and good brings about a flourishing of civilization and that which is harmful leads to cultural decay, poverty, crime and destruction. If the culture we practice is proving harmful, then we must bring it to a halt, 'alter or abolish it', and implement remedies.

Like Scrooge we must end our behavior and begin a new pattern. But how are we to obtain a Scrooge-like transformation, especially on the level of the general society? Scrooge was one man; we are hundreds of millions. What will make us turn away from a harmful path, abandon our substitute religions and embrace true spirituality as a necessary complement to material culture?

Conclusion

Slavery and racism have been supported by a variety of clever and powerful justifications which legalized the oppression of Africans by defining them as part of profane nature, beyond the realm of the Christian law; by condemning nature to be exploited solely for the sake of promoting capitalist enterprise; by identifying Africans as the evil accomplices of the devil and therefore the just targets of society's punishment; by defining whiteness as sacred and therefore as signifying an immunity from sin and a complete freedom of action. These justifications have all drawn a veil over the morality and laws of Christianity.

The justifications seem reasonable to many people because they are seen in the context of substitutes for Christianity, belief systems that sanction materialism, that allow ways of life contrary to the teachings of Jesus while ensuring the ultimate goal of self-confidence and God's favor. Since we do not examine slavery and racism in the Christian moral context, we do not regard slavery and racism as violations of fundamental Christian laws. Christianity, therefore, is either of marginal importance to the development of slavery and racism or of no relevance at all; indeed most histories of slavery and racism lack detailed discussions of Christian morality, even Davis's *The Problem of Slavery in Western Culture*. We have been deceived. First, we believe that separation of Church and state means the Church had no place in the historical development of slavery and racism. Second, we recognize the power of secularism and we accept that if a state declares itself secular then religion from that moment on plays no role and need not be discussed. In fact, if a state changes the rules, as it were, by calling itself secular, it is considered almost *unfair* to apply religious standards in assessing its moral development. Whereas in Christianity slavery and racism clearly constitute violation and corruption, in a secular state they are regarded as rational political and economic decisions. They are justified.

Third, by dismissing the relevance of Christianity we are effectively calling it a myth, for it has no authority in society, no reality. America was faced with two sets of general principles, those of the Bible and those of the slavery-dominated courts. By choosing the latter and ignoring the former America demonstrated by action that its true faith lay in the words of men, not in the Word of God. By turning to the golden calves of slavery and racism, we demonstrated that we had lost faith completely in Jesus' way.

Level Seven: Violent Materialism in America

If we look beneath the laws creating slavery in North America in the 17th century, and the justifications and substitute belief systems supporting them, we find that they were covering up something that the colonists meant to keep secret. What these new laws and justifications were really saying could not be expressed openly because they violated the fundamental principles of civilized society: they were granting permission for whites to be violent, to be greedy, to ignore the laws of Christianity and of civilization. Ultimately these new laws did not represent anyone's fears of strangers with dark skin. Rather they represented the wishes of the new merchant rulers to control their slave labor force, the stability of which was threatened by the tendency of Europeans and Africans to become friends, to intermarry and to unite. The slave codes were not so much about what Africans could and could not do but about what white males could be free to do. C. Vann Woodward identifies an example of this in his description of the economic depression of the 1890s, when southern whites were quick to blame blacks:

> There had to be a scapegoat. And all along the line signals were going up to indicate that the Negro was an approved object of aggression. These 'permissions-to-hate' came from sources that had formerly denied such permission. They came from the federal courts in numerous opinions, from Northern liberals eager to conciliate the South, from Southern conservatives who had abandoned their race policy of moderation in their struggle against the Populists, from the Populists in their mood of disillusionment with their former Negro allies, and from a national temper suddenly expressed by imperialistic adventures and aggressions against colored peoples in distant lands.[206]

These 'permissions-to-hate' were none other than permissions to violate with impunity the Christian law of love. They were very cleverly disguised in powerful legal language that left the African slaves and their descendants, as it were, holding the bag, responsible for all threats to Christianity and civilization. It was all one vast three-century long deception.

The anti-miscegenation laws we saw in Level Four clearly exemplify this deception. They condemned interracial marital and sexual relations in the strongest of terms that resonate hatred even today: such relations are a 'disgrace' to the nation, 'shameful', resulting in 'abominable mixture' and 'spurious issue' – powerful words defining for centuries a moral attitude that prevented the unity of the races. More to the point, this dramatic language prevented the people from recognizing the purpose of the laws; by it the lawmakers were able to avoid being accused of immorality, of pursuing slavery against the laws of Christianity and Christian civilization. Such laws concealed a culture turned towards extreme materialism and a will to extreme violence.

Materialism

In America there is a famous bumper sticker that reads, 'He who dies with the most toys wins', a dumbfounding statement. There are so many questions here. Wins what? Who are the competitors? Why are toys the key to winning? What is it talking about?

The mystery unravels if we start with the toys, which, as any red-blooded American will explain, include virtually everything technological that costs more than pocket change: riding mowers, wide screen digital televisions, computers and other audio-visual equipment, club memberships, automobiles, houses and vacation homes, on up to jets, yachts and so on. The most famous toy of modern times summarizes in one word the meaning, the origin, the purpose and the complete failure of this bumper-sticker philosophy. And the irony is that it actually was a child's toy, named 'Rosebud'.

SATISFYING GREED

While the immediate goal of despiritualization was the legitimization of slavery, the ultimate goal of slavery was the attainment of an endless source of profit primarily from agricultural markets. As we have seen, wealth has been the means in the West's materialistic culture of representing the self's symbolic immortality. But when we speak of the individual's quest for endless profit what we are also talking about is the simple yet profound concept of greed.

Greed is often not given the seriousness it deserves. It is dismissed as being more a political or personal slander rather than a statement of social or psychological fact. It is often laughed off as the accusation of last resort for the market's sore losers. It is rejected as a hopelessly ideological criticism that is either too relative or is premised on an idealism that cannot ever be practiced in the 'real world'. Human society, it is argued, cannot exist without the personal striving of each individual to improve his or her own lot. This is nature. This is universal. This is destiny. To call it greed is to give a partisan political interpretation. In the final analysis, then, greed is simply a myth.

On careful reflection, however, we find that greed, and this conception of it as myth, are not modern but rather ancient characteristics of civilization in decay. All the major religious traditions strenuously and repeatedly warn believers against greed, stating that its practice is not only a reality but can harm, and even bring death to, the human soul.

> Just as the bee takes the nectar and leaves without damaging the color or scent of the flowers, so should the sage act in a village.
> *Dhammapada*[207]

> Verily I say unto you, that a rich man shall hardly enter into the kingdom of heaven. And again I say unto you. It is easier for a camel to go through the eye of a needle, than for a rich man to enter into the kingdom of God.
> *Matthew 19:23–4*

> And let not those who hoard up that which Allah hath bestowed upon them of His bounty think that it is better for them. Nay, it is worse for them. That which they hoard will be their collar on the Day of Resurrection.
> *Qur'án 3:180*[208]

Far from being an ideologically-based illusion, greed is, in the spiritual perspective, a powerful menace to the individual and society. If we acknowledge the reality of spiritual laws in human society we must acknowledge the universal danger posed by the practice of greed.

Echoing R. I. Moore's point regarding the critical historical importance of the reintroduction of a money system, Robert Ergang has noted the importance of greed in the transformation of western culture from Christianity to secularism:

> The unlimited accumulation of wealth at the expense of the buyer was, of course, a far cry from the ideal of brotherly love set up by the Church.
> [The bourgeoisie] were individualistic in their outlook with little sense of social responsibility. Self-interest was for them the highest law, with the profit motive pushing the golden rule into the background.[209]

Of particular importance to our discussion is what might be termed violent greed. When the desire for wealth becomes so powerful that it causes the individual to resort to violence in order to satisfy his craving, greed becomes a force that suddenly affects lives far beyond the greedy individual himself. It becomes greatly magnified in social influence, for it values wealth above the life of humans and other living things on the planet. Whereas greediness might be viewed as a disease of the individual soul, violent greed is more like a plague in the wide-ranging scope of its social consequences.

In order for greed to operate, however, it must disguise itself, because it directly contradicts Christianity's unifying spiritual principles that led to the creation and preservation of modern western civilization. Because of the extreme contradiction between violent greed and Christian ideals, those who have attempted to practice both generally feel obliged to hide their extreme materialism. In nearly all societies and cultures greed is strictly forbidden by religious law. It brings shame upon the perpetrators and abomination to the community. This is so because societies can only be formed on the basis of loving relations and brotherhood. Anything that prevents love and sincere fellowship is anathema and the society's principles are opposed to it. Yet, paradoxically, greed cannot achieve its goal except within a united society, for it is only through social unity that wealth can be generated. Therefore greed is a parasite that depends upon the body of the host, civilization itself.

As a parasite, greed must mimic the unifying social principles that are the foundation of civilization. Otherwise it would be identified as contrary to the law, halted and punished. Greed must adopt a form such that it does not seem related at all to personal acquisitiveness, to wealth or the economy. Here is where the concept of race became useful. If violent greed were practiced against anyone and everyone it would be easy to recognize it as such, for the only thing the victims would have in common would be their economic exploitation. But if violent greed were practiced against a particular group in the society that could in some way be recognized as distinct – by physical or socio-cultural features – then this religiously illegal practice would become confused with the victims' distinguishing features, which are nothing more than red herrings. The perpetrators argue, however nonsensically, that those features *cause* and justify their own actions. The issue at hand, then, becomes not a matter of greed and violence but a matter of the distinctive features. The perpetrators in this way define the terms of the discourse. Violent greed then fades from the discussion as full attention is paid to the red herrings of race or alleged witchcraft.

When violent greed is directed not at the general populace but only at a profaned sub-group of the society, the perpetrators are able to practice the unifying principles of love and brotherhood among the sanctified – whence the duality of society. The African victims see the perpetrators as violent and greedy oppressors. But the European population recognizes them as loving brothers who follow the society's fundamental spiritual laws. If the perpetrators did not create a minority against whom to be oppressive, then the entire society would be victimized and no one would recognize them as faithful to the spiritual laws. Through the creation of a minority, the perpetrators can have their cake and eat it.

To be a Christian slave-holder, then, meant three things: 1) To limit one's violent greed to actions against a sub-group. 2) To redefine that violent greed as the natural and just reaction to the sub-group. Indeed, the sub-group is not composed of victims but rather perpetrators, threateners of civilization. White violence and greed are then seen as a defense of the spiritual laws of the society. 3) A dual society is created. Slave-holders who practice violent greed can, by following this scheme, easily be regarded as the best of men, heroes and upholders of truth, justice and the teachings of Jesus. They appear to be the essence of loving brothers, exemplars of the unity required by any true civilization.

Such a perversion of the Christian spirit and law sounds almost too outrageous to be historically true. Yet it is not so incredible. The history of indulgences is exactly the same: to purchase one's salvation with what was essentially a bribe to clergymen was the very opposite of Jesus' path as defined in the New Testament. It was a perversion that had worked its way into the heart and soul of the Church long before Luther, most notably in the rise of the inquisitions, and would continue long after him. The violent greed and racism of Protestant America was a stage in a long chain of events by which Christianity was transformed: 1) The Crusades justified the use of violence against 'infidels'. Un-Christian hatred became Christianized as the Church became militarized. 2) Likewise, un-Christian behavior was Christianized by the inquisitions and this Christian violence became gradually popularized, so that the elites and the masses accepted it as normal. 3) Witch-hunts, begun by Catholics, were perpetuated by Protestants. 4) The extreme violence of Spanish colonialism was adopted by the English in their colonization of Ireland. 5) Finally, slavery and racism institutionalized all these various forms and purposes of extreme violence in one total system in the New World. With each step in this process we see the widening of the field in which un-Christian violence became defined as acceptable and sanctioned by the Christian and secular authorities.

Before extreme violence became normalized throughout the West, the spirit and law of Christianity had produced an interlude of about seven centuries – from the collapse of Rome until the Crusades – in which violence was moderated if not significantly reduced. The spirit of Christianity, however fitful, had tempered the rise of militarism until the outbreak of the Crusades, followed by the inquisitions and colonialism and the witch-hunts. Militarism therefore created a cultural space in Christianity in which violence and cruelty were not only legitimized but sanctified. Gradually that space expanded, while the space dominated by the imperative of Christian love contracted.

The simple truth is that racism is about violence and greed. Today it may have become merely one or the other – skinheads are mainly violent, while slumlords are mainly greedy – but our current race relations are based on the initial impulse of violent greed planted so many centuries ago and we reap what we sowed.

PRESERVING THE CULTURE OF GREED

It was not long ago that village life in most of the world suffered from dire conditions. Starvation and disease were common. Children often died at an early age. Because it was difficult to raise children, and to assume their survival to a ripe age, the community's economy suffered. If we take the basic formula that wealth is generated by combining land with labor, then the years before World War One were a time in which land was plentiful in most countries yet people were scarce. The sign of a wealthy community or tribe was a large number of residents. Population was precious in those days and the smart community did everything it could not only to preserve it but to increase it steadily as fast as possible. This was the key to wealth.

In the North American colonies there was more than enough land, to be sure; the problem was the lack of manpower. Population was so low that the threat of death and total destruction haunted the colonies for generations. The establishment of slavery enabled the settlers to increase both manpower and population.

Now the question arises: Why couldn't the colonists consider themselves wealthy by bringing Africans over without making them slaves? The goal of raising the population would have been achieved in either case and likewise the goal of increasing cash crop production. Besides the answers that the Europeans wished to maximize profits by minimizing labor expenses and that they derived a sense of spiritual election, there is an important cultural point. Neither the American Indians nor the Africans believed the European myth that wealth was embodied in cash and gold; they would not have labored to produce cash crops had they not been forced to do so. Without this belief the commercial aspect of the colonies would have fallen apart. The Indian and African ways of life were a direct threat to this ideology of material wealth as the be-all and end-all of civilization. The colonists therefore instituted strict segregation and endogamy so that the Indian and African attitudes of harmony with nature and unconcern for material wealth would not 'infect' the culture of European materialism. The power of the Indian culture in this regard was seen over and over again in the preference of whites to remain with adopted Indian tribes. In this case endogamy was essential, for if widespread intermarriage were permitted the whites would have lost a large portion of their settler population to another culture. There would have been no consensus in favor of capitalism or private ownership of land or private control of a labor force, and hence no prospects for the unlimited accumulation of private wealth.

By separating the European population from nature and from the nature-oriented cultures of the Indians and Africans, the colonies were able to maintain the myth that wealth exists only as gold or some other form of cash; that social life is dependent on cash; that civilization is for the purpose, and is defined by, the accumulation of cash. The Europeans feared the great powers of the Indians and Africans in working with nature and so they demonized those powers, just as they had earlier demonized people close to nature in Europe itself, namely midwives and other healers condemned as witches. The American colonists thereby continued the West's long-term development into an anti-nature culture.

There is no doubt that the Europeans brought sophisticated technology to the Americas. Sciences, arts and education, the fruits of the Renaissance, were aspects of European civilization worthy of being preserved. But the question is: Did the Europeans destroy a different form of technological evolution in the Americas? Was it possible that the Indians and the Africans were themselves involved in a different form of technological development that would have yielded its own special fruits? It is significant in this regard that with all their scientific and technological achievements the Europeans were far behind the Indians and Africans in food production skills and understanding of medicines;[210] even to this day some of the most learned experts of medicinal plants are not in the European scientific culture but among indigenous groups.[211]

Racism was a weapon in the European colonists' battle to protect the culture of greed from the strong influence of non-materialistic, pro-nature cultures. By identifying Africans and Indians with nature, and demonizing all three, the colonists were convincing the European newcomers and their progeny to reject the 'back-to-nature' culture of the Indians and Africans and to identify themselves only with the quest for wealth, with a definition of prosperity dependent not on nature but on cash.

'Wealth' itself as defined by western materialism is a myth; there is, in reality, no such thing as wealth, except insofar as nature, the planet, is rich in resources. Personal wealth is nothing more than an illusion; it can only be convincingly sustained by the control of the population. The more the people remain living in harmony with nature, desiring nothing of mythical wealth, the less wealthy the rulers will feel themselves to be; the more the people are crowded into the cities and join in the quest for personal wealth, turning their backs on the freedom and liberty of living in harmony with nature, the more wealthy and powerful the successful rulers will feel themselves to be. Personal wealth does not exist in pure nature; it can only exist in the context of the society. It requires an audience.

Therefore the racist philosophy of the Europeans in America had to achieve two difficult goals: 1) It had to justify the enslavement of Africans for the production of cash crops by arguing their inability to rise to the heights of civilization, their condemnation by God and their indelible association with base nature. 2) It had to prevent the Africans from actually reproducing their traditional pro-nature culture in America, while extracting from them all their skills in working with nature.

The wealthy Europeans wished to preclude an alternative paradigm that would offer working-class and middle-class whites the opportunity to abandon the wealth myth. As we shall see, quite apart from the anti-miscegenation laws, Europeans took draconian measures to dam what threatened to become a flood-tide of colonists crossing over to the Indian culture. Just as the Church feared the healing power of women, so too the Americans feared the economic and political power of the Indians and Africans.[212]

The early American colonists were therefore taking a risk when they brought the Africans to America. Here they had a large population of people who were in harmony with nature, completely unconcerned for the European myth of wealth, and therefore tremendously empowered to overthrow the wealth paradigm. Hence strict segregation was absolutely necessary, otherwise it is clear that the cultural ideas of the Africans and Indians would have convinced at least a significant number of whites of the falsity of the European wealth myth. As it was, a great deal of cultural interchange occurred, most importantly the conversion of whites to American Indian culture, which recent scholarship is only now beginning to reveal.

Conclusion

All that we see in Level Seven is not particularly new to discussions of the origin of racism. Materialism is the centerpiece of the Marxist analysis of society. Marx argued persuasively that social relations between individuals, communities and governments are determined not by ideas, emotions or spiritual truths but by the material aims of the people and the actions they take to achieve them. Therefore it is common for materialist social theorists to explain racism and slavery as the outcome of capitalism's insatiable greed for unlimited profits derived from slave labor. In fact, even most non-Marxist sociologists and historians tend to end their excavation of racism at this level. But we are not going to stop here. For there is yet another question that plainly needs to be answered: Why did the Europeans become so materialistic as to exercise this kind of horrific violence?

Level Eight: Waning of Christianity in Europe

In order to answer the question of violent materialism we must descend further to Level Eight. Here there has been much excavation by previous archeologists but the problem is that few, if any, have unearthed the connections between this level and the previous one.

We can start to answer this question by reviewing one simple and profound fact that we encountered earlier: Slavery never became widespread in Europe and never became the basis of agricultural or industrial production. This is not to say that slavery was completely nonexistent in Europe. It was practiced for fairly long periods in Scotland, Russia, southern Italy, Spain and Portugal in various forms, including serfdom, bonded labor for life, the bondage of children by their parents and the bondage of vagrants.

Throughout the history of the colonial period we find debates raging in Europe itself over whether or not the slave systems being used in the New World and producing such great profits would not also benefit the economic interests of Europeans in the Old World as well. The merchants were often keen to open this door. 'In 1547, the English parliament decided that vagrants should simply be sent into slavery. Two years later, the measure was revoked: parliament had been unable to agree who should receive these slaves and benefit from their labor, the state or private individuals! The idea was certainly in the air.'[213] And it remained current for more than two centuries thereafter.

In 1571-5 efforts to colonize Ulster in northern Ireland inspired some of the leaders to introduce slavery there as was practiced in the New World. In 1662 a proposal was made to reduce habitual thieves and criminals in England to slavery. Thieves and vagrants in Scotland had been forced into slavery since the 16th century and by 1606 in that country a law made even free laborers in the coal mines and saltworks bond slaves, perpetual and hereditary, so as to prevent the workers from suddenly shifting elsewhere for better wages. The law continued in force until 1799.[214]

Each of these steps was a small move towards greater institutionalization of slavery in Europe. Nevertheless, as Fernand Braudel has noted referring to slavery, 'Europe was for the most part free of this evil', for at each turn the advocates of slavery had to contend with Christian scruples against it.[215]

In 1698 the influential Scottish statesman Andrew Fletcher of Saltoun (1655-1716) criticized the notion that Christians could not be enslaved and proposed that 200,000 Scottish beggars be made slaves for life to men of means.[216]

Europe was restrained by its conscience. Christian morality and Christian law forbade slavery. As we have noted, Theodore Allen states: 'It had been received doctrine in England, at least since before the publication of Thomas Smith's *De Republic Anglorum* in 1583, that Christians could not hold Christians in bondage.'[217] Moreover, one of the two primary justifications for the enslavement of Africans in North America was that they were heathen and thus not under the protection of God's laws; the converse means, clearly, that those who were Christian were in fact protected and therefore not enslaveable. Although slavery made significant encroachments on European society, it was primarily on its periphery, both geographically and culturally; those who were furthest from the centers of Christian culture and from the capital cities, and who were least able to assert their rights because of their class disadvantages, were most vulnerable to the creeping cancer of slavery. But slavery's advocates were never able to establish it in the heart of Europe as a standard precisely because it was widely condemned as illegal, shunned as a violation of the Word of God, feared as sin bringing down God's wrath.

We see, then, that Europe was under the influence of two forces. The first was the older influence of Christian law. The second was the newer influence of the capitalist market that demanded ever greater and ever cheaper labor resources. The influence of Christianity remained strong in the cultural centers of Europe but weakened towards the periphery and was weakest of all outside the continent, along the trade routes to other continents and in the colonies. Capitalists and Christianity were therefore inversely related: merchants gained greater freedom, economic rewards and political power as the Church waned. Capitalists did not lament the increasing secularization of European society; it was in their interests to see the spiritual brotherhood of Christianity rolled back and replaced by the secular humanism inspired by the Greco-Roman cultural revival.

American slavery and racism were born out of this gradual rejection of spirituality. Secularization was not a parallel phenomenon in the evolution of slavery and racism; rather it was at the very heart of that evolution.

We can now recognize why the Europeans became so materialistic as to practice violent greed: Their illegal behavior was the product of the despiritualization of the society, the gradual collapse of religious life. The term 'religious life' refers not to the traditions, rituals, institutions and relatively superficial aspects of religion; rather it refers to the inner life of the human soul and the conception of society as the spiritual interaction between souls in relationships of love, compassion and unity. This is not to say that only a return to the closed-minded blind faith of the Middle Ages will solve the problem of racism. As we shall see, true religious life is not only compatible with but actually requires a balance with science and a willingness to evolve, to unfold human potentialities, to avoid cultural petrifaction and the over-emphasis of tradition.

We should also qualify the term 'despiritualization'. It does not mean that spirituality died in Europe and America. Rather, spirituality went underground. It was no longer accepted as a valid basis for decision-making in politics and social life; it was not a legitimate subject of discussion in the public arena. Spirituality was censored by the ruling authorities lest it interfere with the economic interests of the elite. Far from dying a quiet and convenient death, however, spirituality took on a new life as an underground movement, particularly among slaves and their champions, a movement that in time became so powerful that it shook the United States and nations beyond, changing its culture along the way, a movement that has yet to run its full course.

For the European, secularization meant the birth of humanity, the movement of the human being from a secondary, subservient role in the scheme of things to the center of the universe as the king of his own realm. It meant the European was no longer a sinner but an achiever, a creator. It meant the European's sacredness became, as it were, a free agent, no longer dependent on the clergy, the Church or even God Himself.

For African Americans and American Indians, however, secularization meant not more freedom of individual choice and will but less, less than what the Christian teachings would offer them, less than what Europeans prescribed for themselves. It meant despiritualization. It meant that whereas in the past the Church would have recognized their sacredness as children and servants of God, now their sacredness was denied. It meant their service was no longer to God but to the European man and no religious rights or laws could supersede this new secular order.

America's evolution was therefore far more than a secularizing process, for secularization implies the replacement of religious law and authority by civil law and authority under the control of the bourgeois class. Rather, what America engaged in was despiritualization, in which certain groups were transferred out of the potential protection of Christianity, out of the protection of civil government and relegated to a 'no-man's land' in which they literally became *no-men*. This is not secularization. This is the rejection of the sanctity of life. This is spiritual disenfranchisement. As such, the consequences of despiritualization are deep, far-reaching and, as would be expected, universal in the society, affecting all in America, Africa and Europe, black and white.

By the 16th and 17th centuries the corruption of the Catholic Church had progressed so far that its attractive force was well nigh spent. Although it still had tremendous moral authority and was able to provide a significant measure of protection to slaves – even while the Church itself owned slaves – nevertheless materialism was a creeping cancer within the ranks of the highest clergy. By the 18th century, writes Guenter Lewy, this process had gone so far that '173 of the 192 French bishops belonged to the nobility.' 'Around the year 1750 the average annual income of the bishops was estimated at about 37,500 livres, whereas that of the curés [local priests] was about 300 livres.' About half of the highest Church officers lived in Paris. One cardinal was known never to have visited his own archdiocese and some 'abbeys and cathedral chapters were headed by appointees of the crown, who were not even clerics; for them these establishments represented well-paying sinecures'.[218]

This materialism was central to the downfall of the spirit of brotherhood and social solidarity in European culture, which of course powerfully affected not only the development of dissenting religious groups but the American colonies as a whole. The conversion of whites to American Indian culture is very revealing in this regard. James Loewen writes:

> ... many white and black newcomers chose to live an Indian lifestyle. In his *Letters from an American Farmer*, Michel Guillaume Jean de Crévecoeur wrote, 'There must be in the Indians' social bond something singularly captivating, and far superior to be boasted of among us; for thousands of Europeans are Indians, and we have no examples of even one of those Aborigines having from choice become Europeans.' Crévecoeur overstated his case: as we know from Squanto's example, some Natives chose to live among whites from the beginning. The migration was mostly the other way, however. As Benjamin Franklin put it, 'No European who has tasted Savage Life can afterwards bear to live in our societies.'
>
> Europeans were always trying to stop the outflow. Hernando De Soto had to post guards to keep his men and women from defecting to Native societies. The Pilgrims so feared Indianization that they made it a crime for men to wear long hair. 'People who did run away to the Indians might expect very extreme punishments, even up to the death penalty,' if caught by whites. Nonetheless, right up to the end of independent Indian nationhood in 1890, whites continued to defect, and whites who lived an Indian lifestyle, such as Daniel Boone, became cultural heroes in white society.[219]

It is socially and spiritually significant that far fewer Indians chose the reverse path and converted to European culture. Indeed, the historical record clearly shows that the Europeanization of Native Americans, such as it exists, came about primarily by force and the imposition of laws and institutions that stripped away nearly everything on which the Native American culture was based, from language and religion to life itself. Yet even today Indians in the United States, although only a small surviving population of some 2.5 million – down from an estimated 10 to 20 million in North America at the time of first contact with Europeans – retain a deep loyalty to tribal ways and Indian identity.[220] The fact that, if given the choice, even Europeans did not want to be 'white' is one of the central proofs that

Europe's despiritualization afflicted Europeans measure for measure as it oppressed the indigenous peoples they colonized and enslaved.[221]

Converted whites found among the Indians love and harmony, whereas among their own people they found excessive materialism. Surely it would seem a gross exaggeration to say that European society in the 16th and 17th centuries was loveless. Was not Christianity the very heart and soul of society in that period, much more so than today? Were not people marrying and raising children, building coherent communities and carrying out vast projects that required the brotherly unity of large numbers of people? No doubt most of these assertions are true. But on closer examination we see that while Christian love was an important and even defining factor in European culture, it was far from dominant and was in fact rapidly waning.

Consider this second example: In the late 1600s a moral controversy arose between the Dutch Reformed Church and the Dutch East India Company in the Cape Colony. The Church forbade enslavement of Christianized Africans and Asians, yet the Company enslaved them nonetheless. Was the Company punished by the Church? Was it excommunicated? Was it disciplined or brought to heel? No. On the contrary, the Company forced the Church to accept a new way, not vice versa. It was the Church that was effectively threatened with punishment, the Church was altered, the Church was disciplined. It was in effect a second Reformation, this time not by radical clerics but by businessmen. It was the death of Christianity in the Cape Colony.[222]

These two examples illustrate that Christianity was fatefully transformed from a practice into an identity. It was no longer a process of the soul's enlightenment and therefore accessible to all. It was now an inheritance, a legacy exclusively owned by certain groups. Colonists did not want the natives in Ireland or North America to become Christianized, to share in the universal Christian fellowship; the more they were identified with heathenism, the easier it was to exploit them.[223] Christianity was no longer an evangelical, public movement but a privatized club. It was not a spiritual influence at work in the world but a privately-owned birthright. Christianity became a material thing. Even in recent times this characterization applies, for Gordon Allport's research showed that a large percentage of churchgoers looked to the Church primarily for material and social advantages and benefits.[224]

Slavery's Antecedents

The historical record shows, as we have seen, that the extreme violence of American slavery did not suddenly appear full-blown as a spontaneous reaction to the supposed repulsiveness of Africans. Rather it was the descendant of what was, by the beginning of the African slave trade in the 16th century, a fairly long history – stretching back to the 11th century – of extreme violence employed by Christian Europe to achieve religious and political goals. By tracing the history of this violence as it emerged in such stark contrast to Christian teachings, we can expose the roots of racism.

The early colonists in North America were a brave, dedicated and self-sacrificing group. Their heroism as pioneers in an unknown land has been well documented. Yet at the same time, as we have seen, their society had a persistent shadow: It was a society that was cold, harsh and even brutal, to the point where a significant percentage of their own members preferred to live with the American Indians. The Christianity of the New England colonists, as portrayed by Hawthorne's stunning novel *The Scarlet Letter* and as manifested in the Salem witch-hunts, was a perversion of the compassion taught by Jesus.

Christianity had become affected by a long process of secularization and despiritualization. Although its absolute origins are difficult if not impossible to specify, for our discussion we may argue that the process of secularization had its beginnings in the Crusades against the Muslims. Pope Urban II, in calling for this 'holy war', for the first time placed the whole weight and moral authority of the Church behind an action that was directly in violation of Christian principles as taught by Jesus and His disciples. The medieval world was, of course, one of great violence and conflict but this action of the pope officially identified the Church with systematic, legitimized and sanctified social violence. Moreover, some research has pinpointed the Crusades as being the origin of the identity between dark skin and moral difference or enmity in the European mind.[225]

Indeed, Africa as a whole later became seen as a legitimate target of economic exploitation – specifically the capturing of slaves – because Islam had succeeded in pushing Christianity out of the field throughout the regions of the continent known to 15th-century Portuguese traders. A. J. R. Russell-Wood argues that on this basis gradually the Portuguese changed their attitude towards the world and Christianity became militarized. He refers here to India but his analysis applies to Africa as well:

> [The] Portuguese military presence became justifiable as a deterrent to non-Christians who might otherwise spread doctrinal errors. Portuguese attacks became Christian offensives designed to reduce territory held by non-Christians. Christ ceased to be a mystical entity: He took on the guise of a warrior God in whose service the distinction between good and evil became blurred. Such an ideology justified both initiating military actions and securing strong economic bases. To sustain war against the infidel and to bolster the overall economic fortunes of Christendom mandated a spice

trade in Portuguese hands. Pillage, piracy, and wanton destruction were justified as depriving unbelievers of material resources which might other-wise be used against Christianity.[226]

Religious goals were not the only motivation for the Crusades. These were wars in which knights could become the rulers of principalities in the Middle East. Many a prize in land and treasure was to be had. Even the recruitment process for the first Crusades was tinged by material-ism: Itinerant preachers who gave sermons in cities throughout Europe to inspire enthusiasm for the Crusades were unable to attract significant audiences without offering indulgences to those who merely attended.[227]

From the Crusades the process advanced to another stage: Whereas from 1095 until 1270 the object of Church warfare was the foreign infidel, from the 13th century on the targets were in Europe itself and, most significantly, many of them were people who considered themselves Christians. The inquisitions systematized this use of force from 1231 against the Cathars, Albigensians and other perceived heretics and enemies, including Jews. While the object of this warfare was ostensibly the purification of the Church from heretical elements, much of the motivation lay in the desire of the northern French nobility to seize properties in the South. 'From the outset purely political interests were intermixed with the religious.'[228] The materialism of these crusades within Christendom echoed the materialism of the foreign crusades.

In a very real sense this was civil war within the Church. The heretical sects took up arms, built great castles and defended themselves to the death over a number of generations. A. S. Turberville describes the dramatic results:

> The Albigensian wars were the most successful attempt to extirpate heresy known in history. They were successful because they were utterly ruthless and included wholesale massacres. When the town of Béziers fell [1209], it is said that twenty thousand of its inhabitants were slaughtered. There were good catholics as well as Cathari among the populace of the place; but the story goes that when Arnaud of Citeaux was asked whether the catholics were to be spared, in his anxiety lest a single heretic should escape by pre-tending orthodoxy, he replied, 'Kill them all, for God knows His own.'

It was indeed a Pyrrhic victory, for Turberville concludes: 'When the crusaders appeared in Languedoc, toleration vanished out of Western Christendom.'[229]

The next target of holy war did not, and could not, respond with violence in self-defense: Christians in Europe accused as witches, most of whom were poor women of middle age or older. To this subject we shall return presently.

The victimization of poor and marginalized women was in turn followed by the victimization of the poor in general. For many centuries vagrants were considered liable to extreme punishment throughout Europe. Their condition originated in the transition from a rural, agricultural economy to a bourgeois economy. Fernand Braudel writes:

> What appears to have happened in the West was that the great division of labor between town and countryside that took place in the eleventh and twelfth centuries, had left a permanent mass of unfortunates unprovided for, with nothing left to do. The fault lay in society no doubt and its usual evils, but it was perhaps even more to be found in the economy, which was powerless to create full employment. Many of the unemployed eked out a living somehow, finding a few hours of work here and there, a temporary shelter. But the others – the infirm, the old, those who had been born and bred on the road – had very little contact with normal working life. This particular hell had its own circles, labeled in contemporary vocabulary as pauperdom, beggary and vagrancy.

The key point here is that attitudes towards vagrants became hardened, illustrating the waning of religious feelings.

> In the old days, the beggar who knocked at the rich man's door was regarded as a messenger from God, and might even be Christ in disguise. But such feelings of respect and compassion were disappearing. Idle, good for nothing and dangerous, was the verdict passed on the destitute by a society terrified by the rising tide of mendicancy.[230]

Vagrants were subject to dire forms of punishment. They could be publicly tortured and branded at the hands of the executioner and, if caught a second time, hanged without trial or sent to the galleys. By the 16th century, however, the idea arose that it would be more economical to set them to work as slaves rather than have them beaten, banished or executed. As we have seen, it thus became common for vagrants to be rounded up and shipped off to salt works, coal mines, colonies and other places where cheap labor was sorely needed. They had no rights and were bound to work virtually as chattel slaves for life.

In its earliest years the Christian community did not employ violence in order to enforce discipline and maintain purity of doctrine. But gradually the use of physical force and punishments became accepted, particularly from the time of Constantine (ruled 306–37) and the merging of the secular powers of the Empire with the spiritual authority of the Church. 'The Church became possessed of all the enormous power of the imperial authority,' Turberville states, and soon thereafter strong punishments became accepted as part of the Church's method. Even the early controversy between the Arians and the Trinitarians was essentially a war between the two factions involving tremendous violence. 'The Christians, said Julian the Apostate [ruled 361–3], treated each other like wild beasts. The punishments inflicted by one party upon the other included imprisonment, flogging, torture, death.'[231]

From Leo I, who held the papacy from 440 to 461, until the 11th century the fever of violent Christianity subsided as Europe's masses became influenced by Christian teachings and organized under Church authority. But with the revival of independent thought and contact with the Islamic world, new and hot controversies arose that once again disturbed the unity of Christendom. This time the violence became permanent and systematic on a global scale. The punishments for heresy thus grew more severe, frequent and widespread over time: from brotherly admonishment and persuasion in the time of St Paul, to banishment and confiscation of property in the days of St Augustine, to burning at the stake and torture until death. By the 12th century Christendom's capital punishment was 'a particularly terrible kind of death . . . this idea being perhaps derived from the fact that Roman law had at different times meted out this doom for certain kinds of heretics, particularly Manichaeans, and other offenders, such as sorcerers and witches'.[232] With the bull entitled *Ad extirpanda*, issued by Innocent IV in 1252, the systemization and legalization of the Church's violence against heretics was complete. Thus the years that saw the germination of the Renaissance also saw a revival of the dark side of Roman culture. H. R. Trevor-Roper characterizes the Renaissance as a period when 'pagan mystery-religion' was renewed.[233] The true spirituality and brotherhood of the Roman Catholic Church were becoming eclipsed. The ecclesiastical authorities rationalized their return to Roman violence by arguing that heresy itself was the worst of all possible deeds and the need to protect the Church from it warranted the use of any and all means, which in the end, they claimed, would be the greatest blessing to humanity.[234] They cited the New Testament in defense of this violence, as Christ said:

> If a man abide not in me, he is cast forth as a branch, and is withered; and men gather them and cast them into the fire, and they are burned.[235]

Although the British Isles were not ravaged by the inquisitions (nor by the later witch-hunts) to the same degree as in continental Europe, the English were nonetheless fully influenced by these violent movements. For in building their colonies in Ireland and later in the New World the English were consciously following the example of the Spanish and Portuguese. The Iberians' use of violence in the American colonies was similar to that of the inquisitions because it was, in essence, the continuation of the inquisition. As we have noted, the inquisition and subsequent wars against the heretics of southern France were, for northern French nobility, a business opportunity which they did not fail to seize. With gold and silver to be had for the taking, the Spanish and Portuguese had a ready-made justification: If we conquer in the name of protecting and propagating the faith of Christ, we are blessed and we prosper. Thus, from Columbus's first contacts with the Indians of Hispaniola, the accumulation of wealth was built on the same treatment of heretics: torture and execution. Bartolomé de las Casas (1474–1566), in carefully observing the Spaniards, found that they 'thought nothing of knifing Indians by tens and twenties and of cutting slices off them to test the sharpness of their blades'. They were motivated by 'insatiable greed' to the point of 'killing, terrorizing, afflicting, and torturing the native peoples' with 'the strangest and most varied new methods of cruelty'. The systematic violence was aimed at preventing 'Indians from daring to think of themselves as human beings'. 'My eyes have seen these acts so foreign to human nature, and now I tremble as I write.'[236] The great similarity between these acts of the Iberians and those of the Europeans in North America to establish and maintain chattel slavery leads us to conclude that the former set the standard for the latter, that however wide their theological differences their colonial enterprises were bitter fruits on the same tree.

WITCH-HUNTS

The bitter fruits of the inquisitions, and of the enslavement and genocide in the Americas, were soon to be joined by another, one that was even more revealing of the relationship between spiritual corruption and race-based slavery. Las Casas died just at the dawn of the European witch-craze, a period of two centuries, roughly from 1560 to 1760. It was a time in which all that Las Casas saw, all that the Catholic Church had systematized with regard to heretics, came to its ultimate conclusion, the nadir of violence in the name of Christianity in Europe. Perhaps more than any other form of persecution in Christendom, the witch-craze exemplifies the use of accusations of heresy to justify violent greed and stands out as the immediate precursor of the extreme form of slavery in North America.

In the foothills of the Pyrenees in the southwest of France lies Carcassonne, justly famed as one of the best-preserved cities of medieval Europe. Surrounded by a massive crenellated wall, its numerous towers topped by black cones fulfill a stereotypical image of a medieval castle upon a hill,[237] its narrow and crooked lanes are crowded with centuries-old dwellings, still inhabited, and with tourists enjoying a rare, if somewhat commercialized, taste of a complete medieval environment. It is a city that remains foreboding in its starkness, its pure utility as a fortress in a turbulent age. But Carcassonne was not only a defense against violence; it was itself a source of violence, the site of a turning point in European history, the birthplace of a violent movement without parallel in all Christendom. For it was in Carcassonne in 1450 that the Dominican monk, Jean Vineti, in his capacity as inquisitor, produced a document entitled *Tractatus contra Daemonum Invoctores*. This scholarly work became the basis for the Roman Catholic Church's legalization of the systematic hunt for witches.

A key point sets the historical context: The Church of Rome in the Middle Ages had consistently prohibited the persecution of alleged witches and furthermore categorically denied their existence.[238] This fact in itself provides further evidence of the success of early Christianity as a realized ideal in Europe. By Vineti's time, however, passions had become inflamed and he used lawyerly skills, the power of the written word, to change the Church's stance. His work constituted one of the clearest indications of the gradual decline of Christian morality and the rise of violent intolerance in the Church. This, of course, was in the wake of several centuries of the Church's use of extreme violence in inquisitions. Moreover, negative stereotypes of women were already firmly established in the wars against heresy.[239] The method was still the same – except in certain countries like England, where torture was not permitted – but the object was now different: instead of Jews, Muslims and heretics, the Church identified people within the mainstream Christian community itself as the fomenters of spiritual discord, as bearers of evil, as the allies of the devil.

Vineti's *Tractatus* spawned a veritable flood of scholarly work. The revival of Greek and Roman scholarship, and the Church's passion to maintain its purity, conspired to produce an entire genre of works that used classical reasoning and research into Roman law to justify what was obviously contrary to the teachings of Jesus. The revival of Roman law in the 12th century was a highly significant turning point in the history of modern Europe that released the elite from the moral restrictions of Christianity. Barstow states that it also enabled the introduction of the official use of torture into Christendom; it was a legal system that 'rendered European justice more rational but less humane'. One of the main reasons why the witch-hunts were less virulent in England, she argues, was 'its lack of Roman law and an inquisition, thereby permitting a prohibition on torture'.[240]

Scholars reveled in the power bequeathed to them by the philosophers and historians of ancient Greece and Rome, a power that allowed them to make of the Old and New Testaments what they would. They became as prophets and messengers in their own right. Tragically, in taking on the prophets' mantle, these scholars outlined a path to salvation that was paved in the blood of innocents. In reviving the scholarship of Rome they also raised the specter of Roman tyranny, which is fully described in the many treatises and encyclopedias produced on the nature, detection and punishment of witchcraft. One of the first historians in recent times to study this subject systematically was H. R. Trevor-Roper, who wrote of his groundbreaking work as if returning from a perilous and harrowing journey.

> To read these encyclopedias of witchcraft is a horrible experience. Each seems to outdo the last in cruelty and absurdity. Together they insist that every grotesque detail of demonology is true, that skepticism must be stifled, that skeptics and lawyers who defend witches are themselves witches, that all witches, 'good' or 'bad', must be burnt, that no excuse, no extenuation is allowable, that mere denunciation by one witch is sufficient evidence to burn another.[241]

The only solution for the epidemic of witches plaguing Europe, these scholars affirmed, was the application of greater punishment. Trevor-Roper found that throughout their writings they all offered the same solution: 'there must be fire! fire! fire!' To flog a child, for example, as she watched her mother burn at the stake was simply insufficient; better to destroy all witches and their children at once. One scholar, the French lawyer Henri Boguet (1550–1619), exclaimed that witches were a 'miserable and damnable vermin' that was 'multiplying on the land like caterpillars in a garden . . . I wish they all had but one body, so that we could burn them all at once, in one fire!'[242]

Trevor-Roper remarked, 'When we read these monstrous treatises, we find it difficult to see their authors as human beings. And yet, when we look at their biographies, what harmless, scholarly characters they turn out to be!' While their written works were filled with calls for the most horrific violence in the name of protecting Christianity and with images expressing obsessive preoccupation with the human body, these excellent scholars led lives of tranquil elegance, contemplation of nature and art, courtesy and tender consideration for others. One of them, the Jesuit Martin Antoine del Rio (1551–1608),

> had provided himself with a specially constructed combination of desk and tricycle in order to dart, with all his papers, from folio to folio in great libraries. Thanks to such labor-saving devices, he produced an edition of

Seneca at the age of nineteen, citing 1100 authorities, and was hailed by no less a scholar than Justus Lipsius as 'the miracle of our age'. He knew nine languages, was marvelously chaste . . . was devoted to the Virgin Mary, was feared as much by heretics as Hector by the Greeks or Achilles by the Trojans, and died, almost blind with the intensive study which he had devoted to the detection and exposure of witches.[243]

Another scholar, this one Protestant, 'would live to a ripe old age and look back on a meritorious life in the course of which he had read the Bible from cover to cover fifty-three times, taken the sacrament every week, greatly intensified the methods and efficacy of torture, and procured the death of 20,000 persons'.[244]

The scholars behind the witch-craze had plunged into the ocean of Roman thought and culture and come up with the treasures of that world, ignoring the spiritual truths uttered by the simple Prophet of Nazareth who, after all, had penned no book Himself. The spiritual life, the soul, was no longer the center of consciousness. They missed the forest for the trees. They were dazzled by the glories of pagan Rome and the power of the iconic word. They were quick to condemn anyone who opposed the witch-hunts and defended the rights of Christians as witches too, accomplices of the devil, servants of Satan denying the one true God. Yet the greatest irony was that these witch-hunters themselves had abandoned the teachings of Christ and based all their scholarly and political life on the writings of the pagan and often materialistic philosophers of Rome.

Now we can see the parallel between these scholars and those who later wrote the marvelously persuasive tracts and books to defend the institution of slavery in America. Slavery's apologists were the epitome of the scholarly gentleman, highly educated, urbane, pious and loyal, the model citizen and yet what they advocated with their pens was exactly the opposite of what Jesus taught. They were able to do this because they followed the example of the classical scholars of Europe, who in turn were following the example of Romans untouched by the spirit of Christianity and immersed in a morass of materialism.

American slavery and racism on the one hand and European witch-hunts and misogyny on the other are historical twins. Their similarities are too strong to be ignored and yet most students of racism have not noticed them, perhaps because of the overwhelming pressure of academic culture to specialize rather than synthesize. As a result, we have in a way fetishized and mystified racism and slavery, made them seem to be unique and 'peculiar' – as in the title of Kenneth Milton Stampp's classic, *The Peculiar Institution: Slavery in the Ante-Bellum South* – whereas the broader historical vision shows that they descended directly from a culture of violence and exclusion that had long been established in the very heart of the Christian world. In this broader context American slavery was not distinguished by its ideology so much as by the skin color and large number of its victims. We have been blinded by color and hence fetishized it; we have been deceived into thinking that color and Africanness are the keys to understanding slavery and racism, whereas these are only incidental. For example, Joel Kovel, in *White Racism*, bases much of his theory on the equating of black skin with feces in the racist mind.[245] However true this may be, ultimately it is only an epiphenomenon, not the heart of the matter. Race and skin color are nothing but red herrings. The same attitudes and actions were practiced in Europe in the two centuries bracketing the establishment of the North American colonies but there the victims were neither dark-skinned nor African, but European women. Once we realize and accept this parallel we begin to broaden our conception of slavery, to see it as a part of a wider context that is not specific to any particular 'race', nationality or even gender. In fact, all that these victims have in common is that they were treated the same way by the same group of people: with extreme and unjust violence by European males for the purpose of material and political gain. This is yet another reason why the study of racism and slavery needs to focus not on the African slaves but on the mentality and motives of the European males who 'owned' them.

In the period of the witch-hunts European men associated several powerful negative qualities with witches in particular and, more importantly, with all women. They believed women were overly sexual and, indeed, were unable to control their sexual desires. They believed women were susceptible to the seductions of the devil and would even become Satan's sexual partners. They believed women were often guilty of using witchcraft and black arts to accomplish evil goals, including the harming of the most pure and innocent – children. They believed women were capable of conspiring with Satan to overthrow Christianity and deliver the world to his sovereignty. They believed that the bodies of women were dirty, foul, giving off noisome odors, spreading fatal diseases. They believed that women were evil, were corrupters, were the cause of all misfortunes in society, were the opponents of Jesus Christ.[246]

Students of African American history will readily recognize that virtually all of these powerful charges against women in the two centuries of the witch-hunts were neatly projected, with only slight variation, onto the personality and physical body of the African slave in America. An even broader look at European history will show that these charges, almost in identical form, were, in the two centuries before the witch-hunts, leveled against Jews, Muslims and Christian heretics in Europe. We must conclude then that the ideology of slavery, the cultural foundation for its legalization and political enforcement in America, was not an original creation of American colonial society. The oppression of sub-groups had been a theme central to Christian culture in Europe since at least the beginning of the inquisitions; race-based slavery in America was but a variation.

Yet one distinction between the witch-hunts and American slavery is important: Whereas witches were executed, slaves were kept alive for their labor – or rather were killed slowly by hard labor. American slavery was European anti-witch fervor grafted onto the new capitalist program of gaining ever-increasing profits. Why kill a constructed enemy of Christianity when he can be forced to labor, ending eventually in his death and with the bonus of great profits?

The goal of gaining wealth and material advantage, seen in the Crusades against the Muslims and later against the heretics, was also common in the witch-hunts. Male accusers benefited not through the labor of the accused but through the confiscation of their property. Citing recent research, Barstow states that women in New England 'who were inheritors were at high risk for accusation' of being a witch.[247] State and ecclesiastical authorities gained materially in another way: By persecuting witches as scapegoats in times of social and economic instability they consolidated their political authority and power.[248] American slavery likewise created Africans as religious and state enemies so as to own their physical property – that is, their bodies – and to consolidate state power and authority. The distinctive twist or 'peculiarity' of slavery was the use of the lives of the condemned to generate new, capitalistic wealth. Whereas wealth derived from the witch-hunts was static and finite, the wealth derived from slavery was dynamic and unlimited. The economic system behind each was different but the culture and ideology were the same. The outcome of the witch-hunts was about 100,000 executed victims, 85 per cent of whom were women;[249] the transfer of victims' properties to influential men; the long-term terrorization of the entire population of women in Europe; the strengthening of European patriarchy; and the uprooting of the burgeoning culture of women's knowledge and skill in health care and experiential knowledge of natural phenomena in the forests, meadows, agricultural fields and the human body. The outcome of slavery, in economic terms, far transcended the witch-hunts' results. It was a breathtaking accumulation of wealth and ultimately global political power. In this perspective the witch-hunts – and the preceding inquisitions – were a preparation for slavery.

The systematic witch-hunts in Europe and the American colonies completed the foundation of the despiritualization process. Among the most defenseless people in society, the women accused as witches were the easiest targets of violence. Their torture and execution signalized that Christianity was willing and able to apply violent force without scruple or limitation and to do so according to a long-term, seemingly permanent legal doctrine approved by the highest Church authorities. Thereafter, the potential use of violence for the enslavement of Africans and Indians, and the destruction of Indian communities in order to obtain land, did not pique the conscience of the colonial Protestant Christians because it was the letter of the Church's law, the Protestants having adopted wholesale the Roman Catholic culture of holy war. The 'fire! fire! fire!' of the inquisitions and the witch-hunts made slavery look mild and therefore acceptable.

The European populace was thereby accustomed to extreme violence. Hence the Europeans in America believed that society was not properly established and maintained until extreme public violence was systematized. As Barstow writes, 'public witch executions were more even than a purging: they affirmed that the ruler who ordered them was godly, and even more important, that his power was greater than the forces of evil.'[250] Otherwise the Church would be in jeopardy, chaos would ensue, and freedom and equality would allow the devil to enter the community.[251] Although the bourgeoisie in America were a new class, which at every opportunity asserted its independence from the old feudal order and the Church and which jealously guarded its growing domain of private wealth, yet its method was nonetheless not its own, for it inherited and practiced with unprecedented zeal and scientific systemization the Church's harsh and inhumane attitudes against those considered profane.

CRIMINALIZATION OF MASSES

'By the witch hunt,' Ann Llewellyn Barstow states, 'European women as a group were criminalized for the first time.' She also concludes 'that ruling-class European men looked at and treated their women basically as they did their African slaves and Indian serfs and as they had treated Jews and heretics before them, namely, with increasing violence.'[252] Trevor-Roper wrote similarly, identifying the witch-hunts, the inquisitions and modern racism as an organic whole.[253] The period of European history stretching from the first Crusade in 1095 until the establishment of slavery in North America involved the gradual evolution of a process by which a number of different groups in Europe were criminalized by the Church, the state or both: Muslims, Jews, heretics, women, lepers, male homosexuals, female prostitutes, usurers, the mentally disturbed, mutes, idiots, the poor in general, Gypsies and finally, in the colonies, Indians, Africans and other indigenous peoples. R. I. Moore notes that the intolerance of Christianity began with the conversion of the Emperor Constantine, who applied the power of the state to the enforcement of religious orthodoxy. Punishments included loss of civil rights, prohibition from holding public office, coercion and forced conversion. This was consolidated by the Emperor Justinian (ruled from

527 to 565), who, in promulgating the systemic Roman law that was to serve as the basis of an increasingly secular Europe, 'made right belief a condition of citizenship.'[254] The 'machinery' for the hunting and prosecution of heretics devised by the Church at the Fourth Lateran Council of November 1215, argues Moore, 'was to prove adaptable to a much wider variety of victims than the heretics for whom it was designed.'[255] The Church had become transformed from a refuge and cradle of civilization into a social system that, in the name of reform, imposed discipline, punishment and even death upon criminalized groups.

But as the evolution progressed, the protagonist was no longer the Church *per se* but the secularized male, particularly the merchant class. The merchants applied the same concept of discipline and control over not only the members of the Church but the entire world. In the name of reforming all the peoples of the world, and all of nature, they set out for distant shores, applied a strict discipline upon themselves and upon others, and recognized and proved their success by the wealth they accumulated. Moore explains:

> the eleventh and twelfth centuries saw what has turned out to be a permanent change in Western society. Persecution became habitual. That is to say not simply that individuals were subject to violence, but that deliberate and socially sanctioned violence began to be directed, *through established governmental, judicial and social institutions*, against groups of people defined by general characteristics such as race, religion or way of life; and that membership of such groups in itself came to be regarded as justifying these attacks.

In short, around 1100 'Europe *became* a persecuting society.'[256] This is the exact opposite of the New Testament's teachings. The waning of Christianity is evident here. For who can imagine that Christianity would have spread so far and fast across the Roman Empire had its message been conveyed through such systematic persecution?

Negative Christianity

If the inquisitions and the witch-hunts had not existed, would slavery in America have occurred? Of course, no answer can be scientifically proved and yet the question helps us clarify the relationship. What we are arguing here is that at the very least the inquisitions and witch-hunts, while perhaps not directly causing North American slavery, provided the spiritual environment and social conditions in which extreme slavery could exist. These three movements are so similar that one cannot but think they are all forms of the same content. In all three the central argument justifying the inhumane treatment of other people is a religious doctrine. It is a belief that, as Barstow puts it, to be godly is to be anti-Satan – a belief we have seen is a substitute for the true teachings of Christianity.[257] As we have noted, Max Weber wrote that within Calvinism the 'consciousness of divine grace of the elect and holy was accompanied by an attitude toward the sin of one's neighbor, not of sympathetic understanding based on consciousness of one's own weakness, but of hatred and contempt for him as an enemy of God bearing the signs of eternal damnation'.[258] This interpretation of Christianity defines it as a negative program to be *against* something, rather than the original teachings of Jesus to be *for* love and spirituality. Therefore Weber's thesis that the Protestant's material success assures spiritual election has its converse: material failure spells spiritual doom.

OPPOSITION TO THE DEVIL

The history of witch-hunts helps explain why racists in North America have until recently tended to be religious. The religious culture in Europe of the 16th through the 18th centuries made a virtue of suspicion and taught that the heart and soul of faith was to seek out, condemn and destroy the devil. This was a natural inheritance of the Crusades, one of the first great concerted efforts of a self-conscious Latin Christian culture in Europe, a defining action that proclaimed to the world and to the Europeans themselves the identity of European Christendom. It was an identity defined by the negation of Islam, of Judaism, of infidels, of heretics, rather than a positive identity based on the positive actions prescribed in the New Testament. Just as the witch-hunters defined their faith through hunting the devil in the form of the female witch, medieval Christianity had earlier defined itself through hunting the devil in the form of the Muslim and Jewish infidel.

Opposition to the devil, which we can term 'negative Christianity', was at the heart of the ideology of colonialism. By the time the colonies were being established, Europeans had long become accustomed to the definition of religion as war against the devil, a definition in which love and spirituality had little or no place. Colonists justified enslavement and exploitation not as a means to bring love but as a means to purge the heathen, whether by conversion or by destruction. Therefore the engine of capitalism was a vast, globe-spanning weapon, which Europeans regarded as a righteous tool in a righteous war. Materialistic culture was and is essentially a negative enterprise because at its heart is not a will to create but a will to consume and destroy. He who would oppose it would stop the progress of Christianity's war against the devil and thus must be numbered amongst the devil's supporters.

TWISTING THE OLD TESTAMENT

Another of negative Christianity's pillars was the tendency to ignore the teachings of Jesus and base Christian life and discipline on an interpretation of God in the Old Testament: a Creator perceived as harsh, strict and even violent. The compassion essential to Jesus' teachings was replaced by a new method for achieving purity: the righteousness of wrath mirroring that of God. Clearly the meekness and compassion of Jesus were unsuitable to a generation of new capitalists eager to enter the wide-open field of profit-making. The extreme discipline necessary to wring profits from large labor-intensive agricultural enterprises necessitated a conception of Christianity that supported the righteousness of violence and punishment. The New Testament was out and an interpretation of the Old Testament was in. Slavery's defenders consistently referred to passages in the Old Testament, especially those dealing with the laws on slavery.[259] And they neglected the laws promoting the Golden Rule:

> For the LORD your God is God of gods, and Lord of lords, a great God, a mighty, and a terrible, which regardeth not persons, nor taketh reward: He doth execute the judgment of the fatherless and widow, and loveth the stranger, in giving him food and raiment. Love ye therefore the stranger: for ye were strangers in the land of Egypt.[260]

The extreme inhumanity of American slavery cannot be attributed to the slave laws of ancient Jewish society which specifically prohibited such practices as the separation of parents from children, husband from wife.[261]

Throughout most of America's history Christianity has been, among blacks, a religion of joy, salvation and release,[262] while among racially-motivated whites a religion of exclusion, of suspicion, of fear, of condemnation, of the nearness of the devil. This negative interpretation of Jesus' teachings is not true Christianity but a substitute. This is the essence shared by the inquisitions, witch-hunts and slavery. Anti-Satanism paved the way for Christian leaders to be anti-anything and anti-anyone, the opposite of Jesus' teachings calling the believers to love everyone, even sinners and enemies.

FROM SPIRIT TO BODY

A third pillar of negative Christianity was its emphasis on the human body. Protestantism emerged in 16th-century Europe as a reaction to profound corruption and materialism in the Church of Rome. A century later, in the midst of the European witch-hunts, the Protestant American colonies themselves began gradually to adopt a profoundly materialistic interpretation of Christianity. The significance of negative Christianity is not simply that the colonists exchanged true Christianity for making money. Negative Christianity was also about something far less abstract than 'profits': violence. It viewed human beings as physical bodies. Negative Christianity began and ended with the body: the body of the Jew, the Muslim, the European woman, the African. It defined religion as the management of human bodies. Souls were now empty symbols; they were no longer the true referents for action. Inquisitors, witch-hunters and slave masters did not deal with and act upon souls – regardless of their rhetoric. The target and anvil of their actions was always the human body. The clergy reduced the soul and its health, destiny and station to a physical quality: a telltale 'devil's teat' or, in the later development of racism, skin color. It was not just any kind of body but one, conveniently, that a white male generally could not have: one possessing qualities of blackness or femininity.[263]

Clearly this was directly contrary to the teachings of Jesus, who repeatedly rejected any lasting or real value in materiality and who specifically referred to the physical body as a hindrance to the achievement of the true goal, spirituality. Negative Christianity's focus on the human body constituted another aspect of the moral collapse of the Christian leadership in Europe.

THE ROOTS OF SYMBOLIC IMMORTALITY

A fourth pillar of negative Christianity was the quest for symbolic immortality by material means. Violence against the body in negative Christianity was a method whereby ecclesiastical and secular elites gained wealth and political power. But from a spiritual perspective we need to ask more probing questions, and specifically: Why did they desire such material gain?

As we have seen, material success in the world has symbolic meaning. Like negative Christianity it is a substitute for something. The possession of wealth in a materialistic society creates in the people a sense of euphoria, of transcendent victory, of spiritual election and ultimately the magnification of the self into immortality. Robert Jay Lifton argues that the actions of individuals in life are often motivated by a desire to extend and enhance life. We wish to live life to the fullest, savor each day in comfort and enjoyment. In the back of our minds we know that our physical death is inevitable. Ultimately, Lifton argues, we seek to escape from death altogether through symbolic means. We attempt to create immortality through what we hope will be enduring monuments: our work, our children, our name. Wealth, fame and status are used to create not only an enhanced life but an escape from death.[264]

Erich Fromm also argued that the fear of death is one of the key motivators in human action. We feel that we are alone in life, and we face death alone, and therefore we seek to overcome this loneliness by uniting with others. The problem is that unless we have a spiritual attitude our unity with others becomes an unhealthy attempt to escape reality. We do not wish to 'die' to ourselves by leaving a comfortable social environment and moving ahead to something unfamiliar. We are afraid to expand our horizons, to grow, to die to our old selves and be reborn into new experiences. The child seeks safety and security in clinging to the parent; the adult seeks it in clinging to life and running from death symbolically. We build ourselves as eternal: massive mansions and memorial structures; fame; male children to perpetuate our name; works of art; political power. We reject the coming of physical death. The body becomes central and all-consuming. Fromm describes power as a technique that appears to succeed by enhancing the life of the destroyer, by juxtaposing the living self against the destroyed other, a contest which reveals the other infinitely dead and thus the destroyer infinitely alive.[265]

The question then arises: Why did the religious leaders seek symbolic immortality? If we accept the interpretations of Lifton and Fromm the answer is clear and is shown in the historical record of clerical cupidity leading to Martin Luther's rebellion: They did not believe that the immortality of the soul was true. They had no faith in the existence of an eternal life. They were not convinced of a transcendent existence. They called themselves Christians, and they considered themselves true believers, but in reality they did not follow the teachings of Jesus because they did not believe in them. They – not the slaves, not the witches, not the heretics and the adherents of other religions – were the true infidels. Christianity had long ago lost influence among the ranks of the powerful clergy.

The Waning of Morality

If Europe's Christian ideal of brotherly and spiritual unity was only imperfectly achieved, what then was the reality? Europe, as any complex society, came into existence through relations of mutual association and identity that endured over centuries. Conversely, it began to disintegrate when relations of mutual association terminated or became transient. Social problems can be defined as the symptoms of the gradual transformation of association into dissociation, of unity into disunity and the decay of the laws on which mutual association and mutual identity are based.

The popular view of social problems is that they are caused by willful actions: crime by immoral actors, poverty by oppression or laziness, war by hatred or greed, and so on. From this perspective one logically concludes that the solution lies in arresting and subduing the offending cause, be it an individual, class or institution. Were we to seek the causes of immorality, we might identify alcoholism, drug abuse, negative images in the mass media, materialism and the like. This would not be fruitful since these phenomena are themselves symptoms of social decay. Systematic analysis suggests that rather than seeking an isolated 'cause' of each separate social problem, we would gain a truer understanding were we to regard social problems as relatively superficial symptoms of a profound disease, a meta-cause, affecting the very foundation of the social organism. Dissociation in the West is such a meta-cause. It signalizes the ebbing of the original impulse to spirituality and brotherly unity. Therefore, social problems are caused not by the presence of an active force but by the absence of an active force, which in Europe was the unifying influence of Christianity.

In his psychohistory of racism Joel Kovel writes:

> The source of the great influence the Church wielded in all spheres of life lay precisely in its institutional hold over moral judgment. Through its definition of good and evil in all spheres of activity, it held the cords which bound the West into a Christian community. Martin Luther would not have arisen as a great man had not that community been failing in its synthetic function, and this failure was nowhere more explicit than in the inconsistency between the professed values of the Church and its actual corruption. The corruption was primarily venality, an excessive and unbridled greed, itself the signal of a failure in sublimation, and a return to the original drive-centered form of materialistic impulses that were supposed to be held in check by the moral force of the Church. The massive anxiety and despair of the late Middle Ages bore vivid witness to the deterioration of traditional Christian values in the face of new historical phenomena. Clearly, the traditional culture of the West was failing, and a new form of moral restraint was needed.[266]

Western slavery and racism were therefore the social manifestations of the gradual spiritual transformation of Christian Europe, wherein the doctrine of brotherly love – the quintessential law of the Church – faded and was replaced by violent greed. Traces of Christian love still remained but as an ideal becoming increasingly divorced from social practice. As we have seen, this consolidated the formation of a dual society in European culture: one aspect based on religious law and the sanctity of life, the other on the free exploitation of what was perceived as profane nature.

With the weakening of association, not only does community life collapse but also the development of civilized characteristics in the individual. Without the educative influence of association, which stimulates and activates the higher intellectual powers, human beings are not distinguishable from animals.[267] The concept of the id, which refers to the instinctual drives or Kovel's 'materialistic impulses', clearly represents what could be considered man's animal nature. Bruno Bettelheim reasoned that Freud chose the term 'es' (known in our English translations as the Latin 'id') because it means 'it' and thus refers to the thingness or nonhumanness of the unsocialized personality latent within us.[268] As evidenced by the historical documentation of feral children, there is no instinctual drive forcing humans to learn and obey social and cultural practices. While the potential to do so is inherent in us, the realization of this potential is dependent on the influence of enduring association with other humans, which in turn has historically depended upon the practice of spiritual ideals.[269]

There are therefore three possible states of moral life: 1) Amorality. Human beings in the completely unsocialized state are amoral in the same sense that animals are amoral. Immorality *per se* cannot be applied in this case. 2) Morality. Durkheim argued that morality appears only in the context of an established order, an established society: 'Morality begins . . . only insofar as we belong to a human group, whatever it may be.'[270] 3) Immorality. The violation of moral laws appears when *society has become a duality*: one aspect oriented towards the religiously-based legal order, towards the spiritual ideal, and another oriented in the contrary direction, that is, towards nature, towards freedom from the established legal order, towards the animal ideal. It is the contradiction between these aspects that gives rise and meaning to the concepts of immorality and social problems as a whole.[271] Since all human beings are imperfect it is reasonable to assert that everyone is at least to some degree immoral. But the point is that here we are talking not only about individuals but the morality of the civilization itself, which in Europe meant the morality of the Church. The spiritual beauty and power of the Church were precisely in the fact that it was founded and preserved with the intention of expressing the unifying teachings of Jesus Christ; ideally it was to serve as a great signpost guiding European civilization, century after century, in one and only one direction: towards the ideal of spiritual love prescribed in the New Testament. It was an institution that aided imperfect people to transform themselves as much as possible by reducing their animal nature and increasing their spiritual nature. But by the time of Martin Luther a duality was firmly established in the Church itself: the signpost pointed in two opposite directions, not one: towards the life of the spirit and towards the quest for wealth and power.

Sociologists have long acknowledged an inherent relativity of perspectives on social problems: what may be a problem for some is a benefit to others. Indeed, deconstructionism and postmodernism question the possibility of any true sharing and agreement of meaning between different cultures, between different sub-groups in any one society and even between individuals. In analyzing ideological conflict in the West, deconstructionism emphasizes the infinite possibilities of differences and discounts the historical basis of overarching Judeo-Christian continuity. It thus reaches the conclusion that moral values must be regarded as symbols whose meanings disappear outside extremely limited contexts. In applying this reasoning to different cultures and nations within the West, deconstructionism de-emphasizes the persistence and universality of moral values.

Nonetheless, western society does possess a latent religiously-based morality now operating in a secular form – as Emile Durkheim and Harold Berman, among others, have clearly observed[272] – and it is by means of this latent religious context that social problems are identified. Despite secularization, religions in the West serve as the subconscious or conscious frames of reference for orienting social thought. To some extent these frames, according to doctrinal and other particularities, differ in their ideological orientation and thus contribute to the relativity of perspectives on social problems, as deconstructionism rightly argues. Nevertheless, since the majority of religions in the West derive from the Judeo-Christian tradition, their differences are limited and reconciled by a common moral heritage, which has made possible the West's centuries-long agreement on at least the most basic moral values.

We therefore have three basic premises: 1) Civilization is based on enduring relations of mutual identity and association through the influence of spirituality fostered by religion; 2) social problems can be regarded as systemic reactions to the violation of laws of association, that is, the breakdown of mutual association and identity through the waning of spirituality and 3) the ideal, the law and the practice of association in Europe and its American colonies, historically the product of the Judeo-Christian tradition, is not fundamentally relative but fundamentally universal, with only slight, inconsequential variation. We can therefore conclude that western social problems derive from the violation or decay of spiritual ideals in stages: first, decline from unity to duality, in which the freedom of animal nature becomes released from restraints imposed by law; and second, from duality to multiplicity, in which animal freedom creates an endless variety of principles and practices, thus preventing social agreement and unity.

This is not to offer a reductionist view that the rise and fall of western civilization are due solely to the growth and collapse of the Church. It was inevitable that society would grow beyond the Roman Catholic Church and that problems due to this evolutionary growth would arise. Problems are as much because of the rise of new social realities as because of the collapse of old institutions. Rather it is modern social science that has been clinging to a reductionist view. Humanity is far more non-rational than social science would like to admit. We must recognize that human behavior and choices are motivated as much, if not more so, by emotions and by religious and spiritual approaches as by rational, reasoned thinking. It is out of this highly complex matrix, a psychic primeval soup of spiritual aspirations, reasoning and animal desires, that our modern world has emerged and it is within this matrix that we find the origins of racism. From a holistic perspective, looking at the West as an organic structure, we must admit that the fundamental role of spirituality in general, and of Christianity in particular, has been minimized or entirely ignored in discussions of modern social problems, yet the historical record clearly demonstrates that, far from being irrelevant, spirituality and Christianity are essential to unraveling the complex of problems we now refer to as racism.

The Origins of Merchants as Rulers of a New Realm

As moral relativity increased, so grew social freedom. The one class that took the greatest advantage of the new freedom was the bourgeoisie. Until the establishment of the bourgeoisie and the revolutions of the 18th and 19th centuries, virtually all social life required the obedience of the many to the dictatorial authority of one; nearly every individual was the bondsman of a king, queen, lord or chieftain.[273]

Within the womb of the feudal age, however, beginning with the rise of the far-ranging merchant class, the bourgeoisie gradually appeared in the interstices of societies – the geographical and social spaces between one king's realm and another. The bourgeoisie found freedom, wealth and power on the highways and high seas, for there absolute rulers were weak or nonexistent – hence banditry and piracy. The fundamental power of kings and tribal chiefs lay not in constant movement across the earth – although they often did travel regularly throughout their realms – but in claiming a fixed territory. The merchants, like bees, danced from one territory to another, collecting profits and at the same time culturally cross-pollinating all in their paths.

The traders, though legally subjects, were swiftly gaining so much freedom, wealth and power as to transcend the subject class. In order to cement their new status in this interstitial social space they needed public confirmation. Slavery enabled them to display openly and legally confirm this transcendence.

As the new paradigm of freedom, wealth and power arose among the merchants, slavery constituted an opposite paradigm that led to the denial of those values among slaves. Through slavery and racism the merchants created their opposites: a class of people who, like themselves, belonged to no Old World king, who lay permanently suspended in the interstices and yet who never moved – either physically, socially or spiritually – who never grew or evolved, who were the perfect mirror image of the free traders. The merchants and their slaves existed in the same interstitial space and defined that space by their polar relationship. The Africans' status as slaves, contraries, crazy dogs, made the merchants new kings in a new realm.

The merchants did not believe profit-making and spirituality were compatible. Christianity had to be put in its place and thus the spiritual life of the merchants was compromised from the start. Just as missionaries in the early history of Christianity would adapt the teachings to be more compatible with the pagan traditions of the people they sought to convert, so too the Protestant churches attracted merchants by adopting a religious culture that would be acceptable to individuals seeking unlimited wealth. Thus, Kurt Samuelson argues, 'certain leaders of the Free Church movement, confronted with the task of winning over merchants and other business men, find themselves having to adopt as sympathetic a position as possible towards wealth and economic activity'. For their part, the merchants were searching for a platform on which to enshrine their new freedom; they called for 'freedom from governmental coercion in religious matters' to gain 'freedom in economic affairs' and 'the emancipation of trade and industry'. The merchants often claimed that their economic activity was a part of their religious beliefs, when in fact this was but a rationalization putting the cart before the horse. For their motivation was not godly fervor but gold fever.[274]

What makes the West, and especially the American colonies, so striking is the Christian context. It is clear that the United States was *not* founded on Christianity or any other spiritual program. Life, liberty and the pursuit of happiness were code words for gaining wealth – but even on the face of it the American capitalists opposed, by their very selfishness, the Christian way. America's foundation was a pre-Christian ideal, for the pursuit of happiness is an Aristotelian concept, *eudemonia*, meaning the good life in all its aspects. Christianity was permitted for the lower levels of society but not the halls of power and decision-making. Separation of Church and state was not to save the Church from state interference; rather it was to save the ruling classes from Church interference in their inhumane activities for the sake of profit.

The Origins of the Literati

The merchants in their new position as rulers were supported by the simultaneous rise of classical scholars. We have seen the central role that the scholars of Greek and Roman literature, of the Bible and of the law played in the creation of the inquisitions and the witch-hunts in Europe and later

in the justification of slavery in America. R. I. Moore, referring to the rise
of the modern state in the 11th and 12th centuries, provides the historical
background:

> The new order . . . asserted itself not only through a number of emerging
> nation states – not all of them successful – and the nascent papal monar-
> chy, but also in municipal government and even through the households of
> lay and ecclesiastical nobles. Nevertheless it was a single regime. Its foun-
> dation, laid everywhere in Western Europe during these centuries, though
> with some variations of pace and procedure, was the replacement of pay-
> ment in service and kind by payment in cash and of oral process by written
> instrument. It was . . . the expression of fundamental changes in social and
> economic organization. And its establishment required another change, no
> less profound: the replacement of warriors by literate clerks as the agents of
> government and the confidants of princes. It is among these clerks that we
> will see most clearly how the emergence of the state represented a new stage
> in the division of labor, a specialization or professionalization of govern-
> ment – and among them, the agents as well as the theorists of persecution,
> that we will find its origin and *raison d'être*.[275]

Gradually the literati formed a class of their own, conscious of their 'common interests, common values and common loyalties' that were 'expressed
in bottomless contempt for those who did not share their skills'.[276] Moore
argues that 'however [the] tremendous extension of the power and influence of the literate is described, the development of persecution in all its
forms was part of it, and therefore inseparable from the great and positive
achievements with which it is associated'.[277]

The Protestant contempt for the lowly, therefore, became a common
feature throughout western society. It was not only amongst the merchants
in the markets, counting houses and seats of power but also within the
churches, academies and seats of higher learning. Hence the meek would
find no refuge – save among the heathen Indians.

The clerks, lawyers, government functionaries and theologians
possessed exquisite skill in logic and reasoning, in wielding the pen to
convince themselves and others of their righteousness. A great part of
that skill was not so much what they actually wrote, but, like magicians, in
hiding what they did not want people to see. They succeeded by blinding
the people to what had been accepted as fundamental truth for centuries,
namely the Golden Rule of Christianity. The scholars wrote Christian
morality out of the common discourse and in its place they wrote in
everything that could justify slavery, witch-burning and other forms of
persecution: the Roman law, careful selections of the Old Testament, even

mythology. Christopher Columbus's extreme violence towards the natives of Hispaniola was inspired in great part by his fervent belief in his own interpretations of the apocryphal book of Esdras and of *Imago Mundi* written by the mystical theologian Pierre d'Ailly (1350–1420). As we have seen, Thomas Jefferson produced an abridged edition of the New Testament in which he omitted all references to the supernatural, an approach that he believed would put emphasis on morality alone. For him, as for so many of his peers, the true authority was the science, law and philosophy of the classical world defined by Greece and Rome.[278]

The Origins of Secularism: The Romanization of Christian Culture

From Jefferson on down to our time, secularism and racism have been closely associated, though perhaps less obviously than among churched people. Secularists express high ideals of equality but in reality many of them act according to powerful racist principles. What did the Roman Catholic Church, the Protestant Churches and finally even American secularists have in common that encouraged them to adopt this culture of violence? It certainly was not the teachings of the New Testament. Rather, it was the cultural milieu into which Christianity was born: the legacy of Rome itself.

So much scholarly work on slavery and racism focuses on the black man and woman: the life, culture and mind of the slave. But so little focuses on the European's attitude towards himself and the world. This imbalance makes the history of American slavery appear to be all a result of the African's nature, all a reaction or response to the African. We do not think of the European in the New World as having a vision, an agenda, as having constructed for himself a drama to act out. But in fact the ruling class in America took classical Rome as a model, as Meyer Reinhold explains:

> No one may doubt . . . that there occurred in the Revolutionary Age – the golden age of the classical tradition in America – the greatest outpouring of lessons from antiquity in the public arena that America was ever again to witness. The Founding Fathers ransacked the ancient world as a usable past for guidelines, parallels, analogies to present political problems, and indeed for partisan politics. They frequently scoured ancient history and political theory and institutions as 'the lamp of experience' in search of authoritative precedents to legitimate and validate conclusions already arrived at through wide reading in contemporary literature and through the exercise of reason. For the Founding Fathers instinctively associated liberty and republicanism with the ancient commonwealths, 'those free Governments of old, whose History we so much admire, and whose Example we think it an Honor to imitate'. And it was preeminently the Roman republic that

was their exemplar, serving as a timeless model in which the civic virtues as well as corrupting vices stood out with classical clarity. In their quest for good government many among the Revolutionary generation were inspired by this comparative method, this almost ritualistic communion with ancient thought, with high optimism and confidence in the viability of a *novus ordo saeclorum*.[279]

Secularization really means not only a turning away from New Testament beliefs, laws and sentiments but also a *turning towards* something instead: the glories and power of the Roman Empire as a model to be emulated in the formation of society and its expansion through colonization.[280] Here we see the beginnings of the Church's militarization we discussed earlier. The goal of the Roman Empire was ever conquest. Likewise for its successors, the Roman Catholic Church, the princes and kings of Europe and the merchant rulers in America. The imperial ideal of conquest for the sake of material gain and the Christian concept of conquest for spiritual glory gradually converged and thereafter the Roman Catholic and Protestant Churches came to understand that military conquest – by whatever means and however violent – was in fact spiritual conquest.[281] The Word of God became a sword and who better to emulate in the ways of the sword than the Romans, the greatest conquerors of all. Whereas early Christianity remembered Rome as ever doomed and falling, the Church and the bourgeoisie in the colonial age remembered it as ever glorious and rising.

The colonial powers of Europe saw themselves as great nations and patterned their identity after the prototypical civilizations of classical history that had come to light in the Renaissance: Greece and Rome. Glory in history is eternally given to 'the Greeks' and 'the Romans'. It is not possible to give glory to a group that becomes mixed and thus loses its singular identity and becomes multiple – or at least perceived as multiple. Therefore racism emphasizes the need to avoid intermarriage with other groups in part so as to more closely follow the perceived nationalist ideal of the ancients.

But as Frank Snowden's research shows, originally Christianity had no concern for national identity. A sense of national pride could only be acquired by turning to texts other than the Bible, to pagan culture. Christianity taught not nationalism but a transcendent unity, of which the Roman Catholic Church was the guardian in the West. Indeed, the power of the pope arose specifically because tribal and national identities were subordinated to the wider identity with the Church.

The early colonies in North America were a mix of contentious nationalities, of religions and political identities. To forge a national identity they had to be united and in this race played an important part. 'Whiteness', writes Richard Dyer, 'has been enormously, often terrifyingly effective in unifying coalitions of disparate groups of people. It has generally been much more successful than class in uniting people across national cultural differences and against their best interests.'[282] In his study of the history of interracial families in America, Gary Nash draws a clear definition of this aspect of racism:

> Your race does not come from your genes but from the beliefs of the people around you. Racial classifications are definitions placed on already mixed populations in an effort to give these highly diverse groups essential and binding characteristics.[283]

The rise of colonialism, then, signalized the gradual emergence and eventual superiority of national identity over the universal Christian ideal of international or transnational brotherhood. It signalized the *return* of the pagan national identity gloriously exemplified by Greece and Rome, a process that had been flowing in Europe from at least the 12th century.

The Europeans justified this renewed national identity by shifting the focus of religion from God and Jesus to the Greek and Roman heroes. If religion is proved by deed and not by spoken or written sentiment, then clearly the Europeans were not worshiping the God of Jesus but new gods who were mortals yet treated as immortal. It was a worship of other men from the ancient past who, most assuredly, had achieved immortality – assuredly because their eternal glory gave modern Europeans the haunting possibility of achieving a real immortality. They believed that although no one could be like Jesus, anyone who looked and acted like the Greeks and Romans could become immortal like them, either through the glories of conquest or the glories of intellectual achievement. It is from this that we see so many Europeans inordinately devoted to scholarship: they were emulating their idols from Greece and Rome, worshiping them and seeking to become immortal like them.

It is fair to argue that most of the texts, artworks, statues, tableaux and designs in pottery and architecture that came down to the Europeans from Greece and Rome were created by the ancients for the purpose of expressing and glorifying *themselves*. Before capitalism the motive for action was not profit but personal and national glory, the immortality seen in Gilgamesh, Homer and many other works. Thus the relationship between the Europeans and the classical world was as two mirrors facing each other. For in worshiping and emulating the Greeks and Romans – peoples who glorified and deified themselves – the Europeans were ultimately practicing and reflecting *ad infinitum* the same self-worship and self-glorification.

In adopting this form of humanism Europeans were violating the Christian principles, which clearly forbade self-worship as idolatry. They attempted to avoid this sin by reinterpreting their self-glorification as not self-worship at all but as the inferiority and sinfulness of the other.

Of course, the teachings of Jesus also forbid the judgment and condemnation of others, as in the story of Mary Magdalena. But the ever-ready theologians and intellectuals, in a culture in which wordplay had become a fine art of power, overcame this obstacle by referring to the Old Testament instead. Racist ideology among defenders of slavery consistently ignores the New Testament teachings of the Golden Rule. The Old Testament not only permitted slavery – albeit in a far less brutal form than that of the Americas – but it emphasized a national identity, which could easily be misinterpreted in a racist fashion.

This is what filled the moral vacuum left in the absence of genuine Christianity in America: a twisting of the Old Testament, the adoption of Greece and Rome as cultural models, the replacement of universal brotherhood by nationalism, the rise of unbridled greed in the form of capitalism and the legitimization of systematic and extreme violence and hatred against women and slaves. The collapse of Christianity resulted not in a singular replacement but a plethora of ideologies, all reinforcing the fundamental fact that the restrictions of Christianity were to be overthrown. They had one thing in common: they all negated the Golden Rule.

It is no mere coincidence that the philosophy, history and scientific legacy of the Greeks and Romans take pride of place in our schools, colleges and universities of the West. The Bible and the Prophets are relegated to seminaries or are looked upon as objects of philosophical and scientific analysis. We prove what we revere by what we do, and since we have installed the Greeks and Romans in the academies, it is to them that we look for guidance. It is from them that we gain inspiration and justify our actions. The irony is that much of this is done in colleges and universities founded by churches, looking like cathedrals and cathedral schools, originally designed to prepare young men to become priests and ministers.

Because Greek philosophy proved itself in the practical efficacy and power of science and technology, the classical world was able to usurp the throne of Christianity. Science became the fountainhead of glory, honor and immortality. Christianity could never prove its version of heaven, a destiny that could only be reached through faith and which was accompanied by its fearsome twin, hell. The glory of Greece and Rome was tangible, proved by historical record, an immortality that was undeniably real.

THE ROOTS OF MILITARIZATION

The Greco-Roman model was so dominant that the Roman Catholic Church became militarized through the vast process stretching from the Crusades through the inquisitions and the witch-hunts. The Protestant Churches were born in a social milieu in which the militarization of European culture was already in full bloom and the return to the secular culture of Greece and Rome through the rise of classical scholarship had been under way for some four centuries.

Gradually the military culture became diffused throughout society. By the late 16th century militarization had achieved its fully modern form. In that period in the Netherlands the Roman system of regimented, lock-step drill that serves as the basis of military culture even today was revived. This aspect of resurrected Roman culture gradually yet profoundly influenced all of civilian life.[284] The distinction between war time and peace time, between soldiers and civilians, was blurred as never before. Weapons and armed soldier-citizens became commonplace to satisfy the security demands of increasingly wealthy and powerful merchants conducting trade by land and sea. War for the sake of land, trading routes and colonies became constant. The teachings of Jesus faded as the ideal of Rome took hold of the European consciousness. With every battle and blow struck in the name of Christ, the Church – both Roman Catholic and Protestant – was also reforming its own heart and soul into the pre-Christian imperial model inherited from the Latins.

The militarization of society accelerated in America in the 19th and 20th centuries. Pastoral society was decidedly transformed by the industrial revolution and the two world wars. The assembly line culture that followed so closely the exact uniformity of military regimentation became widespread. Military culture followed American veterans home after World War Two.[285] Suburban and urban housing came to resemble army barracks connected by the new national highway system designed to facilitate rapid military and civilian response to threats and invasions. Corporations were modeled directly after military command structures, with officers of various ranks, uniform clothing, price 'wars' and fierce competition ultimately spelling the death of the losing company. Much of the United States economy as it stands today was defined by World War Two, the cold war and the culture of the military.

ROME'S CENTRALITY IN AMERICA

In the 18th and 19th centuries identification with Rome was common throughout all of Europe and informed everything from politics to art, school curricula and even the setting of holidays in a secular calendar.[286]

Romanization was particularly strong among the founders of the United States; in general the 'most educated Americans' were profoundly influenced by an intellectual and political 'consciousness of ancient Rome'.

> From Thomas Jefferson and John Adams down through . . . Henry James and Henry Adams, ancient Rome . . . was for Americans a place of unrivaled cultural significance. The heroes of the Roman Republic – Cincinnatus, Cicero, Cato the Younger – were American heroes because they were champions of liberty, and liberty was the meaning of America.[287]

No surprise, then, that America's sacred secular symbols and its civil saints are evocative of Rome. In Washington DC the visitor finds on every hand massive buildings and temples dedicated to America's greatest historical figures, some actually depicted as Roman heroes in Roman robes. There is, of course, a great National Cathedral representing Christianity but it stands well away from the mall at the city's center. The ideal of Rome predominates in Washington's political architecture, in the symbols by which the city is represented, in the cultural heritage with which the nation aims so openly to be identified. The teachings of Christ exist in America but only in private space. The teachings of Greece and Rome define the public space, the society and the culture. While Las Casas defended the Indians using the arguments of Christianity, his rival Juan Ginés de Sepúlveda (1494–1573) defended racial hierarchy using Aristotelian theories. It was a contest between religious ideals and pagan philosophy.[288] The more Europe and America became Romanized, the more the Christian ideal of humane love was considered unpopular, unwise and ultimately unreal. It was this spiritual vacuum that drove many Europeans to seek refuge among the Indians and that repulsed the Indians themselves.

A Culture of Schism

Europe's return to Roman ideals and culture beginning in the 12th century was not an exact replication but a variation that differed significantly from the original Roman theme. Whereas Rome depended heavily on social unity – for only in that way could great wealth be generated in the ancient world – the neo-classical Renaissance emerged in a period when technology enabled great wealth to be generated by very small groups of people. In that circumstance a monarch's insistence on maintaining a complete social unity under his control was exactly contrary to the bourgeois interest. Admittedly, widespread unity was still indispensable; but the new economy succeeded because this unity was looser, allowing entrepreneurs the freedom to trade beyond the authority of a monarch and to divide society into new classes. Through looser social unity new markets of consumers, laborers, suppliers and traders enabled merchants to seize and maintain the independence and economic advantages they needed. Rivalries between kings enabled tax revenues to slide into the pockets of the merchants, who moved systematically in the spaces between them. Capitalism flourished in northern Europe and North America because it emerged in a milieu of schism, which fostered independence both of ideas and actions.

Furthermore, it could well be argued that Weber's analysis reveals capitalism itself as a form of schism from Catholicism. Rather than regarding it as the economic expression of Protestantism, we can view it as a new religious form in and of itself. In many indigenous cultures around the world money has little or no meaning but in the West we value paper and coin currency so much that we take our reverence for it as only natural. Money is identified with not only life but immortality; as a symbol of immortality, it involves a broad social structure similar to the Christian Church. Banks and corporate headquarters are like temples, churches and cathedrals – many literally so in architectural style. Businessmen are looked upon with degrees of awe and reverence according to their rank, emotions that derive as much from their quasi-religious role in society as from their quasi-military role.

As we have seen, Weber argued that Protestants regard capitalism as a sacred practice. There is not so much a line between capitalism and Protestantism but rather they are twin overlapping forms emerging from the same social forces. If Protestantism has a strong capitalist element, likewise capitalism has a strong religious element. And in the extreme, capitalism becomes a religion, not only an expression of Christianity but a new faith system substituting for it.

We are coming to a conclusion that might not be taken well but must nevertheless be considered: The spiritual unity of Christianity was shattered during the Protestant Reformation and this loss of unity was one of the most harmful setbacks Christendom ever suffered. But by this are we saying that the Protestants were wrong and the Catholics right? Should the Protestant churches and Quaker meeting houses all be replaced by Catholic chapels and cathedrals? Clearly none of these understandings is correct. What this idea means is that while Martin Luther and other reformers were correct in standing up for the revival of morality within the Church and the ending of corrupt practices, the protest, whether inadvertently or not, destroyed the most important aspect of Christianity, which is the unity it fosters. There is no point in correcting certain faults if society is completely disunited as a result. For no matter how morally upright individuals may be, if they do not unite in a way that is spiritually and socially beneficial, there is no fellowship, there is no love, there is no cooperation and there is no civilization; but suddenly there is a tremendous increase in moral and legal freedom, of which the unscrupulous are tempted to take advantage.

The coldness that many observers have noted as typical of Protestant culture in Europe and America has often been attributed to a sense of self-righteousness that Protestants supposedly have earned having corrected the faults of the Catholics. But we are arguing here that the coldness is not due primarily to a sense of superiority – which may nonetheless contribute to it – but rather to the fact that the Protestants instituted a pattern of separation and isolation, of disunity, of schism, which has continued even to this day.

Conclusion

The witch-hunts of Europe established once and for all what has become an unshakeable precedent in the Christian world, a precedent so powerful and contrary that it was one of the main causes of the moral collapse of Christianity. The Roman Catholic Church, beginning in 1450, when Vineti promulgated his *Tractatus*, decreed that witches did indeed exist and were worthy of extreme punishment. This legitimized what was in effect the reversal of Jesus' teaching to love the sinner, the enemy, the outcast, and to have compassion for the lowly. Now the Church, with all its might and power, turned against the meekest in European society, women who were widowed, marginalized and politically and economically defenseless, and shattered the Christian laws that gave them at least a measure of love and protection in the community. This was a precedent that, along with the inquisitions, spawned subsequent evils for centuries thereafter.

Today's popular culture relegates witchcraft to the fun of Halloween, identifies American Indians as mascots for professional, collegiate and high school sports teams and still makes African Americans the target of less than innocent pranks at fraternity gatherings. Most Americans are unaware of the Church's edict and actions against witches and have forgotten the violence, only so recent, against Africans and Indians. But the subtext remains, the superstitious feelings against them linger on, the fear and hatred that go far beyond any logic or civil rights or laws continue. We are captives of an archaic culture that legitimized the most extreme violence and brutality against the innocent and the defenseless in the name of the highest ideal. Soon after the women of Europe were forced down this path, the Africans and American Indians, who were habituated to a relatively calm and peaceful life in their homelands, were made to follow on their heels.[289] From at least 1450 this became our *way of life* in the western world, a pattern set then by which we have lived, made money and ruled for centuries. It is perhaps an ancient practice – to dominate the weak by inhumane force – but what has made it modern is that from 1450 it was done not in the name and at the whim of a tyrant but in the name of the Church, with all the systemic vigor it possessed. This modern twist is what has long caused the oppressed to hesitate, for they are confused: surely we cannot rebel against the Church, which is the source of all goodness and morality. The picture is further complicated by Catholicism's significant efforts to protect slaves and Indians in the Americas.

We can now better understand the reason why there is so much confusion regarding Christian identity and un-Christian behavior in European and American history. On the one hand the European leaders of the colonies always identified themselves as Christians, while on the other they committed acts contrary to the spirit and laws of Christianity. How could they then make such a claim? Were they Christian or were they not? The problem is that to be a true believer requires a two-fold commitment. First, the individual must recognize and accept the Messenger of God. Second, the individual must obey the message. By the early Renaissance period most of the leadership in European society had long left behind the second part of this commitment, while still sincerely remaining steadfast in the first. Recognition of Jesus and love for Him were widespread and perhaps quite strong among all classes of society. But without the second commitment this love was not able to bear the fruit of spiritual unity needed in order for Christian civilization to be firmly established and flourish.

We now understand that the violence and greed of slavery and racism would not have been possible but for the collapse of Christianity's moral authority in Europe and the New World, which left a vacuum filled by the materialistic designs of merchants devoted to amassing personal fortunes. In order for us to appreciate fully this collapse we must see Christianity as it was in its time of strength and fruition.

Level Nine: The Spiritual Unity of Europe

Here on Level Nine we arrive at a period of European civilization before the existence of systemic persecution. Without their unity the Europeans could not have built up the technological and military might that enabled them later to conquer and economically exploit foreign lands. But more importantly, the fact that this unity was spiritual is central to unraveling the mystery of race as a justification for slavery.

The inertia of the unifying tradition in Christianity has been underestimated by sociology, partly due to the downfall of the Catholic Church from its towering position of sovereignty, and partly because modern sociology came into being in support of 19th-century industrialists who desired to release the European economic potential from the fetters of persisting religious and moral traditions. Yet there is no doubt, when the vast panorama of western civilization is considered, that the fundamental principle of brotherly love permeated the consciousness of western society. The early American merchant rulers therefore required, as we have seen, many intricate civil laws and social customs to control, if not eliminate, the Christian impulse promoting fellowship and association between the races.

Furthermore, Christianity has been so central to the functioning of western society that to eliminate it altogether – or even to approach such a state – would have seriously threatened and perhaps destroyed the substructure of communication and cooperation upon which capitalism itself depended. Thus in prohibiting slaves from participation in the Church the capitalist society came close to biting the spiritual hand that fed it, to creating a contradiction wherein capitalism, a superstructural institution, was given priority over the substructure of spiritual unity.

The Critical Role of the Roman Catholic Church

The phrase 'western society' often evokes a vivid image of kings conquering vast realms, ruling large populations from glorious thrones and establishing cities around castles on hilltops. But this picture, although true in part, overlooks a fundamental aspect of western history. For however powerful the European kings have been, or the Roman emperors before them, we notice that the peoples of Europe received little or nothing to unite them from kings who were themselves most often bitter foes. Likewise their inheritance from the Roman Empire was quite limited; indeed, although the Romans laid out a unified system of roads across the continent and spread their language and culture among the colonized Europeans with all the power at their disposal, the collapse of their Empire was so complete that even their language did not survive. Clearly there was something else, then – an essential element that we tend to overlook. This element was none other than Christianity.[290]

Of all institutions in the West, the most enduring, extensive, systematic and, at least during its height from the 11th to the 15th centuries,[291] the most powerful was the Church of Rome. Alongside the antecedent Greco-Roman culture and the later Protestant variation, Roman Catholicism could be considered the central pillar of the rational organization of modern western civilization. Consider Walter Ullmann's description of Frankish society during the Carolingian Renaissance of the 9th and 10th centuries:

> ... the Carolingian age deserves particular attention, because it constituted the period of Europe's gestation and apprenticeship, the period in which the concept of Europe as a cultural, social, religious and especially political entity, sustained by its own forces, became for the first time an operational concept. For Europe was not a geographical expression, but denoted a perfectly well understood conceptual structure characterized on the one hand by the multiform if not heterogeneous complexion of the inhabit-

ants under Carolingian rule, and on the other hand by the unifying and cementing bond of the Roman-Latin, Western as opposed to Byzantine, Christianity . . .

. . . what had hitherto been conceived as a mere conglomeration of families, tribes, conquered peoples, became in the course of the ninth century ideologically and conceptually transformed into one body public, the Church, which *au fond* disregarded the natural, linguistic and tribal differences of peoples and regions.[292]

The Irish historian William Lecky (1838–1903) echoed this point:

The Catholic Church was the very heart of Christendom and the spirit that radiated from her penetrated into all the relations of life. Catholicism laid the very foundations of modern civilization. Herself the most admirable of all organizations, there was formed beneath her influence, a vast network of organizations – political, municipal and social – which supplied a large proportion of the materials of almost every modern structure.[293]

Of all ideologies and belief systems integral to the western social fabric, Christianity in its various forms is doubtless the oldest and most pervasive.[294] Even the crucial scientific and philosophical thought of ancient Greece and Rome was transmitted to the West in part by means of Christian scholars. The categories of thought directly or indirectly shaped by Christianity have long been dominant in the development of the psychological and cultural character of both the individual and the masses, and Max Weber's analysis of the Protestant ethic is but a sampling from this vast and fascinating history.

Above all, the Christian ideal of love must be regarded as the fundamental paradigm of mutual association and identity in the West, the very basis of interaction and communication. Some might object that the Christian Church was too afflicted by internal corruption for its ideal of love to have significant historical impact. This objection is in part valid, for the Church was indeed tottering from corruption. Yet simultaneously it was able to succeed despite itself in spreading the concepts of spirituality and unity enshrined in the New Testament. By the Middle Ages the Church may not have been the best of teachers, yet its message remained of great value to many learned and common folk throughout Europe and they embraced it and put it into practice, however imperfectly. Churches, monasteries, cathedrals and schools were built; the sacred text was painstakingly copied and disseminated; scholarly, scientific, technological and agricultural discoveries were made; lives of great dedication and sacrifice were led; great wealth was accumulated and spent in service to the Church and its community of believers. In short, a vast and powerful culture arose on the foundation of Christianity above the ruins of the Roman Empire, and transcending any particular monarchy. There was corruption but the fact of this corruption does not negate the equally valid historical truth that the teachings of Jesus became popularized and were taken very seriously by the masses. The peoples of Europe became united, as Ullmann pointed out, because of the influence of Christianity, an influence that succeeded where the political and economic might of Rome failed. It was an influence that spiritualized the masses, that enabled them to form bonds of mutual association transcending traditional tribal divisions. This is the significance of the ideal of Christian love in European history. However imperfectly the ideal was practiced, it nevertheless transformed the continent and created a social unity that the modern world has universally recognized.

The Reality of Christian Spiritual Unity

It is impossible to make any sense of European Americans' guilt over slavery, the justifications they created for it, the legal twists they employed to institute it, and the many problems they faced in trying to establish it in the colonial society, without acknowledging that Christianity had succeeded, if imperfectly, in establishing a spiritual unity in Europe. Most Europeans found it difficult to accept slavery because it flew in the face of all that Christianity taught. Only under the severe economic and political pressure of the merchant class, and only on the peripheries of European society and in the remote colonies, was slavery able to take root. The spiritual unity of Christian society was fundamentally incompatible with slavery. Let us then examine the nature of this unity.

There is considerable evidence that originally the ideal of Christian love was regarded by believers as universal. Men and women of all social classes and ranks were treated as brothers and sisters and freely joined the fold. Adolf Harnack clarifies this point:

> It is a mistake to suppose that any 'slave question' occupied the early church...
>
> Still, it would not be true to assert that primitive Christianity was indifferent to slaves and their condition. On the contrary, the church did turn her attention to them, and effected some change in their condition. This follows from such considerations as these:
>
> a) Converted slaves, male or female, were regarded in the full sense of the term as brothers and sisters from the standpoint of religion. Compared to this, their position in the world was reckoned a matter of indifference.
> b) They shared the rights of church members to the fullest extent. Slaves could even become clergymen, and in fact bishops.

c) As personalities (in the moral sense) they were to be just as highly esteemed as freemen. The sex of female slaves had to be respected, nor was their modesty to be outraged. The same virtues were expected from slaves as from freemen, and consequently their virtues earned the same honor.

d) Masters and mistresses were strictly charged to treat all their slaves humanely, but, on the other hand, to remember that Christian slaves were their own brethren. Christian slaves, for their part, were told not to disdain their Christian masters, *i.e.*, they were not to regard themselves as their equals.

e) To set a slave free was looked upon, probably from the very beginning, as a praiseworthy action . . .[295]

Slavery was tolerated in the early Church but clearly it was discouraged. Following ancient tradition, the Church allowed the enslavement of Christians and non-Christians captured in war but in all cases it sought to convert and protect the slaves, to spread the Word of God among slaves and freemen alike.

The protective attitude towards slaves evolved so that by the 16th century the enslavement of Christians, as we have seen, was essentially forbidden in Europe. Only under certain very specific and limited circumstances was it tolerated. But never was the wholesale enslavement of Christian populations permitted.

At no time did the early Church close its doors to any ethnic or racial group. Although it would be an overstatement to assert that the Golden Rule – love thy neighbor as thyself – was practiced flawlessly, at the very least it was taken seriously and applied in daily life. Even the higher ideal of loving one's enemy was also practiced. And despite the logic of Machiavellian political theory, these ideals did not bring about the destruction of the early Church but rather its rapid expansion throughout the Mediterranean world and all Europe. Before the cancer of corruption appeared among the clergy and upper social ranks, before the Crusades, inquisitions and witch-hunts, these high ideals became accepted universal norms in Christendom. Even as corruption spread, the masses of believers continued to follow these principles as best they could, or at least to recognize them as truths. All human beings were considered sacred; there was no sacred–profane dichotomy.

A further significant proof is the fact that before Vineti's *Tractatus* the Catholic Church steadfastly rejected the notion that witches exist. It therefore opposed the oppression of women accused of being witches, most of whom were poor, single and middle-aged or older, lacking protection against the rampant destitution and vulnerability to unscrupulous opportunists following the transition from a rural-based economy to a town-centered one.

The Reality of Interracial Unity

Although there is some controversy about the subject, the historical record is nevertheless quite clear that throughout most of recorded European history the great majority of Europeans did not regard black Africans with anything that can be equated with modern racial prejudice or discrimination. Let us consider four proofs.

First, Frank Snowden's research has definitively shown that Greeks and Romans entertained no such racist notions. On the contrary, many sources show that Ethiopians – the contemporary term for black Africans in general – were highly regarded as being of noble character and as authors of a high civilization. He cites Homer's narrative stating that the gods were attracted to the 'blameless Ethiopians' above all other humans.[296] Homer is not the only source of this praise.

> To Dionysius 'Periegetes' [ca. 300 BCE] the Ethiopians were godlike and blameless. Arnobius [4th century CE] says that the gods are to be everywhere, to pervade all things with their power, not to feast with the Ethiopians and to return to Olympus after twelve days. The Ethiopians, according to Stobaeus [5th century CE], practice piety and justice; their houses are without doors and no one steals the many things left in the streets. Ethiopians, as Diodorus [ca. 90–21 BCE] had said earlier, were the first to honor the gods.[297]

Snowden finds support among other scholars for his views. He concurs with W. den Boer in arguing that the 'modern views . . . have attributed anachronistically to antiquity a nonexistent racial discrimination'.[298]

> The Greeks and Romans attached no special stigma to color, regarding yellow hair or blue eyes a mere geographical accident, and developed no special racial theory about the inferiority of darker peoples qua darker peoples. H. L. Shapiro notes that 'modern man is race conscious in a way and to a degree certainly not characteristic previously', and points out that in earlier societies the ability to see obvious physical differences did not result in 'an elaborate orientation of human relations within a rigid frame of reference'.[299]

Snowden also adds a telling fact:

> The Greeks expressed no astonishment that Ethiopians, a people whom they at times described as black or dark and as having several so-called Negroid physical traits, had conquered Egypt or had constructed great temples. Westerners, it has been pointed out, have traditionally regarded

the civilization of the Napatan and Meroïtic periods as Egypt 'running downhill to an inglorious and too long protracted conclusion'. No such view existed among the Greeks and the Romans.[300]

The Greeks and Romans did distinguish between themselves and others but the others were defined not by skin color or race but rather by the quality of their society. Greeks and Romans saw themselves as civilized and others as barbarians. But there was no identification whatsoever between barbarianism and dark skin color.[301] Moreover, Snowden notes,

> On the whole . . . the number of expressed preferences for blackness and whiteness in classical literature is approximately equal. The evidence, then, shows that, as in several modern societies with white and black peoples, the matter was one of individual preference and that those with preference for blacks had no reluctance in saying so. In short, as Propertius [ca. 50–15 BCE] observed, a tender beauty, whether white or dark, attracts.[302]

It should be noted that Ethiopians in Greece and Rome 'were by no means few or rare sights and that their presence, whatever their numbers, constituted no color problem'.[303]

Moreover, 'No laws in the Greco-Roman world prohibited unions of blacks and whites. Ethiopian blood was interfused with that of Greeks and Romans. No Greek or Roman author condemned such racial mixture'.[304]

Ronald Sanders argues that the Romans 'were beginning to see [Ethiopians] predominantly as slaves by the first century CE'.[305] Nevertheless, it is clear that this must have been a development limited by the rise of Christianity, as we shall now see.

The second proof of the nonexistence of systemic racism in most of European history is the fact that, as Snowden shows, the early Church was completely open to believers of all races.[306] While the black skin of the Ethiopian was usually taken by white Christians 'as a convenient symbol for certain patterns of Christian thought', namely that he was 'the blackest and most remote of men' – remote geographically speaking – yet 'the early Christians made it clear that the Ethiopian's blackness was of no more consequence to them than it had been to the Greeks and Romans'. Indeed, 'the early Christians used the Ethiopian as a prime motif in the language of conversion and as a means to emphasize their conviction that Christianity was to include all mankind'.[307]

Third, there is evidence that European culture did not begin to equate dark skin color with evil until the Crusades and that white skin color was not firmly established as a symbol of virtue and holiness until the Renaissance.[308]

The fourth proof, which we have already noted, is the fact that interracial marriages and families were very common in the colonies of South and North America. This phenomenon is particularly significant in North America, where the colonial authorities did everything they could to try to prevent it but in the end never fully succeeded.

These four proofs show the incorrectness of what Theodore Allen has termed the psycho-cultural argument that slavery and racism were inevitable because it was in the psychic nature of Europeans to fear and hate the Africans, who were so unlike them physically and culturally; that it was psychologically impossible for Europeans to accept them as sisters and brothers and hence it was natural and inevitable that the Europeans would keep them at a distance in a system of slave labor.[309] These four proofs demonstrate clearly that rather than being natural and inevitable, race-based slavery in the Americas was an artificial construct that went directly against Europe's spiritual tradition of ignoring physical and cultural differences, a tradition stretching back to the very heart of Christianity and beyond to the Greco-Roman civilization.

In fact, it is the chief contention of Theodore Allen and others that North America's ruling class created anti-African racism precisely to drive a permanent wedge between the two classes of workers in the colonies, the Africans and the poor Europeans. Aiming to replicate, in a time of turmoil and revolution, the feudal control of labor that was even then collapsing in the Old World, North America's ruling class was ever mindful that these laborers held in their hands the power to revolt.[310] Most whites in the South never did subscribe to slavery and racism the way the slave-holders hoped. They defended the Confederacy but they did not identify with it to the degree that slave-holders did. Of whites in the antebellum South, W. E. B. DuBois found that there were five million who owned no slaves as opposed to two million slave-holders, among whom eight thousand constituted an oligarchy.[311] As one writer recently stated, 'The Confederacy was a slaveowners' coup, not the popular revolution of modern legend.'[312]

Even as late as the turn of the 20th century, when the southern states were establishing new rules to reverse the civil and legal rights gained by the former slaves during Reconstruction, this same strategy of dividing the laboring class was the guiding force of white thinking. In instituting the new legal restrictions that were to prevent blacks from voting, the white establishment had 'to overcome the opposition and divert the suspicions of the poor and illiterate whites that they as well as the Negro were in danger of losing the franchise – a suspicion that often proved justified'. They therefore 'resorted to an intensive propaganda of white supremacy, Negrophobia, and race chauvinism',[313] which was merely a refrain of the original colonial wedge-driving program of the 17th century.

Conclusion

Interracial unity was a long historical reality in the West that, even under the extreme pressures of American slavery and racism, could not be eliminated but only suppressed.

Although in its second millennium the Christian Church suffered extensive corruption, in its earlier stages of evolution it was able to propagate and institutionalize the Christian ideal of spiritual unity across tribal, racial and linguistic boundaries, creating out of thousands of disparate and contending tribes an enduring social unity. The Church spread across the Mediterranean region and all throughout Europe at a time when the peoples took Christian ideals seriously and practiced them. These ideals were the roots of European society itself. The power of this brotherly love, even as it waned, mitigated the harshness of colonial slavery, particularly in South America but to a notable degree even in North America. The violation of Christian spirituality in the Crusades, inquisitions, witch-hunts and slavery constituted a series of revolutions that signalized the gradual moral collapse of the Church and necessitated elaborate justifications in order to avoid public and ecclesiastical opposition. It spelled the dismantling of Christian law and a return to pre-Christian pagan culture.

Level Ten: Paganism

What existed before Christianity? Descending to Level Ten we can trace Christianity's rise in the wake of the Roman Empire's collapse. The teachings of Jesus were a direct counterpoint to nearly all that was held dear in Roman culture. Where Roman society valued wealth, status and power, Christianity taught detachment from material things and humbleness, meekness and submission to God. Where the Romans sought ever to satisfy their earthly desires, Christianity taught its followers to purify themselves of material excesses and to seek only the transcendent existence in God's heavenly kingdom. Where the ultimate aim of Roman life was to achieve the symbolic immortality of the great, Christianity spoke of spiritual immortality, an eternal life not only unrelated to earthly existence but positively opposed to it. For the Romans physical life was an exquisite paradise but for Christians it was a deadly trap from which the soul must remain aloof at all costs. Rome's concern was for physical existence; Christianity's was for the soul. Roman civilization was materialistic; the Christianity of the New Testament was spiritual.

The Quest for Immortality

Of all aspects of materialism, the fear of death has been the most powerful motivator from the very dawn of human civilization. The earliest text describing human society, as opposed to that of the gods, is *The Epic of Gilgamesh*, which dates from the third millennium BCE. The king Gilgamesh was obsessed with the inevitable approach of his death. At that time in Mesopotamian history there was apparently no concept of life after death or of the eternal soul. There were two kinds of human beings: mortals and immortals or gods. Gilgamesh knew of one instance of a mortal becoming immortal; he sought him out in a remote location beyond many obstacles, learned his tale and was given by him the means to live forever – a special plant. However, fate ordained that he would lose the plant on his return to his kingdom and in time he met his death with the greatest regret and sorrow. If anything, this fundamental text testifies to humanity's preoccupation with the fear of death and the search to perpetuate our existence on this planet.

Egyptian civilization gives us even more evidence of the importance of this theme in human history. Temples, pyramids, rituals and technologies were developed in order to satisfy an insatiable desire to defeat death. Yet here, unlike in the story of Gilgamesh, the Egyptians had a clear understanding of another world beyond this one. The kings and queens were buried surrounded by all the equipment and resources they would need to carry on their journey to their next existence: soldiers, tools, conveyances, even food.

Qin Shihuangdi (259–210 BCE), China's first emperor, was buried in a vast tomb complex rivaling and perhaps surpassing those of ancient Egypt; several structures within the complex contain thousands of exquisitely wrought terra cotta soldiers positioned to guard him in the next life. Each of the soldiers is a highly detailed work of art and it is fair to say that there is nothing comparable to this cultural treasure in the rest of the world.

The Greeks and Romans continued this quest for immortality. They emphasized not an existence beyond this planet but the possibility to become an immortal among men through fame and glory. Conquest, gold, triumph on the battlefield and in the arena, wearing the purple – all these achievements were considered the currency with which immortality was bought. As clearly evidenced in his *Apology*, Socrates eventually lost his life in speaking out against the preoccupation of the wealthy with their physical existence and their forgetfulness of the things of the spirit.

The Renaissance was but a reflection of this ancient quest for immortality. The Medicis and other wealthy families fueled the Renaissance by commissioning artists to immortalize them in stone, in color portraits and in word. Architecture became a medium in which the existence of a family name could be given a body that would stand for the ages.

As Pitirim Sorokin has described it, history alternates between periods of high moral and spiritual ideals and periods in which concern for physical existence and physical life dominates.[314] Following the Renaissance the pendulum swung back towards ideals with the rise of the Enlightenment and the Great Awakening. Then with the emergence of the industrial revolution the merchants again came to dictate the direction of culture and to this day we are following the pattern set by the Romans and Greeks in seeking physical symbols with which we can console ourselves that our memory, our existence will be perpetuated. In Levels Six and Eight we examined symbolic immortality as a substitute for Christianity and as an aspect of the waning of Christianity. Here we see that the quest for immortality has existed from the earliest periods of civilization. As did the Romans and Greeks, we glorify ourselves by broadcasting our name, fame and glory, building huge structures in remembrance of ourselves, identifying ourselves with things that seem to perpetuate our existence after we die, things that leave at least a trace. Hopefully, if we are particularly successful, much more than a trace remains, for if we attain the heights of power, we can mold society to reflect our will and thus we become god-like.

But with today's technologies we are gradually moving away from symbols of immortality towards attempts to achieve it literally. We seek methods of genetic manipulation to slow or even stop the ageing process; we alter our bodies to look younger than we are; we dose ourselves, receive implants and transplants, become ever more artificial, 'bionic'. And we even seek to preserve our bodies after death in a cryogenic freeze, hoping that we will awaken in a future society able to conquer death once and for all.

It is in this context that the teachings of Jesus become highly significant. Directly contradicting the cultural dictates of His time, He counseled His disciples to forget the physical body and physical needs, to have no fear of physical death, to recognize this earthly life as a chimera and instead to envision a transcendent existence beyond the physical realm, an existence that is the only true life. The life of the body is as death compared to the eternal life of the spiritualized soul. Jesus called the people to emerge from the prisons of their own selves, to cease dwelling in tombs and building for themselves monuments to personal glory, to cease identifying themselves with stones, names and ephemeral matter. He called them to recognize that, contrary to tradition stretching back to the Egyptians and the Mesopotamians, the life of the body was not true life; the life of the soul was not only true but infinitely greater, infinitely more powerful than physical existence. He declared, in effect, that it was now time to end this ages-long practice of seeking physical and symbolic immortality.

Slavery as Paganism

In the context of these teachings of Jesus, it is clear that slavery was a pagan institution born of a highly materialistic culture which the Roman Catholic

Church did much to control and suppress. The Church's attitude towards slavery was somewhat ambiguous. While it tolerated slavery within the Church membership, it actively discouraged it and encouraged manumission of slaves. It also granted slaves the same spiritual rights as masters, including the right to marry and have a legitimate family. The Church saw slavery as just one of many pagan holdovers from which the community of the faithful would need to be gradually weaned. In short, the Church, while not abolishing it outright, consistently refused to sanction the traditions and laws of slavery inherited from the Romans and Greeks. The point here is that slavery was considered by the central social institution in Europe as an expression of pagan belief. Therefore when we speak of slavery in America we are not talking about Christianity but a pre-Christian institution. We are dealing with an inheritance from ancient Rome that attracted the attention of Romanizing Europeans during and after the Renaissance. No matter how much apologists for slavery try to identify it with Christian belief, we should expose it as having nothing to do with Christianity, neither the Christianity of Jesus as portrayed in the Bible, nor the Christianity as practiced by the pre-corrupted Church. It is true that the corrupted Church itself owned slaves in Latin America and elsewhere; yet the practice of slavery followed by the Church was contrary to the practice of the capitalists and the pagans, for it granted slaves legal status, religious identity and opportunity for social and professional advancement. Two popes had been slaves.[315] William Lecky stated unequivocally: 'In the transition from slavery to serfdom, and in the transition from serfdom to liberty, she [the Catholic Church] was the most zealous, the most unwearied and the most efficient agent.' Another historian, Francois Guizot (1787–1874), also made this point: 'There can be no doubt that the Catholic Church struggled resolutely against the great vices of the social state – against slavery, for instance.' Neither of these scholars was a member of the Roman Catholic Church.[316] The anti-slavery stance of the Church was seen most clearly in the remarkable rise, during the medieval period, of the *societas christiana*, a kind of treaty which Milton Meltzer describes as 'a universal community of Christians who as fellow-countrymen were bound not to war against one another for the purpose of taking slaves'. In England, for example, by 1086 agricultural slaves constituted nine per cent of the population; thereafter their numbers declined and by 1200 'agricultural slavery was gone from England, replaced by serfdom. What slaves were left were confined mostly to household service.'[317] Slavery continued for a much longer period in the Mediterranean region. In the 13th century the Church expressly forbade the trading in Christian slaves, which led to the long-term practice of capturing and trading non-Christians, that is, 'infidels'; in 1455 this was institutionalized by a papal bull granting Portugal the right to enslave all non-Christian peoples.[318] But in the wider view of things, Paul Johnson argues, by the 19th century Christianity had been firmly anti-slavery for more than a millennium and 'had always declared the diminution, if not the final elimination, of slavery to be meritorious'.[319] This statement confirms that slavery faded away in Europe and that the Catholic Church was the primary source of opposition to its practice in both the Old World and the New.

Many people followed Jesus' teachings but many did not, preferring to uphold pagan traditions. Most Christian communities in Europe renounced slavery by the 15th century, reserving it solely for enemies captured in war; even when slavery was revived in the process of colonization most European Christians kept their distance from it. And yet, when the opportunity arose, many were the nominal Christians who eagerly took up the new form of extreme slavery and used it to create vast fortunes that were perpetuated and expanded by their descendants. The question arises: Why do human beings show in all periods of history this unwillingness to follow spiritual ideals? Why are we not attracted to the spiritual life? Why are we so attached to the physical body? Why do human beings repeat and repeat, generation after generation, this futile quest for physical immortality? Why this return to paganism after centuries of Christian spirituality? To answer these questions we must descend to the bottom-most level of our archeological site and confront the innate animal nature, the hidden yet ever-present uncivilized quality, of human being.

Level Eleven: Feral Humanity

Here we are at Level Eleven, the very bottom of the excavation. We feel not even the slightest breath of wind here. It is silent and quite dark. We see very little around us. In fact, there are hardly any artifacts worthy of the name. We are in a period of time that stretches back to the beginnings of human life, to the earliest stages of our existence as a species, for this period represents the qualities of human being that we share with animals.

To this aspect of human being Freud gave the term 'es', the German word meaning 'it', known in English translations as the Latin word 'id'. The id is the thingness of human being, that which is not civilized, which is in essence wild. This aspect is also known as ferality, which is more often heard in the context of domesticated animals – horses, cows, sheep, goats, dogs and cats – that have somehow wandered off and lost their tameness, gone wild.

Ferality can occur in human beings. We know this from historical accounts, perhaps the most famous of which is that of Victor, the so-called 'Wild Boy of Aveyron'.[320] He was not the only case, however. In 1920 Christian missionaries in India discovered two sisters living in the jungle.

The girls, aged about eight and two, were cared for and carefully observed until their premature death. It was clear that they had suffered permanent mental damage owing to their lack of contact with human beings. They were unable to walk properly and never learned to talk. While they remained close to each other, they generally shunned the company of other people. These characteristics are common in cases of feral and isolated children.

Feral children continue to be discovered periodically, most of them the victims of abuse and neglect. The case in California of Genie has become highly significant because her life from the age of 13, when she was discovered, was studied by university researchers and recorded on film. She was found having lived most of her childhood in a room of her parents' home, never having had the benefit of physical and social contact. When she was finally released from this prison it was too late; she exhibited all the permanent damage seen in earlier cases of feral children. Over the succeeding years strenuous efforts were made to help her learn the ways of society and culture but she was able to make only the most rudimentary progress in such basic functions as walking, eating and drinking. She never learned to speak or to communicate in any substantial way.

This indelible aspect of human existence has vast implications which Freud's theory of the id only begins to explore. In contemplating them we stand at the very beginning of history and at the cutting edge, where present meets future. But there are certain conclusions that can be clearly drawn. First, culture and civilized behavior are not automatic functions in human beings. These qualities exist as potentialities in each child but they do not become fulfilled in the personality except through the process of human contact and education.

Second, humanity, both the individual and society, is always just a razor's edge away the abyss of an unsocialized, uncivilized existence. But for the passing on of knowledge through the family, community and formal educational systems from one generation to the next the entire human race could conceivably return to prehistoric cultural levels, even to chaos.

Third, if education through interaction is so vital to the appearance of civilized behavior, then we must acknowledge that whenever we do not adequately educate our children the resulting behavioral problems are symptoms exhibiting their latent ferality, manifesting the imperfect realization of the human potential within them. If social problems are, as we have argued, the manifestation of the gradual transformation of a society from a state of unity to a state of dissociation, we can also argue that they express humanity's latent ferality. For the most important defect found in feral children, we must remember, is that they are unable to come close to other human beings and usually demonstrate fear of them

– they prefer to remain isolated, they shun society. If we have the tendency to regress to materialistic paganism, to periodically reject the spiritual teachings we have inherited from great religions in all ages, it is because the duality of human nature is immutable. If our spiritual nature gives us the power to climb to the endless heights of civilization, our animal nature, our imperfection, makes possible the weaknesses that cause us to fall.

Here on Level Eleven, however far we are down the ladder, we are in a sense right back at the top on Level One. Ferality is always latent in every human being. There is no escaping the animal nature within us. We cannot run from or erase it; we can only exercise our equally innate spiritual and intellectual powers to transcend it. Unlike our feral potential, however, which manifests itself without any effort on our part, the spiritual powers must ever be consciously and diligently cultivated in order to appear, take root, flourish and bear fruit. The garden is rooted in nature's unfathomable depths, yet transcends it through humanity's application of spiritual effort. We possess no instincts that force us to behave as cultured humans. Of all creatures on the planet, we alone must teach each other how to live. Without education we are human, yet our humanity is in a sense stillborn. As the West turned away from the moral education offered by the New Testament and increasingly embraced the extreme materialism – not the high spiritual beliefs – of pagan Greece and Rome, the restraints on human behavior were undone, giving the latent feral nature greater freedom. In the face of the countless descriptions of extreme violence committed in the Crusades, the witch-hunts and colonial slavery, no conclusion can be drawn except that these deeds did not express the conscientiousness of Christianity but rather the licentiousness of the unrestrained violent animal. There can be no darker nightmare, no fiercer war, than humanity's struggle against its own uncivilized self disguised as civilized, roaming freely across the earth.

Conclusion

Historian Kurt Samuelson ascribed the rise of capitalism to a 'new spirit of creativeness, of protest against the old order, of inquiry and widening horizons' and of 'freedom from all external authority, especially that of religion' that appeared in Europe at least several centuries before the dawning of systemic and conscious capitalism in the Renaissance. He attributes this new spirit to the contact made with other cultures outside Europe, particularly the Muslims, but also with others along the various trade routes during the age of discovery.[321] Sociologist Joe Feagin has a complementary view, describing this 'new spirit' as the 'development of a strong acquisitive ethic, an ethic coupled with a missionary zeal convinced of the superiority of European civilization. This was early revealed in the conflicts of European

Christians with Islamic regions that controlled access to spices and gold, land control that spurred European expansion across the oceans.' With the rise of Protestantism the acquisitiveness of the Europeans was not so much created – it had already existed for centuries of trade under Roman Catholic authority – as brought into sharper focus. It involved 'a rather greedy individualism that contrasted with the more collectivistic values of the majority of the world's peoples'. [322]

Indeed, whereas indigenous cultures in Africa, Asia and the Americas – even in the hinterlands of Europe itself – tended on the whole to peacefulness and nonviolence, and certainly had nothing like wholesale slaughter and torture, the European colonists broke new ground in inhumane practices, against both enemies and subjects of their own realms. This was not something they learned from neighboring cultures. It was not a part of the quest for freedom from the Old World, not a matter of inquiry, but rather an independent willingness to oppress others with almost no limit. From where, then, did they get this attitude?

Civilization, the centuries-long association amongst a great population, is not a *natural* phenomenon. Man's *natural* state tends to division and dissociation, as proved by the cases of feral children and by the existence of laws prohibiting divisive behavior in all societies and cultures. Civilization can emerge only by the suppression of the will to dissociate. In saying this we agree with Freud's thesis in *Civilization and Its Discontents* that civilized behavior is the product of sublimation. Where we disagree with him is in his rejection of religion's educational role in raising humanity's standards. For it is through the cultivation of true spirituality in human beings, as we have argued, that the ever greater forms of union – from the family to the tribe, the city, the nation and the planet – are possible. Slavery, racism and violent materialism in the West were caused by the weakening and partial collapse of the Christian laws that fostered spiritual unity. This breakdown was a symptom of spiritual immaturity. The slave-holders shunned Christianity as a hindrance to business. They faced a choice: God's way or profit, spirituality or materialism. And because they sought to maximize profits, there was no middle way.

American racism is not a product of biological or cultural differences, however much these differences may serve to exacerbate and perpetuate it. Rather, it is a result of two simultaneous conditions characterizing a dual society: 1) the carefully limited practice of a doctrine of brotherly love and fellowship among the religiously enfranchised, the godly, the sacred, and 2) the religious disenfranchisement of slaves and their identification with profane nature and evil. The paradox of slavery and racism in America was the attempt to balance a set of laws that unified the society and another set that separated and divided it, an awkwardness that eventually proved an ominous counter-melody to the strong theme of successful capitalist development.

The dual society is caused by, on the one hand, the waning of the religious impulse that has historically provided the means of enduring mutual association and identity in the West, and on the other, the waxing of unbridled materialism. That civil law superseded religious law in the history of American race relations indicates the political superiority of the economic powers that established the colonial economy and government. The schisms disrupting first the Roman Catholic Church and then the Protestant sects themselves evidenced an increasing debilitation of spiritual law and unity, which left a vacuum instantly filled by the rising material powers of secularizing kings, merchants, academics and scientists.

In the Renaissance the paradigm of science and materialism displayed its success in attracting both the elite and the masses. Ever since, and particularly in the critical 19th century, scientific views have been gaining increasing popularity and political prestige to the disadvantage of religious beliefs and institutions. The material interests that systematically explored and colonized the New World rode the rising tide of secular power, a tide that succeeded in defining foreign populations in its own legal terms and not in those of a spiritually healthy religion.

This is not to say that the Christian Church would have perfectly exemplified Jesus' teachings had capitalism not influenced it. For history clearly shows that corruption in the Church reaches back centuries before the colonization of the New World. Rather it is to argue that had the Christian teachings been practiced as the basis of social unity, had the *Christianity* of the Church been stronger, the virulent racism of the North American colonies would not have found a suitable environment in which to germinate and evolve. For the teachings of Christ effectively outlaw violent greed in general and its specific forms in slavery and racism. No greater proof of this can be found than the historical fact that the planters in the North American colonies gathered all their powers to prevent first the conversion of Africans and second the universal application and spread of the Christian law and spirit among Africans and Europeans alike. In the end, the slave codes of colonial America had one purpose: to declare Christianity null and void where commercial enterprise was concerned, so that the European colonists in the New World could pursue material gain unhindered by ethical and spiritual principles.

But the nullification of Christianity was not an open fact. Rather it was done quietly, gradually, behind the scenes of religious life. And as spirituality became less and less central to religion in America it left a vacuum that was filled by substitute beliefs that seemed to be even more effective than genuine Christianity. Throughout history true spirituality has been a highly demanding discipline and human beings have always been tempted to seek the rewards of spiritual life without the struggle and sacrifice it entails. They have always wanted to have their cake and eat it too. As westerners grew more materialistic, as they became despiritualized, as they discarded spirituality along with outmoded religious traditions, they never ceased craving the comfort and certitude that religion gives to the soul. There was nothing for it but to seek substitutes, among the most important of which were racism and unbridled capitalism.

With the firm establishment of the all-encompassing language and symbology of race, of the body and its color, of materialism, the despiritualization of the American society and culture became complete. Of course, many Americans have clung to religion and spirituality yet their spiritual conceptions, their voices, their existence for the most part remain excluded from the discourse at the heart of the society.

In the context of Christian society the race-based exclusion of peoples was a profound change. We know that the teachings of Jesus call for universal love. And our explorations through the strata of western history show that – contrary to the assertions of Freud and others opposed to religion – the pioneering generations of Christians, and many generations thereafter in various parts of the world, strove mightily to live up to this ideal. We must accept this historical fact, that ideals are not necessarily unattainable fantasy. We must recognize the reality of spiritual life. We must recognize that the potentiality for spiritual behavior within each of us is an ever-present truth, not merely a hope or dream. The long process of despiritualization in the West first made us believe that spiritual life was impractical, and then made us believe that it never truly existed in the first place except as myth. Spirituality became seen as the province of fools. How far, then, had the inheritors of Christianity strayed from the religious teachings upon which their own civilization rests. How vast and bewildering the change wrought in their society.

The end of this process of despiritualization is even now calling forth a respiritualization of equal, nay greater power. It is, in its turn, involving the entire world in a change so fundamental and far-reaching that only a glimpse of its characteristics and ultimate implications can be obtained.

3

Respiritualization

Introduction

Let us climb back up to the top and see what we have. Here we are again on Level One. The sun is still high and affords a good overview of the entire dig. We went a long way down, to the very depths of human experience. What have we discovered so far?

Let's face it: From a materialistic point of view racism was a great success. It buttressed slavery and enabled the realization of sky-high profits from agricultural capitalism in the New World. To what was that success due? A number of factors were involved but one of the most fundamental was the elimination of religious scruples and spiritual brotherhood from the law and decision-making. Advocates of slavery worked long and hard to clear religion's influence from the promising field of unlimited capitalism in North America. Since they considered the removal of spiritual unity essential to the success of slavery, spiritual revitalization logically is key to the elimination of racism.

Racism in America centers on keeping African and European Americans separated, and particularly preventing interracial marriage. We fear and even hate each other because of our superstitious feelings regarding such marriage ties. These feelings are rooted in the fact that interracial marriage and brotherhood have been defined as illegal for most of American history. The founders of our society outlawed interracial unity because in seeking unlimited wealth they had turned away from spirituality, which is the means for creating unity in diversity, the indispensable basis of every civilization. Reform of the laws alone will not solve the problem of racism if the underlying cultural base is not spiritual.

From this vantage point it is all too clear that everything we believe in, all that we build today, rests on this entire structure. Each level supports the others above it. Our lives today are directly or indirectly dependent on what was built before, on the traditions that we see in the site below. We see the elements of the persecuting society: money economy, colonization for the extraction of raw materials, a class of literati, a merchant class, consolidation of peasants into landless wage-workers. All of these are not necessarily bad. What is bad is that these combined to *substitute for* the traditional spiritual values. It is not a matter of getting rid of the literati, for example; rather they must spiritualize their profession, make their interests congruent with the interests of humanity as a whole. In this sense, then, the unity of the human race has very practical consequences, for it implies that no longer can a class have its own special interests; indeed, there can no longer be any 'special interests' whatsoever since from a spiritual perspective all interests can and must be reconciled.

America's Continuing Spiritual Potential

There is room for optimism that America's struggle with materialism is not hopeless. In the late 19th and early 20th centuries most Americans were – despite their growing political power, prosperity and international prestige – like most peoples around the world, still quite sensitive to spiritual matters and the wonders of life. They were very simple and unjaded. There are numerous fascinating examples of this. Consider reactions to the introduction of public electric lighting.

> The first large-scale use of electricity was for streetlighting. The new lights were demonstrated and sold at great public spectacles, much like today's manned rocket launches. Charles Brush, an inventor and entrepreneur, promised to make downtown Cleveland 'as bright as day' on the evening of April 29, 1879, with twelve of his own electric arc lights powered by a dynamo of his own design. As a crowd of thousands gathered, Brush motioned for his assistant to throw the switch: 'The first globe flickered with purplish light. Thundering cheers gave way to astonishment as the other lights came on. In the awed quiet the Cleveland Grays band struck up its brass, and artillery boomed along the shorefront. Cleveland became the first city to light its public square with electricity.' A year later in Wabash, Indiana, Brush turned on four 3,000-candlepower lamps atop a 200-foot-high courthouse dome on a moonless night. According to an eyewitness, 'the strange weird light, exceeded in power only by the sun, rendered the square as light as midday. Men fell on their knees, groans were uttered at the sight, and many were dumb with amazement.'[1]

As technology has become more dominant we naturally have become more blasé. Even so, our spirituality endures. While the history of the West from about the time of the Civil War till now has shown increasing environmental and social decay, it has also witnessed a gradual counter-movement, a rise out of that moral collapse, represented most spectacularly by the fight against prejudice in World War Two, in the civil rights and women's movements and in apartheid South Africa. Such movements demonstrate America's sensitivity and gradual spiritual maturation, and this despite the long legacy of racism and gender discrimination imposed by law.

Consider the following examples. Contrary to popular understanding, as we have noted, many southern whites were opposed to slavery.[2] That after several centuries of the harshest totalitarian rule[3] enforcing a racist culture a significant portion of whites remained adamantly opposed to slavery is a powerful evidence of the continuing spirituality of European Americans, 'underground' as it were, in the heart of the South. Mysticism is a long tradition among people in America – not only among African Americans and American Indians but among European Americans as well – we have the well-known examples of Emerson, Thoreau and Muir. And of course, no one can forget that one of the captains of the ideological opposition to slavery was none other than a white woman, Harriet Beecher Stowe. Other writers could be regarded as expressing a spiritual perspective even into very recent times: for example Rachel Carson, the author of *Silent Spring*; Jeremy Rifkin, author of *Beyond Beef*; Marilyn Ferguson, author of *The Aquarian Conspiracy* and Page Smith, author of *Killing the Spirit: Higher Education in America*. This movement towards renewed spirituality has attained a new level of consciousness with the recent publication of Paul Ray and Sherry Anderson's *The Cultural Creatives*.

If ever there were a turning point in the long nightmare of racism in the West, a high water mark to that flood of despiritualization, a moment when its fever finally began to break, there could perhaps be no better choice than the heroism of Elizabeth Eckford and her rescuers during the attempted integration of Little Rock High School in September 1957. Surely her fellows in the 'Little Rock Nine', and others who led the way towards integration and even gave their lives, were equally brave but it was Elizabeth who, unlike the others that day, faced the mob alone, and it was her perilous situation that was captured by still and motion picture cameras. The scene was a microcosm of the entire history of racist persecution, indeed of persecution of all kinds. A defenseless teenage girl, meticulously dressed for school, poised, self-assured, innocent, faced what was literally a howling mob. Rarely has any such mob been caught on film and even rarer its attack on such a helpless figure. Hers was a heroism that one often reads about in accounts of historical events but it is difficult to understand and appreciate its reality without the film documentation; written descriptions seem to the reader to be exaggerations. But what made this scene so particularly powerful and historically significant was that in the end she was rescued by a white woman and a white man, who themselves faced considerable risk: Grace Lorch, a woman whose husband taught at a local college for blacks, and Benjamin Fine, a *New York Times* reporter.[4] Together these three people overturned the ages-old pattern of white mob violence against a lone African American. They stood up against not only the mob but also against what had, until then, been the accepted course of history. And the mob allowed them to do so.

Further examples of America's continuing quest for renewed spirituality abound. Melba Patillo, another of the Little Rock Nine, found sincere support and critical assistance from some white students later that year. Jane Elliott faced long-term opposition from colleagues and citizens of her town, Riceville, Iowa, when in 1968 she began her historic third-grade classroom exercise of dividing the children according to eye color and treating each group in turn with open discrimination to teach them the reality of racism. Her father's business was boycotted and he was eventually forced to close it. Her children were severely harassed. In a word, she and her family were persecuted for many years. She has now become internationally known for presenting this same exercise to professionals in the private and public sectors.[5]

Perhaps one of the most unusual hit songs in American popular music was written by a bearded, long-haired man who, long before the hippy era, wore sandals and lived a simple life in the woods in California. His song, 'Nature Boy', was recorded by Nat King Cole and became a top hit in 1948.

> There was a boy . . .
> A very strange enchanted boy.
> They say he wandered very far, very far
> Over land and sea,
> A little shy and sad of eye
> But very wise was he.
> And then one day,
> A magic day, he passed my way.
> And while we spoke of many things,
> Fools and kings,
> This he said to me,
> 'The greatest thing you'll ever learn
> Is just to love and be loved in return.'
> 'The greatest thing you'll ever learn
> Is just to love and be loved in return.'

The composer's name was Eden Ahbez. He was born into a Jewish family in Brooklyn but lived in California most of his adult life. His song and its great popularity that continues to this day (it was recently recorded by Celine Dion) are evidence that America seeks to reclaim a spiritual heritage.

The following year another song, 'You've Got to Be Carefully Taught', entered popular culture from the stage of Rodgers and Hammerstein's classic Broadway musical *South Pacific*:

> You've got to be taught
> To hate and fear,
> You've got to be taught
> From year to year,
> It's got to be drummed
> In your dear little ear
> You've got to be carefully taught.
>
> You've got to be taught to be afraid
> Of people whose eyes are oddly made,
> And people whose skin is a diff'rent shade,
> You've got to be carefully taught.
>
> You've got to be taught before it's too late,
> Before you are six or seven or eight,
> To hate all the people your relatives hate,
> You've got to be carefully taught!

These famous songs were but the beginning of a new direction in American popular culture following World War Two. They were soon followed by several waves of new mystical and spiritual culture created by the Beat poets, the civil rights movement, the Native Americans, the hippies and the new feminism of the 1950s, 1960s and 1970s.

What is needed if America's spiritual life is to continue to grow and eventually to emerge from its underground exile into the full light of renewed acceptance as the basis for civilization? A complete answer to this question requires volumes but here we can discuss at least some of the main pillars at the heart of a respiritualized society: social thought, daily life, justice and education. Let us explore these four subjects in the hope that they will shed a more general light on respiritualization's broadest, holistic implications.

The Respiritualization of Social Science

In academia love is a four-letter word. We have been taught by our educational systems that, for two reasons, spirituality is not relevant to society.

First, spirituality in general is, by virtue of the powerful tradition of separation of Church and state, considered without any right to exist in the public arena. Religion and spirituality are strictly confined to the private home and the house of worship. At most, as Martin E. Marty, Robert Bellah and others have noted, secular society expresses a kind of civil religion in which reverence is shown towards national symbols such as the flag, the anthem and war monuments. Religion is feared as a potential disintegrator of social unity.

Second, not only do we fear religion, we have decided that it is not real and that science has proved itself to be the only truth. Religion of the Church has been replaced by religion of the intellectual academy and the clergy have been replaced by the new priesthood of natural and social scientists. Social scientists are not only the well-known categories of psychologists, sociologists, anthropologists and political scientists but also those who make use of social science concepts and techniques: journalists, government functionaries, managers in business and other fields. Social science is based on the assumption that human beings and human society are essentially material and therefore the solution to social problems must likewise be material.

However, after almost one hundred years in which its materialist philosophy has dominated public discourse and decision-making, social science has failed to solve the problems it has addressed. This is not to say that the social and natural sciences are useless – their potential to benefit society has been clearly demonstrated. Yet while these sciences may be necessary for modern civilization, they are not sufficient. Social scientists themselves and the public alike are now reassessing the assumption that the human being is essentially material and reconsidering the possibility that the needs of the spirit are real. In 1999 Alan Wolfe suggested that the period of social science inquiry relatively free of explicitly moral issues may have been brief, having its heyday 'from roughly the end of World War Two until roughly the 1980s'.

> But [this] postwar period differed from what came before and after. In the writings of Emile Durkheim and Max Weber, sociology – to cite just one of the social sciences – began at the turn of the twentieth century as an explicitly moral undertaking. In recent years, the moral revival has begun to return the social sciences to those roots. The fact that the social sciences never seem to be able to transcend their historical roots suggests that the study of human beings will never be able to completely ignore the moral dimensions that make its subjects human.[6]

Social Science Must be Dual

Science and religion are not only two different systems of thought but also two systems of values. Science has exercised its freedom from religious constraints to define humanity according to its method of rational investigation. In the process, however, science has obliged itself to reject the benefits of spiritual values in the formation of societies. In seeking so avidly to avoid the limiting conditions of a stifling religious tradition, science – and social science in particular – became deaf to religious knowledge. Scientific culture reasoned that if religious institutions are corrupt, then religious ideas and spirituality are also false. It wished to cleanse the society of corruption but it threw the baby out with the bath water.

ACADEMIA'S MATERIALISM

If an individual can choose the mode of his life, be it material or spiritual, the human sciences can likewise choose to describe human beings as fundamentally material or spiritual – or both. There are important consequences in such a choice, for as a discipline in academia, social science holds significant social power and authority. Moreover, the choice determines not only how social science views humanity but also how it views itself: to consider man a spiritual being would league social science with the traditions of the humanities and the divinity schools – even the religions – and to consider humanity a material being would be to join the camp of the natural sciences. The history of social science in the 19th and 20th centuries shows that it has often been striving towards the ideal of the natural sciences and in so doing has reduced humanity to a material object, or at least a fundamentally materially-oriented being, all of whose characteristics are knowable by means of logic and rational investigation. Whether or not human spirituality is a reality is a question that social science ignores and all human traits generally classified as spiritual are either considered beyond the realm of knowable things or interpreted in terms of materially-oriented behavior.

LIMITS OF MATERIALISM IN SOCIAL SCIENCE

In attempting to emulate natural science, however, social science faces an eternal obstacle. Despite all efforts to measure and quantify human behavior, the experimental method cannot reveal the whole human being. Doubtless the body of the human being is understandable by experimentation, for it is merely one of an infinite number of intriguing material objects in the universe accessible by means of empirical science. Yet it is clear that the human being does not rest solely in the physical body and that the key to understanding human behavior cannot be found in the operation of the body. Though essentially dependent on physical existence, just as the mind depends on the existence of the brain, the behavior of the human being possesses a quality of independence. Though the functioning of the mind is dependent on the functioning of the brain, the mind is not limited or controlled by the brain or any other physical feature of the body. The metaphysical mind, existing by virtue of the existence of the physical body, has the potential to know and to control its own self. The action of no individual is fully predictable even under conditions of extreme social pressure. This is the import of the unique human faculty of free will. The experimental method can be applied to physical entities such as atoms because the realm of possible atomic behaviors is defined by discernable laws. The same method, however, cannot be applied to the human mind, whose behavior is not governed by laws external to it but rather by its own volition.

To a degree, animals also exhibit some independence of will, yet the realm of possible behavior in the animal is severely constrained by the operation of laws commonly referred to as instinct. Similarly, cutting-edge research in the natural sciences is discovering evidence that there are spiritual and therefore unpredictable aspects of nature at the quantum, planetary and higher levels. Yet these are quite limited compared to the spiritual consciousness of human beings.[7] The realm of possible behavior in human beings is infinite, for the mind is free to explore without the fetters of physical or instinctual laws. The observer who prefers to interpret individual human will as constrained by social laws might look again and find that social laws are themselves constantly evolving through epochs of human history and exist in infinite variation. The distinguishing quality of the human being is this very limitlessness which provides both the uniqueness of each individual's personality and the uniqueness of the human species. Perhaps this infinitude is an aspect of what is referred to as the image of God in humanity. How, then, could the experimental method, which makes its way towards understanding by simplifying and consuming finite objects – particles, atoms, molecules, cells, organs – be applied to an infinite entity that cannot be consumed, cannot be encompassed by any finite process? Just as infinity ever remains beyond the possibility of complete observation, so too the human spirit ever remains beyond the grasp of full understanding.

THE INSUFFICIENCY OF MATERIAL SOLUTIONS

We cannot understand the causes of social problems such as racism until we understand the full context in which they occur, a context which necessarily involves spiritual reality. Our non-holistic approaches to social problems have focused intently on physical and material phenomena. We need to widen our scope, to cross the frontier between the physical and the spiritual, to explore fully the vast reality that lies along that frontier. We tend to propose answers on the level of policy and legal measures. We think that a holistic approach involving spirituality is inherently irrational, unscientific and hence *impractical*. There is, therefore, a deep chasm in our consciousness between the realm of the spirit and the realm of practice; we believe that one cannot be affected by the other.

Proof that racism is not fundamentally a material problem can be discerned in the history of our failed attempts to solve it solely by material means. First, we regarded it as a legal problem and instituted new laws. But, as we have noted, *Brown* v. *Board of Education* has not to this day produced success. Voting rights did not lead to the election of many black representatives in local and state government.[8] We've long been looking for 'mechanisms',[9] legal, political and economic; but just as we reach them – leading us to think 'we were at long last going to be able to participate, to be represented' – we find they are ineffective.[10] Some advocate a policy emphasizing enterprise zones and tax breaks. Others suggest affirmative action, *laissez-faire* strategies, head-start programs and so on. But these discussions over policies merely shift money and resources from one pool to another without addressing the sources of racism, sources that, as we saw in the case of the 'rainmaker' African American law partner, can remain even when blacks and other minorities finally become materially successful. Even after the black person achieves everything promised by the American dream and fulfills every duty as a loyal citizen, he continues to face quite virulent forms of prejudice, discrimination and outright hatred. We must conclude, then, that although material values are part of the problem they are not the whole or even the most fundamental issue. Rather, something beyond money, beyond the material, remains unresolved.

Until recently most social research has dealt with the physical needs of the world: food, energy, transportation, housing, jobs, conflict resolution, water, environment. This approach was epitomized by the Worldwatch Institute's annual report *State of the World*. Rarely was there a discussion of how spirituality relates to and plays a role in the solving of such pressing material problems. The need for research along spiritual lines is great and growing, for religion and spiritual ideas, right or wrong, have been for centuries central to nearly every society, culture and civilization. Fortunately, after many decades of being regarded with disfavor – particularly in the academic world – spirituality recently returned to the consciousness of researchers and decision-makers. Worldwatch broke new ground with its 2003 article 'Engaging Religion in the Quest for a Sustainable World'.[11] Several international conferences held by the World Bank have gathered spiritual leaders to discuss the spiritual aspects of social and economic development.[12] The Millennium Summit of the United Nations held in September 2000 was preceded by a complementary conference, the Millennium Peace Summit of Religious and Spiritual Leaders. Prominent international organizations such as the Club of Rome and the Club of Budapest have boldly argued for the inclusion of spirituality within all discourse on the issues of humanity's present and future development. In academia, Mircea Eliade brought a profound, clear and objective yet highly sympathetic view of not only religion but also mysticism to academic language. In a recent interview, literary theorist Terry Eagleton, an ardent Marxist who taught for 30 years at Oxford University, advocated 'a search for absolutes, for norms, for answers to what he calls "fundamental questions of truth and love in order to meet the urgencies of our global situation".[13] In the news today it is not uncommon to hear mention of the spiritual as part of solutions to social problems. Such recognition of spirituality as an integral part of human reality has gradually been gaining strength in the consciousness of leaders of thought over the past several decades and particularly after the collapse of the Soviet Union.[14]

If it is ever to obtain a true understanding of racism, human nature and the evolution of society, social science must inevitably broaden its scope beyond the limits of natural science and embrace spirituality as a legitimate and essential aspect of our self-knowledge. It must favor not one approach over the other but rather unite them.

Spiritual Roots of Classical Social Science

The concept of a spiritualized social science seems an oxymoron. Yet when we look carefully at the issue we see several interesting points. First, as Alan Wolfe has observed, in the earliest years of social science in Europe its practitioners accepted morality and spiritual principles, particularly the need for social unity. They believed these principles are necessary for the stability and growth of society and saw no conflict between religious ideas and rational, scientific exploration of human civilization. Second, the period of intense anti-clericalism, particularly in the mid- to late-19th century, led social scientists to reject religion as a valid source of knowledge and action and to try to translate religious principles into secular terms so that they would be politically acceptable in a secular bourgeois state.[15] Third, as we have noted, social scientists are today increasingly discussing the issues of religion and of spirituality and are beginning to recognize that spirituality is essential for the resolution of social problems.

EARLY SOCIAL SCIENCE

There is no better illustration of the relationship between religion and social science than the work of Karl Marx (1818–83), the most widely read and influential champion of materialist philosophy. What is often most attractive in his writings is that they seem to show us the inner machinery, the immutable laws that determine the way society evolves. Society, he argued, is the expression of the material, economic relations among individuals; if we trace these relations one to another, we will discover the motivation of all history and the inexorable march of destiny. Just as Newton unlocked nature's timeless secret of the movement of physical bodies, Marx gave us a mechanics of the social universe.

Yet somehow the application of his formulas leaves us unsatisfied. His theories do not exactly describe and account for what we observe. Is there a flaw somewhere or are we misinterpreting his ideas?

There is no doubt that Marx was a brilliant thinker and that his ideas about society have enhanced the ages-long discussion concerning humanity. But it is not possible to regard his work as a scientific theory exactly explaining human social phenomena. Its inexactitude could be shown by comparing the statement and predictions of his theory to observable events that contradict it; many have already criticized his theory on the ground that it simply is not accurate, having no predictive capacity as do successful theories in chemistry or physics.[16] A better way, however, to approach the issue of Marx's theoretical inaccuracy is by pinpointing the degree to which his theory was ever meant to be rigorously scientific. For despite Marx's embellishment of his thought with repeated assertions of its scientific character – assertions that serve primarily as political rhetoric – and despite his bitter denunciations of religion, there lies, barely concealed beneath the surface of his work, moral and religious premises.

Marx was the heir of a line of illustrious, venerated social thinkers extending from Adam Smith (1723–90) to Hegel (1770–1831), all of whom regarded the workings of the human world as the fruit of an 'invisible hand', of an unseen metaphysical guide. This evokes images of a shepherd and his flock, a gardener and his garden, a teacher and his students, who progress under the influence of their benefactor wholly ignorant of his presence. Are these not visions of God cast in godless terms so that modern scientific sensibilities may be cultivated undisturbed by old-fashioned sentiments? An invisible hand is surely preferable to God in an anti-religious culture, for we know a hand's form and function; God, however, requires obeisance and humility and, worst of all, defies our rational investigation of His nature.

The concept of an invisible hand that we find in the thought of Smith, Hume, Kant, Hegel and Marx is itself undeniably a metaphysical mystery. If it could not be considered religious *per se* it would be more accurately described as 'sub-theological',[17] meaning that the theological theme is not openly admitted but clearly implied and apparent. These thinkers wrote that life shows to us one aspect and hides from us another that is its true meaning; likewise, our actions have for us a surface meaning and yet within they possess wholly other consequences that lead to purposes transcending our individual lives. Thus there is, as Werner Stark termed it, a 'heterogony of purposes' in social life.[18] The goals for which the individual strives are actually encompassed by and subordinate to the goals of a transcendent entity. A person's struggles actually serve a purpose other than his own.

Adam Smith wrote that human life proceeds as if it were 'led by an invisible hand'.[19] His disciple Frederic Bastiat (1801–50) took up the theme more frankly by ascribing to the social economy an overarching 'harmony', a 'Providence', saying: 'If only each person will look after himself, God will provide for all.'[20] In the work of Immanuel Kant (1724–1804) this theme is described as the will of 'nature':

> Individuals and even whole nations are little aware that they follow unwittingly the designs of nature, which are unknown to them, when they strive for their own ends, each according to his own intention and often against the next man, and that they work for the promotion of those designs in which they would be little interested, even if they were known to them.[21]

In the thought of Georg Hegel we find the concept of 'divine, absolute reason' ruling the world such that 'the living forces of individuals and the nations, when they seek and satisfy their own intentions, are at the same time the means and the tools of something higher and wider of which they know nothing'.[22] What Stark called a heterogony of purposes, Hegel describes as the 'cunning of Reason', the mysterious art by which the unseen Reason, or Geist – meaning Spirit – governs the world and harnesses the purposes of men for its own greater Purpose.[23]

Marx perceived within the chaos of class struggle and the conflict between material progress and oppression a logic that designed a harmonious destiny out of the alienation of man from man: 'we recognize in this antagonism the clever spirit which keenly proceeds in working out all these contradictions'.[24] Karl Löwith specifically notes here that 'the clever spirit' evokes Hegel's 'cunning of reason'. This heterogony of purposes in Marx's theory is manifested in the role of the proletariat, whose membership 'cannot emancipate itself without emancipating itself from all the other spheres of society, without, therefore, emancipating all these other spheres'. In being such a class, it is a 'class which is the dissolution of all classes'.[25] The essence of its existence transcends it and serves a transcending purpose. Charles Taylor explains: 'Marxism seems to speak . . . of a collective intention or purpose, where there is no corresponding individual intention or purpose.' Hence, 'the will of a class becomes something mysterious added on to history, as it were, from the outside.

The theory appears to be an odd kind of supernatural holism.'[26]

How did Karl Marx, the quintessential materialist, develop a world view so replete with mystical and spiritual concepts far from the realm of natural science? Easton and Guddat have shown that the Christian tradition lies at the base of Marx's thought. His education at the Gymnasium in Trier centered on the principles of Christianity and on humanistic philosophy. As a youth his hero was Jesus Christ. After several years of university life his attachment shifted from Jesus to another religiously viewed figure, Prometheus, whom he described as 'the noblest of saints and martyrs in the calendar of philosophy.'[27]

At the age of 25 Marx still respected the Christian tradition, albeit in an explicitly secular form. Here we begin to see the transformation of social science from a form of modern inquiry that blended religion and science to one that reoriented itself away from religion and exclusively towards science. In 'On the Jewish Question' (1843) he wrote:

> The religious spirit can only be realized if the stage of development of the human spirit which it expresses in religious form, manifests and constitutes itself in its *secular* form. This is what happens in the *democratic* state. The basis of this state is not Christianity but the *human basis* of Christianity. Religion remains the ideal, non-secular consciousness of its members, because it is the ideal form of the *stage of human development* which has been attained.[28]

Although it is clear that he rejects the form of religion, he accepts the moral substance of religious ideals and seeks to realize them.

Several years later Marx displayed another aspect of his sub-theological world view. In *The Communist Manifesto* (1848), according to Löwith, Marx reveals his heritage of Jewish messianism, for the *Manifesto* is 'a prophetic document, a judgment, and a call to action and not at all a purely scientific statement based on the empirical evidence of tangible fact.' Löwith emphasizes the point that even though Marx may have been attempting a scientific portrait of society and oppression – it was in this period, the late 1840s, that he was working on the manuscripts that would later be published as *Capital* – his purpose, motivation and approach were fundamentally moral; therefore, scientism must be properly considered a secondary, supportive aspect in his work. 'Marx may explain the fact of exploitation "scientifically" by his theory of surplus-value; exploitation, nevertheless, remains an ethical judgment, something which is what it is by being unjust.'[29]

Erich Fromm, who based much of his work and philosophy on the ideas expressed in this quotation from 'On the Jewish Question', also characterizes Marx's work as being in the messianic tradition, even if fundamentally atheist: 'Marx, like Hegel and like many others, expresses his concern for man's soul, not in theistic but in philosophical language.' And Fromm asks, 'Does not all this mean that Marx's socialism is the realization of the deepest religious impulses common to the great humanistic religions of the past?'[30] Robert Tucker takes the point further by arguing that if Marxism is the fulfillment of religious goals, it can itself be considered a religion:

> [Marx's] atheism was a positive religious proposition. It rules out consideration of Marxism as a religious system of thought only if, with Marx, we equate the traditional religions with religion as such.[31]

The intent here is not to show that Marxism is entirely unscientific. There are, of course, many applications of logic and rational investigation in his work. Rather, we have sought to uncover the metaphysical thread that weaves through Marx's logical theories, be they of his youth or of his maturity, and is part of the basic substance of his ideology. He found a 'clever spirit' governing not only the relations of men but the world's destiny. By means of this spiritual view he constructed a comprehensive vision of history and a dream of the future.

Secularism and the Despiritualization of Social Science

Karl Marx's spirituality was not unusual among social theorists of his time. The question is: What happened? Why did spirituality die in social thought in the West? The answer is that it didn't die. It went underground. The Europeans became influenced by a new social class, the bourgeoisie, who gradually waxed in power and authority as the Church waned and wilted from the long-term effects of its internal corruption.

SCIENTISM

If religion is such a vital part of social life, one might ask, why is it that the West has witnessed a profound movement of irreligion, beginning in the age of revolutions and continuing until today, sweeping away old traditions, norms and institutions? To define spirituality in terms of traditional religions in the West leads to the conclusion that the world is secularizing itself. But spirituality cannot be defined in terms of institutions alone; to do so results in what has been called by Peter Glasner the 'sociological myth' of secularization, based on the 'illusion' of 'modernization'. Precisely, 'The myth of a secularization process can be seen to operate clearly when the basis for defining religion (or religiosity) is institutionally bound.' He also suggests that 'most "theories" of the secularization process are really generalizations from limited empirical findings used by sociologists to bolster an implicit ideology of progress'.[32]

One must wonder exactly why talk of love and spirituality has become not only passé but positively abhorrent in most if not all academic or political discussions of social problems in general and of racism in particular. Our culture no longer accepts such talk as valid. This can be traced to one and only one cultural development in our history: the rise and dominance of scientism. Secular sociology has believed in science but it is a belief that is in fact an ideology more well understood as scientism. Scientistic sociology has inherited the centuries-long feud between science and religion, a war fought over false premises.

Science has been viewed by some as a penetrating light on human existence and religions as the resultant shadow. The light represents truth; the shadow represents unreality or myth. As the light of science grows and pervades society, the shadow of religion, so it is said, will disappear and trouble us no more. But as we are here discovering, social scientists have only half-heartedly dismissed religion, for as they pay great deference to the light of empirical science, they understand that in the final analysis spirituality is a light of another kind whose illumination is natural and necessary in every society. Perhaps the reason why some scientists were determined to dismiss religiosity as a dying anachronism, falling before the cleansing powers of secularism, is that religion's existence, its reality, gave proof that science itself was limited, that the scientific method could not solve all problems, answer all questions, and was therefore unfit to be hailed as the indisputable and exclusive creed of the modern age.

It was the authority of science-based culture that allowed slave-holders and slave-traders to nullify the humanity of Africans and to pursue economic advantage and success with no moral scruples, with the cold-blooded calculation of the miser, the mathematician whose goal is to maximize measurable physical results. Science deals only with material things; it cannot speak about spirituality, the non-material, the metaphysical. We have so fallen in love with science that we have reinterpreted its limitations. We do not wish to acknowledge that science does not speak about the metaphysical because so far it *cannot*. Instead, we say that science does not speak about the metaphysical because the metaphysical is not reality and therefore it is not science that is limited but rather the religious mind.

We desperately need to abandon this interpretation of science, which cannot be the alpha and omega of human endeavor. It alone cannot serve as the foundation of civilization. Granted, science clearly is essential to the evolution of human society but it must be recognized as having its proper place. Once we admit to ourselves the inherent limitations of science we will then be able to foster in a systematic fashion those resources and practices that will answer the metaphysical or spiritual needs of humanity. It is foolish for us to try to do so with science alone; indeed, it is harmful in the extreme. Have we not seen time and time again, and particularly in the decades following the detonations of atomic bombs at the end of World War Two, the failure of science to answer our most urgent questions? Have we not seen countless proofs that science is as much a Pandora's box as a panacea? Have we not seen the failure of technologies alone, of the agricultural 'green revolution', of the computer, of the automobile, of 'weapons of peace', to establish peace and prosperity?

Often commentators have pronounced sciences and technologies as mere tools; the key to our problems, they advise, is to know how to wield these tools and for what purposes. These words of wisdom having been repeatedly said, it is time to take the next step and explore the other side of life, the metaphysical that has been virtually ignored. Our ignorance of spiritual life is the hallmark of western urban culture in the 20th and the 21st centuries. The overemphasis of science has led to the preference for the artificial, the manmade, and the rejection of nature and the natural. Clearly our society must experience a cultural revolution in order for the fundamental spiritual needs of people to be met and for the social problems that have long plagued us to be eliminated.

Slavery in the Americas was unique in the world history of slavery because it was pursued as a scientific and technological matter for the sake of maximizing material gain. It reduced the slaves to less than human – even to non-humans – in a systematic fashion over centuries. It was one long sweeping glorification of science and technology. It was a reveling in new-found power through the use of physical laws. But it was also one long sweeping violation of the spiritual laws upon which human society ultimately depends.

By all means, let science and technologies develop and flourish in such ways that benefit all humanity. Let us develop the wisdom to know what is benefit and what is harm, both in the short term and the long term. Let us achieve a balance between physical development and spiritual development. We must once and for all realize that great questions of morality are often not 'either–or' but both. If a caution is offered against excessive materialism based on science one cannot jump to the conclusion that the cautioner opposes all science and technology and looks forward to all human beings 'going back to nature' and living in the jungles on fruits and nuts. Nor can one assume that the cautioner is a religious fanatic who wishes to see everyone worshiping on bended knees most of each day. Let us be done with this kind of irrational thinking. Let us realize that what we are talking about is balance, holism. What we need is not the exclusive rule of one paradigm over all others but the simultaneous, harmonious balance of many paradigms. The flight of an airplane depends on the delicate balance of many forces operating simultaneously. Likewise we need now understand that the rise of true civilization depends on the delicate balance of no less critical and simultaneous social paradigms.

SECULARISM

When the Berlin Wall collapsed in 1989, one of the most significant results was the return to religious life of millions of people in the former Soviet Union and eastern Europe. This was a historic development, for it showed that after decades of being influenced by the most powerful institutions in the society, people were unable and unwilling to give up religion and they thirsted for spiritual knowledge and understanding. They embarked upon the revitalization of their religious life as one of the very first activities they undertook with their new-found freedom.

Elsewhere a similar revival in interest in religion has appeared. As we have noted, the World Bank has held several conferences dealing with the relationship between religion and development. Native Americans have promoted a renaissance of their indigenous beliefs since the 1960s and they continue to be a strong international voice for the real power of spiritual laws. Legal scholar Stephen L. Carter noted that in the United State Congress of the early 1990s 'over 90 percent of the members say that they consult their religious beliefs before voting on important matters'.[33] Western social scientists and social philosophers are beginning to take heed of this phenomenon and are continuing to strengthen the undercurrent of spirituality in social science.

As we have seen, in his 1995 book *Freedom and Its Discontents*, Peter Marin, who is himself a convinced secularist, provides one of the strongest critiques of secularism in America, admitting that it has led to moral failure. Although he does not believe that religion is a solution, he understands that there are fundamental human needs – which in this discussion we have been calling spiritual – that are consistently unfulfilled in American society, a failure that bodes ill for individual and community alike.

Wade Clark Roof, in a 1998 article, found that Americans are, like the peoples of the former Soviet Union, eagerly and perhaps desperately searching for spiritual fulfillment:

> this quest involves nothing less than a radical protest against the values and outlook implicit in modernity – the post-Enlightenment, highly rational and scientific worldview of the past several hundred years that has privi-leged mind over body, technology over nature, innovation over tradition, knowledge over experience, mastery over mystery . . . Modernity alienates, as when people feel cut off from their natural environments, or when the medical establishment concerns itself only with the body and not with the mind and body, or when human life loses its connections with animal life

and Earth's ecosystems more generally. Fragmented knowledge and highly specialized institutional sectors lie at the very heart of today's spiritual malaise.[34]

Let us trace the origins of modern secularism. Corruption, schism and political machination had marred the Catholic Church's authority and unity from the early Middle Ages and led to the Protestant Reformation in the 16th century. But the process did not stop there. No sooner had Protestants arisen to redefine the purpose and practice of Christianity than their own leaders were at odds with each other, leading to what effectively has been a self-sustaining cyclical process of church formation, criticism and schism continuing to this day. Internal religious protest and schism spilled beyond the church doors into society at large and continued to evolve into profound class war. The nobility and the clergy both were blamed for the corruption that had prevented Europe's economic justice and development. Criticism and protest of the government followed suit, leading to the series of powerful social revolutions beginning in the 18th century.

Social science was born in this milieu of schism in which religious and civil authorities alike were being called into question and overthrown. The traditional structure of knowledge had collapsed and the clergy in particular became the targets of condemnation. The Church and the modern European academy are therefore traditionally irreconcilable, although ironically the former was the founder of the latter. Their views of life are fundamentally different and the competition for authority in society has caused their differences to be exaggerated into an apparently irreversible mutual opposition. Where once the Church held the greatest power in the government of peoples, now the natural and social scientists are attributed the greatest authority by governments, for it is upon material relations that modern societies are established and it is the study and manipulation of materials which form the heart of these sciences.

Social science evolved as the moral arm of the bourgeoisie, a class that had fought its way to independence from government and clergy alike. Rather than turn to the clergy for moral confirmation and legitimization – after all, the clergy remained one of its major rivals – the bourgeoisie created a new moral order based on science. It was science that provided the technology with which the bourgeoisie accumulated wealth, the source of its political power. Therefore science was taken as a higher truth, the ultimate authority. Authority gradually swung away from the Church to the institutions of scientific endeavor, namely the universities and technical institutes. Alvin Gouldner argues that the secular state, in its 19th-century emergence, needed 'an ally in developing its autonomy from religious establishments'. The state therefore 'co-opted' not only science but the entire university and 'mobilized' it 'as an independent font of culture and ideology' – independent, that is, from the Church.[35] As do lawyers seeking to bolster their case with the most prestigious of expert witnesses, the secularists depended upon ostensibly 'scientific' arguments.

Social science absorbed the anti-clerical sentiment and hitched its fortunes to natural science, the uncorrupted truth of the modern age that would dispel the shadows of the Church-based superstitions, dogmas and falsehoods. By removing God and religion from the academy, social scientists accomplished two things. First, following the example of the bourgeoisie, they freed themselves from the restrictions of traditions originating in Church institutions. Second, they became free to define the world according to their own processes, to make humanity in their own image. In this regard social scientists were advancing the line of thought – dating from the Renaissance – that gradually was returning to humanity all the attributes and powers that religion had assigned to God.

Although social science seemed to become completely secular and atheistic, its despiritualization was only partial. The ideals of religion were still needed; the revolutionaries believed in the brotherhood and unity of civilization but they had faith that science would be the means. Religion was thus not erased by social science but rather disguised in secular terms. Meanwhile, academics who believed in God, spirituality and religion went underground, as it were.

The centrality of religion to the evolution of social science, and of western civilization as a whole, has been affirmed by many of the classical sociologists whose professional careers were, ironically, devoted to the creation of a scientific, secular substitute for Christianity. As academics commissioned by and serving at the pleasure of the secular state, many early sociologists, Saint-Simon, Auguste Comte and Durkheim in particular, were charged with the monumental task of refuting the spiritual basis of ecclesiastical authority and transferring the allegiance of the people to the scientifically-based authority of the modern civil government. It was nothing short of a unique revolution, consciously planned and executed, that cut down the tree of religious culture in Europe and planted a new intellectual paradigm in its stead. Their labors and writings testified to the difficulty of their assignment and revealed their own respect for the social powers of religion. In *Secular Religion in France, 1815–1870*, D. G. Charlton argues:

> Nineteenth-century thinkers were, in general, keenly aware of both the moral and social utility and the private consolations of religious or at least philosophical belief. Emile Durkheim's acknowledgment of the social value

of religions and William James's belief in their psychological value were foreshadowed throughout the century . . . For social reformers like the Saint-Simonians, Comte, Pierre Leroux and Etienne Cabet, as for the revolutionaries before them, religion was prized as a cult to spur the masses in society to moral action . . . they . . . saw the chaos and horror of the Revolution as warnings against irreligion.[36]

Writing in 1901, Durkheim himself expressed the great challenge which sociology faced:

> The moral *conscience* of the country [France] must be the same in all classes and in all spheres of society. Moral education, for its part, must be the same at all levels of education . . .
> This pedagogical task, which is always of primary importance, is particularly urgent under present conditions. For the past 30 years, we have undertaken a task, the grandeur of which cannot be justly denied and whose difficulties must also be recognized. We have sought to give the country a strictly rational moral education. We have decided to renounce the religious symbols used by our predecessors and to teach the bare moral truth.[37]

Durkheim's rejection of religious morality in favor of a scientific and rational successor is in itself an acknowledgment of the historical centrality of religion. He became more explicit in *Elementary Forms of the Religious Life*, asserting that the principle categories of thought 'are born in religion and of religion; they are a product of religious thought'. He further argues that 'there is something eternal in religion'.[38]

Writing of the work of Karl Mannheim, Gunter Remmling neatly summarized sociology's ambivalent relationship to religion:

> The programs of conservative sociologists frequently end with efforts to resuscitate the irrational forces of religion. In France Comte and Durkheim praised the regulative power and unifying moral strength of religion; in England it was Benjamin Kidd – an ideological defender of British imperialism – who recommended group constraint and the suprarational sanctions of religion as mainsprings of social progress. In the end Mannheim, as well, came to believe that group survival depended on religion which alone could establish valuational consensus about the ultimate ends of social life.[39]

Alvin Gouldner's sketch of the relationship between religion and sociology during its 'classical period' (1890–1920) is particularly lucid:

Religion continued to be attributed a very special importance in the affairs of men but this was now expressed in the formulations and assumptions of scholarly theory and research. The religious concerns of sociology became sublimated and secularized but they did not disappear. This transition can be clearly seen in the differences between Comte's and Durkheim's treatment of religion.

In the course of his studies of religion, Durkheim developed a conception of the requirements of social order, which premised that society itself was the godhead and that social order depended on the creation and maintenance of a set of moral orientations that were essentially religious in character. In Durkheim, therefore, the religious impulse was no longer expressed, as it had been by Comte, in the formulation of a religion of humanity as a distinct and externalized structure. Durkheim had no religion of humanity as such. He sublimated and depersonalized the manifest religious craving of the Comtian, although he did not eliminate it.

Durkheim thus gave sociology a new, secularized public image. He presented it as a discipline primarily concerned with what is and what has been but not with what ought to be. A 'value-free' conception of sociology emerged in Durkheim's work with greater sharpness. In some part this was stimulated by his effort to distinguish sociology from socialism. It was further strengthened by Durkheim's readiness to relinquish in *practice* the earlier, Comtian expectation that sociology could stipulate and legitimate values, even though Durkheim still maintained in *principle* that this would be possible at some future time.[40]

Social science, therefore, does not reject morality or spirituality. It guards or sublimates its morality because it fears the threat that traditional religion poses to its own modern moral and spiritual constructs. Moral social science is not only inherently religious but also inherently critical and critical in particular of the old religious dogmas it seeks to succeed. Therefore, to a great extent the concept of 'science' and the title of 'scientist' have been used merely as symbols by critics of the old religious order. Moreover, a critique of a world based on religious institutions and principles could gain supporters by enlisting the aid of those who had suffered at the hand of religion. Science, as a primary martyr during the time of religious power, was a political pawn which – by virtue of its success in developing technologies and lending advantages to the practical world – gave highly damaging and influential testimony to the unfitness of religion to rule, to take a major part in the construction of society and even to be considered a true reality.

In the aftermath of their revolutionary victory, however, the secularists have retained an acute memory of religion's original moral fragrance and have striven to diffuse it once again throughout the world by their own designs. It is a changing of the guard: the clergy have failed in their duty to shepherd mankind by means of 'myth' and now the social philosophers and scientists hope to accomplish the task with the tools of logic and rationality. Social science has rejected not morality and spirituality but rather their old religious forms. Its self-appointed task is to revolutionize humanity's spiritual life and in so doing it facilitates the removal of the caretakers of the outmoded religions by instituting a new symbolic language, a new set of laws, a new understanding and a new faith, of which they themselves constitute the new priesthood. This, then, explains the paradox of a social scientific practice that outwardly rejects the idea of religion as a true force in human society yet inwardly speaks of the critical need for moral and spiritual ideals.

Respiritualization of Social Science

In recent decades we have been witnessing a gradual resolution of this ideological dispute. The once bitter division of humanity among rival secular and religious leaders seems to have begun a healing process, for in the 20th century many prominent social scientists acknowledged the validity of both the material and the spiritual aspects of humanity. They found a 'redemption' of humanity, as Claude Levi-Strauss phrased it, in reconstructing it holistically, in returning it to its original, dual yet united spiritual and material nature. In so doing, social science demonstrates a maturity, a self-consciousness by which it is able to transcend the rhetoric of its youth, cease its diatribes against religion and spirituality and emerge from its cradle of fiery social and intellectual revolutions to enter into dialogue with all humanity.

As the 20th century progressed a quiet countercurrent developed beneath social science's mainstream secular and atheistic world view. Prominent social scientists increasingly voiced the same call for understanding the importance of religion and spirituality in social science. The sub-theological theme of social science carried forward by Comte, Durkheim and others in the 19th and early 20th centuries, continued apace. Max Weber, Sigmund Freud, Marvin Harris, Claude Levi-Strauss and Talcott Parsons, to name a representative group, saw their work in social science as, at least in part, moral or theological endeavors. Their theories, though presented in a scholarly, scientific form, nonetheless embrace beliefs in a guiding spirit, an invisible hand; beliefs in the need for rational morality, moral sensibilities, senses of responsibility to humanity, justice and order, loyalty to the whole. Though the morality is there, it is presented in a scholarly, scientific form. In his *Tristes Tropiques*, Claude Levi-Strauss writes that the ethnographer's 'very existence is incomprehensible except as an attempt at redemption: he is the symbol of atonement'. The ethnographer works for the redemption of a humanity – both western and eastern cultures, modern and 'primitive' – that denies its own unity (or 'reciprocity', as Levi-Strauss put it), that ignores the 'total social fact' of humanity's oneness. He refers to humanity's disunity as an 'original sin'. It is not surprising, then, that despite the prevailing view that anthropology is a rational and objective discipline after the fashion of the natural sciences, 'Levi-Strauss has accepted an interpretation of his thought that finds in it *"une dimension spirituelle plus ou moins explicite"*'.[41]

An even more revealing testament is given by another anthropologist, George Murdock (1897–1985):

> Very slowly and very reluctantly, I have come to the conclusion that most of the principles that we have advanced to order our data bear little resemblance in kind to the systems of theory developed in the older physical and biological sciences. They have far more in common with the equally complex but often unverified, and unverifiable, systems outside the realm of science which we know as mythology or perhaps as philosophy or even theology.[42]

Murdock is not alone in this opinion. Sociologist Susan Budd, in interpreting a statement from Talcott Parsons, the grand old man of American sociology, pointed out that any theory of action must take into account humanity's non-material motivations. Undoubtedly the human is a material being, an animal in his or her physical form, and must conform to certain laws of production and reproduction which all animal species share. Nevertheless the human is also a metaphysical being capable of understanding the world in non-material terms and taking action on the basis of non-material motivations.

Parsons considers that religious symbolism does not represent society or empirical reality in any form but rather refers to aspects of significant human experience which are outside the range of scientific understanding. In other words, religion and spiritual experience are real. Quoting Parsons she concludes:

> Religion, because it is the only method of grasping the non-empirical, is a necessary basis for human action. Since the ultimate values which religion represents determine social action, religion is not a social phenomenon; rather 'society is a religious phenomenon'.[43]

We should not, therefore, permit materialist philosophy to cause in social science a division between practical life, calling it reality, and spiritual life or piety, calling it illusion. Both are aspects of one reality we call humanity and to eliminate one or the other is to lead to gross inaccuracy in understanding ourselves. Both the materialists and the clergy have, each in their own times, been guilty of omission. The clergy, having ignored in the past the importance of practical and scientific considerations, were upstaged by the materialists, who strode into the intellectual arena to rectify the situation. But, as the upset pendulum swings beyond the point of equilibrium, the materialists in their turn came to ignore spiritual considerations. The balance must be restored. Inasmuch as humanity is inherently spiritual and material, there cannot but exist dual spiritual and material components in social science. Will Herberg concurs:

> The most empirical society, as the best sociologists themselves are beginning to recognize, cannot operate without presuppositions – presuppositions about reality, about man and human life – which are quite philosophical and like it or not, even theological.[44]

Much research in the fields of psychology and psychoanalysis has dealt more or less explicitly with spirituality, most notably the works of Carl Jung, Erich Fromm and other post-Freudians. And this is increasingly supported by work in other disciplines: Pitirim Sorokin's *Altruistic Love: A Study of American 'Good Neighbors' and Christian Saints* (1950); Robert Bellah et al.'s *Habits of the Heart: Individualism and Commitment in American Life* (1985); Riane Eisler's *The Chalice and the Blade: Our History, Our Future* (1987); Alan Wolfe's *Whose Keeper?: Social Science and Moral Obligation* (1989); Page Smith's *Killing the Spirit: Higher Education in America* (1990); James Collier's *The Rise of Selfishness in America* (1991); and Robert Putnam's *Bowling Alone: The Collapse and Revival of American Community* (2000).

Popular culture, Wade Clark Roof finds, has witnessed the explosion of what must be recognized as an unorganized movement of spiritual seekers.

> As a visit to any large bookstore will demonstrate, interest in spirituality in both the sense of life politics and self-reflexivity is pervasive today. If, as Martin E. Marty says, spirituality as a topic was abandoned in public discourse back in the secular 1960s, then clearly it has returned with a vengeance. On the shelves are found creation spirituality, eucharistic spirituality, Native American spirituality, twelve-step spirituality, Eastern spirituality, feminist spirituality, Earth-based spirituality, women's spirituality, men's spirituality, in addition, of course, to medieval mysticism and any number of Jewish and Christian spiritual traditions. Journey is a major

metaphor, second only to recovery, suggesting the crucial importance of spiritual growth as an ideal.[45]

Roof observes that 'the boundaries of the religious are expanding',[46] meaning that the practice of spirituality is no longer monopolized by established religious organizations, is no longer an 'official' activity that must receive institutional definition, sanction and supervision. Rather it is immediately accessible to all. The mediation of spiritual leaders, professional or otherwise, is no longer deemed necessary. Spirituality has become a grassroots movement. As its boundaries expand it has reached into the staid halls of academe and begun to establish itself as a legitimate category of social thought. As the quest for reviving a sense of wholeness is being fulfilled, we are coming to the point where the extreme relativity of postmodernism is ending – at least to a degree – and making way for some acceptance of universal truths, foremost of which is the recognition of the oneness of the human race. We are therefore witnessing the interaction and mutual support of two separate developments: the original underground spirituality of academia and the popular mass movement of spirituality which is none other than a kind of postmodern enlightenment. This interaction has the potential to transform not only social science and the entire academic tradition but daily life as well.

The Respiritualization of Daily Life
Distinguishing True Spirituality from Idolatry

Is it not naive, or perhaps hopelessly irrational, to argue that if we return to religion all will be well? Is it not foolish to believe that all we need do is go back to 'that old time religion' and follow more closely the footsteps of our devout ancestors? After centuries of religious culture in North America, should we be expected to believe that now a more devoted worship of God will solve our problems, many of which came about through the actions of corrupt religious leaders and institutions? If corrupted religion served as the foundation for slavery and racism in the West, it would certainly make no sense to turn towards the same religious culture for relief from the oppression it has caused for centuries.

A reasonable objection. Nevertheless, if we accept the premise that humanity is as much spiritual as material, then we must revitalize the universal religious beliefs upon which true civilization has always been based, beliefs that have taught us to sanctify life and to practice spiritual unity amongst ourselves. We seek not, however, a return to some nostalgic refuge of 'the good old days' but a renewal of spirituality, a renewal that has nothing to do with nostalgia, just as the farmer's preparation for the planting season has nothing to do with a fixation with the past. What we require is a spirituality that is not limited to past forms of worship but one that encourages the infinite development and creativity of the human being, that fosters our growth beyond what we have known and achieved in the past. Religion that binds us to empty and harmful traditions is not true spirituality but worship of idols, of manmade concepts. We must make a distinction between true spirituality and idol worship and recognize that racism is a product of the latter.

Developing Consciousness of Humanity's Spiritual–Material Nature

When a medical student in the West begins her training she is usually obliged to discover the functioning of the human body by dissecting a cadaver. Many are the accounts of the student's first encounter with a cadaver – one of the best being that of Michael Crichton in his *Travels*. A key to unlocking western medicine's attitude to the human body and to humanity as a whole is the encouragement it gives to students to regard the cadaver merely as a physical object and not as sacred remains. The same attitude is taught to students of physical anthropology, which has led to controversies regarding the remains of Native American and African peoples in North America. When the students enter the dissection room they do not remember the life of these people; they offer no prayers, no call of thanks, no marks of respect; they assign the bodies an anonymity which renders them divorced from humanity and thus later in their careers they tend to do the same to their patients and even to themselves. They tend to regard human beings, living and dead, as physical objects devoid of and completely unrelated to anything resembling a spiritual reality. The same attitude is found in the treatment of animals in slaughterhouses, laboratories and on farms – that is, that they are physical objects of value only as they provide benefits defined by their owners.[47]

How different is this attitude from that of the Native American tradition, which requires that before any animal or plant is taken for food its spiritual value is recognized and duly respected, in prayer and in the offering of a sacrifice.

In the destruction of the natural environment by individuals and companies, the creation of mega-cities that remove the people from any consciousness of spiritual reality, in the production, promotion and consumption of mind-crippling drugs we see that such neglect, nay rejection of spiritual reality is widespread. Society, then, presents itself as a landscape in which the light of spiritual consciousness is dimmed or doused in great swaths throughout the populace. In some places and circumstances spirituality is more strongly represented, while in others it is weak or nonexistent. Like a diseased tree, a society's spiritual health is revealed as subject to harmful forces that strip away fruits, leaves, branches, in patches and nearly random patterns; the tree remains alive yet severely compromised by a disease the effects of which are, though apparently inconsistent, widespread and devastating.

By refining our understanding of spirituality and recognizing that we need to practice it in all aspects of daily life, we can begin to see that the respiritualization of society is a practical possibility. Yet the respiritualization of daily life, far from being simple, involves many unexpected and profound challenges in resetting the proper balance between the private and the public, individualism and collective-consciousness, the roles of Church and state.

Excessive Privatization

The local public library is one of the most successful institutions in American society. It provides not only a means of information, education and entertainment but greatly assists old and young people to prepare the way for the coming years. It is indispensable for true civilization. And yet the public library is not private, not exclusive (at least after the Jim Crow years). It is paid for by public funds. It is shared by all. Far from being associated with communism, it is considered to be central to the American tradition of modern civil life.

Compare this to South Africa, for example, where even today hotels, shops and even airports have signs posted: 'Right of Admission is Reserved'. Such privatization of public space does not occur in most of Europe or in America, at least not so obviously and especially not in public facilities such as airports. South Africa and the American South were notorious for privatizing not only public buildings but also nature itself – the beaches and parks. Apartheid and Jim Crow segregation, therefore, had the same purpose: to make of society a private realm.

Extreme privatization prevents access to resources and hence development suffers. It forces people to move from public schools and public transport systems to private schools and private cars. Sharing is severely diminished. Consider the classic issue of the private club: private organizations have an inalienable right to choose those with whom they wish to socialize. Legally this sounds perfectly reasonable. But spiritually such clubs, when taken to the extremes of privatization and exclusivity in hoarding social and material resources for its members' benefit, violate the fundamental laws on which any sound society is based.

The result of racist law and the illegalization of being African or Indian in America, is to make of America a private society in which the best resources are excluded from these minorities. This is not to say that all privacy is racist and harmful. Clearly certain forms of privacy are essential to civilized life. Withdrawal of public resources from the general society

231

for the exclusive use of a particular sub-group, however, is antithetical to the purpose of civilization.

The encroachment of extreme privatization on the public realm harms all, black and white, but is particularly and historically associated with anti-African racism. Nearly all the so-called white sports depend on private facilities: golf, tennis, skiing, swimming. And all the sports in which blacks have excelled – those associated with schools and universities – do not depend on private resources. Typically one cannot go to a private club to learn basketball or football or baseball or track and field; these are rooted in the state schools. It is not a matter of whether those sports are elitist and these democratic; rather it is a matter of whether the resources are, like libraries, publicly shared.

Moreover, the professions from which blacks are *de facto* excluded – engineering, law, medicine and architecture – have, for most of the past century, been dependent on private training facilities, colleges, universities, graduate schools. Only recently have these professions become accessible to large masses through public universities but even more recently have these public universities become open to minority students.

One could argue that since public primary and secondary schools have long been open to blacks there is no reason why they should not have gained access to the professions. But virtually all public universities barred blacks – even those who were academically outstanding – from attending until after the 1954 Brown decision and more specifically after the 1964 civil rights legislation. Furthermore, public schools are not all the same. Segregation has made predominantly white public schools function as private schools; indeed, it is not a mere coincidence that throughout the country whenever whites have objected to desegregation they have withdrawn their children from the public school systems and created effectively whites-only private schools. Unlike the modern public library, the American school system has not been publicly shared. Privacy, in its extreme forms, has been the backbone of racist society.

The private school concept is now being applied to town life in general, with the emergence of so-called gated communities. This new form of residential development tends to resonate with other pillars of racist society and culture; thus we find gated communities that are centered around golf courses or country clubs, sometimes with their own schools and other civic institutions, laws and security forces.

The centrality of privacy in racist society has not been easily recognizable because the institutions upon which private white society relies are ostensibly part of the public sphere. Whites-only public schools were the quintessential public schools but to blacks they were private. The major universities – many of which ironically have become surrounded by black neighborhoods – were founded for the benefit of the public at large, meaning the white public; the black public, however, was excluded and they therefore regarded them as private property. The publicness of these institutions was an illusion with respect to blacks.

Likewise in business and economic life as a whole. The job market for whites has been wide open, a truly public, shared market, the essential gathering place for all comers. But to blacks and women this was not an open, public market but a private market to which they could in no way gain access. The 'good old boy' system really means a private system of exchange of opportunities and rewards. It is a system that projects the illusion of publicness but in reality functions as a private system excluding all those who do not fit certain materialistic criteria.

GUILDS

Let us give further consideration to the privatization of the job market. What makes the professions so exclusive and difficult to enter is not primarily the academic qualifications. For when we look at the founders of the modern professions we see that many of them, if not most, had no such qualifications at all. Rather, the professions' exclusivity derives from the fact that they are privately held. They do not belong to the United States as a whole but to a small group of Americans who have private control over them. One must be *admitted* to professional school. It is not one's right to enter the school or the profession. The professions are modern day private guilds.[48] A guild usually has two primary goals: to pass on its skill and to keep the skill secret. Knowledge is not freely available but is passed on discreetly from one elite generation to another. Such discretion and secrecy are found not only in academia but also in secret societies, unions, political groups and social cliques.

Indeed it has been argued that the reason why modern education in the West has not been universal or even widespread is precisely because it is a useful tool for social control.[49] Anti-literacy laws against the working classes were promoted in 17th-century England.[50] Education for the benefit of the public is therefore a very recent exception to an ancient historical rule. The miseducation and the enforced illiteracy of blacks in America is merely the natural continuation of an ancient practice. What makes this situation so striking is that whites have progressed into modernity, while the effect of racism is to leave blacks back in that ancient world. In antiquity nearly everyone was subject to barbarities; today only some.

Most formal and informal educational systems in America are guild systems. They prevent free access to knowledge and skills. Harvard's law and medical schools dispense skills and information that *most* people could learn, albeit at various rates of speed. Such knowledge and skill are becoming exposed as not so rarefied and exclusive after all. In the longest legal trial in British history, the McDonald's corporation, though technically victorious, was strategically defeated by two unemployed non-lawyers, a postman and a gardener. Many of the most sophisticated experts in computers and communications are self-taught 'hackers'.[51] Modern history is filled with examples, from the triumph of two bicycle mechanics to the discovery of Lorenzo's oil.

The exclusivity and difficulty of education are artificially created, just as the price of diamonds is artificially inflated by the monopoly of the DeBeers company. It is no wonder that the elite colleges are judged not so much by how well they teach but by how difficult it is to gain admission to them. Tests are designed and examined according to what one *does not* know, not according to one's potential to achieve. Universities and educational systems would like to convince us that we are incapable of learning this special knowledge. One of the attractions of gangs, neighborhood sports such as basketball and the military is that the participants know these guilds are fully open to them, whereas the guild represented by the university is known to be ultimately closed to most aspirants.

Although 'education' is seemingly available to all, we are far from the ideal of universal education in the truest sense. True education goes beyond formal learning. It centers on the *establishment* of every individual in a rewarding and socially beneficial occupation of her choice. By reducing access to skills and opportunities to serve society, guilds stifle and choke civilization. Standing before the university gates most of us are judged *incapable*, that is, 'unqualified'. One must first be 'qualified' to gain the special skill or knowledge. Affirmative action programs offer access to valuable skills regardless of traditional prerequisite 'qualifications'; and, as we shall see, the professional accomplishments of their graduates prove that such prerequisites are irrelevant at best. True education is based on the principles that learning should be available to all and most are capable of learning anything. To base educational and employment opportunities on a record of 'qualifications' is to lock up the future of individuals' lives using a strict set of superfluous criteria. It is a hijacking of the future.

The average European American male is undoubtedly a superb mountain climber. He attains the summit under his own power. Although he received careful training and assistance in preparation, the achievement is his and his alone. Now new climbers aspire to make the ascent. They ask not to be transported up the slopes and cliffs; they too seek to demonstrate and discover their own powers, so as to explore and make assaults on the endless peaks ahead. They do ask, however – and perhaps this is unreasonable – to be able to reach the foothills without being stopped, carded, turned back or arrested by authorities; to begin their climb without having to pay a tax; to go beyond the tree line without having to answer, like Oedipus, the unconstitutional questions of a courthouse Sphinx; to reach the ridge without the need to know about regattas and cotillions. Our European American brother faced none of these restrictions. Affirmative action is about climbing freely up into the mountains, not a free ride; it is about an open path of ascent, clear of locked gates and Sphinxes, tolls and trolls.

Families do not first ask if their children are qualified before raising and training them. If humanity is spiritually a single reality, we cannot afford to make access to knowledge, training and opportunities to achieve conditional on so-called qualifications.

Civilization can flourish only when the life-giving water that is knowledge flows freely everywhere. Otherwise some live in civilization and others do not, whence the dichotomy of slums and mansions.

The length of time over which a guild can hold a skill has shortened. Guilds typically try to prevent change, improvement and paradigm shifts, all of which render their secret skills obsolete. In pre-industrial times guild skills lasted for centuries. Now in the computer age they sometimes exist for only months, as systems and technologies are characterized by rapid turnover rates. Society is increasingly becoming guild-free. In the dawning age of information and globalization guilds are losing their power to localize knowledge. Systems of technology and knowledge are rapidly becoming international and therefore the geographical exclusivity of guilds has gone by the wayside. 'Technology transfer' is natural, mutual and continuous. Solar energy systems are flowing one way; bio-diversity information and resources the other, just as in centuries past Native American concepts of environment, government and justice were shared with Europeans, who in turn offered their own technologies.

Today the rapidity with which valuable skills change is so great that the guild loses its practicality. It preserves nothing but the symbol of itself. It is a real secrecy and exclusivity but with no practical content. In the end the guild itself is the purpose. It is thus that institutional racism becomes exposed as 'racism pure and simple'. What was formerly a denial of entry based on the grounds that blacks *should* not learn and then on the grounds that they *could* not learn, became denial of entry solely on the grounds of maintaining 'racial purity'. At such a point even the guild itself no longer knows why it practices these prejudices and exclusive traditions, except to say that this is the way life is. The function of the guild as such has died but the appearance and form of a guild is maintained, blindly and purposelessly.

Excessive Individualism

Closely related to the extreme privatization of skills, knowledge and resources is the over-emphasis on the individual. Both of these trends reduce and stifle community, interpersonal identity and spirituality. As an example let us consider recent scientific developments.

Health care systems of late have greatly emphasized the manipulation of genes as a potential solution for disease and defects. This approach manifests a philosophy that emphasizes the individual as the key to understanding life and de-emphasizes the environment. It is the old nature-versus-nurture argument, won by the party favoring nature.

Let us compare so-called 'gene therapy' with racism. Both emphasize that there is something wrong with the individual and both turn blind eyes to the environmental causes of suffering. If a person develops a physical problem it is due to a defective gene and not the poisonous environment in which he and his parents have lived or his unhealthy diet. If a person suffers from poverty and a lack of social opportunities it is because of something inherently faulty in him; his social environment has nothing to do with it. The American culture is solidly based on the principle that whatever suffering people experience is due to no one's fault but their own. Environment plays little or no role. Each person is responsible for his or her own destiny. Thus no one is guilty but the sufferer himself. No one need assist another. No one need love another. The Christian principles are defunct and nullified.

Conveniently, the more we blame the individual for his suffering the easier it is for certain groups in society to gain great wealth. Conversely, the more we blame the environment and work to fix it, the less potential there is to accumulate great wealth. The individualist paradigm argues that one suffers because one does not personally *have* something, either a material product, or a skill, or an education, or moral fortitude, or a certain gene. The individualist paradigm then provides a solution: your problem can be solved if you obtain what you do not *have*. And of course, often you can obtain it by buying it. Hence whoever is selling these solutions can make a great deal of money. For this reason it is a vicious cycle because money-making depends on the continuation of problems.

The environmental paradigm provides a quite different solution: your problem can be solved by finding out what in your social and physical environment needs to be changed in order for life in general to flourish. The farmer, for example, looks at her farm from a systemic viewpoint. She wants to make sure that all the elements necessary for life are in the proper measure: light, heat, water, minerals and so on. She does not examine each individual stalk of wheat and treat it individually; rather she studies the entire environment holistically and in that way optimizes the life of all the plants. One of the best examples of this holistic approach is from the career of Dr John Snow, who in 1854 believed that a plague in London, later to be known as cholera, was traceable to a common water source. Instead of treating each individual case like his admittedly brave and selfless colleagues and hoping the epidemic would soon die out, he took the radical step of simply disabling the water pump that was in the very center of the plague-stricken neighborhood.[52] Many of us today are brave and selfless but many of us earn our livelihood from professions that render us systemically dependent on the continuation of disease, crime, pollution, accidents, poverty and other social problems.

If we continue the farm analogy we are immediately struck by the results obtained by the successful farmer. Let us bear in mind that the farmer ensures that the environment for her crops is adjusted and monitored for optimal growth. What happens if she does this? On a farm maintained by a skilled farmer, the thing that strikes one almost immediately is that all the plants are roughly the same height, the same health and the same quality. They are for the most part successful and edible.

But what is the result of a farmer who is careless and unsystematic? That farm will have varied results, depending on accidents of nature and of man. Some plants will be fairly good and others will be wilted and nearly dead. Such is the result in our society today. It is a society that relies, supposedly, on the accidents and fortunes of nature. Let nature and Darwinian competition take their course; forget the religious teachings that will result in a broadly successful society and let the failures fall by the wayside while the survivors enjoy the fruits of life.

To solve racism we must cultivate society like a farmer cultivates crops: she maximizes the optimal conditions. What we are doing today is like creating a farm in which one part of the land is healthy and the other part filled with poison, hoping and expecting that the poison will have no effect on the healthy part. But, of course, experience shows that a wise farmer would not allow any poison anywhere near her farm or even her county. European Americans should realize that racism is a poison seeping into their part of the farm, affecting their supposedly separate lives; for indeed, as John Donne wrote, no man is an island.

We can see by the farm analogy exactly why the anti-communist philosophy has been so strong in America. For if we practice true spirituality success will not be a class or racial monopoly but will be spread more or less uniformly throughout the society, indeed throughout the world. It would eliminate the opportunity to obtain inordinate wealth and power. This is not to say that we should eliminate individualism in favor of an exclusively environmental approach to life. Nor should we strive to make all individuals uniform in income, personal qualities and characteristics. As we have seen with other fundamental principles of social life, the relationship between individualism and the environmentalist view is not either–or but both.

The Government's Responsibility

Some might object that we are mistaken to turn towards spirituality, inasmuch as governments have been the foundation of slavery and racism. After all, the laws which led to the systematic long-term subjugation and oppression of the Africans in America were fashioned, promulgated and enforced by government leaders, from Thomas Jefferson to George Wallace. How then could religion be held accountable for such a development, particularly in the United States where the powers and authority of Church and state have been formally and practically separate throughout the land?

The argument that the origin of the problem is the collapse of the society's religious life in no way absolves government from its moral duty. In the end there is no contradiction between citing religious corruption as the source and citing government as centrally responsible. For from a holistic perspective the corruption of the religious institutions and of the government is a single process inasmuch as the government derives its original authority and powers from the values and ideals of religious teachings.[53] Government is the medium through which religious ideals – and religious corruption – have been carried out. But as this is a holistic analysis, we need not think in terms of either–or; both government and religion are essential to resolving the problem. That we take spirituality as the most fundamental context, the root, in no way minimizes the role of government. In the end the entire tree must be healed, roots, trunk, branches, leaves and all.

The Role of Individuals

If religious corruption is the root of the problem and governmental corruption the trunk, then the branches and leaves are the unhealthy practices among African and European Americans. A sick community cannot help but show its illness. By identifying religious corruption as the root of racism we are not arguing that American citizens be absolved of the duty to reform their own spiritual and moral lives. Again, it is not an either–or situation but rather both. Religious corruption is the root cause *and* individual initiative for spiritual and moral reform must be practiced by African and European Americans. If religious corruption sank the ship of American spiritual society, it is still the duty and need of the survivors to swim up from the bottom of the sea, break the surface, regain land and unite to build a new ship free from defects.

Certainly the victims of racism have their due rights but the need for justice does not substitute for the need to build a renaissance. The attainment of justice is *part* of the renaissance, not the renaissance itself. Renaissance can be achieved only by the emergence, or re-emergence, of the drowned man himself. True renaissance comes from within; no one can do it for another. In a real sense it is conversion and just as no one can force true conversion based on love – for such is not conversion but coercion – likewise no one can force rebirth and emergence, for such is not rebirth but dependency.

Respiritualizing the Human Being

Human beings are part of a wider reality, wider than that we associate with the scientific conception of existence. The Native Americans and mystics of all cultures assert and base their actions on the existence of a spiritual reality that forms with physical reality a whole. Our racist beliefs have come about by ignoring this spiritual reality. Indeed, above all, racism manifests a purely materialistic perspective of life; for this reason it emphasizes physical characteristics, from skin color and other bodily features – going so far as to measure the head in 'craniology' – to the 'measurement' of an 'intelligence quotient' as supposed evidence of genetic difference. Racism clearly ignores any claim to the existence of a spiritual identity among blacks or of a spiritual reality in general. A world that emphasizes or contrives the importance of 'race' is a world of materialism so extreme that it tends to glorify the human body to the point of obsession.

By contrast, the truly spiritual, the mystics who continually seek the connection between humanity and God or a higher reality, make great and constant effort to de-emphasize the human body and to maintain the body in service to the mystic quest. The yogi trains in meditative postures and exercises, the dervish performs a dance filled with symbolic significance, the Zen master likewise studies mystical arts and the Native American seeks out transcendent knowledge in isolation upon a mountain top. In all these actions the body is put to use but to no earthly purpose: its work is of use only to achieve non-practical, other-worldly ends. It seems more than a coincidence that the practice of yoga, the whirling of the dervish and the quest of the Native American are deliberately removed from any 'practical' benefit. In pursuing these strenuous efforts the body's reality becomes submerged in a higher reality, a spiritual reality, dominated by the mind and the soul of the seeker.

Contrast this exacting spiritual discipline of the mystics with the equally exacting, precise and demanding material discipline of western culture. Weber argued that when the Protestants set up their society they quickly developed the belief that wealth signalized God's favor. Business success became a substitute for the wider, holistic spiritual discipline of the Gospels. But American Protestants also developed the belief that the attainment of purity and truth depends on a constant, persevering vigilance to maintain distinction between one type of human body (black) and another (white). Such a discipline involved many social customs, norms, laws and folkways, equally as intricate as a yogi's tradition. It involved the placement of signs for 'colored' and 'white' on all public facilities and institutions; a code of language and gestures to designate one body lower in status than the other; a difference in clothing, in diet, in accent, in spatial separation from birthplace to cemetery; it extended even to textbooks, printed media and eventually electronic media.

The material and racial classification of human beings is so universally and consistently respected in films, advertising, television, even novels and art museums – a classification and separation so precise that the number of black and brown faces, and even their placement, in advertisements, television shows and films can be fairly easily predicted – this material classification is so deeply respected that it takes on the quality of religion and thus can be regarded as nothing other than a materialistic pseudo-religious discipline, the counterpart and substitute for the mystic's spiritual discipline.

In this context, to follow the path of truth is to follow these countless racial observances and to do so willingly and joyfully with the confidence that such is the way ordained by the Creator. To obey this physical ordering of human society is to be disciplined, to be a good human being. Indeed, to follow accurately this racist order eventually became identified with being a good Christian, for both blacks and whites. The extreme material emphasis became so great as to cause the disappearance of the original meaning, purpose and practice of Christianity altogether. Whereas Christianity had been a deeply challenging spiritual discipline, racism was a taxing and demanding material discipline, more in line with taxonomic, 'scientific' reasoning in a world devoted to science.

By focusing so obsessively on humanity's physical traits – by not only speaking and writing of these traits but by creating for them laws, philosophies, sciences, elaborate institutions and complex cultural traditions – we have created another heaven, another 'spiritual' world, contrary to the heaven described by the religions. In effect, then, heaven itself has been stolen or colonized and remade into something reflecting the wishes of the population in power. Heaven is indeed brought to earth, for it is defined as the predominance of all things white, of all things Protestant. Thus the infinite qualities of the spiritual world become completely lost.

FROM THE FINITE TO THE INFINITE

It is becoming more and more clear, then, that racism cannot be solved solely on the level of public policy, social engineering, sociological inquiry, legal argument and all other efforts based on pure reasoning. This, of course, is not to say that systems of rational thought are useless; rather that they are necessary but insufficient. They look at human society as a machine, a complex of interacting forces and entities, whose malfunctions can be resolved simply by the manipulation of its parts. The problem is that this way of thinking is an expression of the secular world view that gave birth to slavery and racism themselves. It is as if we would put out a fire by using materials that helped make the fire possible, as if yin can be balanced with yin and not yang. Indeed, racism and slavery reached the height of their perniciousness when rational arguments and systematic, even scientific programs were applied to them. The yin of material development must be balanced by the yang of spirituality. In orienting ourselves to respiritualization it is helpful to recall that many if not most traditions and cultures have looked forward to a transcendent life following the death of the physical body. If we take such a transcendent existence as fact, we immediately begin to view humanity in much broader terms; and physical qualities, which disappear upon death, become not only less important but ultimately irrelevant. It is our challenge, then, to bring this sense of the irrelevance of physical characteristics into practice in our daily lives.

We must put the issue of prejudice in the wider spiritual context. That is, we must bear in mind that life on earth is but a prelude to what many religious traditions describe as a transcendent existence after death, a state in which the familiar, earthly human reality is shed and a higher reality, a metamorphosis of unimaginable loftiness, is revealed.

Within this wider transcendent context of the afterlife is a subtle and yet highly influential facet of life: a sense of wonderment. If beyond the intellectual realm is the spiritual realm, it may be said that beyond the spiritual realm lies the realm of pure wonder. Here the words, concepts and 'realities' of the physical world are seen not only to be misleading and false illusions, they are completely forgotten. For how can issues of black and white even come to mind when the mind beholds transcendent splendors? It is perhaps for this reason that we are naturally attracted to the glories of nature, the limitlessness of the oceans, the night sky, the universe – we are compelled to wonder. And if it is in our nature to wonder, over-emphasis of the physical world stifles and even extinguishes that natural impulse. The large cities are filled with sophisticated citizens who believe they have seen and understood everything: they have 'been there, done that'. And who could fault them, for they are surrounded by an environment which, far from being the creation of an almighty Creator, is their own handiwork, the essence of the mundane.

One might argue, however, that some of the strongest forms of prejudice have occurred in periods when the rural life predominated. No doubt this is true; but the rural life in America, South Africa, India and other centers of prejudice involved deliberate attempts by an agricultural society to impose an order – a manmade order – on a natural and social environment that was originally boundless in scope and potential. The racist leadership was determined to reduce the infinite to the finite, just as a new resident makes his own home according to a preconceived plan. In this way the natural and social environment are no longer nature's or God's but his alone. His world is created in his own image and he is a god on earth. No doubt this was the covert belief of many racists and the overt belief of a good many others, most notably the Nazis.

The manmade world, then, must be recognized as a superficial façade, like a two-dimensional movie set. It is our destiny to go beyond it, to explore the infinitely broader, infinitely deeper spiritual context in which we exist. We must allow that faculty of wonderment at the infinite variety of human being and natural phenomena to flourish freely, inspiring humility, a desire to learn and the ability to recognize the humanity of others.

THE HUMANITY OF AFRICAN AMERICANS

One of the most difficult issues in racism is the question of how to respond to the claim that African Americans are not fully human. This is not simply a charge made by uneducated bigots. It has been confidently defended by educated persons, such as the popular novelist William Gilmore Simms (1806–70), who wrote that the regular raping of African slave women was a 'beneficial institution because it protected the purity of white women by allowing slaveholders to vent their lust harmlessly upon slave women'.[54] The attitude is captured in a statement by a New England clergyman, Samuel Hopkins, in the year of the American colonies' independence, 1776:

> we have been used to look on them [African slaves] in a mean, contempt-ible light; and our education has filled us with strong prejudices against them and led us to consider them, not as our brethren, or in any degree on a level with us; but as quite another species of animals, made only to serve us and our children . . .[55]

It is enshrined in the United States Constitution, which in Article 1, Section 2, states that representatives to the federal government and taxes 'shall be apportioned among the several States' according to the population of each state, 'which shall be determined by adding to the whole Number of free

Persons, including those bound to Service for a Term of Years and excluding Indians not taxed, three-fifths of all other Persons'. This is a clever way to avoid referring to slaves and slavery while at the same time giving slaveholders extra voting power and access to tax revenues on the grounds that they had to manage a large population of slaves. Here the most sacred document in the history of the United States defines Africans as three-fifths of a free white person. The American Indians, who along with women were not given the right to vote, were at least not reduced to a fraction of white humanity. The sub-humanity of Africans became a major theme of racist thought during slavery, as Stephen L. Carter explains:

> One popular justification for the African slave trade – including by leading clergy – was that the black Africans were subhuman or even nonhuman. This view made it quite simple for many of the Founders of the Republic to maintain what today is seen as racist hypocrisy – to affirm in the Declaration of Independence that all men are created equal, while at the same time keeping in thrall substantial numbers of 'kidnaped Africans' (as the antebellum Supreme Court, in a rare moment of candor, described Africans taken for import). Indeed, a principal task of the mid-nineteenth-century abolitionist literature was to demonstrate that the slaves were human beings.[56]

The three-fifths clause was not nullified until ratification of the Fourteenth Amendment in 1868 yet symbolically it still has power in that it remains in the text of the Constitution. It still reminds us. It permanently labels Africans as inferior in the mind if not in the law.

Even in our time it is clear that the abolitionists did not completely succeed in the mission to redefine African Americans as fully human. As late as the 1960s at least one high school carried on debates between students over the question of 'whether blacks were human beings and deserved civil rights or a lower species that could be denied civil rights'.[57]

In an analysis of right-wing racist militia groups in the 1990s in the United States, James Ridgeway points out the continued belief among racists in the sub-humanity of African Americans and in the necessity of a dual society:

> In fact, many members of the militias and other far-right groups draw a distinction between what they call 'organic sovereigns' or 'common law state citizens' – the white people mentioned in the Constitution's preamble, who have inalienable rights derived from God – and 'Fourteenth Amendment citizens' – who 'do not have inalienable rights, only limited statutory "civil rights" that Congress has seen fit to grant them'.[58]

By an extension of this reasoning, 'organic sovereigns' are not bound by federal law but only by the common law of the individual states. Only for 'Fourteenth Amendment federal citizens' who do 'not have access to the Common Law' do federal laws prevail. A 1990 issue of *Patriot*, a California newsletter that circulates widely in the militia movement, explained this theory to its readers and asked: 'So are you a White Common Law Citizen of the State or a federal citizen of the District of Columbia?'[59]

The definition of blacks as not fully human, and the concomitant challenge to blacks that they must prove their humanity, has power because it rests on the authority of the iconic word. A text becomes iconic when it is perceived over time to possess innate authority, a power of truth that derives not from any meaning or reality it represents but from itself alone, merely by the fact that it is written in ink or stone, preserved in libraries and archives, sold in bookstores, placed on syllabi, handled with great care, revered, worshiped. It is a word that becomes sacred and holy whether or not it deserves to be so regarded.

Because the laws of the country – from local ordinances to the United States Constitution – established the inferiority of Africans in America, this group has been forced either consciously or unconsciously to prove itself equal to whites. The underlying problem is one of defining who is of base nature and who is of the human, sacred world. How could Africans ever *prove* their humanity to whites, so that at last the doors to civilization would be opened wide?

But this is a false dilemma. For two reasons there is no need for blacks to prove their humanity. First, we can begin to unravel this knotty problem by first noting that all the arguments claiming African sub-humanity are academic. The most recent of them has come in *The Bell Curve*. But academia can in no way prove or disprove the humanity of anyone. The essence of humanity is not the province solely of academic argument, the purposes of which are extremely limited and cannot yet encompass or master such lofty fields. Rather, humanity is self-evident. Academia's claim to be able to define humanity in purely intellectual terms is not valid inasmuch as human being is part of the spiritual realm that transcends the intellectual realm. Such arguments are no different than those dealing with angelic pinhead dancers.

Second, whites never proved their own humanity. But then how did their humanity become accepted as undoubted fact? Not by dint of achievement but by declaration. Religious ceremonies, marriage, baptism and so on are in essence public announcements identifying the participants as having a sacred status. People *make* themselves sacred by saying so in public, as seen in cleansing ceremonies that restore sanctity and balance in cases of crimes or social problems among indigenous communities in the

Americas, Africa and elsewhere. The difficulty is that European Americans never allowed Africans a forum in which such declarations could be heard by all. The religions in North America played a key role by withholding this recognition from the slaves.

The civil rights movement succeeded because at last African Americans were able publicly to declare and assert their own sacredness. They realized they did not need to prove their humanity to whites; they realized they needed only to declare themselves so, which they increasingly did through a variety of symbolic and literal means. One African American man participating in a street protest carried a sign on which was written the simple message 'I am a man'.

The spiritual significance of lynching and all other racist violence is that it is the opposite of the public declaration of sacredness. It is a public declaration of profaneness, of unholiness, of evil vanquished. Similarly the Klan's cross burnings were public declarations that the victims were unholy. Therefore, to remedy such a crime it is not sufficient to arrest the perpetrators, although that is necessary. It also requires that we, the community, renew the victims' sacredness by restating it publicly in some way. When we say we feel violated after even a relatively minor theft, what we are really saying is that our sense of self-sacredness has been diminished; we no longer are confident that the community regards us as holy, or that we regard ourselves as holy. The community as a whole must renew that sense of sacredness in the victim.

Reparations for victims of genocide, slavery and other crimes against groups and nations are not about money. Our payment of reparations is a proof of our desire to sacrifice ourselves to renew the garment of sacredness that was ripped away by the crime against the collective. And by doing so we renew our own sacredness. America is not merely a *secular* state; it is a state that has forfeited its sense of sacredness, which must be redeemed sooner or later.

Justice
Beyond Affirmative Action

In 1998–9 the Stephen Lawrence affair in the United Kingdom – a controversy over the failure of police authorities to prosecute successfully the alleged murderers of a teenage boy of African descent – led to a government admission that the police force in Britain suffered from institutional racism and measures were to be adopted to remedy the situation. Among the remedies was the recruitment to the force of enough minority people so as to reflect the racial distribution of the population it serves. An immediate objection to this solution, however, was that such a move amounts to a quota system.

A number of assumptions and significant implications lie hidden within this criticism. Minority people who are not qualified will be hired. People who are better qualified will be prevented from rightfully obtaining a good job. The quality of work done by the force will decline. The force could not thereafter be trusted by the people. The politicians would be as much to blame as the minorities. The politicians would lose their positions and the minorities would bring greater hate down upon themselves.

Underlying these ideas are further arguments commonly used to defend racism. People have a natural right to hold racist or any other beliefs, inasmuch as such convictions are equivalent to religious beliefs. Fear of the unknown is natural. People have a natural right to choose their friends. They have a natural right to choose the color of the skin of their spouses, of their children and grandchildren. They have a natural right to choose the socio-economic class to which they wish to belong. Love and fellowship between races cannot be forced through legislation and law.

Arguments of this nature are difficult to oppose. But we need to look at them more carefully. They are popular because they assign blame to the minority population, the 'others'; they remove responsibility from the shoulders of the accusers and place it on those of the minority and the government. In short, they absolve the accusers of all fault, of all 'sin', for creating and practicing racism.

The most important goal of these arguments, however, is to function as red herrings in order to hide the fact that by affirmative action, fairness and justice minority populations would prosper and progress. Harvard law professor Lani Guinier has spent much of her career proving this point. She cites as a prime example the success of affirmative action at the medical school of the University of California at Davis, where affirmative action was dealt a severe blow by the Bakke case in 1978:

> A study of doctors trained at the medical school of the University of California, Davis, published in October 1997 in the *Journal of the American Medical Association*, found that students admitted to Davis between 1968 and 1987 with race, ethnicity, or unusual experience as a consideration went on to careers that were indistinguishable from those admitted on academic grades or test scores alone.[60]

Racism opposes affirmative action not because it fails to help blacks but because it succeeds in proving African Americans' equality with European Americans.

Although affirmative action has been clearly demonstrated as a successful method for the removal of many barriers to minority success, it has failed, like all essentially material approaches to the race problem, to remedy the fundamental disease. Successful African Americans remain surrounded by a social environment that continues to reject them despite and often especially because of their success.

In America we exhibit a range of responses to African American achievement. We may

1) accept and reward the achievement
2) ignore the achievement
3) question it, raise doubt about it
4) dispute it
5) oppose and punish it

As we move from the first to the fifth response we see that the attitude becomes increasingly racist. The punishment of achievement is the quintessential experience of racism in America. Far from receiving a vote of confidence or exclamations of 'Bravo!' and 'Well done!' whether in the school, the work place or the mass media, African American achievement is, apart from a few token gestures, met with cold silence or active discouragement and punishment. Many examples of this are documented in a number of recent works.[61] Here we must keep in mind that we are not talking about the black media stars – the Oprah Winfreys, Michael Jordans and Tiger Woodses – but the average person living an average life and wishing to gain prosperity for his or her family. While the mass media bestows a *conferred sanctity* upon black stars, the average black retains an identity that racism regards as *innate profaneness* from which he cannot escape until the society becomes spiritualized.

Traditional racism in America places African Americans in a neat conundrum, an elegant catch-22. Simply put, they are damned if they do and damned if they don't. If they succeed they are treated harshly. They are often hounded out of their success, as was the case among masses of blacks in the South during the post-Reconstruction period, who faced the greatest form of intimidation and terrorism in American history short of genocide: lynching. Blacks were lynched in record numbers after their liberation from slavery and again after World War One, precisely because *they were succeeding* economically, socially, culturally – without any affirmative action programs; *they were* building up farms, educating their children, gradually attaining parity with the white population; *they were* demonstrating the limitless spiritual powers of human being.

The damned-if-they-do paradigm continued alive and well after World War Two. The first efforts to integrate schools were important because here were black children who had done everything according to white definitions, from dress to academic expectations and demeanor. Their rejection signalized that the game was over, the long game played by whites that said acceptance is readily forthcoming as soon as you meet our standards and criteria. A very small percentage of blacks are able to find success today through the few remaining affirmative action programs. But as for the masses of blacks, racism could not tolerate such an open demonstration of the oneness of the human race. The steady trickle of affirmative action successes has been acceptable primarily because it is kept hidden from the public eye, maintaining the illusion of white superiority. What is fatal to white identity is *public* black success, which, especially in large numbers, would proclaim and prove that the concept of 'whiteness' is an illusion. Whites have a three-century-old emotional and psychological investment in the concept of white superiority and black inferiority, of white sacredness and black profaneness. They have fought for centuries to deny black success and achievement, to maintain the *status quo*. They have fought for their very lives and they have fought to save themselves from oblivion; for they knew themselves only as *white humanity* and not as *humanity*.

The only way to unravel this seemingly intractible problem is to go beyond affirmative action to a spiritual understanding. If humanity is one, then society at large must act as one family. But what does that mean, practically speaking, in a case such as this? It means: in a family, those who are more qualified try to assist those who are less so. The parents dedicate themselves to strengthening their children to succeed and surpass them. The older siblings do the same for the younger ones. It would not only be absurd for the senior members to withhold such assistance, it would mean the collapse and disintegration of the family itself. The senior members never ask whether the younger ones are 'qualified' or not to learn. This is not an issue. The one and only issue is that the younger ones must advance, prosper and fulfill their potential. Therefore the real issue is not 'quotas' and being 'qualified'. Spiritually we *know* that all human beings are virtually endowed with infinitely varied talents and skills. We know this, also, because racist societies have always feared the *success* of the minorities, not their inadequacy. Rarely if ever are the success stories of the affirmative action programs, or even pre-affirmative action achievements, trumpeted and lauded by the public.

Rather the real issue is that we do not wish to be joined as a family with the minority people. Most of us do not feel any urge to commit physical violence against minorities. Many of us do not even mind living in close proximity with them. But to grant them access to public success, to assist them to attain that success, requires a heart that wishes them success, as a true brother or sister would. It requires our recognition that they are our brothers and sisters, yet we are repulsed by the thought because of long years and generations of ingrained beliefs that have taken on the authority and power of religious doctrine and truth. In this point we are referring of course to people and places that stubbornly cling to racism; we are not dealing with the growing interracial movement – a cause for optimism, yes, but also a cause for renewed determination and opposition on the part of racists.

Thus we return to the old conundrum: How can we fulfill the need for spirituality? We believe we cannot, because such brotherly love cannot be forced upon people. It would be a forced conversion and doomed to fail like the inquisitions. Hence social scientists and legal thinkers are duty bound to avoid this topic since, they argue, it cannot be a part of any realistic action plan.

Implied in this resignation is the belief that the races will remain unbrothers *ad infinitum*. Or that racism can never be attacked directly. Brotherhood can only come about, if ever, as the sort of 'trickle-down' result of social policies that attack non-spiritual factors and conditions, policies such as school desegregation, right-to-vote laws, income generation schemes. The pattern of these approaches is that if we just repair one or another factor our troubles will be over. But the disappointments are absolutely consistent: every success of this kind is quickly followed by renewed determination of racists to preserve disunity. Perhaps the greatest example of this persistence in racist belief is the resurgence of Nazism and xenophobia in Europe.

By saying that spirituality is the missing factor, we are not saying that now we must drop everything else we are doing and focus our efforts and attention exclusively on religion and spirituality. We must continue to work on better laws, a fair economic system, education, cultural reform and the material needs and goals of an evolving civilization. But we need to add the factor of spirituality into the process. The law must become spiritualized. This means, first, that justice must be not only a negative force that punishes but also a positive, constructive force that rewards, that strengthens, protects and cultivates the development of civilization. Second, love and spirituality must be recognized as part of the essence of the law, as part of the ultimate goal of the law. Third, the law must rest not on compromise but on fundamental, inviolable truths. Fourth, our attitude towards justice and the law must be elevated through universal recognition of their inherent sanctity.

POSITIVE ACTION

Let us take several examples to illustrate how this process can work. These are simple acts of individuals, yet we can well imagine the impact they would have if large numbers followed suit without interference from racist institutions and traditions. From the author Richard Wright we have a classic depiction of the workings of racism in the deep South dating from the late 1930s. After completing grammar school he obtained a job at an optical company, where he was promised that he would not only do menial work but would eventually move up to learn the craft of grinding lenses. When the promise went unfulfilled he reminded his supervisor, who had until then been friendly to him. But from that moment the supervisor and another man turned against him, saying, 'This is a white man's work around here and you better watch yourself!' Eventually they forced him by violence and threats to quit his job and leave altogether.[62]

By contrast, in 1950, 24-year-old Hans Massaquoi, the son of an African prince and a German woman raised by his mother in Germany throughout the war – a remarkable story in itself – traveled to the United States where he was welcomed by his mother's relatives in Illinois. Having become a highly skilled machine tool operator for the Nazi war machine, he was offered a job as a lathe operator at the Elgin Watch Company. 'Interestingly, all the lathe operators were white; the few blacks I saw were pulling hand trucks and operating forklifts.' Shortly after beginning his job and proving himself expert in his work, he was told by the foreman: 'I am really ashamed to tell you this but we have learned that most of the operators have walked off their jobs because we hired you. We never had a colored lathe operator before.' In Richard Wright's case, the manager was unable to oppose the will of the machinists who refused to accept him. In Hans Massaquoi's case, however, the response to the racists was quite effective. The foreman continued: 'I don't want you to be upset. You seem to be doing fine. Just keep working as if nothing has happened. In the meantime, management has taken a very firm stand and informed the operators who walked out that if they don't return right after lunch break, they can look for other jobs.' Results were soon forthcoming:

> At lunchtime I was sitting dejectedly beside my lathe . . . when several workers, including some women, stopped by to chat. They wanted me to know that they strongly disapproved of their colleagues' action and told me to hang in there because not all of the people at the plant were bigots.
>
> That was encouraging news to me but even more encouraging was the fact that gradually the machine shop started to fill up as workers who had walked out returned to their machines. The firm stand taken by the . . . management and with it common decency, had won out. Within a few days the incident seemed forgotten. At least nobody openly challenged my right to work in the shop. While I was convinced that the company's action did not change any hearts, it certainly went a long way to change behavior.[63]

Here we see how effective the application of law can be in resolving rac-ism and injustice. The white machinists insisted that they could tolerate no compromise of their racist beliefs. The management countered with a clear, equally uncompromising ultimatum. As the society had impercep-tibly changed since the days of Richard Wright's youth, primarily due to the dramatic years of World War Two, the firm stand of the Elgin manage-ment was enough to overthrow a racist regime that had never before been questioned. Here we see that the resolution of much of racism – Massaquoi himself notes that the entire problem was not yet resolved, for hearts had yet to change – does not involve converting racists to a new way of thinking but rather the upholding of the law. Is such an approach effective? In this case there is no doubt that it is. And this was the original aim of affirma-tive action. The hearts of the management had been changed and that was enough to make a tremendous difference – between night and day – in the life of the black worker. The management were not only the business leaders but also the leaders of thought; their conversion acted like a lever by which the entire workforce could be moved to accept a new program of racial unity. Above all, the contrast between these two examples shows that racial justice is a curious but elegantly simple mix of spiritual belief and practical action. The dismantling of racism is a matter of the simplest acts.

One final example will serve to confirm this point. Here we have an incident in 1953 from the field of political life, witnessed by former president Jimmy Carter. An old family friend, an African American man named Willis Wright, was chosen by the local black community to be the first to attempt to register to vote in their rural Georgia county. He sought Jimmy's advice.

'. . . early this morning I went over to the courthouse to the registrar's office and found that it was closed. I waited until almost dinnertime and he finally unlocked his office and I followed him in. He asked me what I wanted and I said I wanted to register to vote. He told me to wait a few moments and walked down the hall. When he came back, he brought out some papers and said I would have to answer some questions about citizenship.'

I interrupted to say, 'I'm familiar with those questions and I couldn't answer them myself. There are thirty of them and they're used only to keep Negroes from voting . . .'

'Yes, sir,' Willis agreed. 'We discussed this at the church and the man from Washington said that we no longer have to answer them in order to vote. I told the registrar this and then he pulled a pistol out of a drawer and laid it on the counter. He was nervous but he said, "Nigger, you better think this over for a few more days, then let me know what you decide."'

251

Carter offered to accompany Willis in a second effort to register; Willis declined, saying, 'It wouldn't mean nothing if you was there with me.' Carter recalls,

> I advised Willis to tell the registrar that he had discussed the matter with me and that I told him to go back and register. He did so and the next time I saw him he said he hadn't had any problem. Times were changing in Georgia but slowly.[64]

The pistol on the table. Normally that would have trumped the law and justice as defined by the Constitution and newly-enforced voting rights legislation. But a simple conversation between one man and another, a simple gesture, a simple word, is enough to overturn the process when the culture, having been shaken to its core by two world wars, has become uprooted from its centuries-old racist belief system. If such simple acts were effective 50 years ago, certainly they can be even more effective now. We often think of affirmative action as a giant bureaucracy of paper-pushers in flourescent-lit anonymous office blocks in the District of Columbia. But within and beyond affirmative action are simplicities that untie knots centuries old.

LOVE AND THE LAW

Let us go to the heart of the matter. African Americans, like all other human beings, wish to be loved. They suffer because they are hated by many European Americans. Racism is the systematic expression by some European Americans of disdain, disrespect or fundamental hatred towards African Americans. It may be subtle or blatant, latent or manifest. But in whatever form, it is felt everywhere by African Americans. The fact that many European Americans do not have prejudice and do not hate people of other ethnic groups unfortunately does not alter the spiritually deadly atmosphere in which African Americans must survive. The many anti-racists are yet not enough to turn the tide. We are still working on achieving the critical mass of anti-racists that will cause the entire culture in America to reject racism and prejudice once and for all. As part of that work we must struggle to understand why this hatred, this lack of love, exists in the hearts of European Americans. Through the power of understanding, this spiritual storm will abate.

Love is a human reality. Human history and society simply cannot be understood without taking into account the fact that love is a key motivating factor in the decisions and actions of individuals, groups and cultures. Perhaps the most obvious example is the love of parents for each other and their children. On the basis of this love the family rests and upon the family in turn the local community and, ultimately, civilization as a whole are founded. Only someone far removed from social reality, deeply entangled in academic abstractions, immersed in the material discourse from which religious ideals are excluded, could ever claim that love is irrelevant to the understanding and resolution of social problems. As we have seen, it has long been a tradition of social science to avoid discussion of love and spirituality; such things were branded as emotions and irrational qualities, the rightful province of poets and romantics, which cloud the judgment of the scientist and prevent the recognition of truth. Virtue for the scientific priests lay in a new kind of chastity: abstinence from the life of the heart. Fortunately, as we have seen, scholars are beginning to acknowledge this wrong turn and make up lost ground.

We use many words to describe the problem: racism, discrimination, intolerance, prejudice, segregation, bias and so on. But what we really mean by these terms is *hatred*. Why do we not call this attitude hatred when we confront it? It is in part because as soon as we refer to hatred, we also by implication refer to love. For the victim of racism to accuse a racist person of not loving is to put himself in a weak position, to ask publicly, 'Why won't you love me?' Instead we refer to bias, prejudice and other such terms because they refer not to matters of the heart but to legal issues. By referring to justice and legality we try to avoid the charge 'You can't legislate love'. But in the end what we need is love. Indeed, justice is inextricably intertwined with love. We practice justice, we are fair, because we respect human life and regard it as sacred, because we love. We attempted to have justice without love for most of the 20th century. We assumed long ago that love was out of the question, not a legal matter.

The essence of the Jim Crow and slave laws was the prohibition of love between European and African Americans. Once blacks and whites were permitted to socialize together, become open friends and marry, the proof was finally shown to the masses that indeed black people are loveable. The mass of whites would not believe that blacks were worthy of their love unless they had seen it demonstrated by a white exemplar. Theorists can talk and argue *ad infinitum* without convincing the ardent racist; the demonstration of such deep love is proof beyond words, far more powerful, because it reveals an aspect of essential human reality that had been purposefully concealed by these laws.

To the argument that love and progressive ideas in general cannot be legislated we can reply that history is full of instances where the hearts of the masses have been changed by legislation. A primary example is the rise of North American slavery itself. For until slave laws were instituted there was no racism as is now known. Anti-African feeling and racism were created, engineered and cultivated by means of these laws. If unspiritual

253

attitudes can be created by law, so can spiritual attitudes. Likewise, the whole system of modern education is founded on the premise that beliefs, habits and emotions can be changed, molded and trained to suit the needs of the time.

Abolitionists and civil rights activists focused on eliminating the negatives of slavery and segregation. What has been needed ever since is not the elimination of further negatives but the creation of positives, namely unity: a conception and a declaration enforced by law that we are one people.

FUNDAMENTAL TRUTHS

In order for justice to be established we must first agree on a set of basic truths about the nature of the human being. Those truths must explicitly acknowledge that one of the principal motivations for our actions is our spiritual life: love, the desire for unity with fellow human beings, respect for the natural environment. They must also include the recognition of the oneness of humankind, that is, however different human beings may be physically and materially, from the spiritual perspective we cannot be regarded as separate. We must formally and informally, officially and personally, recognize that injustice and oppression against one is injustice and oppression against all.

The elimination of racism and prejudice must be brought to the level of a fundamental principle. In practical terms this means that schools, organizations, companies and communities must declare themselves strictly in favor of the concept of the oneness of humankind and vigorously uphold that principle. The parallel is what we see today with regard to the green movement. Environmentalism is no less an ideal than the oneness of humankind. Why then has the former been embraced by the masses and the latter not? First, the green movement, although spiritual in many ways, has as one of its chief goals the attainment of a material benefit, whereas anti-racism's primary goal is spiritual. Second, being pro-green was never illegal, whereas being pro-black was for centuries illegal in the United States.

Policy today is formed by means of compromise. But there can be no compromise when it comes to a fundamental principle such as the oneness of the human race. If a truth exists, it must always be upheld. The very meaning of the term 'fundamental principle' is that it is taken as an inviolable law; its violation threatens the well-being of the entire society and must therefore bring upon the violator corrective action.

The key, once humanity's oneness is recognized, is to act on the basis of that principle, to eliminate systematically all social forces that prevent it from emerging. If humanity's oneness is reality, then the lack of its expression in the real world must be due to our imposition of a false reality on the world, a mask, a poisonous environment that prevents the seed from rooting, sprouting and flourishing. The true nature of human being must be permitted to express itself. It is for this reason that racism utterly and completely depends on artificial constructs which are contrary to human nature. We must go far out of our way, as it were, to inhibit the natural evolution of humanity, to prevent ourselves from achieving maturity. The history of human folly proves that rarely do we embrace and safeguard fundamental truths. We are all too quick to compromise. Just as an individual demonstrates maturity by wholehearted acceptance of the realities of life, so too the human race attains maturity by ceasing once and for all its prevarication. We have feared that without the freedom that compromise gives we will enter the future unable to shift and sham our way through the obstacles and shadows of the unknown. Compromise, we believe, places in our hands the essential tools with which to construct the imperfect progress that is the best we can expect. Nothing could be further from the truth. For compromise, in science, would not unlock mysteries but seal them up; in the arts, would reveal more of the mundane; in education, would bring hemlock to everyone's table; in civilization, cause us to ignore the summits and triumph in the valleys. While compromisers concentrate on the next bit of craftiness with which to turn a difficult corner, mature civilization sets sail across a boundless sea. Fundamental truth is not the cast iron law of the ideologue or the oppressive system of the totalitarian. Rather it is the gift of power that exists everywhere yet remains unrealized until we, like farmers, cultivate it. By committing ourselves to this work we will find ourselves upraised by a civilization advancing in powerful waves of prosperity and achievement. Therefore, we must not only conscientiously undo what we have done, we must hold fast to the truth of humanity's oneness forever into the endless future.

SANCTITY OF LAWS

All constitutions, no matter how well written and heartfelt, are dependent on sincerity. None of the ideals or principles or laws of any constitution have integrity and validity if this condition is not fulfilled. The intent of the framers, interpreters and enforcers of those laws must be sincere to the point of self-sacrifice.

The issue of absolute sincerity is a more profound one than racism itself. It is a vague, murky realm of human will and spirit. It is the realm in which faith lives and dies, in which conversion, conviction and consecration come into being. The problem of racism does not lie in the intellect or the mind but rather in this soul world wherein one's true beliefs are created and maintained. It is this realm that must be exposed, not the realm of intellectual argument and legalistic maneuverings, as seen in the works of the academics and literati. We write books about arguments and debates because they are easier to approach; these are sets of words and ideas linked to each other in a more or less logical fashion and all the scholar need do is unravel them. But the realm of sincerity is beyond logic, beyond law, beyond history. How can we write of the growth and evolution of the soul? How can we capture the spirit?

A secret society, for example – an exclusive club, a fraternity, a gang – creates a realm of sincerity amongst its members. They then have the opportunity to plant in that realm a set of ideas, ensure their firm rooting and thereafter tend their growth, while at the same time uprooting all other ideas considered undesirable. What this secret society represents is not the separation of Church and state but rather the concealment of reality behind a false façade. A member might say at the drop of a hat that he believes in exactly what he was taught in civics class (honor the flag) and religious class (the Ten Commandments). Yet in his heart of hearts he truly believes in only what he does, not what he says. In eliminating spiritual principles from government and public life the principle of Church–state separation left a vacuum that secret societies and other private groups filled with alacrity. In the place of spirituality other convictions were established, most of which are quite contrary to religion. The challenge for spiritual society, then, is to expose these beliefs to the light of day and ensure that laws do not become a mask concealing duplicity.

The sanctity of laws in America is variable. They are put on the books, vigorously enforced, ignored, forgotten, used as symbols, played with for the sake of politics. In our society today we tend not to shrink from the idea of compromising the law. Bending the laws, treading the borderline and 'creative accounting' are now often the standard in conflict resolution, legal disputes and business. Far from being upheld as sacred, laws are seen as tools that can be manipulated for the sake of gaining advantage. Such compromise and manipulation are signs of our immaturity.

Derived from the Prophets and originally obeyed because of its divine origin, the law was gradually co-opted and perverted for the sake of material purposes. Historically people have obeyed the law because they associate it with the holy. Corrupted figures seeking power seize upon this association and exploit it for their earthly benefit. Harold Berman interprets history not as 'a series of transitions from feudalism to capitalism to socialism but rather as a series of transitions from plural corporate groups within an overarching ecclesiastical unity to national states within an overarching but invisible religious and cultural unity and then to national states *without* an overarching Western unity, seeking new forms of unity on a world scale'.[65] The key, then, is to revive our sense of the sacredness of the law in this new global context.

The Baháʼí writings, as do the American Indian traditions, explain that all things in the universe are connected and just as there are physical laws there are also spiritual laws. ʻAbduʼl-Bahá explained:

> ... this limitless universe is like the human body, all the members of which are connected and linked with one another with the greatest strength. How much the organs, the members and the parts of the body of man are intermingled and connected for mutual aid and help, and how much they influence one another! In the same way, the parts of this infinite universe have their members and elements connected with one another, and influence one another spiritually and materially.
>
> For example, the eye sees, and all the body is affected; the ear hears, and all the members of the body are moved. Of this there is no doubt; and the universe is like a living person. Moreover, the connection which exists between the members of beings must necessarily have an effect and impression, whether it be material or spiritual.[66]

When spiritual laws are broken there are consequences. Racism, although a spiritual violation, has both spiritual and physical consequences. To take only one of many examples: racism was instrumental in the emphasis on private automobiles in America, which led to the creation of segregated suburbs, which contributed greatly to the destruction of the cities. Indeed, any spiritual disunity in America is manifested in physical, historical consequences. In this sense 'environmental racism' should not be a surprising concept, inasmuch as all spiritual disunity has environmental consequences.[67]

In order to reach maturity, therefore, we must recognize that as spiritual beings we are subject to the operation of spiritual laws and that whenever we break those laws we suffer consequences. In our contemporary culture, however, the body of laws is regarded as standing outside the reality of the individual. People consider laws troublesome obstacles to be avoided, oppressive burdens, even irrelevancies. In the spiritual perspective the law is an essential aspect of the innermost reality of each individual; it is directly relevant to and essential for the growth of one's soul. Hence we should shun its violation as an athlete would shun a harmful diet. We must study the law and accept it explicitly as part of our basic principles. Its violation must become overwhelmingly repugnant to us, beyond toleration, beyond contemplation.

Laws should therefore be viewed not as impositions but as emerging from the unfolding reality of humanity itself. Just as we discover new physical laws and apply them to improve our life through advances in technology, so too we must discover spiritual laws and apply them to our society so to unfold previously unknown potentialities within us.

This then is the reason why we must be law-abiding. It is not so we avoid punishment but so that we achieve our humanity. We must regard laws as helpers, just as an athlete or musician regards practice and training as the keys to the attainment of expertise and excellence. Fortunately in this era of globalization it is becoming easier to discover the spiritual laws that humanity requires. They can be defined through the consultation of leaders of thought, who can identify those universal values and truths they have in common. Perhaps the Millennium Peace Summit of Religious and Spiritual Leaders was a true beginning.

Education
A True Panacea

As we have noted, it is often said, 'You can't legislate love' or morality or any spiritual ideal. This cliché is based on historical reasoning that cites as a prime example the failure of the laws to prohibit the production, sale and transportation of alcoholic beverages in the United States between 1920 and 1934. But what this cliché ignores is that in order for any laws to be effective the citizenry must have attained a level of spiritual maturity that enables them to understand and obey the law as a benefit to themselves. It is, in the end, a matter of education. Perhaps the most important practical step regarding the principle of the oneness of humanity, other than its legal enforcement, is that it must be taught to all children in their schools, just as they are taught that the earth is not flat but spherical and that it orbits the sun. Difficult new ideas have indeed been instituted in schools, so the question is not whether such a thing is possible. Rather the question concerns the collective will to do so.

The subject of education usually fails to excite the collective imagination. It is identified with flat, lusterless images of four-walled classrooms, hours of boredom, days of cold institutionalized discipline, the banishment of true fellowship, the suppression of the natural enthusiasm and boundless creativity of youth. The identification of education with the modern school prevents us from recognizing a fact of human life: contrary to the oppressive scholastic culture that has arisen on the model of the industrial factory – with its time checks, horns and bells, assembly-line order and lock-step methods – the desire to learn is one of the fundamental qualities of human nature, expressed in all cultures and throughout all periods of our social evolution. To be human means to grow from one stage to another, to mature through a life-long series of births into ever higher stages of ability and accomplishment. The individual's powers gradually emerge, leading in turn to her ability to speak, read and write, coordinate her physical and mental actions in ever more complex tasks, take on more challenging responsibilities, become detached from her original family, form a new family of her own and eventually accept the end of physical life. Not only is the individual evolving, so too is humanity as a whole; throughout these millions of years of its existence the human race has continually sought, gained and applied knowledge in an endless pattern of creativity. The desire to learn is an essential quality of the spiritual life of human beings.

As important and fundamental as is the desire to learn, the more subtle and perhaps more powerful motivation is the desire to improve. Our desire to create is most satisfied when our creation transcends in some way what we and others have already created. This is not a simplistic, politicized concept of 'progress' but rather the constant search by humanity for greater use of its powers, for the discovery and rediscovery, through action, of the boundlessness of its potentialities.

Human history traces the search for and the achievement of transcendence in human knowledge and creativity. The periods when civilization has flourished in both East and West can be regarded as humanity's coming into conscious recognition of its powers. In periods of high civilization humanity understood that, despite all appearances of its exceeding weakness in the face of the overwhelming powers of nature, it held within itself transcendent powers that could be wielded on demand. From the Renaissance until today this consciousness has reached a higher level wherein we have recognized that not only are these powers wide and deep but they are boundless. The greatness of humanity's creativity in the Renaissance was the recognition that humanity's creative powers are infinite. In shifting from a finite to an infinite self-definition, humanity crossed a critical threshold in the process of its maturity.

While there may be a law of diminishing returns in economics, in education there is a law of increasing accuracy. The archer becomes better over time, the approximation becomes more exact, less and less to either side, more along the straight path. And the definition of true civilization is that this increasing accuracy obtains not only in the career of the individual but also intergenerationally. A true civilization fosters the transmission from one generation to the next of increasing success, understanding, accuracy in approximating the ultimately unattainable goal of perfection.

Over the centuries of modern Europe's development from the first glimmerings of the Renaissance to the establishment of an independent United States of America and its rise to prominence in the 20th century, education in all its forms has been recognized by society's leaders as essential to the well-being and advancement of the individual and community alike. Under the influence of Muslim scholars, whose successes in sciences and humanistic studies set the example for the entire Mediterranean region and set the stage for the Renaissance itself, Christian clergy gained a heightened appreciation for formal learning. Kings and clergy worked together in founding cathedral schools, which eventually became the great medieval universities, the progenitors of our thousands of modern institutions of higher learning. From the late medieval period education was closely identified with social progress, religious well-being and the fruits of true civilization. It gradually influenced the lives of the masses and by the time of the Protestant Reformation the notion that the common man, as an individual believer, should express and strengthen his faith through the independent study of the Bible was firmly established. While the masses for the most part were to remain illiterate for generations to come, the basic principle that education is vital to the unfoldment of humanity's social and spiritual potentialities had become recognized. The quest for a teacher, which for those few hardy seekers after knowledge had for so long been an adventure filled with uncertainty and often failure, now became increasingly facilitated through the establishment of schools in the cities. In the place of the hermitic monks sitting isolated upon a distant mountain there appeared an educational system, an institutionalization of the intergenerational learning process. In the place of remote monasteries and hidden libraries there appeared universities located in the centers of Europe's most populated cities. Learning became routine and pervasive. If the Renaissance was anything it was the birth of a culture of learning, of a humanity confident in its understanding that the wells of human potential are infinitely deep and that through the medium of literacy and through diligent study the bucket could be dipped and drawn at will. Inexorably the consciousness of the unfailing efficacy of education – a true panacea – became universal.

A Remedy Withheld

This same consciousness of humanity's essential and inherent power to learn led slavers purposefully to bar the African slaves from access to education. In the 17th and 18th centuries the slavery-based governments in the North American colonies prohibited the education of African slaves in order to suppress their infinite human powers and qualities. We often reduce our conception of this fact to a lesser reality, that is, that the slaves were forbidden to learn to read. But the deeper meaning of this is they were forbidden to become educated, which is a far broader outcome. The effect, as we know, was profound. Freedom is very precious to every human being. It is not the freedom of unbounded license that we seek. It is the freedom to grow to our full potential, to have a clear unobstructed view of the path leading to the infinite horizon of our creative powers as individuals and as a collectivity. This is the freedom called for in the Declaration of Independence and sung about by the African Americans for so many generations before and after they had won freedom from slavery.

If anything epitomizes the consequences of slavery and racial segregation as practiced in America, beyond chains, fetters, whips and the slave-auction notice, it is the laws prohibiting the education of Africans in America. Of all the many impressive images of the civil rights era caught on film perhaps the most poignant and meaningful were of the efforts of a small band of black students in Little Rock to gain entry to their public school, the doors of which were legally open to them yet shut by virtue of the opposition of the public.

Racism creates an environment opposite to that necessary for education. It deliberately aims to maintain African Americans in social isolation and in an undeveloped state. It subverts the principles of civilization by barring education in trades and professions; barring literacy and general education; violating the sanctity of the family; destroying childhood. If we carefully list all factors needed for civilization we find that racism deliberately suppresses each one of them.

From the founding of the nation America's rulers were very conscious of the civilizing powers present in all races and were determined to manipulate those powers, to control the reins of history and humanity's evolution. By allowing some groups to surge forward into the future and forcing others to remain in a primitive stage, the merchants were able to reap profits. They could become 'modern' artificially, by creating a primitive class. The pro-slavery lawmakers, like experienced surgeons, deftly separated one group based on an older paradigm of finiteness from another based on the new Renaissance paradigm of infinite possibilities and harnessed the former to the service of the latter. The Renaissance had already become integrated in European and American culture, yet they were able to isolate an entire sub-population from its growth-inducing and boundlessly creative effects. Such an act, enforced for some 15 generations upon a captive population, beyond its obvious social significance, resulted in the most profound spiritual consequences for slave-owners and slaves alike. Two social paradigms, two stages of social evolution, were artificially caused to operate side by side, at times even intermeshing so finely as to be indistinguishable – what with, on the one hand, educated slaves who advanced science, technology and commerce and on the other hand slave-holders who barely could be distinguished from the slaves for their ignorance. These lawmakers were aware that changes in history and changes in societies are organic processes evolving one from the other and they sought mightily and successfully to prevent this natural evolution from occurring among the captive population. History and social evolution had, in their minds, become a farm whose tools and resources they exploited with the greatest efficiency rational law could allow. The infinity of humanity allowed them to assert and create at their whim. Indeed the finiteness of the slave was used to define and confirm the infiniteness, the ongoing renaissance and ultimately the holiness, of the slave master.

We cannot regard the anti-literacy law as merely one among many legal measures adopted to facilitate the control of Africans during and after slavery. We cannot regard their lack of access to formal education as simply a two-century delay in their development, which was nullified when the first schools for blacks opened. We somehow regard anti-literacy laws as almost harmless, a neutral restraint that neither cuts nor pains in any way. From a spiritual perspective, however, such a deliberate neglect of the African Americans' spiritual needs – especially in the 20th century, living as they did in a society in which the vast majority were able to receive some form of education, be it learning to read the Bible or learning a craft – was not merely a passive measure but one that distorted their development just as binds distorted the feet of Chinese women. Although the Emancipation Proclamation signalized a bright and glorious day for the African American, spiritually he lay prostrate, sick, unable to draw back the curtains, his infinite potentialities – and those of his children – unrealized, unknown. By withholding the right to literacy and formal education, whites created an artificial wilderness, a poisonous atmosphere, an environment that thwarted the growth of the entire country.

Of course, European Americans could claim that even they did not have universal access to education. Doubtless this was true in America's early history but with increasing democratization and liberalization the institutions of learning and culture were increasingly built exclusively for them. The pro-slavery lawmakers were as farmers who, having taken great pains to ensure the proper and sustainable cultivation and harvesting of one part of the farm, dedicated themselves with equal if not greater vigor to establish in another part conditions the exact opposite of those necessary for sustainable growth. There they deprived the soil of nearly all nutrients, allowed only the least amount of rain or irrigation water to flow to the plants, covered the fields and orchards to prevent all but the least amount of sunlight from reaching the leaves and in the harvest time allowed nearly all the fruit to rot and fall to the ground ungathered. The suffering of the slaves was more than material. They lived out their lives in a holistically poisonous environment in which the infinite potentialities of the mind and soul withered.

While the basis of this environment may have been a relatively small number of discrete, apparently unconnected legal decisions, the outcome was vast and complex. For these legal actions gradually began to interact and reinforce each other – as was, no doubt, the intention of the lawmakers – creating a structure, a whole transcending the parts, an organic social environment with its own myriad evolutions like the endless unfolding of an intricate ecosystem, until every aspect of the slave's life that would naturally express his infinite creativity was suppressed, poisoned and forced to wither and die prematurely. Like Don Quixote, who sought to tilt at windmills, the slave who aimed to break his chains could never do so, insofar as his chains were the very clouds, rivers, fields and landscape of his social environment. The 'freedom' gained in escaping from the master's chains was lost when he could not learn to read and his children could not enter schools, for the infinite potentialities remained folded up, seeds sown on stones.

On the one hand, the Africans were defined by the laws and philosophy of the slave-holders as *inherently* lacking these boundless creative potentialities of the spirit; on the other hand, whenever slaves and freedmen demonstrated their abilities, proving that they indeed possessed these potentialities, the slave-holders and segregationists acted vigorously to nullify this evidence by usurping or destroying the fruits of African creativity and labor, agriculture and commerce. Thus a long-standing cultural war has been in progress since the slaves' emancipation. African Americans in their new-found personal freedom began to fulfill the spiritual desire of every human being to realize the infinite creative potentials within and, furthermore, to do so in a process of unending improvement of skill, little by little, from one generation to the next. Each freed slave and each of his descendants, without any formal declaration or instruction but merely motivated by his spiritual nature, sought to improve his lot and his children's with every passing day. Such is a desire of the spiritual life, a desire universal in all humanity. Yet it was the aim of racists to prevent that desire from achieving expression among blacks. Racists reached deep within the mysterious heart of the seed and then the sapling and then the young tree, attempting at every stage to suppress its growth, its flowering and fruition.

Education, or rather its lack, was and still is the key tool used by racists in their effort to prevent the unfolding of African potentialities. For without education, Africans could more easily be convinced that they did not possess such potentialities. Without education, the racists hoped, the Africans would remain ignorant of their own spiritual nature. It is for this reason that racism is so closely bound up with expressions – folk sayings, proverbs and especially jokes – that identify Africans with animals and material things. These are all part of the constant efforts of the racist society – like the desperate and futile actions to halt the cracks in a weakening dike – to renew at regular intervals in daily life the doctrine of the absence of spirit among Africans. By convincing themselves the racists hoped to convince the Africans and in this, for a time, they partly succeeded.

But the complete and final extinction of the human spirit amongst a community has never been achieved, even in the harshest of conditions. The efforts of the racists are always material and the material has no complete and ultimate power over the transcendent realm of the spirit. Generations of former slaves and their descendants, many of whom may well have believed in their finiteness as defined by the racists and many of whom were so convinced that they lamented their freedom and wished to remain with their masters – these seemingly lost generations, weak and unempowered in every sense, were nonetheless able to grow spiritually, morally and materially and have continued to do so despite the enforcement of the harsh environmental conditions in which they are obliged to live. For the material efforts of racists, however comprehensive – reaching into the most intimate aspects of the African American's life from cradle to grave – can never destroy the infinite spiritual world to which all human beings naturally belong.

We can only speculate what might have occurred had education been made freely available to slaves and their descendants. But no doubt any vision of the possibilities, however speculative, shows that the labor and intelligence of a nation of well-educated people of all races would have far transcended our present-day achievements.

4

Civilization

The Maturation of Human Society

Here we come to the final element of this discussion: civilization. It seems out of place, does it not, in the context of a discussion of racism? Social problems like racism are always associated with policy questions and historical circumstances and so religion, law and even science naturally enter the debate. But civilization? We usually associate civilization with the technicolor glories of Greece and Rome, of Antony and Cleopatra. That such a vast panorama has anything to do with separate drinking fountains in Sleepy Town, Alabama, seems to be an absurdity.

'We as a people will get to the promised land!' So exclaimed Martin Luther King, Jr., in his last speech. But what is this promised land? It could be interpreted in many ways. Perhaps Dr King himself would describe it from multiple perspectives. One thing is certain, however: the African American conception of the promised land includes a life that allows each person the freedom to grow and develop, both spiritually and materially. Such freedom refers to nothing less than true civilization. It is in the building of true civilization that racism ends. Racism does not end in mere policies and strategies, workshops and focus groups, however important and useful they may be. All that we have discussed thus far shows that the very existence of racism is due to the collapse of true civilization as a whole. Therefore African and European Americans are not waiting for the Godot of a strategy, policy or concept to rectify the wrongs of American society; rather they are waiting to build a true civilization, the civilization that was the road not taken when in the 1600s the American colonists went for the gold. African and European Americans are waiting for the chance to use their own hands and minds to create what should have been created 350 years ago. Getting to the promised land is a matter of getting to work on a vast and profound scale. The final and permanent union of the 'races' lies down that as yet unknown road of cooperative and infinitely creative action to raise up, out of the darkness of ignorance, a civilization of transcendent power, dignity and splendor, a civilization that will expose the empires of the past as aborted attempts to unlock the infinite potentialities of the human race. Therefore when we speak of the elimination of racism ultimately we refer to eliminating the conditions that make it possible; this in turn implies no less than the dawning of a new stage in the social evolution of humanity. As long as we hesitate at the threshold of this new era we will be obliged to suffer racism and its myriad ramifications. By committing ourselves not to rebuilding what we have but to creating true civilization we leave racism forever behind us.

A hopelessly utopian vision? From a traditional academic perspective, yes indeed. But one of the central points of our discussion is that human being is far greater than any academic definition, far more than mind or material. It is also spiritual, and it is the spiritual element that makes the achievement of ideals and lofty goals possible. We seek not absolute perfection but the unlocking of our potentialities, the freedom to improve without end. This freedom has, after a long struggle, been established in the sciences, arts and crafts; now it must be established in the spiritual and social realms.

We have tended to see racism at the local level. We see it as an expression of what one person or group did to another. We do not draw the camera back to gain a broader view, for then we do not see racism in particular. Yet it is in this broader perspective that racism will be resolved, in the perspective wherein African Americans and European Americans become simply human beings; and they can only be seen as such, and see each other as such, in the wider panorama of the evolution of human civilization, not in local politics. Sleepy Town is therefore destined to be overtaken by a broader movement, a rise of civilization so profound that all Sleepy Towns and backwaters, the dark corners, in rural lands, suburbs and cities, will be fundamentally transformed. What kind of civilizing transformation are we anticipating? What kind of threshold are we crossing? It is not possible to say with any precision, as is the case with any anticipation of the future. But if all that we have discussed thus far is any indication, particularly in the light of recent developments in the elimination of barriers to interracial unity, it is fair to say that we are on the threshold of a very profound change indeed, one comparable to a complete evolutionary shift, as when neolithic societies began systematic agriculture. At the very least, simple logic suggests that widespread acceptance of the fundamental unity and oneness of the human race is comparable to the historical shift from polytheism to monotheism, and we certainly can appreciate the profound evolutionary change that shift entailed.

Once we resolve to respiritualize our society, and launch ourselves upon that process, we can expect many positive changes to occur. It is useful to anticipate these changes, to make an effort to draw at least some of the outlines of future spiritualized civilization, so that we can have a clearer understanding of the meaning of our present efforts.

Recognition of Complexity

In order to make and enjoy a cup of tea many preparatory steps must be taken. It cannot be produced in an empty house. We must provide a regulated heat source, dry tea leaves, pure water, a pot, a cup, a spoon, a table, a place to sit. Together these constitute what is essentially quite an involved process. Although apparently among the simplest of daily activities, producing a cup of tea can be regarded as a profound cultural form in both the East and the West, as witnessed in the reverence and perfection with which tea ceremonies in Japan are conducted and in the ideal of gracious living associated in England with high tea. The creation of fine porcelain, of silverware and of handcrafted furniture, all for the purpose of contributing to the effect of the beverage and its richness as a cultural expression, has spawned whole industries and technologies and set standards which have been followed for centuries. Tea has inspired vast movements of merchants and sailors, machinery and treasure, and has been the cause of spilled blood, of colonial and post-colonial conflicts between peoples in various regions of the world. The simple cup of tea is, from a wider historical perspective, not simple at all.

The complex reality of tea, which is normally hidden amidst the rest of our daily activities, has three lessons for us in our anticipation of a spiritualized civilization. First, we can see from this example that even the most elementary aspect of human life cannot be understood until we recognize the totality of its reality and not merely its surface appearance. So often in discussing matters of race we hear someone confidently proclaim, 'It's all politics' or 'It's all economics' or 'It's all human psychology', from which we must conclude that the solutions lie exclusively within the bounds of these respective fields. But taken from a holistic perspective we can readily see that many elements went into the making of what we now know as modern racism and prejudice. Many factors are listed in the ingredients, as it were, and they have been combined in a number of different ways according to local historical circumstances. Racism is therefore not one phenomenon, identical in all its manifestations, but a set of branches of similar phenomena, produced by circumstances which are themselves the product of manifold causes.

Even in this discussion we have taken care to point out that although despiritualization may be the root of the problem we must address all the different parts – the spiritual and the material – of the massive tree we call civilization in order for it to flourish.

The primary reason why we need to recognize the complexity underlying racism is not to catalogue an endless genealogy of the causes that led down through history to its current forms but to understand that the solution to the problem of racism is necessarily going to involve dealing with a number of factors, not merely one or two. A corollary of this concept is that differing perspectives on the causes and solutions of racism need not be opposed; on the contrary they may be complementary, each dealing with a different aspect of a complex reality. Such recognition of the multiplicity of social phenomena is equivalent to the acceptance of the theory of relativity in physics; that is, the principle that different observers may be correct in their apparently divergent and contradictory observations, and only a transcending perspective can reconcile them, or vice versa, only through reconciling them can a transcending perspective be achieved.

One of the signs of maturity in human life is an ability to deal with complexities. It is an interesting phenomenon, and quite a perplexing one, that a technologically advanced, well-educated population, habitually dealing with subtleties and complexities – from the launching of space vehicles to the making of a gourmet cup of tea – is unable to regard racial issues except in the most superficial and simplistic terms. Maturity begins when the same attention to detail, the same diligent and rigorous application of rational thought, is applied to racism as to the building of a computer. A racist society, despite its wholehearted embrace of science and technology, completely renounces its own powers to be humane, to be civilized when, like Dr Jekyll, it surrenders to baser instincts; and it does so justifying its actions by referring to what are widely accepted, and hence authoritative, superstitions. A child or teenager is considered immature not solely or even primarily because of his incomplete physical development but rather because he does not have full control over his emotions; the immature person is one who, however great his powers of rational thought, still allows himself to be governed by unreasonable impulses, refuses to evolve. An adult who appears to be, in speech and actions, fully mature may actually be like an electric light whose switch turns on and off from one situation to the next. Such a person is mature only to a limited degree. He demonstrates not full maturity but a dual character, one that accepts and manifests both maturity and immaturity with great power and effect.

Such a dual character can be recognized in the modern racist society, as seen in Nazi Germany, for on the one hand it displays all the talents and skills of a highly refined civilization, yet on the other it bases many of its actions on pure superstitions which no form of reason or scientific thought can accept. Superstitions prevent the recognition of the complexity of solutions to racism; they reduce the complexity to an absurdly abstract simplicity ('all blacks are less intelligent') which, like a light switch, turns off the practice and application of rational thought and prevents our recognizing and dealing with the complex reality.

The second lesson from the example of making tea is that in the final analysis the experience of having tea is more than the sum of its material parts. The essence of high tea in England and the Zen tea ceremony in Japan lies beyond the preparation and consumption of a beverage for the sake of physical well-being. Offering tea is more than offering nutritious food: it is offering hospitality. It is not an act of cooking but an act of grace and love. Generosity, kindness and grace are spiritual terms indicating that the reason for the complexity in producing tea – and ultimately the complexity in all our cultural acts – is to produce a spiritual atmosphere, renew a spiritual connection, reinforce a spiritual reality in daily life, refresh the soul as well as the body. The tea-maker does not rest until this spirituality comes to life and fills the home.

The same perseverance and diligence must infuse our efforts to bring together the multiple elements needed to create unity between the races, to eliminate the slums and to build in their place enlightened civilization. Our actions in putting the material elements together, once they have been chosen, are not motivated by a desire to witness clever designs or to satisfy some intellectual, financial or political victory but to invoke in the end a spiritual atmosphere in the renewed city. What do we mean by 'spiritual atmosphere'? Very simply, we mean that the place must reflect not merely respect for the residents but a deep reverence for them, must show that the builders regard them as sacred beings. Such reverence is the hallmark of true civilization.

The third lesson is that in order to achieve a complex yet healthy civilization we must overcome the immaturity of pessimism and lack of will. Every aspect of culture that made possible the preparation and presentation of the tea requires tremendous exertion and focused will – the meticulous cultivation of tea, the movement of a tea plantation's harvest across oceans, the artist's creation of pottery, the weaving of fine linen, the mining of silver and gold. In modern society skills have for generations been devoted to the accomplishment of very difficult tasks, from the creation of vast, mammoth infrastructures across the face of the globe – railroads, water systems, communications systems – to the study of such arcane subjects as are all too common among graduate theses in contemporary universities. Yet with all this tremendous talent and energy devoted to countless tasks, we turn ourselves off, like a light switch, when we come to the challenge of uniting ourselves across racial, religious and other social boundaries simply because we say, 'It has never been done and therefore it never will be done.' Surely the will involved in all the many difficult processes necessary to produce and enjoy a civilized cup of tea can be directed to our social ills. It is, in the end, a matter of maturity, which in turn is a matter of willingness to embrace constant change.

Liberation from the Tyranny of Tradition

Alongside the ability to deal with complexity, mature society must also liberate itself from blind obedience to tradition.

One of the greatest inventions is the modern eraser-tipped pencil. It creates but it also corrects. By its means nothing is written in the permanent ink of the medieval scholars or in the stone tablets of the ancient all-powerful priests who preceded them. By it, and the flexible education it promotes, we learn to adapt, change and grow. In primary and secondary schools we are able to admit error and go unhesitatingly to the process of correction. We are encouraged to seek out our own errors and correct ourselves. Schooling thus involves a culture of *openness to correction*. Why, then, do we regard oppressive laws and traditions as immutable? In the adult world this openness mysteriously disappears. We no longer admit errors. We become defensive of our beliefs and cherished theories to the bitter end, fearful that we might be proved wrong. As Thomas Kuhn noted, scientific revolutions or paradigm shifts are strongly opposed by those who stand to be proved wrong. When this openness to correction narrows, learning slows; when it closes completely, learning ends.

It is in our nature, especially when we are in immature stages of development, to imitate our parents, elders and leaders. Imitation is the simplest form of learning and indeed most effective for the immature. The challenge arises when we realize that we are mature, meaning that spiritually we are fully empowered, and we do not need to imitate past generations; indeed such imitation would be harmful.

One of the many great paradigm shifts implied by the end of racism is that increasingly humanity will not fight new ideas but will quickly prove their truth or falsehood and without delay make use of whatever good they have to offer. The recognition and use of good ideas will become like a fluent language, rather than the slow, stuttering, broken and halting speech we attempt now. Fortunately we can see the historical trend. The United States Constitution, for example, and most others in the modern world are written with the possibility of future amendment in mind.

We should take a scientific approach to our own evolution. In science we respect, honor, love and value past achievements but we are not limited by them. The dominance of tradition has no place in science. We must approach our social evolution with a similar attitude, not making idols of past events and heroes but using them as stepping-stones for our own advancement. We, not generations long dead, are the creators of our tomorrows. While each minute we create scientific breakthroughs, it is absurd to think that we believe the greatest philosophy and social thoughts were those of Plato, Aristotle and Socrates and that we'll go no higher.

Fusion of the Human Race

If prejudice against Africans had never existed or had faded completely by the mid-17th century, several aspects of American society would have been profoundly different from what we see today. Interracial marriage and family life would be commonplace, not exceptional. Communication among people would be much more fluent. Cultural unity in diversity would have been established as the standard. Skin color would not be related to, and would not define, roles, class and status. There would be a different consciousness of the meaning of American citizenship. In short, Americans would have become one people instead of a collection of disparate and disputing groups.

The idea of a united United States, however, sparks fear in the hearts of many. We fear that our identities would be lost in an unnatural 'amalgamation' that would destroy our potential and the potential of the human race, that would betray our future and our God. Only by addressing it will this fear fade and eventually disappear.

Human history can be interpreted as analogous to the development of the fertilized human egg, a cell that divides and multiplies, becoming in the process a more complex structure while retaining its unity and integrity. Human society began as a single community, or 'cell', undiversified and limited to a relatively tiny region on the face of the planet. In the course of millions of years gradually the original population multiplied and dispersed to different climates and continents. In the process each sub-population acquired unique physical and cultural characteristics, as if they were cells dividing from the original single cell. With the increasing tendency in modern times of populations to migrate in large groups, the effect is as if these cells are fusing. America, for example, was the province of native peoples; they were suddenly joined by Africans and northern and western Europeans; thereafter by eastern and southern Europeans, and Japanese and Chinese, each group reproducing its own culture and representing its own unique characteristics; and today America is composed of virtually all the races and ethnicities of the world, a multi-celled organism, as it were, of maximum diversity and continuing structural unity. In the past 50 years, as a result of World War Two and colonial and post-colonial economic forces, many other nations of the world have witnessed a similar influx of different ethnic groups either as migrant workers or as refugees. Diversity has become the hallmark of the modern state.

The stage we are now entering surpasses previous levels of fusion. This is the significance of interracial, interreligious and intercultural marriages; they are a final stage in the ages-long process of human society's evolution from a single undifferentiated 'cell' on the plains of Africa, to a widely diverse set of distinct 'cells' or races and now to the reunification of these cells to form not a simple structure, as in its origin, but an infinitely complex unity, as in the fully formed human body that emerges out of the process of cellular division, multiplication and fusion within the mother's womb.

In this regard we can address a long-standing objection: that in the process of this ultimate fusion distinct ethnic groups will lose their identity and will eventually become extinct. Such a fate indeed no group could view with favor. But the reality of such a fusion, when considered from a spiritual and holistic perspective, is that the unique qualities and characteristics are never lost to history but rather are eternal contributions to the development of the human race as a whole. The analogy of the development of the human body is illustrative of this principle: All the original cells eventually multiply and diversify to such an extent that they no longer can be considered to dominate the structure, rather they become subsumed, yet their essence remains forever in the transcendent entity which is the resulting complex yet organically united being. All organic processes involve such transcendence from simple to complex levels and such retention of the unity of the whole. The caterpillar that metamorphoses into a butterfly, and the seed that becomes a tree, do not lose their identity; on the contrary, the essence, the potential within them, becomes fulfilled. Indeed, were the seed or caterpillar to insist on remaining unmetamorphosed, far from preserving its true identity it would in fact be denying it and causing its own death.

In exactly the same sense, for an ethnic or racial group to reject its unity and fusion with other races of the world would mean its rejection of that very destiny which its own Prophets, poets and seers longed to witness, that very fulfillment towards which its own historical evolution is inexorably moving, that very emergence into a transcendent reality it is their spiritual nature to experience. Only the blindness of ignorance, tradition and superstition prevents us from embracing this inevitable metamorphosis of the particular into a transcendent whole.

What distinguishes humanity's metamorphosis from the metamorphosis in nature is that it will develop only through our conscious will. Cells divide, multiply and form a united complexity according to laws of nature the functioning of which is automatic and requires no conscious involvement. But the meta-being that is the human family cannot emerge except by means of the uniquely human spiritual power of consciousness.

Imagine a tree. It is a unified, single organism. Clearly it is one entity.

Yet it is composed of literally countless diverse elements, including leaves, blossoms, seeds, branches, bark, roots, rhizomes – and we can go further into the cellular level, the molecular level and so on. What brought these diverse elements into such a powerful and united harmony? This was a result of the operation of nature. It was not the result of the conscious will of the tree itself. The formation of global society, however, will not occur as a result of the automatic functioning of nature. All the elements of global society are today present. The diversity required for the creation of a complex, united global organism exists. Yet global society remains only a potential. It will not emerge until human beings decide consciously to create this unity. We see the same action of conscious will in lower forms of human unity, namely the nation, the city, the tribe and the family. These groupings are possible not because nature dictates their existence but rather because humans will them into existence. A new leap of consciousness is now required in order for global unity and the elimination of racism to be achieved.

The conflict between globalization and localization is really between two forms of consciousness: one that recognizes humanity's emergence in the fusion of its parts and one that believes the limit of social organization is at the level of the tribe, clan, nation or race. The irony is that even these local forms of social organization are themselves the product of the fusion of previously disparate, simpler elements: distinct families united to become a clan; clans united to become a tribe; tribes united to become a city; cities united to become a nation. These earlier forms of fusion in no way negated the elements on which they were based; in fact systems philosophy argues that it is not possible to have greater complexity, broader forms of unity, without the preservation of diversity. Family and tribal identities remain even in the context of national unity. Each of these unities did not cause the destruction or loss of the unique qualities of its elements. New York does not cease to be New York simply because it is part of the same country as Los Angeles – or Boston for that matter.

Unity has been integral to all human social evolution. To object to its continued operation would mean to object to its past operation and would require us to return to a primitive, even atomistic social life. What would happen if we carried the practices of segregation, anti-miscegenation and apartheid to their logical conclusion? All the peoples of the world would remain within their own groups. We would not only marry within our own group but we would go to school only with 'our own', work only with them, associate and socialize only with them, worship only with them, die amongst them and be buried amongst them. The world would be a set of individual cells, each having no association with any other. The sharing of knowledge and technology would cease, suffering would increase, freedom of motion would be severely curtailed, leading to wars over territories and mutual destruction. The transcendent power of the group would be reduced to a very small scale. Civilization would end.

The fusion of human groups on a global scale is in some ways unlike previous levels of social fusion. It involves for the first time the totality of the human race. It commences the primacy of a transcendent human reality, a global human identity that takes priority over but does not negate local identities. If previous, relatively local social fusions were paradigm shifts in human organization, the coming establishment of global fusion is none other than a meta-shift, just as the organs constitute a whole which is a 'meta-being', the human.

How will this united human family affect the problem of racism and its many consequences? Let us turn our attention to the most powerful and destructive manifestation of racism: the segregated, impoverished American city. If spirituality and unity are ever to prove their efficacy, their healing powers will have to be clearly demonstrated here.

Despiritualized Cities

Much of our modern life is fake. The 'marble' facades of buildings; plastic 'wood veneer'; 'beef' and 'milk', nay 'food' in general; 'music'; 'houses' and 'architecture' – such things constitute a two-dimensional Hollywood set. Most of us don't know, for example, that 'Much of the taste and aroma of American fast food . . . is now manufactured at a series of large chemical plants off the New Jersey Turnpike.'[1] We have fake houses and neighborhoods ('tract housing', 'housing developments', 'housing projects'); fake families ('The Nelsons', 'Eight is Enough', 'The Partridge Family', 'The Brady Bunch'); fake towns (Levittown); fake cities (Las Vegas); fake parks (Disney); fake culture (Disney) and fake education (Channel 1, Disney). Yet we convince ourselves that everything is great: great food, great house, great concert. We will ourselves to believe; we try to convince ourselves of the authenticity of what we very well know is fake. This is a form of mass insanity.[2] In Japan, Alex Kerr reports, this has become a runaway process so extreme that it is common to find people who believe that handmade traditional crafts made of natural materials, no matter how neat and clean, are actually dirty.[3]

Why has everything become false? Why did the genuine disappear? A primary reason, of course, is the increasing destruction of natural resources, necessitating the substituting of the real by plastic imitations. But this accounts for only part of the problem and leaves the question of fake culture unanswered. Perhaps a more comprehensive answer is that in our materialistic society the city is no longer regarded as a community of human beings but rather as a machine. When an urban society becomes despiritualized the consciousness of people as souls is lost and all that remains is the consciousness of the city's material quality: its machine-like ability to generate tremendous wealth.

As cities have dramatically expanded in the past half-century the process of urban despiritualization has likewise accelerated. Cities around the world have experienced a mass inward migration of rural people, what could be termed a population implosion. Consequently, the cities exceed the carrying capacity of their natural environment; they cannot sustain the lives of the people in a systemically healthful way; there is a gradual collapse of the infrastructure, the economy, the culture and the mental and physical health of the city's inhabitants. That such cities have not yet collapsed completely is due to an ever-growing process: These cities artificially sustain themselves by exploiting increasing quantities of natural resources and manufactured goods from the surrounding region and eventually from distant lands. In the process, manufacturers, keen to satisfy the ever-quickening mass demand of these consumer black holes, exert every effort to tailor their products so as to meet demand as rapidly as possible, for extreme demand requires nearly instant supply, which in turn implies simplification of the product for mass production, transportation and consumption. It is no longer *food* that is eaten but rather boxes of this, cans of that, crates of one thing and gross of another. The actual food is no longer of primary importance, for in the final analysis it is not human beings who consume these products but the city – a vast machine. The process is so enormous that producers of food and other goods have long ago oriented their products to the city-as-machine, which is their primary customer. An inadvertent consequence is that people in the countryside are often obliged to go along: when dealing with the mainstream market and producers, rural people cannot but accept the situation, the demand as defined by New York, London, Mexico City, Tokyo. Hence rural and suburban people find in their local retail markets shoddy goods produced in haste for a distant city with no human beings in mind. The despiritualization of the city affects all, near and far.

THE DRIVE TO UNIFORMITY

As to be expected, there is a direct relationship between the false culture of the modern city and racism. The great historian Arnold Toynbee perceived in history a two-fold pattern: civilizations that are growing tend 'towards differentiation and diversity' while those in decline tend 'towards standardization and uniformity'.[4] What we see as the mass production of standardized goods to be consumed by a machine-like urban society Toynbee interprets as the symptoms of a civilization approaching collapse. In such a society it is no wonder that racial and cultural groups that divert from the norm are punished and those that adhere to the standard are rewarded. Just as a dying tree eventually reaches the point where it can put out leaves on only one branch, so too a despiritualized city tends to favor only one group and is incapable of embracing humanity in all its infiniteness.

But how then do we explain the great diversity of the modern city? Contrary to the process of decay and collapse, the process of respiritualization is having increasing effect. Racial diversity in the world's cities is indeed growing, despite the fact that the masses of minority groups are confined to slums and ghettos, abandoned in vast tracts that are nothing but rubble-strewn war zones. We are therefore in a transition stage in which the elements of diversity exist and are gradually moving toward fusion into a transcendent whole and yet they are restrained by the continuing influence of despiritualization that favors uniformity. Let us examine some of the ways in which uniformity manifests itself in the modern urban society.

Starting in the late 1800s a movement emerged in the United States and parts of Europe that sought to replace haphazard urban development with planned neighborhoods, towns and cities. The concept of the suburban community as a garden village was born and spread rapidly, particularly in the region between America's East coast and Chicago. But following World War Two the pressure to build suburban housing for tens of thousands of returning veterans and their baby-boom families meant that beauty and elegance were sacrificed to expedience and the garden village became overwhelmed by Levittowns, cookie-cutter-colonial neighborhoods characterized by sterility, alienation, culturelessness and even mental depression. Zoning laws instituted a new pervasive uniformity by breaking up the natural unity between local commerce and homes, disallowing 'Mom and Pop' stores on the corner, apartments over shops, carriage-house apartments and alleys in the backyards. In many cases even large shade trees were expressly forbidden. In place of the ages-long harmony between small commercial establishments and residential areas the new zoning philosophy married houses with driveways, streets and highways in order to facilitate the use of the private automobile at the highest possible speeds. The result was more than aesthetically atrocious; it was positively suffocating. In short, the home front became militarized into a uniform, standardized and racially segregated military barracks culture that allowed the automobile to flourish but spelled the doom of community in most of suburban America.

In a fascinating parallel, Alex Kerr has found that Japan's extreme attachment to the artificial and the unnatural, its excessive devotion to things technological and its manic destruction of its own natural beauty can be traced to a military culture 'that ruled Japan for many centuries', and that demanded 'total control over every branch and twig'.[5]

Such imbalanced urban life expresses what Dyer calls 'extreme whiteness', those cultural qualities that exhibit the social pathology of European Americans derived from an over-emphasis on material life. The culture of extreme whiteness claims that virtues of civilization are unique to itself and not inherently present in any other culture. These virtues include orderliness, systematism, cleanliness and freedom from all forms of 'dirt', a rational and even scientific approach to the management of all aspects – all aspects – of social and personal life. Extreme whiteness manifests itself in an ideal personality that is 'taut, tight, rigid, upright, straight (not curved), on the beat (not syncopated), controlled and controlling'.[6] This describes nothing other than a militarized society. The ideal white male is a military officer in uniform or in civilian clothing, the stern Marlboro Man. Manifested in the community and wider environment it is a culture that destroys the wildness of nature and replaces it with orderly rows of crops, streets, houses, power lines, desks in classrooms and offices – a unity in uniformity. Orderliness and discipline are important for any civilization; the problem is that in the culture of extreme whiteness they are not counterbalanced with the equally important qualities of diversity, creativity and respect for nature.

Jeremy Rifkin explains how despiritualized society forfeits its relationship to the natural environment:

> In the cold calculating domain of the modern world, we have substituted material self-interest for eternal salvation, expediency for renewal, and production quotas for generativeness. We have flattened the organic richness of existence, turning the world around us into abstract mathematical equations, statistics, and bottom-line performance standards. Cold evil is perpetuated by institutions and individuals bound by rational organizing principles, with only market forces and utilitarian goals to guide their choices and decisions. In such a world, there is little opportunity to honor the creation, empathize with our fellow creatures, steward the environment, and protect the rights of future generations.[7]

John Howard Griffin also found this same drive to uniformity in his experience traveling as a black man in the South:

> . . . it is an utter distortion to claim the freedom to deny someone else's freedom. This attempt to gobble everyone up, to make everyone conform to our individual or group prejudices, our religious or philosophical convictions – and seeking to suppress them if they do not – is the deepest cultural neurosis I know.[8]

The Rockettes, the famous dance troupe at the Radio City Music Hall in New York City, was always all white until October 1987. But even then the first black dancer to be hired was only a stand-in for unexpected absences of the regular dancers. The reason no blacks were ever hired was openly stated by the group's director, who said that the dancers should be 'mirror images' of each other. 'One or two black girls in the line would definitely distract. You would lose the whole look of precision, which is the hallmark of the Rockettes.' Patricia J. Williams sees in this statement an allegory: 'all of society pictured in that one statement'.[9] The mere presence of an African American person has what she calls a 'ghostly power' that renders everything ugly, imbalanced and sloppy, no matter how she may be as a dancer. The physical presence of the dancer is perceived to signify a deeper, more sinister reality that evokes from the whites an emotional response. This whole construct, as we have seen, traces its roots to the superstitions and excesses of the late Middle Ages. It is just such a situation that causes African Americans, as Ralph Ellison wrote, to be invisible. For the only way to succeed in the white world, Williams argues, is to deny and hide one's blackness:

> What the middle-class, propertied, upwardly mobile black striver must do, to accommodate a race-neutral world view, is to become an invisible black, a phantom black, by avoiding the label 'black' (it's all right to be black in this reconfigured world if you keep quiet about it).[10]

European Americans also suffer from the culture of extreme whiteness. The sociologist William H. Whyte argued that post-World War Two America was a society that suppressed true individual creativity and promoted 'the Organization Man', a technocrat or bureaucrat who would, like a soldier in an army, achieve success through conformity and obedience. That is still the norm in America today, a society in which public space and public discourse have been 'corporatized', reduced to facilitating the individual's role as a passive consumer.[11]

But there is one glaring exception and this exception proves the possibilities that lie ahead. America has no greater business success of its own making today than the computer industry. Silicon Valley thrives because it has allowed the highly talented individual, in his or her own way, however eccentric or odd, to be creative, to search and build, without pressure to be 'normal'.[12] One wonders what harm would come to America were it to allow this same kind of creative freedom in all fields of endeavor.

Balanced Cities

The respiritualization process is gathering momentum to the point where even now the quest to transform cities no longer seems to be a utopian dream. A new movement of the garden village style of architecture and urban planning arose in the 1990s in reaction to the growing conscious-ness that the ills of the American city and suburb must be corrected before it is too late. We long for 'the good old days' when neighbors spoke amongst themselves on a daily basis, knew each other well, borrowed from each other, gave to each other, helped each other, laughed together. The New Urbanism school of planning has in the past decade demonstrated its skills in numerous projects around the United States and abroad. It is attracting a large following among architects, urban designers, city governments and home buyers. It is being hailed as the savior of American culture, as the resurrection of the genuine America in the midst of a plastic culture col-lapsing under the weight of its own phoniness.

There is only one problem: In New Urbanist communities alienation stubbornly persists. The spiritual problems of the wider society are quite present, only less obviously so.

Consider the most famous of all New Urbanist developments, the town of Celebration, Florida, created by the Disney corporation. Of course, one obvious uniqueness about Celebration is that Disney has played a dominant role in all decision-making and cultural aspects of the town, specifying issues ranging from the colors of draperies permitted in homes to the level of ethnic and economic diversity of the residents. In fact, the omnipresence of Disney prevents the town from developing as a true community. And this is precisely the point. For Celebration is not so much a new direction in America's social evolution as a more clear and focused expression of the way we have been living since World War Two. New Urbanism is being co-opted by business interests in the same way America's small town life and rural countryside were transformed by car manufacturers, oil companies, electricity monopolies and other powerful corporations.

Before going any further in our discussion of Celebration, let us note that we will have many positive things to say about it.

Built on pasture and swamp just outside the Disney World theme park, Celebration, which opened in 1996, is characteristic of most New Urbanist communities in tending towards the culture of extreme whiteness. Douglas Frantz and Catherine Collins are professional journalists who lived in Celebration for over a year before publishing a book about their experience. As they described it:

> The one- and two-story houses were variations on a limited number of designs, so they seemed to fit together like pieces of an architect's puz-zle. Garages were tucked discreetly behind the houses along alleys that ran parallel to every street. Lawns were clipped, and there was no sign of litter anywhere.

So far so good. A bit limited in architectural freedom but otherwise nothing to complain about. Everybody likes to live in a neat, clean and beautiful environment. But they continue:

> The streets themselves were laid out on a modified grid plan, attesting in that singularly American way to order, virtue, and rectitude.[13]

The problem here is that somehow Americans have equated military order with virtue and rectitude. Any thoughtful visit to the exquisitely beautiful villages of Europe, from the British Isles to France to the Czech Republic, convinces us that order and harmony are not at all dependent on this American caricature of stiff, grid-plan suburban life. And those European villages are 'white' cultures too. In fact, morality, rectitude, order and civilization have nothing to do with this sterile conception of community.

Let us take Switzerland, for example, the wealthiest nation in the world – depending on the exchange rate. Switzerland, as far as we know, has been throughout modern history a place where 'white people' have lived, built their villages, towns and cities, established their cultural and religious norms and traditions, traded, farmed, produced and flourished. It is a country famous the world over for its orderliness, as expressed in the stereotypical Swiss watch and the train systems it governs. The entire country does indeed run like a watch in the sense that services are extremely reliable, laws are enforced and obeyed, new laws evolve systematically according to need and are smoothly introduced. This is not to say that Switzerland is a perfect country. There is crime, there are social problems, there are divisions. But nowhere in Switzerland will the visitor find towns that resemble sprawling American grid-plan suburbs, and this despite the fact that Switzerland, like all western Europe, has a very high population density. Forests come to the edge of villages, towns and cities. Open waterfronts of lakes and rivers are common in heavily populated areas. Agricultural fields and vineyards are often lying at the back and front doors of apartment buildings and houses. A vast network of bicycle routes and footpaths, marked by accurate and well-maintained signage and complemented by sets of detailed maps, crisscross the entire country through all kinds of terrain, from the peaks of snow-covered mountains to the centers of business districts. Swiss people of all ages are regularly out and about making use of them and the sports equipment needed to enjoy nature: bicycles, roller blades, downhill skis, cross-country skis, kayaks, canoes, sail boats, wind surfers, hiking boots, climbing boots, snowshoes, gliders, hang gliders, paragliders, walking sticks, climbing axes, packs, ropes, tents, Swiss army knives and chocolate.

Who says civilized life must be dry, dull, sterile, empty and removed from the 'dirt' of nature?

Many American 'developers' say so. One observer who works for and supports Disney in Celebration nevertheless complained:

> Any county would be thrilled to have a development of this quality. But it has been a professional failure for me. I have a job to do, to integrate the development with the environment, and I can't get it done. They are designing with the mind-set of the fifties and sixties. Clear, mow down, level, start all over again, replant. Instead of trying to design by using the natural amenities.[14]

Frantz and Collins are positive about the Celebration project, yet they have their reservations: 'There is a fine line between harmony and conformity, and too often we felt that the residents of Celebration had come down on the side of conformity.'[15] One of the more disturbing aspects of Celebration's uniformity, they discovered, is its racial homogeneity. No significant effort had been made to attract minority buyers and to provide housing in the town for low-income families and individuals. As a result only a small handful of minorities lived in the town when Frantz and Collins were there. It is significant that in the mid-1940s Celebration's 'grandfather', the real estate company that built the prototypical, factory-made Long Island suburb of Levittown, refused to sell any of its houses to blacks. Now some 50 years later, the newest town of the future, created by the corporation that made an international hit of a theme song about unity in diversity – 'It's a Small World', the lyrics of which call for 'friendship to everyone' and proclaim 'there's so much that we share' – maintains more or less the racial *status quo*, as if the civil rights movement had never existed.[16]

Disney has apparently gone too far in reaching back to the past to revive lost qualities of American culture. It resurrected a number of aspects that are best laid to rest. The nostalgia for the peaceful small town life seems to be remembered with a racial tint. New Urbanism of this sort is more retro-urbanism. It not only builds old-fashioned towns but creates within them a narrow-minded, closed-borders culture no longer possible or healthy in an inexorably globalizing world. Frantz and Collins found many fellow residents who shared their belief that racial homogeneity in Celebration was a serious problem that should be corrected for the sake of the town's future and to provide the town's children the necessary experiences for living in a world of ever greater cultural and ethnic diversity. Although their voices were in the minority, the very fact that they were vocal about the subject in their homes and town meetings shows the rising consciousness of global citizenship – a phenomenon that was not in evidence at the founding of Levittown half a century ago.

There are other causes for hope in Celebration. The town's designers had in mind the goal of integrating residential areas and commerce so that cars would not be needed to do most daily tasks. In this they succeeded. Frantz and Collins were able to sell one of their two cars and drove the remaining one less than a thousand miles a month. Celebration's planners also succeeded in making it easier for townspeople to interact more frequently and informally. Civil society is able to flourish there because the typical barriers to social interaction in suburbia – the cars and roadways, the large and isolating yards – have been removed through careful planning. In their stead are a town center with shops and services, convenient meeting places, front porches, footpaths and sidewalks, attractive streetlights, benches, pedestrian- and bicycle-friendly streets and greenery everywhere. One resident, an urban planner by profession, remarked:

> It is just easier to be a part of this community. I am more involved here than I ever was in Tampa, despite my long commute, because there, being involved meant getting back in the car. Here it is just a matter of, do I want to have a pleasant walk down the street? Well, of course. You turn the TV on and notice on the local cable channel that there is a PTSA meeting, and even if you didn't plan to go, it is so easy that you tend to do it. It is almost as if modern society puts all these hurdles in front of behaving in a good way, like being involved in your kid's school. Here the obstacles are removed.[17]

Reviewing their time in the town, Frantz and Collins realized that 'one of the most positive things was a vibrancy that we had not experienced any-place else. People were bound together in an endeavor that ran counter to the overall decline of civil society in America. Celebration had something important to say to the rest of the country about how we live as friends and neighbors.'[18]

There is no doubt that much of the rest of the country is listening. The authors cite the fact that 'there are 225,000 planned communities nationwide', many of which are so-called gated communities for affluent whites who 'are willing to swap certain freedoms in order to live in what they think are safer, better communities'.[19] But there is also a growing number of more creative, less fortress-minded planned towns designed by New Urbanists. If nothing else, these efforts are raising consciousness of the need to create a sense of unity between households in a community, to end once and for all the dominance of the private automobile, to have a town center. And they have also clarified for all of us the choice that stands before us: Do we choose the barracks culture of the grid-plan, militarized society? Or do we opt for the kind of community that seeks harmony with nature and with all peoples? Do we prefer the false peace of a 'secure' closed fortress or the true peace of a balanced city? Do we seek unity in uniformity, or unity in diversity?

The answer is clear. From what we have discovered in our journey through western history, and as Toynbee also cautions, we must restore the balance of unity in diversity if we are to grow as a true civilization. In this regard there are two simple implications of such a choice. First, the balance between nature and civilization must be restored. Towns must be built within and become part of nature; they must be built in parks, not only parks built into towns. If the urban landscape is not traversed by greenways that connect to each other and to open spaces on all sides, there is a disruption in the flow of nature in, around and through the city. Just as a dammed river leads to serious environmental consequences, so too a damming of green space causes serious material and spiritual consequences.

Second, we must re-examine and revise our motivation. A balanced city cannot be built through the quest for wealth alone. It is not merely coincidental that the world's most beautiful villages, towns, cities and architecture were built *before* the dominance of the profit motive. Ironically, the faction of American society most commonly known as 'conservatives' has tended to be quite radical, for in the pursuit of capital they have willingly swept away all traces of the past and have eagerly created what we now call the postmodern world – a world in which traditional values, or any values, have been abandoned in favor of extreme freedom. Conversely, the alternative movement of what Paul Ray and Sherry Anderson call 'cultural creatives'[20] – which includes New Urbanists, environmentalists, organic farmers, revivalists of local and indigenous arts and crafts, practitioners of alternative non-invasive healing methods – is in many ways truly conservative, aiming to preserve old values that the radical capitalists have discarded. Of course, this is not to say that spiritualized civilization must forbid profit-making, market activity and individual enterprise. Rather, there should be a balance: the economic freedom of the individual should be encouraged, the motivation transformed from the quest for self-enrichment to the desire to benefit oneself, one's family and the community as a whole and ultimately to make lasting contributions to civilization.

Having introduced here the idea of balanced cities and of the process of respiritualization that must be established amongst the citizens, let us now explore more deeply this subject by turning to one of the goals of spiritual civilization: the ending of the ghetto and slum.

Urban Metamorphosis

One of the most famous songs sung by Lou Rawls is 'Tobacco Road', a symbolic stretch of urban squalor in which the singer/narrator was raised from childhood and which he determines in his maturity to raze so that he can 'start all over again'. It would not be surprising to learn that most African Americans have envisioned themselves participating in the momentous process of the cleaning of the urban slate, purifying the land and resting their eyes on a sight of clear horizons ready for solid homes of dark brick and heavy wood, tree-shaded and flower-bedecked walkways and an urban farm close to hand. This is all well and good and many people dream of doing so. But how?

The structural cause of urban poverty is twofold: unemployment and lack of land rights. African Americans came from a rural society, culture and economy in the South. They settled in the urban North, expecting to transfer to industrial jobs. As industry collapsed or moved away the African Americas were left abandoned in a post-industrial society with no jobs. The natural thing for them to have done would have been to return to a rural economy, to agriculture. But this was not possible in an urban setting for one reason: they did not have control over the land on which they were living. They could not transform the land from sterile concrete jungle to productive farms with complementary rent-free housing built from materials produced from the land itself. If they could have done so, the problems of food, housing and employment would have been readily solved. Agricultural productivity could have easily brought in cash as well; we need only have a quick glimpse of the jumping early morning activity at the fresh produce markets in Manhattan, Philadelphia and Boston to get a clear idea of the economic potential of urban farms.

As it is now, however, African Americans and other urban minority groups stand unempowered in a no-man's land between an industrial structure and an agricultural one. Our society has made it appear normal that large masses of people, the poor and the homeless, do not have access to land. We think it is natural for human beings to have no control over any land anywhere. We do not question this. We take for granted that rent is natural, inevitable and well-nigh universal. Because of the despiritualization of the city we cannot imagine the urban poor obtaining control over large areas of land. Through the process of respiritualization, however, it would become not only imaginable and possible but inevitable.

But assuming the urban poor were able to become custodians of the land on which they live, what would it really take to start anew in an American slum? The first thing that might come to mind is the razing of all the ugly, decrepit structures: the squalid housing projects and tenements, derelict factories, toxic waste sites, repulsive schools, crude commercial centers. Then would follow the digging up of tens of square miles of concrete, of sewage systems and the debris of decades that lies upon and is imbedded within the soil: bits of broken glass, metal, plastic, of all shapes and colors.

Whether done all at once or in stages this process of cleaning the slate is inevitable, for everything in the slum is damaging to human health. The outcome would be square miles of good, healing earth, perhaps not yet rich in nutrients but quickly becoming so.

Demolishing unwanted buildings and clearing the land is, of course, the easy part of the job. Not because construction is more costly, time-consuming and painstaking than deconstruction but primarily because construction involves the establishment of a new organic social system – institutions, infrastructure, habits, practices, rules and laws. Eliminating a slum is akin to diverting a powerful river from one channel to another; the new course must first be well prepared before the actual diversion takes place. The institutions and infrastructure of the new neighborhoods must be carefully planned so as to ensure not only the elimination of the slum but also the endless unfoldment of a healthy, progressing social order. This in turn would involve a program to maintain social balance and unity with the wider society.

Such a concept of regular monitoring of the city, its suburbs and its surrounding rural region, has been adopted by the city of Portland, Oregon, where the city government is assisted and to a degree supervised by a new governmental body that plans development at the metropolitan or regional level. The citizens of Portland have realized that for their city to function according to sustainable principles they must closely coordinate with the suburban and rural populations with whom they are organically united.[21] Recognition of the organic unity between peoples is the essence of the spiritual quality of mature civilization.

But the creation of such a complete and sustainable infrastructure, the re-creation of a city from the ground up, involving thousands of complex tasks and the harmonious interaction of hundreds of institutions in order to provide food, water, health care, energy, shelter, clothing, education, professional training and administrative and maintenance services – to provide all this overnight in one package, as it were, is perhaps too artificial an approach to the solving of the problems of Tobacco Road. And maybe that is the reason why it has not and cannot be done in this way. To do so is an artifice, the work of engineers and urban planners, the work of technology, not the work of families, human beings with a personal stake in the outcome, not the work of minds and hearts. To rebuild Tobacco Road in this manner is to involve the sale and purchase of technology; it would be, in the end, a consumer transaction, a material endeavor. No one can purchase or create a new community on behalf of the people of Tobacco Road. The world of consumerism is far removed from the reality of social life, for it centers on the relationship between people and money, not the relationships between people themselves.

Rather, a truly revived Tobacco Road would be a community naturally and organically created by the people of that place, with the assistance of the wider society. Through their own labor the slum would be cleared and a new, lasting community would rise in its place. In the end, it is always the input of human labor that makes a thing valuable. Whereas reconstruction by technology and consumerism would be artificial and doomed to fail, reconstruction by the people themselves would be a holistically empowering endeavor. Ultimately it would become their work of art.

Refinement

Art in most western societies today is relegated to a very small part of social life. It is created by a limited group of highly specialized artists and their work is appreciated by the public only in certain special circumstances – at museums, concerts, galleries and so on. It is not generalized in the society. Moreover, the society itself is not considered an artistic creation but rather something utilitarian, like the bureaucracy of a business or the administration of an army. Society is associated with the need for survival, for the organization of food, water, shelter and other economic and life resources. To consider the construction of society an art work is to be misconstruing serious business; it is to confuse the frivolous with the essential. We tend to look at the founding of our societies as heavy drama, filled with death, destruction and suffering. We never seem to overcome this shadow of the past; we are tied to it and remain, like participants in a memorial for the war dead, in perpetual mourning.

If we begin to regard society as an art work in progress we will adopt a completely different attitude towards our own activities. It will no longer be sufficient simply to 'make do'. We will attempt to perfect what we build, to improve continually upon it as a musician constantly works to produce a purer, more accurate and evocative sound from his or her instrument. The musician's goal, like the tea-maker's, is beyond the music itself; it is for the performer and the audience to attain a higher spiritual state. So too the creation of any aspect of society, whether it be a transportation system or an educational program, a hotel or a park, a building or a business, will be to elevate the spiritual state of the entire community – indeed, ultimately it will aim to contribute to the spiritual elevation of the entire human race. Our motivation will be not the quest for wealth or some form of symbolic immortality that wealth implies. Rather we will seek to serve humanity and will derive the deepest satisfaction in seeing that our labors have provided a valuable assistance to others, solved a problem, improved upon work done by predecessors, made the way to future advancement all the easier to travel.

American society behaves much like an imprecisely tuned guitar. At first it seems to function as it should but a more careful inspection proves that its 'harmonics' are not true. Many people feel it is indeed a society in tune and they play it with vigor all their lives, not understanding why people object to the music they make. This is why we seem to have two Americas: one in tune, that is, fair and just, and one out of tune, unjust and unfair. People are becoming more mature, more sensitive to the subtleties of life, more able to hear them and consequently they need to have them in tune and in balance. We therefore cannot appeal to minorities to accept their lot as the past generations have. Some critics of African Americans have argued that the protests of the 1950s and 1960s were due primarily to their 'rising expectations', as if to have such expectations is to be spoiled and unworthy. It is only natural to expect a better life for oneself and one's children; indeed this is a defining quality of a healthy, progressing civilization. In the course of its evolution, humanity naturally loses sensitivity to certain values and increases or acquires new sensitivities to others. Our sensitivity towards prejudice and racism was weak some two centuries ago; they were considered a normal part of life. Now it is a point of controversy. But it is only natural that as humanity matures it becomes more sensitive to injustices, more intolerant of and opposed to them, just as a musician becomes with experience more sensitive to the subtleties of pitch and harmony. In this context it is not reasonable to ask a segment of humanity to 'stop being oversensitive', nor is it fair to ask them to stifle their 'rising expectations'. Sensitivity is a proof of awareness, of consciousness, of constant growth.

To refine America's sense of justice is to raise its standards, not lower them. It would be far better to play a well-tuned instrument and make some mistakes than one poorly tuned with great virtuosity; the former is pure while the latter is not. Many people feel it is unrealistic – utopian – to seek greater precision in society's fine tuning, that crude tuning is all we can expect. Yet why do we practice fine tuning in every sphere – family, art, science, sports and even the minutiae of everyday life – but not in the organization and balance of the whole society?

Everywhere today people are energetically pursuing their quest for refinement and beauty. Even from the earliest civilizations the creation and enjoyment of beauty has been one of the universal and central goals of human activity, as any viewer of the treasures of King Tutankhamun's tomb would testify. Beauty is difficult to define, no doubt, but such difficulty does not prove its nonexistence. Are there any people who would prefer to live in squalid surroundings rather than clean, spacious and verdant towns? Is there anyone who would choose to wear filthy rags instead of spotless, well-tailored clothes?

A sense of refinement is innate in human beings and with our historical evolution this sense has become stronger, more widespread and more prominent as a guide and motivator in individual and community actions. With each new generation the peoples of the world are refining and sharing their senses of beauty across cultural boundaries, further confirming the universal nature of this vital aspect of human culture. Conversely, by the same intercultural process we are also refining our sense of what is not beautiful. Many people today make the acquisition of beautiful things their chief aim: homes, vehicles, art, clothing, work places, gardens, parks. We wish to fill our daily lives with beauty and eliminate all traces of unattractive and unseemly qualities.

Ours is a culture of beauty and refinement permeates our society even to the most seemingly trivial details of our daily lives. Whole careers and educational programs are devoted to the design of jewelry, stamps, paper shopping bags, bathroom fixtures, pens and pencils, lawnmowers, type fonts, musical instrument cases, pet accessories and tissue dispensers so that they will be pleasing to the eye and comfortable to use. Perhaps one of the greatest ironies in this age of technology is that our tastes are increasingly inclining towards handcrafted products from around the world. We are swimming in a sea of refined consumer goods, the exquisiteness of which is limited only by the shopper's budget.

How utterly bewildering, then, is the panorama which confronts us, beyond the well-appointed suburban home in its beautifully landscaped neighborhood, when we stand back and see that within nearly every American city lies a large and sometimes dominating slum which epitomizes all that is undesirable in life, all that is unattractive, all that is decrepit, decaying, rotting and dying. The slums of American cities are malignant cysts that grow even as our search for beauty becomes more earnest, particularistic and far-reaching.

No one likes these slums, neither those who live in them nor those who live near them. Yet while we train people to design and manufacture ever more refined and attractive credit cards, ATM machines, and aprés-ski boots, we ignore the challenge of reclaiming these areas, making the city whole and healthy again. Why?

Is it that the task of designing a more beautiful kitchen takes less skill than beautifying a city slum? No. The skills involved in creating comfortable, attractive dwellings amidst a pleasing landscape and in renovating decaying structures are well known and routinely practiced.

Is it that designing and producing an exquisite kitchen leads to profit, whereas the revitalization of a slum does not? No. Such urban revitalization creates value where little or none had existed. Hence we see the very telling phenomenon of gentrification. The renovation work, and the maintenance of the beautified area, generates many long-term and perpetual business and employment opportunities. It contributes to the strengthening of the economy as a whole. Indeed this work is not only a challenge but a hidden economic boon.

On the other hand, the question arises: Who will pay for these profit-making renovation and maintenance services? We know who will buy a new kitchen but who will invest in a complete makeover for South Central Los Angeles?

Here we encounter a fundamental problem: the profit motive. The economic philosophy of free market systems jealously guards the right of companies and entrepreneurs to act on their own behalf for the sake of gaining profit. On the surface of it there would seem to be nothing wrong with this approach. For by the strong incentive of self-interest most of the landmark achievements of the modern West have come into being and the spirit of technological creativity and problem-solving has permeated the most minute aspects of our daily lives – hence the ever new and improved toothbrush holder, the Shinkansen and TGV, lightweight shoes and high-tech ski bindings.

But the profit motive is not relevant to tasks that are socially necessary yet not within the boundaries of the market. For the poor have no money to offer in exchange for goods and services. They are in the country but not in the market.

The problem of the profit motive, then, is that it prevents goods and services from reaching those people who need them most. Of course, ideally a system of taxation could be instituted in order to redistribute wealth, endow the poor with financial resources and enable them to pay for their needs and satisfy the profit requirements of service providers. But ultimately isn't such a system only an illusion? The haves seem to be paid by the have-nots but in reality the money is coming from the pockets of the haves themselves. Collectively they seem to gain nothing by serving the poor. As this is well known, the market vigorously and persistently works to prevent such a system of taxation from being established. Meanwhile the slums continue to grow.

Perhaps another approach can be considered. If we analyze from a holistic perspective the economic relationship between a slum and a wealthy city, we find that in reality the rich pay a great deal of money – are in effect heavily taxed – to allow slums to exist. They pay in several ways: 1) in lost profits from a population of potential customers too poor to pay for goods and services, 2) in the cost of maintaining such a large population in a state of non-productivity and near-chaos, the costs of police, medical care and fire protection, which certainly far outweigh whatever benefits may be derived, 3) in the time and effort spent by lawyers and governmental institutions to establish rules and systems to maintain segregation and 4) in the lost prestige and foolishly ignored social value of once bustling and now derelict downtowns, whose locations are often priceless for their strategic positions on waterways and rail lines. In the mid-1990s a Fortune 500 company estimated that racism, sexism and other sources of social disunity reduced its profits by $20 to $40 million.[22] One scholar likens all these expenses as equivalent to the cost of an ongoing war against an external enemy.[23] Joe Feagin adds that the suburbs themselves, the refuge primarily of whites seeking to live far away from blacks and from the squalor created by urban segregation, are a tremendous financial burden on the country.

> In the process white families have paid a price in terms of higher hous-
> ing costs, long-distance commuting, pollution from automobiles, and
> the social problems associated with metropolitan growth and central city
> decline. Thus growth is costly in terms of infrastructural costs – for trans-
> portation, water, and sewage systems – that increase greatly with sprawling
> and leapfrogging exurban development.[24]

Purely from a material perspective European Americans suffer a great financial burden in tolerating the existence of vast slums in literally every major American city. They suffer financial losses because the society as a whole loses. Their sense of separation from the poverty of the slums is only an illusion. They pay for it out of their own pockets every day. We can conclude, then, that European Americans have nothing to lose and only greater prosperity to gain by working together with African Americans to bring an end to the slums.

It is not accidental that the wealthiest countries in the world in terms of per capita income have virtually no slums. Let us again take for example Switzerland. The Swiss economy is inherently more restricted and ultimately weaker than that of the United States. By all standards Switzerland is a very small country. Its 41,000 square kilometers is only 0.4 per cent of the area of the United States and its population of 7.4 million is only 2.5 per cent that of the United States. It is landlocked. More than half the country is mountainous terrain that is not conducive to intensive and varied agriculture. The Alps are a difficult obstacle to trade. Compared to the United States, Switzerland's economic situation is positively precarious. How, then, is it possible for such a country to rival and even surpass the United States in economic productivity?

The answer can be summed up in the proverb 'Waste not, want not'. Even before the Swiss banks became international powerhouses in the 20th century, Switzerland was rapidly rising in economic strength. The Swiss have, since at least the 19th century, developed a habit of meticulous usage of the few resources they do possess. Every resource in the country is put to good use and often multiple uses simultaneously or in series. No resources are left idle out of neglect. All are accounted for, monitored, preserved and exploited in a fairly sustainable fashion. This meticulousness is found right across the country, from the highest Alps to the agricultural flatlands, from suburb to urban center. Everywhere the land and the people are at work generating wealth and prosperity. The Swiss know that they cannot afford to do otherwise. For a large section of Zurich or Geneva to collapse into slums would be out of the question.

While this firm stance against urban blight expresses what may be regarded as common sense, it also signifies spiritual qualities of the Swiss of which Americans need to take note. First, it demonstrates their love for their country beyond the normal patriotism. The Swiss love their land as most people love their own homes.

Second, their love includes also respect for the *people* – not in a sentimental sense but in a very down to earth, practical, action-oriented sense. This is perhaps a startling concept for Americans. American society is used to the idea that the powers that be do not *love* the people *per se*, do not wish to protect them, shepherd them and safeguard their interests. Switzerland is particularly relevant because it is, like the United States, a country based on the free market system. Despite its materialistic culture and all the problems that entails, Switzerland is able to overcome many of the worst aspects of materialism because it retains this basic simple respect that the United States either lost or never had.

One might argue, of course, that Switzerland, like other similarly prosperous small countries – Sweden and Japan, for example – is able to respect its people because the native population is ethnically homogeneous. This homogeneity makes respect easy, so the argument goes. But the historical record shows that this is not necessarily the case. The Swiss federation includes four official language groups and several powerful religious traditions, to say nothing of the cultural diversity across cantons. Moreover, ethnic or racial homogeneity has not prevented many instances of harshness around the world, including 19th-century industrial England and China's Cultural Revolution.

But the point is that the Swiss still preserve what the European Americans expunged from their laws and culture: the obligation to respect the sanctity of life. European Americans have only to respiritualize their education and apply it. There is no doubt that the Swiss success can be duplicated anywhere. The question then is how to start.

Peace Street

The answer begins with a vision of what we want our cities to become and of the role that spirituality is to play in their development. A house is attractive because it is well designed and maintained, and if old, reno-vated to a perfect state. Its walls, floors, ceilings, fixtures and electrical and plumbing systems evidence great care, which is an expression of love for the natural things of which the house is made and the people who live in it. Therefore, our motivation for seeking beautiful kitchens, gardens and parks for Tobacco Road is not to honor our own sense of taste. Rather our motivation for seeking them is to honor the people, to recognize them as sacred and deserving and, ultimately, to invoke a spiritual atmosphere in Tobacco Road.

When Tobacco Road is cleansed and rebuilt – preserving of course any worthy and historic structures – through the labor of the people living there and the help of others, when a new social order is established there that unites a diverse population, when a culture of constant and endless artistic refinement emerges that ensures the healthful evolution of the community, when these processes create a spiritual atmosphere and redefine all the diverse residents, of whatever race, as equally sacred and honored members of one human family, it will become what we can call Peace Street. How will it be to live in an American urban environment such as this? A complete picture is not possible as it involves human potentialities yet beyond our understanding. Nevertheless we can consider several basic aspects that give us a glimpse of the beginning of this new world emerging on the horizon. Since on Peace Street race will no longer be a cause of difference, social relations will be universal as if racism had never existed. As social relations become universal the individual and the community become much more powerful. And lastly, these new-found powers will be both in the material realm and, more importantly, in the spiritual realm. What, then, can all this mean in practical terms for the residents of Peace Street? Let us do something here that is unforgiveable: allow our imaginations to run free.

Peace Street itself will not resemble a street as we know it. It will be a garden with beautiful houses situated within it. Each house will be an evolving work of art but the garden will dominate, not the houses. Not only will flowers adorn the homes and the street itself but there will be towering trees in the woods at the end of the street. Surprisingly, soon after its transformation Peace Street will be so integrated into the garden that its age will appear to be much greater.

Organic waste will not simply be removed but swiftly, safely and efficiently recycled into the nutrients necessary to nourish vegetation in the surrounding woods, farms and meadows. Likewise non-organic refuse will be completely recycled. The purity of Peace Street, and the entire city, will be maintained, for in its essence it is a sacred place.

On the street, day and night, the predominant sound will be people's voices and footsteps, with some musical instruments occasionally. Farms, businesses and workshops of all kinds will be nearby, established in such a way that they will be completely integrated and in harmony with the neighborhoods. People will be in easy contact with each other, informally, light-heartedly. Day and night the streets will be alive with chance encounters and the creativity of unstructured activity, through which the arts and ideas will flourish. People will be involved in educating themselves and each other throughout their entire lives. The doors of educational institutions will always be open to everyone and the old and new knowledge they disseminate will flow in endless waves throughout the neighborhood and the city. The evenings will be filled with a wide choice of musical concerts, theater and dance performances, communal dances, games and song festivals, spiritual gatherings and consultative assemblies. The individual will move among a series of social settings to which she will contribute ideas and creative work: the family, the neighborhood, councils at work and school, and even gatherings for all in the town center. At times in the day, and at night, she will freely seek solitude for the purpose of spiritual reflection and meditation and she will find quiet solitary places close at hand: in the woods bordering the neighborhood at the end of Peace Street, woods that lead on to farmland; in houses of worship; and in her home, where at night the cityscape will be filled with the sounds not of machines but of gardens as they turn through the seasons. Beyond the windows of Peace Street will be heard the wind and rain, the silence of snowfall, the summer sounds of birds and insects.

The street will have access to a transportation system that will allow an individual to walk out of his door, roll a suitcase five or ten minutes, catch a light rail tramway and travel to any part of the world with an amount of pollution and noise that decreases, and of speed and comfort that increases, decade by decade. Conversely, that same system will allow anyone from the world over to be welcomed and to live on Peace Street.

Hopelessly utopian, romantic, naive and saccharin? The truth is that all of these qualities and urban practices are existing realities in various places in America and other countries. There is no greater proof than this that the racially segregated slums of America's cities exist not because of the lack of material powers but because of the lack of spiritual consciousness.

Conclusion
Racism as Theater

Only at great cost across centuries, through the devotion of the strongest characters and scientific minds even to the point of self-sacrifice, has our society overcome many false beliefs held since the Dark Ages. Yet we continue to cherish destructive fantasies and fallacies grounded in the distant past. Racism today is perpetuated by the same unquestioning acceptance that blindly endorsed the superstitions of old and to oppose it is to fight against a powerful current. Although racism began as a very simple artifice, created out of whole cloth by the crudest of laws, instituted and enforced by and for the small slaveholding class, it evolved into a bewilderingly intricate and subtle matrix of volatile emotions: hatred, fear, anger, suspicion. The simple original lie became so complex, vast and overwhelming as to constitute an alternative universe, utterly false yet apparently real. It is not a natural phenomenon, not the will of God, not an inevitability. It is a set of roles written for us by long-dead legal literati and we have been playing those parts only because we believe that if we do not we shall face punishments that are themselves written into the script.

Many of us find that now is the time to break character, give up our roles, remove our masks and costumes, renounce our prescribed lines written so long ago for us, look at each other for the first time and acknowledge the formerly hidden reality. The play is over. The script has been thrown away. The curtain has been permanently raised, the house lights have come up, the theater doors have been opened wide, the false scenery has been stored away and we now emerge into the wide open space beyond, smell the fragrances on the wild breeze, hear the trees, feel the sun. Having abandoned memorized lines and mechanically learned behaviors, we now consort with each other in true fellowship and share a richly laden table.

The Birth of True Humanity

One of the best young writers to capture the spirit of the emerging process of global society is Pico Iyer, who describes himself as 'a person with an American alien card and an Indian face and an English accent' who lives in Japan.

> Everywhere is so made up of everywhere else – a polycentric anagram – that I hardly notice I'm sitting in a Parisian café just outside Chinatown (in San Francisco), talking to a Mexican-American friend about biculturalism while a Haitian woman stops off to congratulate him on a piece he's just delivered on TV on St Patrick's Day. 'I know all about those Irish nuns,' she says, in a thick patois, as we sip our Earl Grey tea near signs that say City of Hong Kong, Empress of China.[25]

Iyer feels himself part of a new world and yet he notes that the idea of a unified global society is not so new at all. He refers to many past writers: Teilhard de Chardin, who believed that humanity necessarily converges as it advances in its evolution; Thomas Paine, who wrote, 'My country is the world, and my religion is to do good'; Ralph Waldo Emerson, who saw in humanity a 'universal soul'; Hugo of Saint Victor, a 12th-century monk who wrote, 'The man who finds his homeland sweet is still a tender beginner; he to whom every soil is as his native one is already strong; but he is perfect to whom the entire world is as a foreign land'; José Vasconcelos of Mexico, who spoke of a cosmic race, the mixing of all races into one; C. J. Cameron of Canada, who in 1913 wrote that the 'final race will not be any one nationality but will be composed of elements from all races'; and A. N. Whitehead, who described loyalty to the world as a whole as the core belief of religion.[26]

Iyer himself speaks with the authority of experience, as one of the first to actually represent this new humanity that visionaries have long anticipated: 'as the British Empire has given way to the American and then the International one, as the classic colonial refugee has given way to the Global Soul, what was once a binary relationship is now many-pronged, spraying out into every direction at once.'[27]

In this quickly globalizing world, the lack of spirituality in relations between human beings in society is gradually becoming recognized as the root cause of racism and all social problems. We are beginning to understand that spirituality and science are not contradictory but complementary. Many forms of spiritual living are now being practiced and spiritual principles are being taken seriously in a wide variety of forums, from alternative health care to development work at the World Bank.

In a spiritualized society, although we retain our identities, we also paradoxically lose ourselves, for we come closer to a reality within and beyond us that is infinitely transcendent. In that context material life becomes recognized as merely a means to an ineffable end. Our traditional, materialistic concept of humanity disappears and in its stead we find ourselves to be a reality of transcendent power. We are beginning to see the signs of this power realized in our social life and we are beginning to see how this process of spiritualization will transform the planet. The material categories into which we had sorted ourselves by color, 'race', nationality, language, are all being obliterated. *The Remains of the Day*, a quintessentially British tale, was written by a man from a Japanese family who grew up in England from the age of two. One of the greatest golfers in the history of the game is of so many ethnic backgrounds that it is virtually impossible to categorize him. Interracial families are speaking out in unprecedented numbers, publishing accounts of their lives, voicing a different reality never before heard and insisting on the abrogation of racial categories in America's national census. Now a mother can assert: 'My son and daughter are biracial, but they are not half white and half black, or half Irish-American and half African-American: they are all white and all black, all Irish-American and all African-American.'[28] These are the signs that true humanity is about to be born.

We are all inherently infinite and yet we are only now claiming this birthright to create ourselves free from the limitations imposed by distant ancestors. As we emerge into maturity, we renounce forever racism and prejudices, the false gods of our collective childhood. We celebrate, for the last war, the global nightmare, the spiritual storm is ending and the peace of poets, philosophers and dreamers has begun. Their vision, which has ever been dismissed as utopian and naive, is finally being proved. They never accepted what was called great in their days; to them, every renaissance, however glorious, was but a dark age and every civilization a false dawn. In a global society in which the oneness of humanity is recognized as fundamental truth, their patience is rewarded at last.

Bibliography

'Abdu'l-Bahá. *The Promulgation of Universal Peace: Talks Delivered by 'Abdu'l-Baha during His Visit to the United States and Canada in 1912*. Wilmette, IL: Bahá'í Publishing Trust, 1982.
— *Some Answered Questions*. Wilmette, IL: Bahá'í Publishing Trust, 1987.
Albrecht, Donald (ed.). *World War II and the American Dream: How Wartime Building Changed a Nation*. Washington DC: National Building Museum, 1995.
Allen, Theodore. *The Invention of the White Race, Volume One: Racial Oppression and Social Control*. London: Verso, 1994.
Allport, Gordon W. 'The Religious Context of Prejudice'. *Journal for the Scientific Study of Religion*, vol. 5 (1966).
Alvord, Katherine. *Divorce Your Car!: Ending the Love Affair with the Automobile*. Gabriola Island, BC: New Society, 2000.
Appleby, Joyce O. (ed.). *Materialism and Morality in the American Past: Themes and Sources, 1600–1860*. Reading, MA: Addison-Wesley, 1974.
Archives of Maryland, Proceedings of the General Assembly, 1637–1664, quoted in Carter G. Woodson, 'The Beginnings of the Miscegenation of the Whites and Blacks'. *Journal of Negro History*, vol. 3, issue 4 (October 1918).
Arvigo, Rosita. *Sastun: One Woman's Apprenticeship with a Maya Healer and Their Efforts to Save the Vani*. San Francisco: Harper, 1995.
Bahá'u'lláh. *Gleanings from the Writings of Bahá'u'lláh*. Wilmette, IL: Bahá'í Publishing Trust, 1983.
— *Tablets of Bahá'u'lláh Revealed after the Kitáb-i-Aqdas*. Wilmette, IL: Bahá'í Publishing Trust, 1988.
Baldwin, John W. and Richard A. Goldthwaite (eds.). *Universities in Politics*. Baltimore: Johns Hopkins University Press, 1972.
Barstow, Anne Llewellyn. *Witchcraze: A New History of the European Witch-hunts*. San Francisco: HarperCollins, 1994.
Beals, Melba Patillo. *Warriors Don't Cry: A Searing Memoir of the Battle to Integrate Little Rock's Central High*. New York: Washington Square Press, 1994.
Bellah, Robert N. 'Durkheim and History'. *American Sociological Review*, vol. 24 (1959).

Bellah, Robert N. et al. *Habits of the Heart: Individualism and Commitment in American Life*. Berkeley: University of California Press, 1996.

Berman, Daniel and John O'Connor. *Who Owns the Sun?: People, Politics, and the Struggle for a Solar Economy*. White River Junction, VT: Chelsea Green, 1996.

Berman, Harold. *Law and Revolution: The Formation of the Western Legal Tradition*. Cambridge: Harvard University Press, 1983.

Bertrand, Marianne and Mullainathan, Sendhil. 'Are Emily and Greg More Employable Than Lakisha and Jamal? A Field Experiment on Labor Market Discrimination'. *The American Economic Review*, vol. 94, issue 4 (2004).

Bettelheim, Bruno. *Freud and Man's Soul*. New York: Knopf, 1982.

Blakey, Michael. 'The New York African Burial Ground Project: An Examination of Enslaved Lives, A Construction of Ancestral Ties'. *Transforming Anthropology*, vol. 7, no. 1 (1998).

Bloom, Marc. 'Kenyan Runners in the United States Find Bitter Taste of Success'. *The New York Times*, 16 April 1998.

Bolgar, R. R. (ed.). *Classical Influences on Western Thought, AD 1650–1870*. Cambridge: Cambridge University Press, 1979.

Bonazzi, Robert. *Man in the Mirror: John Howard Griffin and the Story of Black Like Me*. New York: Maryknoll, 1997.

'Bones reveal little-known tale of New York slaves'. *CNN*, 12 February 1998. <http://www.cnn.com/TECH/9802/12/t_t/burial.ground/>.

Boskin, Joseph. 'Race Relations in Seventeenth Century America: The Problem of the Origins of Negro Slavery'. *Sociology and Social Research*, vol. 49 (July 1965).

Bowser, Benjamin and Raymond Hunt. *Impacts of Racism on White Americans*. Thousand Oaks: Sage, 1996.

Bradley, Bill. *Life on the Run*. New York: Vintage, 1995.

Braudel, Fernand. *Civilization and Capitalism, 15th–18th Century, Volume II: The Wheels of Commerce*. New York: Harper and Row, 1986.

Budd, Susan. *Sociologists and Religion*. London: Collier–Macmillan, 1973.

Burgess, Ernest W. and Paul Wallin. 'Homogamy in Social Characteristics'. *American Journal of Sociology*, vol. 49 (1943).

Bush, Jonathan A. 'The British Constitution and the Creation of American Slavery', in Paul Finkelman (ed.). *Slavery and the Law*. Madison: Madison House, 1997.

Butsch, Joseph. 'Catholics and the Negro'. *Journal of Negro History*, vol. 2, issue 4 (October 1917).

Candland, Douglas. *Feral Children and Clever Animals: Reflections on Human Nature*. New York: Oxford University Press, 1993.

Canny, Nicholas P. 'The Ideology of English Colonization: From Ireland to America'. *William and Mary Quarterly*, vol. 30, no. 4 (October 1973).

Carney, Judith. *Black Rice: The African Origins of Rice Cultivation in the Americas*. Cambridge: Harvard, 2001.

Carter, Jimmy. *An Hour Before Daylight: Memories of a Rural Boyhood*. New York: Simon and Schuster, 2001.

Carter, Stephen L. *The Culture of Disbelief: How American Law and Politics*

Trivialize Religious Devotion. New York: Anchor, 1994.

Charlton, D. G. *Secular Religion in France, 1815–1870*. London: Oxford University Press, 1963.

Chisholm, N. Jamiyla. 'Fade to White: Skin Bleaching and the Rejection of Blackness'. *Village Voice*. Week of 22–8 January 2001. <www.villagevoice. com/issues/0204/chisholm.php> and <www.betweensistersfoundation. org/Sisters_Magazine_Articles/skin_bleachings.html>.

Clark, Terry. *Prophets and Patrons: The French University and the Emergence of the Social Sciences*. Cambridge: Harvard University Press, 1973.

'Con Edison Crew Unearths Bones Near Early Black Graveyard'. *New York Times*. Sunday Late Edition, 14 February 1993.

Cornford, Francis M. *From Religion to Philosophy: A Study in the Origins of Western Speculation*. New York: Harper, 1957.

Cose, Ellis. *Color-Blind: Seeing Beyond Race in a Race-Obsessed World*. New York: HarperPerennial, 1997.

— *The Rage of a Privileged Class*. New York: HarperCollins, 1995.

Cox, Oliver C. *Race Relations: Elements and Social Dynamics*. Detroit: Wayne State University Press, 1976.

Coyote, Peter. *Sleeping Where I Fall: A Chronicle*. Washington DC: Counterpoint, 1999.

Davies, K. G. *The North Atlantic World in the Seventeenth Century*. Minneapolis: University of Minnesota Press, 1974.

Davis, David B. *The Problem of Slavery in Western Culture*. New York: Oxford University Press, 1988.

Dhammapada: The Sayings of the Buddha. Trans. by Thomas Cleary. New York: Bantam, 1995.

Dubin, Steven. 'Symbolic Slavery: Black Representations in Popular Culture'. *Social Problems*, vol. 34, no. 2 (April 1987).

DuBois, W. E. B. *Black Reconstruction in America, 1860–1880*. New York: Atheneum, 1979.

Durkheim, Emile. *Elementary Forms of the Religious Life*. New York: Collier Books, 1961.

— 'The Role of Universities in the Social Education of the Country'. *Minerva*, vol. 14, no. 3 (Fall 1976).

Dyer, Richard. *White*. London: Routledge, 1997.

Dynes, Russell R., Alfred C. Clarke, Simon Dinitz and Iwao Ishino. *Social Problems: Dissensus and Deviation in an Industrial Society*. New York: Oxford University Press, 1964.

Eastman, Max. *Marxism: Is it Science?* New York: W. W. Norton, 1940.

Easton, Lloyd and Kurt Guddat. *Writings of the Young Marx on Philosophy and Society*. New York: Doubleday, 1967.

Eisler, Riane. *The Chalice and the Blade: Our History, Our Future*. New York: Harper and Row, 1987.

Elkins, Stanley. *Slavery: A Problem in American Institutional and Intellectual Life*. Chicago: University of Chicago Press, 1976.

Equiano, Olaudah. *The Interesting Narrative of the Life of Olaudah Equiano or*

Gustavas Vassa, The African, Written by Himself. New York: New American Library, 1987.

Ergang, Robert. *The Renaissance.* Princeton: D. Van Nostrand, 1967.

Evans, William M. 'From the Land of Canaan to the Land of Guinea: The Strange Odyssey of the "Sons of Ham"'. *American Historical Review,* vol. 85, no. 1 (February 1980).

Feagin, Joe R. *Racist America: Roots, Current Realities, and Future Reparations.* New York: Routledge, 2000.

Feagin, Joe R. and Melvin P. Sikes. *Living with Racism: The Black Middle-Class Experience.* Boston: Beacon Press, 1994.

Feinstein, John. *Hard Courts: Real Life on the Professional Tennis Tours.* New York: Villard Books, 1991.

Finkelman, Paul (ed.). *Slavery and the Law.* Madison: Madison House, 1997.

Finley, Moses. *Ancient Slavery and Modern Ideology.* Princeton: Markus Wiener, 1998.

Fox, Robin Lane. *Pagans and Christians.* New York: Alfred Knopf, 1987.

Frantz, Douglas and Catherine Collins. *Celebration, USA: Living in Disney's Brave New Town.* New York: Henry Holt, 1999.

Fredrickson, George M. *Racism: A Short History.* Princeton: Princeton University Press, 2002.

— *White Supremacy: A Comparative Study in American and South African History.* Oxford: Oxford University Press, 1982.

Freud, Sigmund. *Civilization and Its Discontents.* New York: W. W. Norton, 1961.

Friedrichs, Robert. *A Sociology of Sociology.* New York: Free Press, 1970.

Fromm, Erich. *Beyond the Chains of Illusion.* New York: Simon and Schuster, 1962.

— *Marx's Concept of Man.* New York: Frederick Ungar, 1966.

— *To Have or To Be.* New York: Harper and Row, 1976.

— *The Sane Society.* New York: Henry Holt, 1990.

Frost, Peter. 'Fair Women, Dark Men: The Forgotten Roots of Colour Prejudice'. *History of European Ideas,* vol. 12, no. 5 (1990).

Gardner, Gary. 'Engaging Religion in the Quest for a Sustainable World', in Worldwatch Institute, *State of the World 2003.* New York: W. W. Norton, 2003.

Genovese, Eugene D. *The Political Economy of Slavery: Studies in the Economy and Society of the Slave South.* Middletown, CT: Wesleyan University Press, 1989.

— *Roll, Jordan, Roll: The World the Slaves Made.* New York: Vintage, 1976.

Girard, René. *Violence and the Sacred.* Baltimore: The Johns Hopkins University Press, 1977.

Giroux, Henry A. *The Mouse that Roared: Disney and the End of Innocence.* Lanham, MD: Rowman and Littlefield, 1999.

Glasner, Peter. *The Sociology of Secularization.* London: Routledge and Kegan Paul, 1977.

Goings, Kenneth W. *Mammy and Uncle Mose: Black Collectibles and American*

Stereotyping. Bloomington: Indiana University Press, 1994.

Gouldner, Alvin. *The Coming Crisis of Western Sociology.* New York: Avon, 1970.

Greenberg, Jack. *Race Relations and American Law.* New York: Columbia University Press, 1959.

Greenhouse, Steven. 'Going for the Look, But Risking Discrimination'. *The New York Times,* 13 July 2003.

Griffin, John Howard. *Black Like Me.* New York: Signet, 1996.

Guinier, Lani. *Lift Every Voice: Turning a Civil Rights Setback into a New Vision of Social Justice.* New York: Simon and Schuster, 1998.

Hacker, Andrew. *Two Nations: Black and White, Separate, Hostile, Unequal.* New York: Ballantine, 1995.

Handlin, Oscar and Mary Handlin. 'Origins of the Southern Labor System'. *William and Mary Quarterly,* Third Series, no. 7 (April 1950).

Harnack, Adolf. *The Mission and Expansion of Christianity in the First Three Centuries.* New York: Harper, 1962.

Hegel, Georg W. F. *The Philosophy of History.* New York: Dover, 1956.

Higginbotham, Jr., A. Leon. *In the Matter of Color: Race and the American Legal Process.* New York: Oxford University Press, 1978.

— *Shades of Freedom: Radical Politics and Presumptions of the American Legal Process.* Oxford: Oxford University Press, 1998.

Holladay, Marvin 'Doc'. *Life, On the Fence: An Autobiography.* Oxford: George Ronald, 2000.

The Holy Bible. Authorised King James Version. London: The Gideons, International, 1957.

Ignatiev, Noel. 'Immigrants and Whites', in Ignatiev and Garvey, *Race Traitor.*

Ignatiev, Noel and John Garvey (eds.). *Race Traitor.* New York: Routledge, 1996.

'Into the Sunset: The Age of Cultural Theory'. *International Herald Tribune,* 8 January 2004.

'Ireland', vol. 21. *The New Encyclopaedia Britannica.* Chicago: Encyclopaedia Britannica, 1995.

Iyer, Pico. *The Global Soul: Jet Lag, Shopping Malls, and the Search for Home.* New York: Knopf, 2000.

Jamieson, Russ. 'Alabama Town Fears New School Superintendent's Alleged Bigotry'. *CNN,* 2 July 1997. <http://www.cnn.com/US/9707/02/humphries.return/>.

Jarman, T. L. *Landmarks in the History of Education.* London: Cresset, 1951.

Jernegan, Marcus W. 'Slavery and Conversion in the American Colonies'. *American Historical Review,* vol. 21, no. 3 (April 1916).

Johnson, Paul. *A History of Christianity.* New York: Atheneum, 1976.

Johnston, Douglas and Cynthia Sampsan (eds.). *Religion, The Missing Dimension of Statecraft.* New York: Oxford University Press, 1994.

Johnston, James H. *Race Relations in Virginia and Miscegenation in the South, 1776–1860.* Amherst: University of Massachusetts Press, 1970.

Jordan, Winthrop D. *White Over Black: American Attitudes Toward the Negro, 1550–1812.* Chapel Hill: University of North Carolina, 1968.

Jump, John D. 'Introduction,' in Christopher Marlowe, *Doctor Faustus*, edited by John D. Jump. London: Methuen, 1968.

Kaeser, Gig and Peggy Gillespie. *Of Many Colors: Portraits of Multiracial Families*. Amherst: University of Massachusetts Press, 1997.

Kay, Jane Holtz. *Asphalt Nation: How the Automobile Took Over America and How We Can Take It Back*. New York: Crown, 1997.

Kenan, Randall. *Walking on Water: Black American Lives at the Turn of the Twenty-First Century*. New York: Alfred Knopf, 1999.

Kerr, Alex. *Dogs and Demons: Tales from the Dark Side of Japan*. New York: Hill and Wang, 2001.

Kiernan, Victor. *Lords of Human Kind: European Attitudes to Other Cultures in the Imperial Age*. London: Serif, 1995.

The Koran. Trans. J. M. Rodwell. London: Dent (Everyman's Library), 1963.

Kovel, Joel. *White Racism: A Psychohistory*. New York: Columbia University Press, 1984.

Kunstler, J. H. *The Geography of Nowhere: The Rise and Decline of America's Man-Made Landscape*. New York: Simon and Schuster, 1994.

Laszlo, Ervin. *Macroshift: Navigating the Transformation to a Sustainable World*. San Francisco: Berrett-Koehler, 2001.

Lazarre, Jane. *Beyond the Whiteness of Whiteness: Memoir of a White Mother of Black Sons*. Durham: Duke University Press, 1996.

Lewis, Michael. *The New New Thing: A Silicon Valley Story*. New York: W. W. Norton, 2000.

Lewy, Guenter. *Religion and Revolution*. New York: Oxford University Press, 1974.

Lifton, Robert Jay and Eric Olson (eds.). *Explorations in Psychohistory: The Wellfleet Papers*. New York: Simon and Schuster, 1974.

Loewen, James. *Lies My Teacher Told Me: Everything Your American History Textbook Got Wrong*. New York: Simon and Schuster, 1996.

Löwith, Karl. *Meaning in History*. Chicago: University of Chicago Press, 1949.

Malcolm X. *The Autobiography of Malcolm X*. Harmondsworth: Penguin, 1968.

Malson, Lucien. *Wolf Children and the Problem of Human Nature*. New York: Monthly Review Press, 1972.

Mann, Michael. *The Sources of Social Power, Volume I: A History of Power from the Beginning to AD 1760*. Cambridge: Cambridge University Press, 1986.

Marin, Peter. *Freedom and Its Discontents: Reflections on Four Decades of American Moral Experience*. South Royalton, VT: Steerforth Press, 1995.

Mason, Jim. *An Unnatural Order: Uncovering the Roots of Our Domination of Nature and Each Other*. New York: Simon and Schuster, 1993.

Massaquoi, Hans. *Destined to Witness: Growing Up Black in Nazi Germany*. New York: HarperCollins, 1999.

McNeill, William H. *The Pursuit of Power: Technology, Armed Force, and Society Since A.D. 1000*. Chicago: University of Chicago Press, 1982.

Meeks, Kenneth. *Driving While Black: Highways, Shopping Malls, Taxicabs, Sidewalks: How to Fight Back If You Are a Victim of Racial Profiling*. New

York: Broadway Books, 2000.

Meltzer, Milton. *Slavery, A World History.* New York: Da Capo, 1993.

Mendelsohn, Robert. *Confessions of a Medical Heretic.* Chicago: Contemporary Books, 1979.

Montague, Ashley. *Touching: The Human Significance of the Skin.* New York: Harper and Row, 1986.

Moore, R. I. *The Formation of a Persecuting Society: Power and Deviance in Western Europe, 950-1250.* Oxford: Blackwell, 1994.

Morgan, Edmund S. *American Slavery, American Freedom: The Ordeal of Colonial Virginia.* New York: W. W. Norton, 1975.

Morris, Thomas. *Southern Slavery and the Law, 1619-1860.* Chapel Hill: University of North Carolina Press, 1996.

Morrison, Toni. *Playing in the Dark: Whiteness and the Literary Imagination.* Cambridge: Harvard University Press, 1992.

Nash, Gary. *Forbidden Love: The Secret History of Mixed-Race America.* New York: Henry Holt, 1999.

Nelson, Jill. *Straight, No Chaser: How I Became a Grown-Up Black Woman.* New York: Penguin, 1997.

The New Encyclopaedia Britannica. Chicago: Encylopaedia Britannica, 2002.

Nisbet, Robert A. *The Sociological Tradition.* New York: Basic Books, 1966.

Olwell, Robert. *Masters, Slaves, and Subjects: The Culture of Power in the South Carolina Low Country, 1740-1790.* Ithaca: Cornell University Press, 1998.

O'Meara, Molly. 'How Mid-Sized Cities Can Avoid Strangulation'. *World Watch*, vol. 11, no. 5 (September–October 1998).

One Country: The Online Newsletter of the Bahá'í International Community, vol. 9, issue 4: January–March 1998; vol. 10, issue 4 (January–March 1999); vol. 11, issue 3 (October–December 1999). <www.onecountry.org>.

'Oregon to Vote on Constitution's Racist Language', 27 September 2002. <http://www.salon.com/politics/wire/200>.

Patterson, Orlando. *Rituals of Blood: Consequences of Slavery in Two American Centuries.* Washington DC: Civitas, 1998.

— *Slavery and Social Death: A Comparative Study.* Cambridge, MA: Harvard University Press, 1982.

Perry, Nick. *Hyperreality and Global Culture.* New York: Routledge, 1998.

Peters, William. *A Class Divided: Then and Now.* New Haven: Yale University Press, 1987.

Pickthall, Muhammad Marmaduke. *The Meaning of the Glorious Qur'án.* Beirut: Dar Al-Kitab Allubnani, 1970.

Ploski, Harry A. and James Williams (eds.). *The Negro Almanac: A Reference Work on the African-American.* Detroit: Gale, 1989.

Price, Don K. *America's Unwritten Constitution: Science, Religion, and Political Responsibility.* Cambridge: Harvard University Press, 1985.

Ray, Paul and Sherry Anderson. *The Cultural Creatives: How 50 Million People are Changing the World.* New York: Harmony Books, 2000.

Reddy, Maureen. *Crossing the Color Line: Race, Parenting, and Culture.* New Brunswick, NJ: Rutgers University Press, 1997.

Reinhold, Meyer. 'Eighteenth-Century American Political Thought', in Bolgar, *Classical Influences on Western Thought*.

Remmling, Gunter W. *The Sociology of Karl Mannheim*. Atlantic Highlands, NJ: Humanities Press, 1975.

Rice, C. Duncan. *The Rise and Fall of Black Slavery*. London: Macmillan, 1975.

Ridgeway, James. *Blood in the Face: The Ku Klux Klan, Aryan Nations, Nazi Skinheads and the Rise of a New White Culture*. New York: Thunder's Mouth Press, 1995.

Rifkin, Jeremy. *Beyond Beef: The Rise and Fall of Cattle Culture*. New York: Plume, 1993.

Riley-Smith, Jonathan. *What Were the Crusades?* London: Macmillan, 1992.

Ringer, Fritz K. *The Decline of the German Mandarins: The German Academic Community, 1890–1933*. Cambridge: Harvard University Press, 1969.

Robinson, Randall. *The Debt: What America Owes to Blacks*. New York: Dutton, 2000.

— *Defending the Spirit: A Black Life in America*. New York: Dutton, 1998.

Rogers, J. A. *World's Great Men of Color*, vol. 2. New York: Simon and Schuster, 1996.

Roof, Wade Clark. 'Modernity, the Religious, and the Spiritual'. *The Annals of the American Academy of Political and Social Science*, vol. 558 (July 1998).

Rubio, Phil. 'Civil War Reenactments and Other Myths', in Ignatiev and Garvey, *Race Traitor*.

Russell-Wood, A. J. R. 'Iberian Expansion and the Issue of Black Slavery: Changing Portuguese Attitudes, 1440–1770'. *American Historical Review*, vol. 83, no. 1 (February 1978).

Rymer, Russ. *Genie: A Scientific Tragedy*. New York: HarperCollins, 1993.

Samuelson, Kurt. *Religion and Economic Action*. Stockholm: Alb. Bonniers, 1961.

Sanders, Ronald. *Lost Tribes and Promised Lands: The Origins of American Racism*. Boston: Little, Brown and Co., 1978.

Scales-Trent, Judy. *Notes of a White Black Woman*. University Park, PA: Pennsylvania State University Press, 1995.

Schlosser, Eric. *Fast Food Nation: The Dark Side of the All-American Meal*. Boston: Houghton Mifflin, 2001.

Sickels, Robert J. *Race, Marriage and the Law*. Albuquerque: University of New Mexico Press, 1972.

Slatalla, Michelle. *Masters of Deception: The Gang That Ruled Cyberspace*. New York: HarperPerennial, 1996.

Sleeter, Christine. 'White Silence, White Solidarity', in Ignatiev and Garvey, *Race Traitor*.

Snowden, Frank M. *Blacks in Antiquity: Ethiopians in the Greco-Roman Experience*. Cambridge: Harvard University Press, 1970.

'A Solitary Sojourn'. *College Park* [University of Maryland Alumni Magazine], Spring 1995.

Solomon, Joshua. 'Skin Deep; Reliving "Black Like Me": My Own Journey Into the Heart of Race-Conscious America'. *The Washington Post*, Sunday 30 October 1994.

Solomon, Norman, and Jeff Cohen. *Wizards of Media Oz: Behind the Curtain of Mainstream News*. Monroe, ME: Common Courage, 1997.

Sorokin, Pitirim. *The Crisis of Our Age*. Oxford: Oneworld Publications, 1992.

Spiegel, Marjorie. *The Dreaded Comparison: Human and Animal Slavery*. New York: Mirror Books, 1996.

Stark, Werner. *Social Theory and Christian Thought*. London: Routledge and Kegan Paul, 1958.

Steinhorn, Leonard and Barbara Diggs-Brown. *By the Color of Our Skin: The Illusion of Integration and the Reality of Race*. New York: Dutton, 1999.

Tawney, R. H. *Religion and the Rise of Capitalism: A Historical Study*. Gloucester, MA: Peter Smith, 1962.

Taylor, Charles. 'Marxism and Empiricism', in Williams and Montefiore, *British Analytical Philosophy*.

Taylor, Mark. *Beyond Explanation: Religious Dimensions in Cultural Anthropology*. Macon: Mercer University Press, 1986.

Thomas, John L. 'The Factor of Religion in the Selection of Marriage Mates'. *American Sociological Review*, vol. 16 (1951).

Toynbee, Arnold. *A Study of History*. Abridged by D. C. Somervell, vol.1. New York: Oxford University Press, 1947.

Trevor-Roper, H. R. *The European Witch-Craze of the Sixteenth and Seventeenth Centuries and Other Essays*. New York: Harper and Row, 1969.

Tucker, Robert. *Marx–Engels Reader*. New York: W. W. Norton, 1978.

— *Philosophy and Myth in Karl Marx*. London: Cambridge University Press, 1972.

Turberville, A. S. *Mediaeval Heresy and the Inquisition*. London: Archon Books, 1964.

'UC Law Professor Named One of Most Notable Asians in America for 2001', 6 December 2001. <http://www.uc.edu/news/chinalst.htm>.

Ullmann, Walter. *The Carolingian Renaissance and the Idea of Kingship*. London: Methuen, 1969.

Vance, Norman. *The Victorians and Ancient Rome*. Oxford: Blackwell, 1997.

Vance, William L. *America's Rome, Volume One: Classical Rome*. New Haven: Yale University Press, 1989.

Verlinden, Charles. *The Beginnings of Modern Colonization: Eleven Essays with an Introduction*. Ithaca: Cornell University Press, 1970.

Vidal, John. *McLibel: Burger Culture on Trial*. New York: New Press, 1997.

Watkins, Steve. *The Black O: Racism and Redemption in an American Corporate Empire*. Athens, GA: University of Georgia Press, 1997.

Weber, Max. *The Protestant Ethic and the Spirit of Capitalism*. New York: Charles Scribner's Sons, 1958.

Weisz, George. *The Emergence of Modern Universities in France, 1863–1914*. Princeton: Princeton University Press, 1983.

Williams, Bernard and Alan Montefiore (eds.). *British Analytical Philosophy*. London: Routledge and Kegan Paul, 1966.

Williams, Juan. *Eyes on the Prize: America's Civil Rights Years, 1954–65*. New York: Penguin, 1988.

— *Thurgood Marshall: American Revolutionary*. New York: Random House, 1998.

Williams, Patricia J. *The Alchemy of Race and Rights: Diary of a Law Professor*. Cambridge: Harvard University Press, 1991.

Wolfe, Alan, 'The Revival of Moral Inquiry in the Social Sciences'. *The Chronicle of Higher Education*, 3 September 1999, Opinion and Arts section.

Wood, Forrest G. *The Arrogance of Faith: Christianity and Race in America from the Colonial Era to the Twentieth Century*. Boston: Northeastern University Press, 1991.

Woodson, Carter G. 'The Beginnings of the Miscegenation of the Whites and Blacks'. *Journal of Negro History*, vol. 3, issue 4 (October 1918).

Woodward, C. Vann. *The Strange Career of Jim Crow*. New York: Oxford University Press, 1966.

Wright, Richard. *Black Boy: A Record of Childhood and Youth*. Cleveland: The World Publishing Company, 1945 (1937).

Zimmerman, Christopher. 'A Conversation with Jonathan Kozol'. <http://sun2539.sph.umich.edu:2000/public_html/heros/kozol/k2.html>.

Zinn, Howard. *You Can't Be Neutral on a Moving Train: A Personal History of Our Times*. Boston: Beacon Press, 1994.

Zucchino, David. *Myth of the Welfare Queen*. New York: Touchstone, 1999.

References and Notes

Chapter 1: Introduction
1. Sickels, *Race, Marriage and the Law*, pp. 74–5.
2. ibid. pp. 64, 155.
3. A 1691 Act of Virginia's statutes referred to 'that abominable mixture and spurious issue . . . by Negroes, mulattoes and Indians intermarrying with English or other white women'. Quoted in Higginbotham, *In the Matter of Color*, p. 44.
4. See for example: Feagin and Sikes, *Living with Racism*; Cose, *The Rage of a Privileged Class*; Steinhorn and Diggs-Brown, *By the Color of Our Skin*.
5. Steinhorn and Diggs-Brown, *By the Color of Our Skin*, p. 123.
6. Reddy, *Crossing the Color Line*, p. 132.
7. Griffin, *Black Like Me*, pp. 137–8.
8. Williams, *The Alchemy of Race and Rights*, p. 73.
9. Williams, *Thurgood Marshall*, p. 188.
10. Chisholm, 'Fade to White: Skin Bleaching and the Rejection of Blackness'.
12. Solomon, 'Skin Deep; Reliving "Black Like Me": My Own Journey Into the Heart of Race-Conscious America', p. C–1; 'A Solitary Sojourn', p. 6.
13. Nash, *Forbidden Love*, p. ix.
14. ibid.
15. Williams, *The Alchemy of Race and Rights*, p. 61.
16. Quoted in Zimmerman, 'A Conversation with Jonathan Kozol'.
17. Ignatiev, 'Immigrants and Whites', in Ignatiev and Garvey, *Race Traitor*, p. 15.
18. Dyer, *White*, pp. 15–18.
19. Matthew 23:25, 19:16–23, 8:21–2, 10:28, 16:26, 6:19.
20. See, for example, Wood, *The Arrogance of Faith*.
21. Bahá'u'lláh, *Gleanings*, p. 215.
22. ibid. p. 286.
23. Bahá'u'lláh, *Tablets*, pp. 129–30.
24. ibid. p. 125.

25. Freud, *Civilization and Its Discontents*, p. 36.
26. Marin, *Freedom and Its Discontents*, p. 198.
27. ibid. pp. 195–265.
28. See Bellah et al., *Habits of the Heart: Individualism and Commitment in American Life*; Sorokin, *The Crisis of Our Age*; Johnston and Sampsan, *Religion, The Missing Dimension of Statecraft*; 'An Unusual Meeting of Bankers and Believers', in *One Country*, vol. 9, issue 4 (January–March 1998); 'Second Summit between World Bank and World Religions Focuses on Projects' in *One Country*, vol. 11, issue 3 (October–December 1999). Also of relevance are the works of legal scholar Stephen Carter on the relationship between law, religion and civil society.
29. Quoted in Woodward, *The Strange Career of Jim Crow*, p. 71.
30. Quoted in ibid. pp. 103, 139.

Chapter 2: Despiritualization: The Archeology of Racism

1. Price, *America's Unwritten Constitution*.
2. Reddy, *Crossing the Color Line*, p. 37.
3. Quoted in ibid.
4. Higginbotham, *In the Matter of Color*, p. ix.
5. Robinson, *Defending the Spirit*, p. xiv.
6. John Dovidio refers to this as 'aversive racism'. See Cose, *Color-Blind*, pp. 190–1.
7. Dubin, 'Symbolic Slavery: Black Representations in Popular Culture', pp. 122–38. See also Goings, *Mammy and Uncle Mose*.
8. Steinhorn and Diggs-Brown, *By the Color of Our Skin*, p. 110.
9. Juan Williams, *Thurgood Marshall*, p. 398.
10. Robinson, *Defending the Spirit*, pp. 284–5.
11. Quoted in Kenan, *Walking on Water*, p. 217.
12. Quoted in Feinstein, *Hard Courts*, p. 333.
13. Bloom, 'Kenyan Runners in the United States Find Bitter Taste of Success', *The New York Times*, 16 April 1998, p. A1.
14. Bradley, *Life on the Run*, p. 18.
15. Cose, *The Rage of a Privileged Class*, pp. 47–51.
16. Meeks, *Driving While Black*, pp. 82–3.
17. Watkins, *The Black O*, pp. 205–6.
18. Malcolm X, *The Autobiography of Malcolm X*, p. 118.
19. Williams, *Thurgood Marshall*, pp. 22, 25; Carter, *An Hour Before Daylight*, p. 149.
20. Beals, *Warriors Don't Cry*, pp. 110–11.
21. Zucchino, *Myth of the Welfare Queen*, pp. 33–4.
22. Carter, *An Hour Before Daylight*, pp. 229–30.
23. Kenan, *Walking on Water*, p. 198.
24. Juan Williams, *Thurgood Marshall*, pp. 132–3.
25. Williams, *Thurgood Marshall*, p. 158.
26. Holladay, *Life, On the Fence*, pp. 15–16.

27. Feagin, *Racist America*, p. 58.
28. Fredrickson, *Racism: A Short History*, p. 2.
29. Qur'án 24:33.
30. Quoted in Feagin, *Racist America*, p. 49.
31. The term 'miscegenation' was coined in the mid-1800s.
32. Zinn, *You Can't Be Neutral on a Moving Train*, p. 31.
33. Jamieson, 'Alabama Town Fears New School Superintendent's Alleged Bigotry', *CNN*, 2 July 1997.
34. Lazarre, *Beyond the Whiteness of Whiteness*, p. 34.
35. *Archives of Maryland, Proceedings of the General Assembly, 1637–1664*, quoted in Woodson, 'The Beginnings of the Miscegenation of the Whites and Blacks', pp. 339–40.
36. Theodore Allen refers to Virginia as 'the pattern-setting colony'. Allen, *The Invention of the White Race*, vol. 1, p. 83.
37. Quoted in Woodson, 'The Beginnings of the Miscegenation of the Whites and Blacks', p. 343.
38. Sickels, *Race, Marriage and the Law*, pp. 64–7.
39. Allen, *The Invention of the White Race*, vol. 1, p. 21.
40. Johnston, *Race Relations in Virginia and Miscegenation in the South*, p. 186.
41. Bush, 'The British Constitution and the Creation of American Slavery', in Finkelman, *Slavery and the Law*, p. 382.
42. Elkins, *Slavery*, pp. 37–9; Handlin, 'Origins of the Southern Labor System', in *William and Mary Quarterly*, Third Series, No. 7 (April 1950), pp. 199–222.
43. Boskin, 'Race Relations in Seventeenth Century America: The Problem of the Origins of Negro Slavery', in *Sociology and Social Research*, vol. 49 (July 1965), p. 447.
44. Johnston, *Race Relations in Virginia*, pp. 184–5.
45. Verlinden, *The Beginnings of Modern Colonization*; Frost, 'Fair Women, Dark Men: The Forgotten Roots of Colour Prejudice', p. 674.
46. Quoted in Allen, *The Invention of the White Race*.
47. Quoted in Appleby, *Materialism and Morality in the American Past*, p. 60.
48. ibid.
49. ibid.
50. ibid.
51. ibid.
52. ibid. pp. 60–1.
53. Sanders, *Lost Tribes and Promised Lands*, p. 94.
54. Feagin, *Racist America*, p. 71; Frost, 'Fair Women, Dark Men', p. 672.
55. Feagin, *Racist America*, p. 71.
56. Rogers, *World's Great Men of Color*, vol. 2, pp. 11–15.
57. Morgan, *American Slavery, American Freedom*, p. 333.
58. Johnston, *Race Relations in Virginia*, p. 186.
59. Nash, *Forbidden Love*, pp. 37–8, 40, 66–7.

60. Rice, *The Rise and Fall of Black Slavery*, p. 52.
61. Woodson, 'The Beginnings of the Miscegenation of the Whites and Blacks', p. 349.
62. Woodward, *The Strange Career of Jim Crow*, p. 15.
63. ibid. pp. 42–3.
64. Quoted in Genovese, *Roll, Jordan, Roll*, p. 414.
65. Morgan, *American Slavery, American Freedom*, pp. 330–1.
66. Woodson, 'The Beginnings of the Miscegenation of the Whites and Blacks', p. 349.
67. Barstow, *Witchcraze*, p. 57.
68. Hacker, *Two Nations*, p. 7.
69. Nash, *Forbidden Love*, p. 37.
70. Fritz Hirchfeld, quoted in Feagin, *Racist America*, p. 54.
71. See 'Ireland', *The New Encyclopaedia Britannica*, vol. 21, p. 1009.
72. Dyer, *White*, p. 66; Ignatiev, 'Immigrants and Whites', p. 16.
73. Kiernan, *Lords of Human Kind*, p. 204.
74. Quoted in Bonazzi, *Man in the Mirror*, pp. 109, 150.
75. Johnston, *Race Relations in Virginia*, p. 185.
76. Jernegan, 'Slavery and Conversion in the American Colonies', p. 524.
77. See, for example, Olwell, *Masters, Slaves, and Subjects*, pp. 110–11.
78. Thomas, 'The Factor of Religion in the Selection of Marriage Mates', pp. 487–91; Burgess and Paul, 'Homogamy in Social Characteristics', pp. 109–24.
79. Morgan, *American Slavery, American Freedom*, p. 336.
80. Johnston, *Race Relations in Virginia*, pp. 185–6.
81. Allport, 'The Religious Context of Prejudice', pp. 447–57.
82. Genovese, *Roll, Jordan, Roll*, p. 422.
83. Morgan, *American Slavery, American Freedom*, p. 336.
84. *Race Relations in Virginia*, p. 183.
85. Cox, *Race Relations*, pp. 158–9.
86. Kovel, *White Racism*, pp. 69–70.
87. 'The American environment was viewed . . . as a fallen world, a chaotic wilderness that needed to be beaten back, tamed, and harnessed. The conquest of the American frontier took on all the trappings of an ancient morality play, with the forces of light battling against the dark satanic underworld.' Rifkin, *Beyond Beef*, p. 251.
88. Bush, 'The British Constitution', p. 401.
89. ibid. pp. 381, 397–9.
90. ibid. p. 386.
91. ibid. p. 379.
92. Higginbotham, *Shades of Freedom*, pp. 14–15.
93. Quoted in Feagin, *Racist America*, p. 15.
94. Note in brackets is Higginbotham's.
95. Quoted in Higginbotham, *Shades of Freedom*, pp. 69–70.
96. Quoted in ibid. pp. 68–9.
97. Nash, *Forbidden Love*, p. 37.

98. Reinhold, 'Eighteenth-Century American Political Thought', p. 230.

99. Woodward, *The Strange Career of Jim Crow*, p. 17.

100. Quoted in Williams, *The Alchemy of Race and Rights*, p. 160.

101. Morrison, *Playing in the Dark*, p. 52.

102. Nash, *Forbidden Love*, pp. 98, 103.

103. Recently such actions have been taken in South Carolina, Alabama, Kansas, Wyoming, Oregon and New Mexico. The national movement is led by Professor Jack Chin of the University of Cincinnati College of Law. 'UC Law Professor Named One of Most Notable Asians in America for 2001', 6 December 2001. <http://www.uc.edu/news/chinalst.htm>; 'Oregon to Vote on Constitution's Racist Language', 27 September 2002. <http://www.salon.com/politics/wire/200>.

104. Barstow, *Witchcraze*, p. 10.

105. ibid. p. 12.

106. 'Con Edison Crew Unearths Bones Near Early Black Graveyard,' *New York Times*, 14 February 1993, p. 43.

107. Blakey, 'The New York African Burial Ground Project', p. 54.

108. ibid. pp. 56–7.

109. 'Bones reveal little-known tale of New York slaves', *CNN*, 12 February 1998.

110. Nelson, *Straight, No Chaser*, p. 92.

111. Watkins, *The Black O*, p. 113.

112. Quoted in Finley, *Ancient Slavery and Modern Ideology*, p. 168.

113. Feagin, *Racist America*, p. 54.

114. ibid. p. 199.

115. Genovese, *The Political Economy of Slavery*, pp. 318–19.

116. Greenberg, *Race Relations and American Law*. See also McLaurin v. Oklahoma State Regents for Higher Education (1950) in Ploski and Williams, *Negro Almanac*, pp. 309–34.

117. Williams, *Thurgood Marshall*, p. 71.

118. Woodward, *Strange Career of Jim Crow*, p. 98.

119. ibid. pp. 68–9, 98, 102, 117–18.

120. Kenan, *Walking on Water*, p. 306.

121. 'The racial economic gaps in this country have been locked open at constant intervals since the days of slavery. The gaps will not close of themselves. To close them will require, as Norman Francis, president of Xavier University of Louisiana, has said, a counterforce "as strong as the force that put us in chains".' Robinson, *The Debt*, p. 229.

122. Kenan, *Walking on Water*, p. 556.

123. Sickels, *Race, Marriage and the Law*, p. 68.

124. ibid. p. 72.

125. See Montague, *Touching*.

126. Rymer, *Genie*; Candland, *Feral Children and Clever Animals*.

127. As we have noted, slavery continued throughout the South in practice if not in name for some years after the Emancipation Proclamation, which had no effect in the states of the Confederacy and even after the

end of the Civil War in 1865.

128. Holladay, *Life, On the Fence*, pp. 175–6.

129. Coyote, *Sleeping Where I Fall*, pp. 195–6.

130. Morris, *Southern Slavery and the Law*, p. 441.

131. Evans, 'From the Land of Canaan to the Land of Guinea', pp. 15–43.

132. Dyer, *White*, pp. 14–15.

133. For a discussion of white conceptions of Africans as apes and beasts, see Jordan, *White Over Black*, pp. 29–32.

134. Turberville, *Mediaeval Heresy and the Inquisition*, p. 131.

135. ibid. pp. 156–7.

136. Rice, *Rise and Fall of Black Slavery*, pp. 17–18.

137. Meltzer, *Slavery*, part 2, pp. 20–3; Paul Bohannon, quoted in Meltzer, *Slavery*, part 2, p. 20.

138. Quoted in ibid. part 2, p. 22.

139. Quoted in ibid. part 2, pp. 27, 29.

140. 'Both nineteenth-century Southern judges and Northern abolitionists agreed that slavery had never been legally created or initially authorized. Historians agree. Slavery simply evolved in practice, as a custom, and then received statutory recognition.' Bush, 'The British Constitution', p. 382.

141. Higginbotham, *Shades of Freedom*, p. 49.

142. Elkins, *Slavery*, p. 40.

143. During the colonial period in England, 'Public opinion . . . was well acquainted with blacks and the growth of black slavery. Blacks had been in London since at least the late sixteenth century, and by the mid seventeenth century their presence came to be well known. Even more widely known was the systematic use of slaves in the colonies. Indeed, it is a measure of how broadly diffused information was about slavery and conditions in the plantation colonies that many of the poorest English and Irish men and women – prospective emigrants – resisted private blandishments and public campaigns to remove them to the colonies because they expressly did not want to be worked like slaves.' Bush, 'The British Constitution', p. 391.

144. Rice, *Rise and Fall of Black Slavery*, pp. 54–5, 57.

145. Canny, 'The Ideology of English Colonization', pp. 575–98; Allen, *Invention of the White Race, Volume One*.

146. Canny, 'The Ideology of English Colonization', pp. 583–6, 592.

147. Davies, *North Atlantic World in the Seventeenth Century*, p. 5.

148. Girard, *Violence and the Sacred*, pp. 78–86.

149. Clearly it is not only blacks who are and have been identified with the devil; so too have women, the elderly, other minorities, the ill, the mentally and physically handicapped. We see, then, that a great percentage of people are among the suspect; furthermore, it is always too easy to *become* suspect, either through illness, accident or marriage. For this reason the members of society constantly exert tremendous effort in two ways: 1) to avoid becoming suspect – i.e. by running away from

anyone or anything identified with evil, an act of fear, a constant pressure of fear; 2) to gain entrance to the very center of society, as far from the evil-identified periphery as possible, also motivated by fear but as well by hope – a hope for immortality.

150. Richard Dyer, *White*, p. 19.
151. Sleeter, 'White Silence, White Solidarity', in Ignatiev and Garvey, *Race Traitor*, pp. 261–3.
152. Davis, *Problem of Slavery in Western Culture*, p. 204.
153. Elkins, *Slavery*, pp. 64–6, 73–4; Tannenbaum, quoted in Cox, *Race Relations*, p. 161.
154. Meltzer, *Slavery*, part 2, p. 82.
155. Nash, *Forbidden Love*, pp. 47–8.
156. Genovese, *Roll, Jordan, Roll*, p. 179.
157. Elkins, *Slavery*, p. 74; Rice, *Rise and Fall of Black Slavery*, pp. 283, 371.
158. Allen, *Invention of the White Race*, p. 80.
159. Nash, *Forbidden Love*, pp. 46–9.
160. Butsch, 'Catholics and the Negro', p. 403.
161. ibid. p. 404.
162. Patterson, *Slavery and Social Death*, p. 276.
163. Jordan, *White Over Black*, pp. 206–10.
164. Elkins, *Slavery*, pp. 43, 49–51. As the European Renaissance unfolded, 'Many who were active in the various fields chafed under the restrictions imposed on them by the traditional sanctions of religion. Consequently there was a widespread demand either stated or implied for independence from ecclesiastical control . . . The desire to be free from ecclesiastical prescription also became manifest in economic life. The rising merchant, industrial and banking class believed that the sphere of economic affairs should be divorced from religion and governed by its own principles.' Ergang, *The Renaissance*, pp. 34–5.
165. Jernegan, 'Slavery and Conversion in the American Colonies', p. 517.
166. ibid. p. 512; Davis, *Problem of Slavery in Western Culture*, chapters 10–12.
167. See Kovel, *White Racism*, pp. 86–9.
168. See Kunstler, *Geography of Nowhere*.
169. Cornford, *From Religion to Philosophy*, pp. 158–9.
170. Elkins, *Slavery*, p. 43.
171. Jump, 'Introduction', pp. lix–lx.
172. Moore, *Formation of a Persecuting Society*, p. 105.
173. Barstow, *Witchcraze*, pp. 99, 103–4.
174. ibid. pp. 104–5.
175. Higginbotham, *Shades of Freedom*, p. 33.
176. Barstow, *Witchcraze*, pp. 11–12.
177. Quoted in ibid. p. 160.
178. Quoted in Feagin, *Racist America*, pp. 28–9.
179. Weber, *Protestant Ethic and the Spirit of Capitalism*, pp. 109–10.

180. ibid. pp. 111–12.
181. ibid. p. 122.
182. See Dyer, *White*, pp. 70–81.
183. Meeks, *Driving While Black*, p. 252.
184. Quoted in Zinn, *You Can't Be Neutral on a Moving Train*, p. 28.
185. Kaeser and Gillespie, *Of Many Colors*, pp. 3, 5.
186. Reddy, *Crossing the Color Line*, p. 109.
187. Barstow, *Witchcraze*, pp. 70, 76.
188. Fredrickson, *White Supremacy*, p. 81.
189. Jordan, *White Over Black*, p. 97.
190. Nash, *Forbidden Love*, p. 73.
191. Peggy McIntosh, 'White Privilege and Male Privilege: A Personal Account of Coming to See Correspondences through Work in Women's Studies', quoted in Dyer, *White*, p. 9.
192. Reddy, *Crossing the Color Line*, p. 35.
193. Lazarre, *Beyond the Whiteness of Whiteness*, pp. 49–50.
194. See Ringer, *Decline of the German Mandarins*, especially p. 263.
195. Tawney, *Religion and the Rise of Capitalism*, pp. 240–1.
196. 'Abdu'l-Bahá, *Promulgation*, p. 299.
197. Note especially that Brabantio clearly charges Othello of having cast a spell upon Desdemona. See the discussion in Jordan, *White Over Black*, pp. 37–9.
198. Cose, *Color-Blind*, p. 159.
199. Fromm, pp. 36–8.
200. Girard, *Violence and the Sacred*.
201. See Patterson, *Rituals of Blood*, pp. 203–8.
202. National Institute for Literacy website <http://www.nifl.gov/nifl/faqs.html#literacy rates>. Viewed 10 July 2004.
203. Bertrand and Mullainathan, 'Are Emily and Greg More Employable than Lakisha and Jamal?'
204. Greenhouse, 'Going for the Look, But Risking Discrimination', p. 12.
205. McNeill, *Pursuit of Power*.
206. Woodward, *Strange Career of Jim Crow*, pp. 81–2.
207. *Dhammapada*, p. 21.
208. Pickthall, *Meaning of the Glorious Qur'án*, p. 92.
209. Ergang, *The Renaissance*, pp. 35–6, 55.
210. See, for example, Carney, *Black Rice*.
211. See, for example, Arvigo, *Sastun*.
212. Barstow, *Witchcraze*, p. 82.
213. Braudel, *Wheels of Commerce*, p. 508.
214. Allen, *Invention of the White Race, Volume One*, pp. 72–3, 219.
215. Braudel, *Civilization and Capitalism*, p. 506.
216. Allen, *Invention of the White Race, Volume One*, p. 219.
217. ibid. p. 80.
218. Lewy, *Religion and Revolution*, pp. 349–50.
219. Loewen, *Lies My Teacher Told Me*, p. 109.

220. ibid. pp. 85, 109–10; Resident Population Estimates of the United States by Sex, Race, and Hispanic Origin: April 1, 1990 to July 1, 1999, with Short-Term Projection to November 1, 2000, <http://www.census.gov/population/estimates/nation/intfile3-1.txt>. Viewed 19 September 2001.

221. See Nash, *Forbidden Love*, pp. 189–90, regarding white captives in early colonial America.

222. Fredrickson, *White Supremacy*, p. 81.

223. See Canny, 'The Ideology of English Colonization', pp. 585–6.

224. Allport, 'The Religious Context of Prejudice', pp. 452–5.

225. Richard Dyer, *White*, p. 67.

226. Russell-Wood, 'Iberian Expansion and the Issue of Black Slavery', pp. 24–5, 27.

227. Riley-Smith, *What Were the Crusades?*, p. 39.

228. Turberville, *Mediaeval Heresy and the Inquisition*, p. 138.

229. ibid. pp. 138–9.

230. Braudel, *Wheels of Commerce*, pp. 506, 508.

231. Turberville, *Mediaeval Heresy and the Inquisition*, pp. 125–6.

232. ibid. p. 135.

233. Trevor-Roper, *European Witch-Craze*, p. 90.

234. Turberville, *Mediaeval Heresy and the Inquisition*, pp. 157–8.

235. John 15:6. Turberville, *Mediaeval Heresy and the Inquisition*, p. 158.

236. Quoted in Solomon and Cohen, *Wizards of Media Oz*, p. 184.

237. Carcassonne was renovated in the 19th century.

238. Trevor-Roper, *European Witch-Craze*, pp. 91–2, 103.

239. Barstow, *Witchcraze*, p. 62.

240. ibid. pp. 32–3, 76.

241. Trevor-Roper, *European Witch-Craze*, p. 151.

242. Quoted in ibid. p. 152.

243. ibid. pp. 152–3.

244. ibid. p. 159.

245. Kovel, *White Racism*, pp. 87–8.

246. Barstow, *Witchcraze*, pp. 15–29, 129–45.

247. ibid. pp. 31, 37, 78.

248. ibid. pp. 39, 143–5.

249. ibid. p. 25.

250. ibid. p. 143.

251. ibid. pp. 61–2.

252. ibid. pp. 142, 164.

253. Trevor-Roper, *European Witch-Craze*, pp. 99–100.

254. Moore, *Formation of a Persecuting Society*, p. 12.

255. ibid. p. 10.

256. ibid. pp. 4–5. Emphasis in original.

257. Barstow, *Witchcraze*, p. 77.

258. Weber, *Protestant Ethic and the Spirit of Capitalism*, p. 122.

259. For a specific example see the 1700–1 debate between Samuel Sewall and John Saffin in Appleby, *Materialism and Morality in the American*

Past, especially p. 57.

260. Deuteronomy 10:17–19

261. Meltzer, *Slavery*, part 1, p. 43.

262. Sociologist Orlando Patterson argues that 'in the middle of the twentieth century a religion emerged that, for the first time since the death of Jesus, actually succeeded in creating a faith and a community of believers that came fairly close to the gospel of love, fellowship, commitment, and radical engagement that he preached. This was the revitalized Afro-American Christianity that took shape in the church-directed protest movements culminating in the Southern Christian Leadership Conference led by Martin Luther King Jr.' Patterson, *Rituals of Blood*, p. 230.

263. There are rare documented instances in which male witches were identified by the discovery of the 'devil's teat'.

264. Lifton, 'The Sense of Immortality', p. 276.

265. Fromm, *The Sane Society* and *To Have or To Be*.

266. Kovel, *White Racism*, pp. 123–4.

267. Malson, *Wolf Children and the Problem of Human Nature*, pp. 10, 12.

268. Bettelheim, *Freud and Man's Soul*.

269. Malson, *Wolf Children*, pp. 37–82.

270. Nisbet, *Sociological Tradition*, p. 90.

271. See Dynes, Clarke, Dinitz and Ishino, *Social Problems*, pp. 3–17.

272. Bellah, 'Durkheim and History', p. 459; Berman, *Law and Revolution*.

273. Braudel, *Civilization and Capitalism*, pp. 258–62.

274. Samuelson, *Religion and Economic Action*, pp. 29–30, 42.

275. Moore, *Formation of a Persecuting Society*, p. 136.

276. ibid. p. 139.

277. ibid. p. 153.

278. Sanders, *Lost Tribes and Promised Lands*, pp. 77, 100; Price, *America's Unwritten Constitution*, p. 25.

279. Reinhold, 'Eighteenth-Century American Political Thought', pp. 224–5.

280. 'One of the factors which promoted secularization in the realm of politics and statecraft was the revival of Roman Law, a development which began toward the end of the eleventh century ... Thus Roman law was an effective force in exciting self-consciousness in the rising national states and in impelling them to assert their independence from papal supervision.' Ergang, *The Renaissance*, pp. 36–7.

281. Las Casas found it difficult that official Portuguese historians of the 15th century routinely described the extreme violence and rapacity of the colonial enterprise 'as great sacrifices made in the service of God'. Quoted in Russel-Wood, 'Iberian Expansion and the Issue of Black Slavery', p. 29.

282. Dyer, *White*, p. 19.

283. Nash, *Forbidden Love*, p. vii.

284. McNeill, *Pursuit of Power*, pp. 125–6.

285. See for example, Albrecht, ed. *World War II and the American Dream*.

286. Vance, *Victorians and Ancient Rome*, pp. 11–12, 25–6.
287. Vance, *America's Rome, Volume One*, p. 2.
288. Rice, *Rise and Fall of Black Slavery*, p. 41.
289. In addition to the European explorers' accounts of the relatively gentle and sympathetic character of the native peoples of the Americas, we also have the revealing description of the slavers' violence in the autobiography of the former slave Olaudah Equiano (1745–97): 'I had never seen among any people such instances of brutal cruelty: and this is not only shewn towards us blacks, but also to some of the whites themselves.' Equiano, *Interesting Narrative of the Life of Olaudah Equiano*, p. 34.
290. Ergang, *The Renaissance*, pp. 12–13.
291. Berman, *Law and Revolution*, p. 2.
292. Ullmann, *Carolingian Renaissance and the Idea of Kingship*, pp. 1, 8.
293. Quoted in Butsch, 'Catholics and the Negro', p. 399.
294. Detailed analyses are found in Berman, *Law and Revolution* and in Mann, *Sources of Social Power, Volume I*, chapter 10.
295. Harnack, *Mission and Expansion of Christianity in the First Three Centuries*, pp. 167–70. For a description of the wide diversity of social ranks in the early church, see Fox, *Pagans and Christians*, pp. 293–312.
296. Snowden, *Blacks in Antiquity*, p. 144.
297. ibid. p. 148.
298. ibid. p. 1.
299. ibid. p. 176.
300. ibid. p. 120.
301. ibid. pp. 169–71.
302. ibid. p. 179.
303. ibid. p. 186.
304. ibid. p. 195.
305. Sanders, *Lost Tribes and Promised Lands*, p. 49.
306. Snowden, *Blacks in Antiquity*, pp. 196–207.
307. ibid. p. 196.
308. Dyer, *White*, pp. 67, 72–3.
309. Allen, *Invention of the White Race, Volume One*, pp. 5–7.
310. ibid. pp. 16–21. The new power and will to rebel was most clearly evidenced in the American colonies by Bacon's Rebellion, a 1676 uprising of white farmers who, in prosecuting wars against local Indians, moved towards independence from the feudal style of colonial government which they felt was inadequate and unresponsive to their needs. Morgan, *American Slavery, American Freedom*, pp. 250–70.
311. DuBois, *Black Reconstruction in America*, p. 26.
312. Phil Rubio, 'Civil War Reenactments and Other Myths', in Ignatiev and Garvey, *Race Traitor*, p. 185.
313. Woodward, *Strange Career of Jim Crow*, p. 85.
314. Sorokin, *The Crisis of Our Age*.
315. Butsch, 'Catholics and the Negro', p. 395.
316. Quoted in ibid. pp. 399–400.

317. Meltzer, *Slavery*, part 1, pp. 207, 217.
318. ibid. part 1, p. 223; part 2, p. 1.
319. Johnson, *History of Christianity*, p. 437.
320. The story of Victor formed the basis of two feature films: *L'Enfant Sauvage* (1969), and *The Wild Child* (1991), starring Jodie Foster.
321. Samuelsson, *Religion and Economic Action*, pp. 48–51.
322. Feagin, *Racist America*, p. 72–3.

Chapter 3: Respiritualization
1. Berman and O'Connor, *Who Owns the Sun?*, p. 67.
2. Rubio, 'Civil War Reenactments and Other Myths', *Race Traitor*, pp. 183–93.
3. Joe R. Feagin characterizes slavery in North America as 'a totalitarian system in which whites controlled the lives of black men, women, and children – a total racist society protecting white interests'. Feagin, *Racist America*, p. 41.
4. Williams, *Eyes on the Prize*, p. 102.
5. Peters, *A Class Divided*.
6. Wolfe, 'The Revival of Moral Inquiry in the Social Sciences', p. B4.
7. Laszlo, *Macroshift*.
8. Guinier, *Lift Every Voice*, pp. 71, 185.
9. Dayna Cunningham, quoted in ibid. pp. 90–1.
10. Victoria Gray, quoted in ibid. p. 90.
11. Gardner, 'Engaging Religion in the Quest for a Sustainable World', *State of the World 2003*.
12. *One Country*, vol. 9, issue 4 (January–March 1998); vol. 10, issue 4 (January–March 1999).
13. 'Into the Sunset: The Age of Cultural Theory', p. 18.
14. For a more detailed discussion of the renewed interest in spirituality see Laszlo, *Macroshift*, pp. 122–4.
15. Weisz, *Emergence of Modern Universities in France*, pp. 10, 115–16, 293–4; Clark, *Prophets and Patrons*, pp. 162–3.
16. See for example Eastman, *Marxism: Is it Science*.
17. Stark, *Social Theory and Christian Thought*, p. 36.
18. ibid. p. 52.
19. Quoted in ibid. pp. 36–7.
20. ibid.
21. Quoted in ibid. p. 38.
22. Quoted in ibid. p. 43.
23. Hegel, *Philosophy of History*, p. 33.
24. Quoted in Löwith, *Meaning in History*, p. 36.
25. Quoted in Tucker, *Marx–Engels Reader*, p. 64.
26. Taylor, 'Marxism and Empiricism', in Williams and Montefiore, *British Analytical Philosophy*, pp. 236, 242.
27. Easton and Guddat, *Writings of the Young Marx on Philosophy and Society*, pp. 3, 5.

28. Quoted in Tucker, *Marx-Engels Reader*, p. 39.

29. Löwith, *Meaning in History*, p. 43.

30. Fromm, *Beyond the Chains of Illusion*, p. 12; *Marx's Concept of Man*, pp. 63–4.

31. Tucker, *Philosophy and Myth in Karl Marx*, p. 22. Tucker views the structure of Marxism as one which 'invites analysis as a religious system', particularly in its 'aspiration to totality of scope', in its provision of 'an authentic philosophy of history', in the prophecy of a 'new man' and in its 'unity of theory and practice'. ibid. pp. 22–4.

32. Glasner, *Sociology of Secularization*, p. 64.

33. Carter, *Culture of Disbelief*, p. 111.

34. Roof, 'Modernity, the Religious, and the Spiritual', p. 216.

35. Gouldner, *Coming Crisis of Western Sociology*, p. 136.

36. Charlton, *Secular Religion in France*, p. 28.

37. Durkheim, 'The Role of Universities in the Social Education of the Country', p. 385. Emphasis in original.

38. Durkheim, *Elementary Forms of the Religious Life*, Introduction, section 2, p. 22; Conclusion, section 2, p. 474.

39. Remmling, *Sociology of Karl Mannheim*, p. 122.

40. Gouldner, *Coming Crisis of Western Sociology*, pp. 134–5. Emphasis in original.

41. Claude Levi-Strauss, quoted in Taylor, *Beyond Explanation*, pp. 186, 187, 234.

42. George Murdock, quoted in ibid. p. 205.

43. Budd, *Sociologists and Religion*, p. 47.

44. Will Herberg, quoted in Friedrichs, *A Sociology of Sociology*, p. 353.

45. Roof, 'Modernity, the Religious and the Spiritual', p. 218.

46. ibid. p. 222.

47. See Mason, *Unnatural Order*; and Marjorie Spiegel, *The Dreaded Comparison: Human and Animal Slavery*.

48. The first modern university, at Bologna, was patterned after the guild system, in which students, instead of learning through an individual tutor – common in the monastic form of education – learned in groups that 'closely corresponded to the hierarchy of the guilds'. Baldwin and Goldthwaite, *Universities in Politics*, pp. 5, 8.

49. See, for example, Jarman, *Landmarks in the History of Education*, pp. 218–25.

50. Genovese, *Roll, Jordan, Roll*, p. 561.

51. Vidal, *McLibel*; Slatalla, *Masters of Deception*. In recommending that lay people become familiar with the *Physicians' Desk Reference*, the late Dr Robert Mendelsohn, who was a well-known associate professor of medicine at the University of Illinois, wrote in his classic work *Confessions of a Medical Heretic*, p. 40: 'Of course, you don't have to buy the book. Almost every public library now has it. You shouldn't worry about understanding it. Anybody with an eighth grade education and a dictionary can read *any* medical book. Even doctors will testify that

patients always seem to be able to pick out and understand the parts that they *must* know.' Emphasis in the original.

52. There is some controversy as to the details of this historical account but it nonetheless illustrates the point.

53. See, for example, Berman, *Law and Revolution*, pp. 39, 45.

54. Quoted in Lazarre, *Beyond the Whiteness of Whiteness*, p. 7.

55. Quoted in Jordan, *White Over Black*, p. 276.

56. Carter, *Culture of Disbelief*, p. 233.

57. Steinhorn and Diggs-Brown, *By the Color of Our Skin*, p. 183.

58. Ridgeway, *Blood in the Face*, p. 14.

59. ibid.

60. Guinier, *Lift Every Voice*, p. 297.

61. See Cose, *Rage of a Privileged Class* and Feagin and Sikes, *Living with Racism*.

62. Wright, *Black Boy*, pp. 163–9.

63. Massaquoi, *Destined to Witness*, pp. 417–18.

64. Carter, *An Hour Before Daylight*, pp. 260–1.

65. Berman, *Law and Revolution*, p. 45.

66. 'Abdu'l-Bahá, *Some Answered Questions*, pp. 245–6.

67. Regarding the contribution of suburbs and car culture to racist social structures see Kay, *Asphalt Nation*, pp. 229–31; and Alvord, *Divorce Your Car!*, pp. 38–9.

Chapter 4: Civilization

1. Schlosser, *Fast Food Nation*, p. 7.

2. See Perry, *Hyperreality and Global Culture*, p. 78.

3. Kerr, *Dogs and Demons*, pp. 32–7.

4. Toynbee, *A Study of History*, p. 555.

5. Kerr, *Dogs and Demons*, p. 36.

6. Dyer, *White*, pp. 210, 222.

7. Rifkin, *Beyond Beef*, p. 285.

8. Quoted in Bonazzi, *Man in the Mirror*, p. 169.

9. Williams, *The Alchemy of Race and Rights*, p. 116.

10. ibid. p. 119.

11. See, for example, Giroux, *The Mouse that Roared*, pp. 23–5, 44, 64, 156.

12. Lewis, *New New Thing*, p. 57.

13. Frantz and Collins, *Celebration, USA*, p. 14.

14. Quoted in ibid. p. 230.

15. ibid. p. 269.

16. ibid. pp. 216–25.

17. ibid. pp. 247–8.

18. ibid. p. 256.

19. ibid. p. 152.

20. Ray and Anderson, *Cultural Creatives*.

21. See O'Meara, 'How Mid-Sized Cities Can Avoid Strangulation', pp. 8–15.

22. Bowser and Hunt, *Impacts of Racism on White Americans*, p. 157. See

chapters 3 and 8 for a more detailed discussion.
23. Scales-Trent, *Notes of a White Black Woman*, pp. 131–2.
24. Feagin, *Racist America*, p. 199.
25. Iyer, *Global Soul*, p. 11.
26. ibid. pp. 16–17, 37, 167, 175.
27. ibid. p. 252.
28. Reddy, *Crossing the Color Line*, p. 101. Emphasis in the original.

Index

This index is alphabetized letter by letter, thus 'civilization' comes before 'civil rights'. Articles, prepositions and conjunctions in entries are ignored.

through scapegoating, 93–4, 102
universe, interconnectedness of, 257
universities, 78, 127, 128, 232–4, 260
University of California at Davis, 246
Urban II, Pope, 257
urbanites, 100–1

vagrancy, 159
values, 211
  moral , xii
    moral vacuum, 64–6
    as symbols, 175
  spiritual, 206
Vasconcelos, José, 295
victims, 118–21
villages, European, 280
Vineti, Jean, 162, 186, 191
violence, 37, 71, 170–1, 179, 201
  against African Americans, 39–40,
    73, 109, 114, 167, 182
  against women, 73, 166–7, 182, 242
  culture of, 73, 179, 186
  and death, 133–4
  in Europe, 157–61, 166–7, 168
  violent materialism, 144–51, 202
  in witch-craze, 161–7
Virginia, 60
  anti-miscegenation laws in, 47–8, 56
voting rights, 194, 213, 243

Wallace, George, 238
war, 141
  and peace, 183
Washington, George, 57
Washington DC, 184
Watkins, Steve, 78
wealth, 12, 107, 111, 123, 136, 145–51,
  166, 171, 174, 177, 183, 184, 239, 283,
  286
  redistribution of, 289
weapons, 183
Weber, Max, 104, 108, 109, 110, 124,
  131, 169, 185, 189, 210, 226, 239
West, the
  culture of, xi, 108, 147, 173, 175, 220,
    239–40
  ideological conflict in, 175
West Africa, creation of slavery in, 90
White, Walter, 7–8
white backlash, 27–8
Whitehead, A.N., 295
'white male privilege', 126–30
whiteness, 127, 180–1, 193
  'extreme', 277–8
  as heaven, 109–11, 117

White Over Black (Jordan), 86
White Racism (Kovel), 165
whites, 248
  first use of term, 59
  humanity of, 244
  men, 63–4
  opposition to slavery, 207
  women, *see* women, white
  see also European Americans
white superiority, 10, 132, 248
white supremacy, 41, 134–5
Whitney, Eli, 141
Whyte, William H., 278
'Wild Boy of Aveyron', 199
will, 269–70, 272
Williams, Juan, 28, 39
Williams, Patricia J., 5, 278
Williams, Venus, 31, 80
Wilson, Woodrow, 44
witch craze, 72, 74, 161–7
witches/witchcraft, 86, 94, 104–6, 115,
  137, 158–9, 186
witch-hunts, 73, 106, 112, 132, 148, 158–
  9, 161–7, 169, 177, 186, 191, 195, 201
  effects on women in Europe, 73,
    104–6, 167
  men as witch-hunters, 129–30
  Salem, 2, 7, 81, 94
Wolfe, Alan, 210, 214, 228
women, 85, 151
  accused of witchcraft, 104–6, 158–9,
    165–6, 191
  black, 63, 242
  criminalization of, 167
  disadvantaged, 127
  effect of witch-hunts on, 73
  equated with evil, 107, 165
  negative stereotypes of, 162
  oppression of, 191
  raping of slave, 242
  violence against, 163, 166–7, 186
  white, centrality of, 62–4, 242
Woodard, Isaac, 40
Woods, Tiger, 31, 80, 247
Woodson, Carter G., 54–5, 56
Woodward, C. Vann, 55, 69, 74, 144
words
  iconic word, 71–2, 164, 244
  Word of God versus word of man,
    70–2, 143–4
working class, 73, 233
World Bank, 213, 221, 295
World War One, 43
World War Two, 36, 40, 43–4, 46, 114,
  183, 209, 210, 220, 271, 276